SOLIDARITY IN INTERNATIONAL DISASTER RESPONSE LAW

This is the first book to comprehensively explore the role of solidarity in international disaster response law (IDRL), offering a timely and transformative vision for this regime governing cooperation in disaster response.

As disasters intensify due to climate change, solidarity is increasingly invoked by states and others as a principle guiding disaster response. Yet its role remains underexplored and underutilised, risking solidarity to function as a mere rhetorical device. This book responds to that gap, offering a comprehensive examination of the meaning, legal status and implications of solidarity in IDRL. It demonstrates that solidarity can reorient IDRL from a sovereignty-centred regime characterised by state autonomy and voluntarism to one focused on the protection of disaster-affected persons through differentiated international cooperation and assistance.

The book further explores how solidarity could reshape specific legal and practical issues that challenge international disaster response. By analysing these issues through the lens of solidarity, the book offers novel perspectives that can break new ground in finding concrete solutions for persistent challenges within the regime.

This analysis comes at a pivotal moment. In 2024, the United Nations initiated negotiations for a multilateral convention for international disaster response, signalling growing recognition of the need for a universal treaty in this area. Against this backdrop, the book is both timely and ambitious. It not only exposes the untapped potential of solidarity but also provides a practical roadmap for its implementation, seeking to shape the development of IDRL to meet the demands of an increasingly disaster-prone world.

Volume 106 in the series Studies in International Law

Studies in International Law

RECENT TITLES IN THIS SERIES

Global Lawmaking and Social Change: The Varieties of Customary International Law Gregor Novak

The Effectiveness of the Inter-American Court of Human Rights: The Case of Indigenous Territorial Rights Gabriela CB Navarro

Individuals in International Humanitarian Law: A Historical Analysis
Sarina Landefeld

The Pathology of Plenty: Natural Resources in International Law
Lys Kulamadayil

The United Nations Security Council and the Authorisation of Force: Form, Character and Nature Marko Svicevic

Protecting the Right to Leave in an Era of Externalised Migration Control
Emilie McDonnell

Pluralising Actors and Norms in Human Rights Treaties: Beyond Monolithic States
Hinako Takata

Systemic Economic Offences as International Crimes: Theorising a New Paradigm of Mass Criminality Nicole Citeroni

A Central Asian Perspective on International Law
Sergey Sayapin

Responsibility for the Crime of Aggression under International Law
Nikola Hajdin

Judicial Discretion in the Interpretation of International Crimes: Revisiting the Legality Principle
Ligeia Quackelbeen

Solidarity in International Disaster Response Law
Thomas Mulder

For a complete list of titles in this series see www.bloomsbury.com/uk/series/studies-in-international-law/

Solidarity in International Disaster Response Law

Thomas Mulder

•HART•
OXFORD • LONDON • NEW YORK • NEW DELHI • SYDNEY

HART PUBLISHING
Bloomsbury Publishing Plc
Kemp House, Chawley Park, Cumnor Hill, Oxford, OX2 9PH, UK
1385 Broadway, New York, NY 10018, USA
Bloomsbury Publishing Ireland Limited, 29 Earlsfort Terrace, Dublin 2, D02 AY28, Ireland

HART PUBLISHING, the Hart/Stag logo, BLOOMSBURY and the Diana logo are trademarks of Bloomsbury Publishing Plc

First published in Great Britain 2026

1

A catalogue record for this book is available from the British Library.

A catalogue record for this book is available from the Library of Congress.

ISBN: HB: 978-1-50999-407-6
ePDF: 978-1-50999-409-0
ePub: 978-1-50999-408-3

Typeset by Amnet

Acknowledgements

THIS MONOGRAPH IS BASED on my PhD thesis, completed at the University of New South Wales in 2023. Words cannot adequately express my gratitude to my supervisors, Sarah Williams and Aline Jaeckel, for their invaluable guidance, insightful feedback and generous encouragement throughout this journey. They consistently challenged me to produce my best work while supporting my development as an early career academic. I have deeply appreciated our open and honest conversations and their unwavering faith in me finding my own path on this journey. I am also grateful to the examiners of my PhD thesis, Giulio Bartolini and Dug Cubie, for their generous and constructive feedback that have made this monograph only better.

I am also grateful to the colleagues with whom I work at UNSW and the Kaldor Centre for International Refugee Law. I thank Natalie Klein for giving me the opportunity to launch my career as a postdoctoral fellow and for encouraging and guiding me in the development of this book project. I owe special thanks to Jane McAdam, whose mentorship means the world to me. Together with Regina Jefferies, she continually pushes me outside my comfort zone to see the concepts behind the law, elevating my research beyond my doctrinal instincts. Working at the Evacuations Research Hub has been a joy every single day. I am also grateful to Jane for allowing me the space and time to work on this book. This research was partially supported by her Australian Research Council Laureate Fellowship (FL230100011), *Evacuations in International Law: Disasters, Conflict and Humanitarian Crises*, funded by the Australian government.

Finally, I wish to thank my family and friends. The irony is not lost on me that many disasters challenged Sydney and the world as I worked on this book. I would be remiss not to acknowledge the family and friends who kept me going through bushfires, floods and a global pandemic. I am deeply thankful to my parents for their unfaltering love and support from many time zones away, especially when the world kept us apart. Special thanks to Carmel for her unrelenting understanding and support, to Sophie for her unfailingly candid feedback and to Emma for her unwavering cheerleading. I am also grateful to my friends in Sydney for reminding me of what matters most in life – from swimming and trivia to having new food experiences. Lastly, my heartfelt thanks to Eugene for keeping me grounded and for playing the devil he was born to be.

Contents

Abbreviations

AADMER	ASEAN Agreement on Disaster Management and Emergency Response
ASEAN	Association of Southeast Asian Nations
CDEMA	Caribbean Disaster Emergency Management Agency
CESCR	Committee on Economic, Social and Cultural Rights
CRC	Convention on the Rights of the Child
CRPD	Convention on the Rights of Persons with Disabilities
EU	European Union
GFDRR	Global Facility for Disaster Reduction and Recovery
IAEA	International Atomic Energy Agency
IASC	Inter-Agency Standing Committee
ICCPR	International Covenant on Civil and Political Rights
ICISS	International Commission on Intervention and State Sovereignty
ICESCR	International Covenant on Economic, Social and Cultural Rights
ICJ	International Court of Justice
ICRC	International Committee of the Red Cross
ICTY	International Criminal Tribunal for the Former Yugoslavia
IDI	Institut de Droit International
IDRL	International Disaster Response Law
IFRC	International Federation of Red Cross and Red Crescent Societies
IHL	International Humanitarian Law
IHRL	International Human Rights Law
IHR	International Health Regulations
IIHL	International Institute of Humanitarian Law
ILC	International Law Commission
IPCC	Intergovernmental Panel on Climate Change
IRU	International Relief Union
NGO	Non-Governmental Organisation
NIEO	New International Economic Order
OCHA	Office for the Coordination of Humanitarian Affairs
R2P	Responsibility to Protect
UNDAC	United Nations Disaster Assessment and Coordination
UNDRR	United Nations Office for Disaster Risk Reduction
UNFCCC	United Nations Framework Convention on Climate Change
WHO	World Health Organization

Table of Legal Materials

Treaties

Cases

UN Documents

1

International Law in the Response to Disasters

I. THE CALL FOR SOLIDARITY IN INTERNATIONAL DISASTER RESPONSE

Disasters pose a significant threat to humanity, affecting millions of people worldwide each year.[1] While not every extreme event warrants an international response, major disasters often demand concerted efforts from the global community to avert or alleviate human suffering. In the face of the devastation and despair they leave behind, calls for solidarity have become a recurring feature of international disaster response.[2] Such appeals are often used in calls for action, serving as urgent pleas for generous assistance to support response and recovery efforts. Recent experiences highlight this pattern. During the COVID-19 pandemic, for example, solidarity played a central role in calls for mutual assistance and ensuring equitable access to resources and vaccines.[3] Solidarity also features prominently in appeals for aid following major disasters. For instance, in the wake of the Turkey-Syria earthquake in 2023, the United Nations (UN) Secretary-General urged the international community to provide generous support 'in an enormous show of solidarity'.[4]

The recurring invocation of solidarity in international disaster response raises important questions about its role in international disaster response law (IDRL), the specialised regime of international law governing the facilitation and regulation of international disaster assistance.[5] Consistent references to solidarity frame disaster response as a shared responsibility, urging states to act not only out of compassion but also from a collective duty to avert or alleviate

[1] Disasters impacted more than four billion people globally between 2000 and 2019: UN Office for Disaster Risk Reduction (UNDRR), 'The Human Cost of Disasters: An Overview of the Last 20 Years (2000–2019)' (2020) 9.

[2] See examples in ch 3, section IV.

[3] A Rahman-Shepherd et al, 'Solidarity in Response to the COVID-19 Pandemic' (Chatham House, 2021).

[4] UN, 'Secretary-General's Press Encounter on the Earthquake in Türkiye and Syria' (9 February 2023) www.un.org/sg/en/content/sg/press-encounter/2023-02-09/secretary-generals-press-encounter-the-earthquake.

[5] International Federation of Red Cross and Red Crescent Societies (IFRC), 'International Disaster Response Law' https://disasterlaw.ifrc.org/IDRL.

human suffering. Over time, this language of solidarity has become increasingly embedded in IDRL. Often portrayed as a foundational principle of collective action in addressing global needs in international law,[6] solidarity is now regularly referenced in both binding and non-binding instruments of IDRL such as regional treaties and the International Law Commission's (ILC) Draft Articles on the Protection of Persons in the Event of Disasters (Draft Articles),[7] as well as in statements by states and other actors.[8] Notably, the Draft Articles, which form the basis of a forthcoming treaty on the protection of persons in the event of disasters, expressly recognise the 'fundamental value of solidarity' as a 'key concept underlying the topic [of the Draft Articles]'.[9]

Yet, despite its intuitive and normative appeal, solidarity remains underexplored and underutilised in IDRL. Although frequently invoked, its meaning, legal status and practical implications are largely undefined, raising the risk that solidarity functions merely as lip service expressing sympathy or urgency rather than representing meaningful commitments to cooperation and assistance. While existing scholarship has examined solidarity in particular contexts,[10] a systematic analysis of its role within IDRL is missing. This book seeks to close that gap by offering a comprehensive examination of the meaning, legal status and implications of solidarity in this field of international law.

This analysis comes at a pivotal moment as solidarity in international disaster response is arguably more important than ever before in order to meet the needs of people affected by disasters and uphold their human rights and dignity. According to the International Federation of Red Cross and Red Crescent Societies (IFRC), more than 130 million people affected by disasters annually required international humanitarian assistance between 2010 and 2019.[11] Projections suggest that these figures will rise, given experts' predictions of increased frequency and intensity of disasters worldwide due to the effects of climate change.[12] If current trends continue, it is estimated that the number of

[6] Maarten den Heijer and H van der Wilt, 'Global Solidarity and Common But Differentiated Responsibilities' in Maarten den Heijer and Harmen van der Wilt (eds), *Netherlands Yearbook of International Law 2020* (TMC Asser Press, 2022) 3, 4.

[7] ILC, 'Draft Articles on the Protection of Persons in the Event of Disasters' (27 May 2016) UN Doc A/CN.4/L.871 (Draft Articles).

[8] See examples in ch 3, section IV.C.

[9] ILC (n 7) preamble; ILC, 'Commentaries on the Draft Articles on the Protection of Persons in the Event of Disasters' (2016) UN Doc A/71/10, 18.

[10] See, eg, T O'Donnell, 'Solidarity, Duties to Assist and the Potential of the ILC Draft Articles on the Protection of Persons in the Event of Disasters' in M Aronsson-Storrier and SC Breau (eds), *Research Handbook on Disasters and International Law,* 2nd edn (Edward Elgar, 2024) 274; F Zorzi Giustiniani, *International Law in Disaster Scenarios: Applicable Rules and Principles* (Springer, 2021); T O'Donnell and C Allan, 'Identifying Solidarity: The ILC Project on the Protection of Persons in Disasters and Human Rights' (2017) 49(1) *George Washington International Law Review* 53; T O'Donnell and C Allan, 'A Duty of Solidarity? The International Law Commission's Draft Articles and the Right to Offer Assistance in Disasters' in S Breau and K Samuel (eds), *Research Handbook on Disasters and International Law* (Edward Elgar, 2016) 453.

[11] IFRC, 'World Disasters Report 2020: Come Heat or High Water' (2020) 153.

[12] The Intergovernmental Panel on Climate Change (IPCC) predicts with high confidence that the effects of global warming will raise the likelihood of extreme events with 'increased

disasters will surge by 40 per cent by 2030 compared to 2015.[13] As a consequence, the IFRC has warned that by 2050, more than 200 million people affected by disasters annually could become reliant on international humanitarian assistance.[14] These projections underscore the urgent importance of international cooperation in preparing for and responding to future disasters.

Responding to 'the increasing number of disasters in the world, as well as their intensity and impact on affected populations', states are expected to adopt the first global treaty on the protection of persons in the event of disasters in 2027.[15] This treaty is needed to establish 'a comprehensive global legal regime to better address the protection of persons in the event of disasters'.[16] The negotiation of this instrument presents a unique and timely opportunity to closely examine the role of solidarity in IDRL. It offers states the chance to move beyond merely paying lip service and instead embed solidarity in a meaningful way through obligations of international cooperation and assistance in disaster response. This book seeks to seize that opportunity by demonstrating how solidarity can be conceptualised and implemented across IDRL, advancing a forward-looking vision for the future of international disaster response in an increasingly disaster-prone world.

Next, this chapter outlines how the book pursues its objectives. Section II sets the stage by introducing IDRL, providing an overview this specialised regime of international law. Building on this foundation, section III considers the place of solidarity within IDRL, showing that while references to it are increasing, it remains underexplored and underutilised. This section also sets out the case for a dedicated analysis of solidarity in IDRL. Finally, section IV outlines the methodology, scope and structure of the book, explaining how its analysis of solidarity is carried out.

II. WHAT IS INTERNATIONAL DISASTER RESPONSE LAW?

While IDRL has attracted considerable attention in academia and practice in recent years,[17] it remains a relatively unfamiliar regime to a broader audience of international law scholars, practitioners and others. To address this,

intensities, durations and/or spatial extents [that are] unprecedented in the observational record': IPCC, 'Summary for Policymakers' in IPCC, *Climate Change 2021: The Physical Science Basis. Contribution of Working Group I to the Sixth Assessment Report of the Intergovernmental Panel on Climate Change* (Cambridge University Press, 2021) 27.

[13] UNDRR, 'Global Assessment Report on Disaster Risk Reduction – Our World at Risk: Transforming Governance for a Resilient Future' (2022) 17.

[14] IFRC, 'The Cost of Doing Nothing' (2019) www.ifrc.org/document/cost-doing-nothing, 3.

[15] UN General Assembly Res 79/128 (4 December 2024) UN Doc A/RES/79/128.

[16] ibid preamble.

[17] For instance, the *Yearbook of International Disaster Law* was launched in 2018, with the aim to 'foster the interest of academics and practitioners on legal and institutional issues relevant to all forms of natural, technological/human-made disasters, including rapid and slow onset events, but excluding armed conflicts or political/financial crises per se': 'Yearbook of International Disaster Law Online' https://brill.com/view/journals/yido/yido-overview.xml?contents=journaltoc.

the following sections introduce IDRL as a legal regime. Section II.A situates IDRL within international law, outlining its general nature, purposes and scope of application. Section II.B outlines the fragmented sources of IDRL, shedding light on its scattered character. Section II.C then turns to the substantive content, discussing five fundamental principles that govern international disaster response.

A. A Legal Regime for International Disaster Response

Historically, the legal dimension of disasters has been largely overlooked in international law. For a long time, cooperation in disaster response has rested on principles of humanitarianism and goodwill rather than on binding legal agreements.[18] However, there is now increasing recognition that 'a significant body of practice has developed at the international and national levels devoted to addressing the legal and institutional issues relevant in disaster settings'.[19] From this practice, IDRL has taken shape as the specialised international law regime governing the immediate response to disasters, encompassing all 'actions taken directly before, during, or immediately after a disaster to save lives, reduce health impacts, ensure public safety, and meet the basic subsistence needs of the people affected'.[20] Within this phase, IDRL is primarily concerned with the protection of persons affected by disasters by mobilising and distributing humanitarian aid, securing access to affected communities, and facilitating and coordinating response activities.

IDRL is situated within the broader regime of international disaster law, which addresses key legal and institutional issues across all phases of disaster management.[21] The scope of international disaster law thus extends beyond the immediate response to also encompass mitigation and preparedness as well as recovery and rehabilitation. The pre-disaster phase focuses on reducing vulnerabilities and disaster risks, emphasising proactive measures such as risk assessments, early warning systems and resilience-building initiatives to prevent or mitigate the impact of hazards.[22] The Sendai Framework for Disaster Risk Reduction (Sendai Framework) stands as the leading global instrument in

[18] ILC, 'Preliminary Report on the Protection of Persons in the Event of Disasters, by Mr. Eduardo Valencia-Ospina, Special Rapporteur' (5 May 2008) UN Doc A/CN.4/598, para 14.

[19] G Bartolini, 'Charting an Emerging Subject: The Role of the Yearbook of International Disaster Law' (2019) 1(1) *Yearbook of International Disaster Law* 1, 1.

[20] UNDRR, 'Response' www.undrr.org/terminology/response.

[21] Center for Disaster Philanthropy, 'Disaster Phases' (2021) https://disasterphilanthropy.org/cdp-resource/disaster-phases/.

[22] ILC (n 7) art 9. See also M Aronsson-Storrier, 'Exploring the Foundations: The Principles of Prevention, Mitigation, and Preparedness in International Law' in KLH Samuel, KN Bookmiller and M Aronsson-Storrier (eds), *The Cambridge Handbook of Disaster Risk Reduction and International Law* (Cambridge University Press, 2019) 52.

this area.[23] By contrast, the post-disaster recovery phase centres on rebuilding affected communities, enhancing long-term resilience and addressing systemic inequities and injustices that disasters often exacerbate or expose.

Unlike international humanitarian law (IHL), which regulates humanitarian aid in situations of armed conflict, IDRL applies to disasters occurring in peacetime. Determining what constitutes a 'disaster' is therefore critical to defining the scope of IDRL's application. There is, however, no single, universally accepted legal definition; instead, most instruments provide their own definitions.[24] For the purposes of this book, the definition provided in the Draft Articles is used:

> [A] calamitous event or series of events resulting in widespread loss of life, great human suffering and distress, mass displacement, or large-scale material or environmental damage, thereby seriously disrupting the functioning of society.[25]

This definition is drawn from a wide range of binding and non-binding instruments, and incorporates three elements common to various adopted definitions.[26] First, the definition focuses on the consequences rather than the cause(s) of a disastrous event.[27] It does not differentiate between natural or human-made disasters 'in recognition of the fact that disasters often arise from complex sets of causes that may include both wholly natural elements and contributions from human activities'.[28] It also does not distinguish between sudden-onset (for example, earthquakes or hurricanes) and slow-onset events (for example, droughts or sea-level rise).[29] Second, a disaster must be an extreme event with 'calamitous' consequences, such as 'widespread loss of life, great human suffering and distress, mass displacement, or large-scale material or environmental damage'.[30] This excludes minor events that do not cause severe impacts, as well as political or economic crises per se.[31] Third, the cumulative consequences of a disaster must meet a qualitative threshold: the event must cause 'serious disruption of society'.[32] For example, the ILC explained that a major earthquake on an uninhabited island is unlikely to qualify as a disaster in legal terms because it may not cause societal

[23] World Conference on Disaster Risk Reduction, 'Sendai Framework for Disaster Risk Reduction 2015–2030' (18 March 2015) UN Doc A/CONF.224/L.2 (Sendai Framework).

[24] ILC (n 18) para 46. See also G Bartolini, 'A Taxonomy of Disasters in International Law' in F Zorzi Giustiniani et al (eds), *Routledge Handbook of Human Rights and Disasters* (Routledge, 2018) 10, 11; U Toshiya, 'Natural Disasters and the Theory of International Law' in DD Caron, MJ Kelly and A Telesetsky (eds), *The International Law of Disaster Relief* (Cambridge University Press, 2014) 21, 24.

[25] ILC (n 7) art 3(a).

[26] ILC, 'Commentaries' (n 9) 22–24. See also ILC (n 18) para 44; A de Guttry, 'Surveying the Law' in A de Guttry, M Gestri and G Venturini (eds), *International Disaster Response Law* (TMC Asser Press, 2012) 3, 6; Bartolini (n 24) 14.

[27] Bartolini (n 24) 15.

[28] ILC, 'Commentaries' (n 9) 23. See also Bartolini (n 24) 15.

[29] ILC, 'Commentaries' (n 9) 23.

[30] ILC (n 7) art 3(a).

[31] ILC, 'Commentaries' (n 9) 24.

[32] ILC (n 7) art 3(a). See also Bartolini (n 24) 17–18.

disruption.[33] However, it is difficult to define this threshold in abstract terms due to the subjective nature of what constitutes a 'serious disruption'. Therefore, discretion is needed in determining what amounts to a serious disruption of society in practice, with the caveat that this threshold should not be interpreted too rigidly, to avoid the unnecessary exclusion of events that may not disrupt all of society, such as localised disasters (for example, wildfires, landslides or industrial accidents).[34]

When an event constitutes a disaster, the core purpose of IDRL is to promote and facilitate international cooperation in response, primarily serving the humanitarian objective of protecting affected persons, reducing loss of life and alleviating human suffering.[35] While the term 'protection' varies in meaning across different contexts in international law,[36] the Inter-Agency Standing Committee (IASC) provides an authoritative definition adopted here: protection encompasses safeguarding the rights of persons affected by disasters, including 'all activities aimed at ensuring full respect for the rights of the individual in accordance with the letter and spirit of the relevant bodies of law'.[37] Protection thus extends beyond providing access to resources and services critical for survival and the fulfilment of essential needs, and also covers action to ensure that rights and human dignity are respected and upheld. However, protecting persons through international cooperation is not the sole objective of IDRL; some instruments also aim to facilitate cooperation for other purposes, such as reducing damage to property, infrastructure and the environment, and preventing or mitigating spill-over effects and transboundary harm caused by disasters.[38]

IDRL pursues these objectives primarily by defining the roles and responsibilities of actors involved in disaster response – including states, international organisations, non-governmental organisations (NGOs) and private actors – establishing mechanisms for international cooperation and providing technical guidance on domestic legal and institutional frameworks. This guidance seeks to remove common administrative and regulatory barriers to international assistance,[39] such as delays in customs clearance, visa restrictions for relief personnel,

[33] ILC, 'Commentaries' (n 9) 23.

[34] ibid 24. See also Bartolini (n 24) 17; T Stephens, 'Disasters, International Environmental Law and the Anthropocene' in S Breau and K Samuel (eds), *Research Handbook on Disasters and International Law* (Edward Elgar, 2016) 153, 155.

[35] ILC (n 7) art 2.

[36] ILC, 'Memorandum by the Secretariat on the Protection of Persons in the Event of Disasters' (11 December 2007) UN Doc A/CN.4/590 para 251.

[37] Inter-Agency Standing Committee (IASC), 'Protection of Internally Displaced Persons – Inter Agency Standing Committee Policy Paper' (December 1999) 4. See also S Giossi Caverzasio, *Strengthening Protection in War: A Search for Professional Standards* (ICRC, 2001) 19; ILC (n 18) para 51; D Cubie, *The International Legal Protection of Persons in Humanitarian Crises: Exploring the Acquis Humanitaire* (Hart Publishing, 2017) 23–25, 75–86.

[38] *ASEAN Agreement on Disaster Management and Emergency Response* (26 July 2005) (AADMER) art 2; *Tampere Convention on the Provision of Telecommunication Resources for Disaster Mitigation and Relief Operations* (18 June 1998) preamble.

[39] IFRC, 'Guidelines for the Domestic Facilitation and Regulation of International Disaster Relief and Initial Recovery Assistance' (2007) (hereinafter 'IDRL Guidelines').

and other regulatory obstacles to the deployment of relief operations.[40] By clarifying roles and responsibilities and promoting legal preparedness, IDRL helps ensure that aid reaches those in need without unnecessary delay, while safeguarding the dignity and rights of affected persons throughout the response.

In recent years, there has been a shift to expand IDRL beyond its traditionally state-centric focus, reflecting a broader trend in international law that increasingly recognises the legal position of actors beyond nation-states, particularly individuals.[41] Non-binding instruments and scholarship advocate for complementing the traditional needs-based approach to disaster response, which focuses on meeting the acute needs of disaster victims, with a rights-based approach that emphasises the protection and fulfilment of the human rights of those affected.[42] This rights-based approach challenges the state-centric nature of IDRL by drawing attention to the rights of individuals in disaster settings. It underscores that IDRL ought to operate along two axes: a horizontal axis that relates to the rights and obligations of affected states, third states and, to some extent, non-state actors in relation to one another, and a vertical axis that concerns the rights of persons affected by disasters and the corresponding obligations of states to ensure the enjoyment of these rights.[43]

While IDRL aims to promote and facilitate international cooperation, it has historically adopted a decentralised approach to disaster response, with the state(s) affected by a disaster bearing primary responsibility. Unlike other regimes of international law, IDRL lacks international institutions with a formal mandate to direct or oversee cooperation in disaster response or to promote, develop and enforce IDRL. Past attempts to centralise disaster response under a single international organisation were unsuccessful (see section II.B). However, two institutions have assumed a de facto leadership role in international disaster response, though their institutional influence remains comparatively underdeveloped.[44] First, the UN plays a key role through its Office for the Coordination of Humanitarian Affairs (OCHA), which supports affected states and facilitates international

[40] For a comprehensive overview of legal and practical issues in the operationalisation of international disaster response, see D Fisher, 'Law and Legal Issues in International Disaster Response: A Desk Study' (IFRC, 2007) https://disasterlaw.ifrc.org/sites/default/files/media/disaster_law/2020-08/113600-idrl-deskstudy-en.pdf.

[41] W Kälin, 'The Human Rights Dimension of Natural or Human-Made Disasters' (2012) 55 *German Yearbook of International Law* 119.

[42] See eg ILC, 'Commentaries' (n 9) 20; Kälin (n 41); Cubie (n 37) 109.

[43] ILC, 'Commentaries' (n 9) 18. See also W Kälin, 'Protection of Victims of Disasters: The "Vertical" Dimension of the Draft Articles on the Protection of Persons in the Event of Disasters' (2019) 1(1) *Yearbook of International Disaster Law* 28; G Bartolini, 'A Universal Treaty for Disasters? Remarks on the International Law Commission's Draft Articles on the Protection of Persons in the Event of Disasters' (2017) 99(906) *International Review of the Red Cross* 1103, 1115 ff; D Tladi, 'The International Law Commission's Draft Articles on the Protection of Persons in the Event of Disasters: Codification, Progressive Development or Creation of Law from Thin Air?' (2017) 16(3) *Chinese Journal of International Law* 425, 429 ff.

[44] T Mulder, G Simm and S Williams, 'Regime Interaction and the Protection of Refugees during COVID-19' (2020) 3 *Yearbook of International Disaster Law* 92, 109–10.

cooperation in disaster response. OCHA serves as a central focal point for states, international organisations and other assisting non-state actors, offering support on mobilising and coordinating international assistance.[45] However, OCHA is not operationally active in disaster-affected areas and lacks a mandate to direct international response efforts. The IFRC is another leading actor in international disaster response. As part of the International Red Cross and Red Crescent Movement, the IFRC is the largest global humanitarian aid organisation active in peacetime disaster response.[46] Unlike OCHA, the IFRC is operationally active in affected areas, often supporting national Red Cross and Red Crescent societies, and has shown particular interest in the normative development of IDRL, similar to the International Committee of the Red Cross (ICRC) in IHL, but without a formal mandate from states. The IFRC has produced a number of soft law instruments to address legal and regulatory issues in facilitating international disaster response; however, these instruments are non-binding (see section II.B).[47]

In addition to OCHA and the IFRC, regional intergovernmental organisations (or their subsidiary bodies) are increasingly engaged in coordinating international disaster response. Examples include the European Union (EU) in Europe,[48] the Association of Southeast Asian Nations (ASEAN) in Southeast Asia[49] and the Caribbean Disaster Emergency Management Agency (CDEMA) in the Caribbean.[50] These organisations primarily play facilitative and supportive roles, fostering cooperation among states, but they do not centralise, direct or carry out international response efforts.

Finally, while IDRL is the specialised regime governing international disaster response, it is important to note that it is not the only body of international law that applies in disaster settings. Depending on the specific circumstances – such as the nature, impact and location of the disaster – other regimes of international law may apply concurrently,[51] including international human rights law (IHRL), international environmental law, international refugee law and global health law.[52] So-called 'complex emergencies', where a disaster occurs in an area

[45] UN General Assembly Res 46/182 (19 December 1991) UN Doc A/RES/46/182, para 35.

[46] The International Red Cross and Red Crescent Movement comprises the IFRC, the International Committee of the Red Cross (ICRC) and the national Red Cross and Red Crescent societies. See IFRC, 'The International Red Cross and Red Crescent Movement: The Three Parts of our Movement' www.ifrc.org/international-red-cross-and-red-crescent-movement.

[47] See, eg, IDRL Guidelines (n 39).

[48] *Decision No 1313/2013/EU of the European Parliament and of the Council of 17 December 2013 on a Union Civil Protection Mechanism* (20 December 2013) (hereinafter 'EU Civil Protection Mechanism') (last amended in May 2021).

[49] AADMER (n 38).

[50] *Agreement Establishing the Caribbean Disaster Emergency Management Agency* (4 July 2008) (CDEMA Agreement).

[51] ILC (n 7) art 18(1).

[52] G Venturini, 'International Disaster Response Law in Relation to Other Branches of International Law' in de Guttry, Gestri and Venturini (n 26) 45; D Cubie, 'An Enchanted Tool: Humanitarian Assistance and the ILC Draft Articles on the Protection of Persons in the Event of Disasters' (2009) 4 *Irish Yearbook of International Law* 119, 128. See also Mulder, Simm and Williams (n 44).

where there is an armed conflict, are regulated by both IHL and IDRL, although the former takes precedence over the latter as *lex specialis*.[53]

B. Sources

IDRL is not codified in a single treaty, but consists of a collection of binding and non-binding instruments, alongside longstanding practices, that seek to promote and facilitate timely and effective international disaster response. Its sources are notably fragmented compared to other regimes of international law. In the absence of a 'flagship treaty',[54] IDRL has evolved through 'a patchwork of norms rather than a coherent body of law'.[55] The piecemeal development of the regime creates challenges in identifying universally applicable rules and principles that could form a coherent and comprehensive legal framework for IDRL.

Unlike other regimes of international law that are anchored by a flagship treaty – such as the *Geneva Conventions* in IHL or the 1951 *Refugee Convention* in international refugee law – IDRL lacks a universally ratified treaty that establishes core rules and principles for disaster response. Past attempts to create such a treaty failed, hindered by insufficient political momentum, a limited sense of urgency among states and persistent sovereignty concerns. States have generally been reluctant to accept binding obligations that could constrain their discretion in how to respond to disasters or impose duties beyond voluntary cooperation.[56] The first major attempt came in 1927, when the League of Nations adopted the *Convention and Statute Establishing an International Relief Union* (IRU Statute).[57] Intended to create an international framework for disaster response under a newly established institution tasked with overseeing and facilitating relief efforts, the IRU Statute was the first multilateral treaty to provide a comprehensive legal and institutional framework for disaster response.[58] The IRU was

[53] ILC (n 7) art 18(2); IDRL Guidelines (n 39) art 1(4). See also S Williams and G Simm, 'Assistance to Disaster Victims in an Armed Conflict: The Role of International Humanitarian Law' in Zorzi Giustiniani et al (n 24) 43; A Perez, 'In Defense of Concurrent Application: The ILC Draft Articles on the Protection of Persons in the Event of Disasters and International Humanitarian Law' (2018) 46(3) *Denver Journal of International Law and Policy* 259; G Venturini, 'Disasters and Armed Conflict' in de Guttry, Gestri and Venturini (n 26) 251; D Gavshon, 'The Applicability of IHL in Mixed Situations of Disaster and Conflict' (2009) 14(2) *Journal of Conflict and Security Law* 243; T Rodenhäuser and G Giacca, 'The International Humanitarian Law Framework for Humanitarian Relief during Armed Conflicts and Complex Emergencies' in S Breau and K Samuel (eds), *Research Handbook on Disasters and International Law* (Edward Elgar, 2016) 132.

[54] D Fisher, 'The Future of International Disaster Response Law' (2012) 55 *German Yearbook of International Law* 87, 89; S Sivakumaran, 'Techniques in International Law-Making: Extrapolation, Analogy, Form and the Emergence of an International Law of Disaster Relief' (2017) 28(4) *European Journal of International Law* 1097, 1098; Bartolini (n 43) 1104.

[55] Sivakumaran (n 54) 1098.

[56] Bartolini (n 43) 1104–05.

[57] *Convention and Statute Establishing an International Relief Union* (12 July 1927).

[58] JF Hutchinson, 'Disasters and the International Order – II: The International Relief Union' (2001) 23(2) *International History Review* 253.

designed to effectively function as a central 'clearing house for international aid', where funds and resources would be collected and directed to disaster-affected states and populations.[59] Yet, despite ratification by nearly 30 states, the IRU never lived up to expectations. It was hampered by insufficient funding, limited state support and fractured international relations, becoming defunct by the 1930s and rendering the IRU Statute effectively obsolete.[60] A second attempt followed in the 1980s, when the UN sought to address recurring legal and practical challenges in disaster response. This effort culminated in the 1984 *Draft Convention on Expediting the Delivery of Emergency Assistance*.[61] Unlike the IRU Statute's centralised, top-down model, the Draft Convention proposed a bottom-up legal framework to facilitate international cooperation during disasters. However, despite initial expressions of support, the Draft Convention lost momentum and was never adopted.[62]

In the absence of a flagship treaty, IDRL has developed in a piecemeal fashion through a 'potpourri' of subject-specific and disaster-specific treaties,[63] regional and bilateral agreements, ad hoc arrangements for cooperation, soft law instruments and domestic laws.[64] Several universal treaties are open to all states, but these are narrowly focused on particular types of disasters (such as nuclear accidents,[65] desertification[66] or oil pollution)[67] or particular aspects of disaster response (such as telecommunications[68] or civil defence)[69] and suffer from low levels of participation.[70] Regional treaties tend to be more comprehensive,[71] but their effectiveness is limited by restricted geographical scope and minimal ratification by signatory states.[72] Alongside these, IDRL encompasses a wide range of bilateral agreements, though many are not publicly accessible. Those that are available reveal significant variation in scope and content, with some

[59] M Eburn, 'International Law and Disaster Response' (2010) 36 *Monash University Law Review* 162, 166.

[60] See generally P Macalister-Smith, 'Reflections on the Convention Establishing an International Relief Union of July 12, 1927' (1986) 54(4) *Legal History Review* 363.

[61] UN Disaster Relief Coordinator, 'Draft Convention on Expediting the Delivery of Emergency Relief' (18 June 1984) UN Doc A/39/267/Add. 2.

[62] Cubie (n 37) 251.

[63] C Allan and T O'Donnell, 'A Call to Alms? Natural Disasters, R2P, Duties of Cooperation and Uncharted Consequences' (2012) 17(3) *Journal of Conflict and Security Law* 337, 345.

[64] For an overview of instruments, see ILC (n 36) annex II.

[65] *Convention on Assistance in the Case of a Nuclear Accident or Radiological Emergency* (26 September 1986) (hereinafter 'Nuclear Accident Convention').

[66] *United Nations Convention to Combat Desertification in those Countries Experiencing Serious Drought and/or Desertification, Particularly in Africa* (14 October 1994).

[67] *International Convention on Oil Pollution Preparedness, Response and Cooperation* (30 November 1990).

[68] Tampere Convention (n 38).

[69] *Framework Convention on Civil Defence Assistance* (22 May 2000).

[70] For instance, only four and 49 states have ratified the Framework Convention on Civil Defence Assistance (ibid) and the Tampere Convention (n 38) respectively.

[71] G Simm, 'Disaster Response in Southeast Asia: The ASEAN Agreement on Disaster Response and Emergency Management' (2018) 8(1) *Asian Journal of International Law* 116, 117.

[72] Bartolini (n 43) 1105.

amounting to little more than the 'exchange of good practices and information between states'.[73] At the national level, domestic law plays a crucial role in facilitating international disaster response by defining the roles and responsibilities of relevant actors, and enabling the prompt and effective influx of international assistance, if needed. Yet reports indicate that most states still lack adequate legal and institutional frameworks to fully support such responses.[74]

Beyond treaty law, IDRL cannot draw from a comprehensive body of customary international law or general principles either. Although international disaster response has a long and rich history in practice, customary international law plays a limited role in this regime. While certain individual rules, such as the obligation to protect foreign disaster relief personnel and equipment, are likely to have attained customary status,[75] they do not collectively form a coherent or comprehensive legal framework capable of substituting for a flagship treaty.[76] The development of customary norms is hindered by the nature of international disaster response, where state practice is often driven by humanitarian considerations, politics and voluntarism rather than by a perceived legal obligation (see Chapter 3, section IV). As Macalister-Smith observed:

> It should be apparent that the individual nature of at least some disaster situations, the uncertainty as to the general character of humanitarian practices and, above all, the influence of political factors in relief, work firmly against the crystallisation of particular customary international rules in this area.[77]

Similarly, the role of general principles in IDRL remains underdeveloped. While the regime draws on some principles of international law – such as the humanitarian principles of humanity, neutrality, impartiality and independence – it has not yet established a comprehensive set of norms derived from general principles.[78] That said, Cubie has highlighted the potential of general principles in shaping specialised regimes of international law and calls for exploring potential principles that might be applicable in the context of disasters.[79] This

[73] ibid. See also de Guttry (n 26) 11 ff.

[74] Fisher (n 40) 14. See also IFRC, 'Law and Public Health Preparedness and Response: Lessons from the COVID-19 Pandemic' (2021) https://disasterlaw.ifrc.org/sites/default/files/media/disaster_law/2021-07/SNAPSHOT%20Law%20and%20Public%20Health%20Emergency%20Preparedness%20and%20Response%20Lessons%20from%20the%20COVID-19%20Pandemic%20-%20GLOBAL_0.pdf.

[75] LM Ulrich, 'The Customary International Law Obligation to Protect Foreign Disaster Relief Personnel and Their Equipment' (2014) 22 *Willamette Journal of International Law & Dispute Resolution* 343.

[76] MH Hoffman, 'What is the Scope of International Response Law?' in V Bannon (ed), *International Disaster Response Laws, Principles and Practice: Reflections, Prospects and Challenges* (IFRC, 2003) 13, 16.

[77] P Macalister-Smith, *International Humanitarian Assistance: Disaster Relief Actions in International Law and Organization* (Kluwer Academic Publishers, 1985) 54.

[78] Sivakumaran (n 54) 1110; D Cubie, 'Sources of IDL: Focus on General Principles of Law' (2024) 5 *Yearbook of International Disaster Law* 493.

[79] D Cubie, 'Identifying Principles of International Disaster Law' in M Aronsson-Storrier and S Breau (eds), *Research Handbook on Disasters and International Law*, 2nd edn (Edward Elgar, 2024) 11.

book answers that call by examining the potential of solidarity as a principle of IDRL.

In the absence of a unified legal framework, IDRL has been shaped significantly by a range of soft law instruments.[80] Three stand out for their efforts to create a coherent and comprehensive framework for international disaster response. The first is UN General Assembly Resolution 46/182. Adopted in 1991, this resolution was one of the first globally adopted instruments to set out guiding principles on humanitarian emergency assistance. Noting that 'humanitarian assistance is of cardinal importance for the victims of natural disasters and other emergencies',[81] the resolution outlines several key principles for the provision of international assistance, including the humanitarian character of emergency aid,[82] respect for the territorial integrity and sovereignty of states[83] and the importance of international cooperation.[84] It also establishes a framework for the role of the UN in disaster response, leading to the creation of OCHA. The second key soft law instrument is the Guidelines for the Domestic Facilitation and Regulation of International Disaster Relief and Initial Recovery Assistance (IDRL Guidelines), adopted by the IFRC in 2007.[85] Taking a 'bottom-up' approach, the Guidelines recommend how states can strengthen their domestic legal and institutional frameworks to facilitate disaster response.[86] They clarify the responsibilities of affected states, third states and assisting non-state actors, and set out the legal facilities that states are encouraged to adopt to expedite international relief operations. The third is the Draft Articles on the Protection of Persons in the event of Disasters (Draft Articles), adopted by the ILC in 2016.[87] Drawing on existing binding and non-binding instruments, as well as other regimes of international law,[88] the Draft Articles set out a basic legal framework for IDRL. They address core issues such as the affected state's primary responsibility to protect its population, respect for human rights and dignity, the duty to cooperate, the duty to seek assistance and the principle of consent. Although lacking binding force, the IDRL Guidelines and the Draft Articles both enjoy broad support among states and shape the regime normatively.[89]

[80] For a list of non-binding instruments, see ILC (n 36) annex II.
[81] UN General Assembly Res 46/182 (n 45) para 1.
[82] ibid para 2.
[83] ibid para 3.
[84] ibid para 5.
[85] IDRL Guidelines (n 39).
[86] C Clement, 'International Disaster Response Laws, Rules, and Principles: A Pragmatic Approach to Strengthening International Disaster Response Mechanisms' in DD Caron, MJ Kelly and A Telesetsky (eds), *The International Law of Disaster Relief* (Cambridge University Press, 2014) 67, 78.
[87] ILC (n 7).
[88] Sivakumaran (n 54) 1108; A Pronto, 'Codification and Progressive Development in Contemporary International Law-Making: Locating the Draft Articles on the Protection of Persons in the Event of Disasters' (2019) 1(1) *Yearbook of International Disaster Law* 148.
[89] D Cubie, 'An Analysis of Soft Law Applicable to Humanitarian Assistance: Relative Normativity in Action?' (2011) 2(2) *Journal of International Humanitarian Legal Studies* 177.

The relative success of these soft law instruments has generated renewed momentum for establishing a flagship treaty in IDRL. Despite earlier failed attempts, there is now a growing appetite for a binding universal instrument to serve as the foundation for international cooperation in disaster response. In 2024, the UN General Assembly endorsed a negotiation process with the goal of concluding a 'legally binding instrument on the protection of persons in the event of disasters' by the end of 2027.[90] The ILC's Draft Articles will serve as the basis for these negotiations. If successful, the treaty could mark a turning point in the development of IDRL, moving towards unifying this fragmented regime under a universal framework that sets out the core rules and principles of international disaster response.

C. Five Fundamental Principles

Having situated IDRL as a specialised regime and scoped its sources, this section turns to its substantive content. At its core, IDRL is founded on five fundamental principles that govern international disaster response: (1) the sovereignty of the affected state must be respected; (2) the affected state is primarily responsible for the protection of persons during disasters; (3) human rights and dignity must be upheld in the event of a disaster; (4) states have a duty to cooperate in disaster response; and (5) international assistance must be facilitated promptly and effectively. These principles have emerged as widely accepted norms based on existing instruments and practice, although it should be noted that IDRL encompasses additional topics.[91] As such, this section serves only as a broad overview of the regime.

i. State Sovereignty

State sovereignty is a cardinal principle underpinning IDRL, affirming the exclusive competence of states to exercise authority over all matters within their jurisdiction without external interference.[92] In the disaster context, this principle establishes that the state affected by a disaster – whether within its territorial boundaries or under its jurisdiction – holds exclusive authority over disaster response efforts. Respect for state sovereignty is firmly embedded in both binding and non-binding instruments of IDRL. Some instruments explicitly enshrine the principle, underscoring the

[90] UN General Assembly Res 79/128 (n 15). See also G Bartolini, 'Toward a Universal Treaty on "Protection of Persons in the Event of Disasters"' *EJIL:Talk!* (17 December 2024) www.ejiltalk.org/toward-a-universal-treaty-on-protection-of-persons-in-the-event-of-disasters.

[91] Some other topics include quality assurance of assistance, the use of foreign military and civil defence assets, the protection of vulnerable groups, data sharing and information management, coordination, and liability and insurance issues.

[92] S Besson, 'Sovereignty' in *Max Planck Encyclopedia of International Law* (Oxford University Press, 2011).

affected state's exclusive authority and responsibility in managing disaster response,[93] while others affirm it more indirectly by recognising the 'primary role of the affected state' in coordinating and directing relief efforts.[94]

The principle of sovereignty translates into certain sovereign rights of the affected state that must be respected by other states and assisting actors – the term used in this book to refer to 'competent intergovernmental organization, or a relevant non-governmental organization or entity, providing assistance to an affected State with its consent'.[95] Prominently among these is the right to give consent to the provision of international aid. This right is widely recognised in binding and non-binding instruments and supported by state practice,[96] which treat consent as a sovereign prerogative of the affected state, serving as 'the expression of the will of the sovereign who permits activities on its territory that may otherwise constitute violations of the principle of non-intervention'.[97] As such, it is a key tool of the affected state to regulate disaster response and safeguard its sovereignty and territorial integrity.[98] Third states and assisting actors must respect this requirement and refrain from providing humanitarian assistance directly to affected communities without permission.[99] If consent is given, the affected state retains the sovereign right to oversee all aspects of disaster response within the state's jurisdiction, including the initiation, coordination, direction, implementation and supervision of relief activities.[100] This

[93] For example: 'The sovereignty, territorial integrity and national unity of States must be fully respected in accordance with the Charter of the United Nations' (UN General Assembly Res 46/182 (n 45) para 3). See also ILC (n 7) preamble; IDRL Guidelines (n 39) art 3(3); AADMER (n 38) art 3(1); Framework Convention on Civil Defence Assistance (n 69) art 3(b).

[94] For example: 'The affected State has the primary role in the direction, control, coordination and supervision of such relief assistance' (ILC (n 7) art 10(2)). See also UN General Assembly Res 46/182 (n 45) para 4; IDRL Guidelines (n 39) art 3(3); Tampere Convention (n 38) art 4(8); AADMER (n 38) art 3(2); *Inter-American Convention to Facilitate Disaster Assistance* (6 July 1991) art IV(a); *Agreement among the Governments of the Participating States of the Black Sea Economic Cooperation (BSEC) on Collaboration in Emergency Assistance and Emergency Response to Natural and Manmade Disasters* (15 April 1998) (hereinafter 'BSEC Agreement') art 8(1); *Agreement between Governments of Member States of Shanghai Cooperation Organization on Cooperation in Delivery of Assistance for Emergency Liquidation* (26 October 2005) (hereinafter 'Shanghai Agreement) art 6(1); CDEMA Agreement (n 50) art XXII(1); EU Civil Protection Mechanism (n 48) art 15(5).

[95] ILC (n 7) art 3(d). The IDRL Guidelines use the term 'assisting humanitarian organization', referring to 'a foreign, regional, intergovernmental or international non-profit entity whose mandate and activities are primarily focused on humanitarian relief, recovery or development': IDRL Guidelines (n 39) art 2(12).

[96] ILC (n 7) art 13(1); IDRL Guidelines (n 39) art 10(1); Tampere Convention (n 38) art 4(5); Framework Convention on Civil Defence Assistance (n 69) art 3(a); AADMER (n 38) art 3(1); *SAARC Agreement on Rapid Response to Natural Disasters, 2011* (26 May 2011) art III(1).

[97] ILC, 'Fourth Report on the Protection of Persons in the Event of Disasters, by Mr. Eduardo Valencia-Ospina, Special Rapporteur' (11 May 2011) UN Doc A/CN.4/643 para 52.

[98] Bartolini (n 43) 1125.

[99] ILC, 'Commentaries' (n 9) 61; Eburn (n 59) 188.

[100] UN General Assembly Res 46/182 (n 45) para 4; IDRL Guidelines (n 39) art 3(3); Tampere Convention (n 38) art 4(8); AADMER (n 38) art 3(2); Inter-American Convention (n 94) art IV(a); BSEC Agreement (n 94) art 8(1); Shanghai Agreement (n 94) art 6(1); CDEMA Agreement (n 50) art XXII(1); EU Civil Protection Mechanism (n 48) art 15(5).

right affirms that, even when overwhelmed by a disastrous event, the affected state retains its sovereignty and that all actors involved in disaster response must operate within the boundaries established by local laws and policies.

The principle of sovereignty grants the affected state a degree of discretion in exercising its primary role and sovereign rights, suggesting it has 'the freedom to adopt whatever measures it sees fit' in determining its approach to disaster response, including decisions on whether to cooperate with other states and assisting non-state actors.[101] However, this discretion is not absolute; it is constrained by other obligations under international law.

ii. Duty to Protect Persons in Disasters

One of these obligations is the duty of the affected state to protect persons in disasters. This duty is widely recognised. For example, UN General Assembly Resolution 46/182 states that: 'Each State has the responsibility first and foremost to take care of the victims of natural disasters and other emergencies occurring on its territory.'[102] The Draft Articles provide: 'The affected State has the duty to ensure the protection of persons and provision of disaster relief assistance in its territory, or in territory under its jurisdiction or control.'[103]

The duty to protect persons in disasters arises from both states' sovereignty and obligations under IHRL. The protection of the population is increasingly recognised as a core responsibility stemming from state sovereignty.[104] This notion builds on the interpretation of sovereignty put forward by the International Commission on Intervention and State Sovereignty (ICISS) in 2001, which asserts that 'state sovereignty implies responsibility, and [that] the primary responsibility for the protection of its people lies with the state itself'.[105] The duty to protect disaster victims also arises from states' obligations under IHRL, particularly concerning the right to life.[106]

The duty to protect persons in disasters constrains the affected state's sovereignty-based discretion in terms of how to respond to disasters. While the affected state enjoys some freedom in determining how it responds, it must ensure that adequate protection is provided to those affected. Where the affected

[101] ILC, 'Third Report on the Protection of Persons in the Event of Disasters, by Mr. Eduardo Valencia-Ospina, Special Rapporteur' (31 March 2010) UN Doc A/CN.4/629 para 74.

[102] UN General Assembly Res 46/182 (n 45) para 4.

[103] ILC (n 7) art 10(1). See also IDRL Guidelines (n 39) art 3(1).

[104] ILC, 'Commentaries' (n 9) 51.

[105] ICISS, 'The Responsibility to Protect: Report of the International Commission on Intervention and State Sovereignty' (2001), XI.

[106] *International Covenant on Civil and Political Rights* (16 December 1966) (ICCPR) art 6; *Convention on the Rights of the Child* (20 November 1989) (CRC) art 6; *Convention on the Rights of Persons with Disabilities* (13 December 2006) (CRPD) art 10. The European Court of Human Rights affirmed that the right to life 'lays down a positive obligation on States to take appropriate steps to safeguard the lives of those within their jurisdiction': *Budayeva and Others v Russia* App Nos 15339/02, 21166/02, 20058/02, 11673/02 and 15343/02 (European Court of Human Rights, 20 March 2008) para 128.

state's capacity to provide adequate protection is overwhelmed, some instruments suggest that it must seek international assistance to meet its obligations;[107] however, such an obligation is controversial as it infringes on the affected state's sovereignty by mandating international involvement in disaster response (see Chapter 5, section III.B).

The duty to protect also places limits on the right to withhold consent, particularly where states are unable or unwilling to ensure adequate protection for affected populations. This issue arises, for instance, when states reject international aid for political reasons. Following the 2023 Turkey-Syria earthquake, for example, Syria withheld consent for the delivery of international aid to opposition-controlled regions, exacerbating the humanitarian crisis in those areas.[108] Similar concerns arose after Cyclone Nargis in Myanmar in 2008, when authorities rejected international assistance for weeks while affected communities suffered.[109]

While the duty to protect persons in disasters suggests that the affected state's discretion to withhold consent should be restricted in such cases, it remains deeply contested when, how and to what extent such limitations should apply, given their implications for state sovereignty (see Chapter 5, section III.C). Equally contentious are the consequences of unlawfully withholding consent when international aid is essential to protecting disaster-affected populations. Some states have argued that such conduct could trigger intervention under the doctrine of Responsibility to Protect (R2P), though this interpretation remains highly disputed (see Chapter 6, section III.A).

iii. Respect for Human Rights and Dignity

The respect for human rights and dignity during disasters constitutes the third fundamental principle of IDRL. This principle seeks to ensure that disaster response efforts place people's inherent rights and dignity at the centre, especially in times of emergency. It is recognised across IDRL instruments, emphasising that humanitarian assistance must be delivered in a manner that respects human rights, avoids discrimination and addresses the specific needs of vulnerable populations.[110] For instance, the Draft Articles explicitly state that 'the inherent dignity of the human person shall be respected and protected in the event of disasters'.[111] The ILC further explained that it considers human dignity to serve as 'a guiding principle for all actions related to disaster relief, disaster

[107] See, eg, ILC (n 7) art 11; IDRL Guidelines (n 39) art 3(2); Institute de Droit International (IDI), 'Resolution on Humanitarian Assistance' (2003) 86(856) *International Review of the Red Cross* 874, art III(3).

[108] L Doucet, 'Crisis upon Crisis: Why it's Hard to Get Help to Syria after Earthquake', *BBC* (11 February 2023) www.bbc.com/news/world-middle-east-64600913.

[109] A Selth, 'Even Paranoids Have Enemies: Cyclone Nargis and Myanmar's Fears of Invasion' (2008) 30(3) *Contemporary Southeast Asia* 379, 390 ff. This case is discussed in more detail in ch 5, section III.C.

[110] ILC (n 7) arts 4–5; IDRL Guidelines (n 39) art 4(1).

[111] ILC (n 7) art 4.

risk reduction, and the evolution of relevant legal frameworks'.[112] This principle entails both negative obligations to refrain from actions that would harm the inherent dignity of individuals and positive obligations to actively protect and uphold human dignity.[113] By embedding these obligations, IDRL aims to balance the urgency of disaster response with the imperative to uphold fundamental rights, reinforcing that disaster response is, above all, about protecting the rights and dignity of those affected.[114]

While only a few human rights treaties explicitly reference disasters,[115] it is widely recognised that international human rights obligations remain applicable in disaster settings.[116] These include commonly affected rights such as the right to life,[117] food,[118] water,[119] health[120] and housing.[121] Although states' obligations under IHRL may be temporarily limited or derogated during disasters and the progressive realisation of economic, social and cultural rights may result in a temporary reduction in the level of protection provided, particularly when the state's capacity to respond is overwhelmed,[122] General Comments of UN human rights treaty bodies emphasise that states retain core non-derogable obligations to ensure the minimum essential levels of enjoyment of these rights that 'continue to exist in situations of conflict, emergency and natural disaster'.[123] Courts and human rights treaty bodies have also paid attention to the human rights obligations of states in the context of disasters,[124] and several non-binding instruments provide guidance on how to ensure the protection of the rights of the people affected by disasters.[125]

[112] ILC, 'Commentaries' (n 9) 28.

[113] ibid 30.

[114] Kälin (n 43).

[115] See, eg, CRPD (n 106) art 11; *African Charter on the Rights and Welfare of the Child* (1 July 1990) arts 23(1), 23(4), 25(2)(b).

[116] ILC (n 7) art 5. See also Kälin (n 41).

[117] ICCPR (n 106) art 6.

[118] *International Covenant on Economic, Social and Cultural Rights* (16 December 1966) (ICESCR) art 11.

[119] *Convention on the Elimination of All Forms of Discrimination against Women* (18 December 1979) art 14(2)(h); CRC (n 106) art 24(2)(c).

[120] ICESCR (n 118) art 12.

[121] ibid art 11.

[122] ICCPR (n 106) art 4(1); ICESCR (n 118) art 2(1). See also E Sommario, 'Limitation and Derogation Provisions in International Human Rights Law Treaties and Their Use in Disaster Settings' in Zorzi Giustiniani et al (n 24) 98.

[123] Committee on Economic, Social and Cultural Rights (CESCR), 'Poverty and the International Covenant on Economic, Social and Cultural Rights' (10 May 2001) UN Doc E/C.12/2001/10 para 18; CESCR, 'General Comment No. 3: The Nature of States Parties' Obligations (Art. 2, Para. 1, of the Covenant)' (14 December 1990) UN Doc E/1991/23 para 10. See also E Sommario, 'Derogation from Human Rights Treaties in Situations of Natural or Man-Made Disasters' in de Guttry, Gestri and Venturini (n 26) 323, 348. Also note that the right to life is non-derogable – see ICCPR (n 106) art 4(2).

[124] M Hesselman, 'A Right to International (Humanitarian) Assistance in Times of Disaster' in Zorzi Giustiniani et al (n 24) 65. The *Budayeva* case (n 106) is one example of a case addressing state obligations in disasters.

[125] For example, IASC, 'IASC Operational Guidelines on Human Rights and Natural Disasters' (June 2006).

The application of the humanitarian principles of humanity, neutrality and impartiality to the delivery of disaster assistance further reinforces the respect for human rights and dignity.[126] The principle of humanity ensures that disaster response prioritises alleviating suffering, protecting life and preserving human dignity.[127] Neutrality demands that assistance be delivered without taking sides in political, religious or ideological disputes, ensuring that aid remains focused solely on the needs of affected individuals.[128] Impartiality requires that aid be provided based on need alone, without discrimination of any kind.[129] The humanitarian principles apply to all actors – both states and assisting actors – delivering disaster assistance.[130] Together, they seek to ensure that the provision of disaster assistance upholds and respects the inherent rights and dignity of affected populations.

iv. Duty to Cooperate

The fourth fundamental principle of IDRL asserts that states have a duty to cooperate with other states, the UN and assisting actors in disaster response.[131] States have long engaged in cooperation following disasters, showing a particular willingness to assist when another state's national response capacity has been overwhelmed. For example, UN General Assembly Resolution 46/128 explicitly recognises this reality, affirming that: 'The magnitude and duration of many emergencies may be beyond the response capacity of many affected countries. International cooperation to address emergency situations and to strengthen the response capacity of affected countries is thus of great importance.'[132] Most IDRL treaties acknowledge and respond to this imperative, often identifying cooperation as a core objective.[133] For example, the *ASEAN Agreement on Disaster Management and Emergency Response* (AADMER) lists among its objectives the commitment 'to jointly respond to disaster emergencies through concerted national efforts and intensified regional and international co-operation'.[134]

[126] ILC (n 7) art 6; IDRL Guidelines (n 39) art 4(2); UN General Assembly Res 46/182 (n 45) para 2.
[127] ILC, 'Commentaries' (n 9) 33.
[128] ibid.
[129] ibid 34.
[130] IDRL Guidelines (n 39) art 4(2).
[131] ILC (n 7) art 7; Tampere Convention (n 38) art 3(1); Nuclear Accident Convention (n 65) art 1(1); AADMER (n 38) art 4(a); Shanghai Agreement (n 94) art 2(1).
[132] UN General Assembly Res 46/182 (n 45) para 5.
[133] See, eg, Tampere Convention (n 38) preamble; Nuclear Accident Convention (n 65) preamble; Civil Defence Assistance Convention (n 69) preamble; AADMER (n 38) art 2; Inter-American Convention (n 94) preamble; BSEC Agreement (n 94) preamble; Shanghai Agreement (n 94) preamble; *Agreement between Member States and Associate Members of the Association of Caribbean States for Regional Cooperation on Natural Disasters* (16 April 1999) (hereinafter 'ACS Agreement') art 2; *Arab Cooperation Agreement on Regulating and Facilitating Relief Operations 1987* (3 September 1987) (hereinafter 'Arab League Agreement') preamble. See also ILC (n 7) preamble; UN General Assembly Res 75/124 (11 December 2020) UN Doc A/RES/75/124 preamble.
[134] AADMER (n 38) art 2.

Some treaties also explicitly establish a duty for states parties to cooperate both among themselves and with relevant non-state actors involved in disaster response.[135] The *Tampere Convention on the Provision of Telecommunication Resources for Disaster Mitigation and Relief Operations* (Tampere Convention), for instance, provides: 'The States Parties shall cooperate among themselves and with non-State entities and intergovernmental organizations, in accordance with the provisions of this Convention, to facilitate the use of telecommunication resources for disaster mitigation and relief.'[136]

The Draft Articles seek to further codify the duty to cooperate, stating: 'In the application of the present draft articles, States shall, as appropriate, cooperate among themselves, with the United Nations, with the components of the Red Cross and Red Crescent Movement, and with other assisting actors.'[137] The ILC commented that '[e]ffective international cooperation is indispensable for the protection of persons in the event of disasters',[138] calling it an 'underlying principle' in the protection of persons in disasters and one of the 'key concepts underlying the [Draft Articles]'.[139] Cooperation in this context is broadly defined and may include 'humanitarian assistance, coordination of international relief actions and communications, and making available relief personnel, equipment and goods, and scientific, medical and technical resources', depending on the circumstances and particular needs and priorities of the affected state and populations.[140] The duty to cooperate encompasses both pre-disaster cooperation on risk reduction and cooperation during the response and recovery.[141]

The ILC relied on the duty to cooperate – alongside states' obligations to protect persons within their jurisdiction – as the basis for the duty to seek and accept international assistance when an affected state's national response capacity is overwhelmed.[142] In such circumstances, international cooperation becomes imperative for protecting disaster-affected populations. However, corresponding duties of third states remain contentious.[143] Despite broad support for the duty to cooperate, many states continue to interpret this duty as fundamentally voluntary for non-affected states.[144] This interpretation reflects a long-standing tradition of

[135] See, eg, Nuclear Accident Convention (n 65) art 1(1); AADMER (n 38) art 4(a); Shanghai Agreement (n 94) art 2(1).

[136] Tampere Convention (n 38) art 3(1).

[137] ILC (n 7) art 7.

[138] ILC, 'Commentaries' (n 9) 36.

[139] ibid 18; ILC, 'Second Report on the Protection of Persons in the Event of Disasters, by Mr. Eduardo Valencia-Ospina, Special Rapporteur' (7 May 2009) UN Doc A/CN.4/615, para 50.

[140] ILC (n 7) art 8.

[141] ibid arts 8–9.

[142] ILC, 'Commentaries' (n 9) 53.

[143] See further discussion in ch 6, section III.C.

[144] During discussions on the Draft Articles in the UN General Assembly's Sixth Committee, several states expressed general support for the duty to cooperate, but opposed the imposition of specific binding obligations to partake in cooperation: ILC, 'Eighth Report on the Protection of Persons in the Event of Disasters, by Mr. Eduardo Valencia-Ospina, Special Rapporteur' (17 March 2016) UN Doc A/CN.4/697, para 146.

disaster response grounded in humanitarian concern rather than binding legal obligations. In this tradition, voluntarism serves as the starting point for international cooperation and assistance. While state practice demonstrates a general willingness to cooperate – often through widespread and generous offers of aid following disasters – such cooperation is typically motivated by compassion or a sense of moral duty rather than a perceived legal obligation.[145]

v. Facilitation of International Assistance

The fifth fundamental principle of IDRL emphasises the prompt and efficient facilitation of international assistance once it has been accepted by the affected state.[146] The affected state must ensure the smooth processing and delivery of aid to the affected communities by removing or minimising administrative and regulatory barriers, ensuring that assistance reaches those in need without unnecessary delays (see Chapter 7, section III.B). In addition, states and assisting actors involved in disaster response must coordinate their activities to ensure that the needs of all affected communities are met, avoiding the overserving and/or underserving of communities. This is essential to ensure that disaster relief efforts are timely, coordinated and responsive to the urgent needs of affected populations.

To facilitate international assistance, states should establish appropriate domestic legal and institutional frameworks at all levels of government to coordinate and facilitate disaster response.[147] This is particularly crucial in addressing common practical issues that could hinder the entry and delivery of international aid, such as issuing visas for relief personnel, clearing resources in compliance with customs procedures, and authorising foreign relief workers to operate in disaster-affected areas.[148] The IDRL Guidelines provide valuable guidance to states on how to effectively resolve these challenges, aiming to 'enhance the quality and efficiency of international disaster relief and initial recovery assistance'.[149] While non-binding, these guidelines serve as a key resource for improving coordination and facilitation, ensuring that international aid reaches affected communities in a timely and organised manner.[150]

Yet, despite these efforts, practice shows that administrative and regulatory challenges remain a recurring concern, often hindering the prompt and efficient response to disasters.[151] For example, in the aftermath of the 2015 Nepal

[145] This argument is made in ch 3, section IV.

[146] ILC (n 7) art 15.

[147] IDRL Guidelines (n 39) art 8; UN General Assembly Res 78/120 (8 December 2023) UN Doc A/RES/78/120 para 21.

[148] Fisher (n 40) 13. See also Cubie (n 37) 253.

[149] IDRL Guidelines (n 39) art 1(3).

[150] Besides the IDRL Guidelines, the IFRC has also developed other guides for states to use in preparing legal and institutional frameworks for disaster response; see, eg, IFRC, 'Model Act for the Facilitation and Regulation of International Disaster Relief and Initial Recovery Assistance' (March 2013).

[151] For a comprehensive overview of legal and practical issues in the operationalisation of international disaster response, see Fisher (n 40).

earthquake, Nepalese authorities were significantly overwhelmed and heavily reliant on international aid. Yet, they were ill-prepared to facilitate and coordinate the influx of assistance, resulting in concerns over mismatches between aid and needs, aid diversion, a lack of control over the distribution of funds and supplies, as well as congestion and customs delays at local airports and border crossings.[152]

III. EXAMINING SOLIDARITY IN INTERNATIONAL DISASTER RESPONSE LAW

The overview of IDRL demonstrates that the international legal framework for disaster response is firmly grounded in the principles of sovereignty and voluntarism. At its core, the affected state bears the primary responsibility for protecting the human rights and dignity of persons impacted by disasters. While international cooperation is encouraged, the affected state is only obliged to seek assistance when it cannot provide adequate protection on its own. Likewise, although most states (and assisting actors) are willing to assist when called upon, they generally do so out of humanitarian concern rather than legal duty. Yet, as section I noted, the language of solidarity is increasingly invoked, framing international disaster response as a collective duty to avert or alleviate human suffering – one that emphasises shared responsibility for protecting affected populations.

The increased attention to solidarity in IDRL is part of a broader trend. In recent years, solidarity has experienced a notable resurgence in international law and relations, spurred on in particular by the COVID-19 pandemic and the climate crisis.[153] Increasingly, it is being advanced as a guiding principle for collective responses to global needs and challenges. The UN Human Rights Council, for example, has called for solidarity to be recognised as 'a new foundational principle underpinning contemporary international law'.[154] While solidarity has not yet established itself as a mainstream principle of international law,[155] it is gaining traction: growing support from states in a rising number of resolutions and statements suggests that it is becoming 'widely endorsed in the international community as an indispensable principle that should underpin common efforts to resolve global challenges'.[156] Scholars have likewise observed its growing presence across various regimes of international law,[157] and some treaties

[152] See ADB Cook, M Shrestha and ZB Htet, 'An Assessment of International Emergency Disaster Response to the 2015 Nepal Earthquakes' (2018) 31 *International Journal of Disaster Risk Reduction* 535.

[153] Den Heijer and van der Wilt (n 6) 3.

[154] UN Human Rights Council Res 41/5 (11 July 2019) UN Doc A/HRC/RES/41/5 para 5.

[155] See the examples in ch 3, section IV.A.

[156] Den Heijer and van der Wilt (n 6) 4.

[157] See generally K Wellens, 'Solidarity as a Constitutional Principle: Its Expanding Role and Inherent Limitations' in R StJ MacDonald and Douglas M Johnston (eds), *Towards World Constitutionalism: Issues in the Legal Ordering of the World Community* (Martinus Nijhoff Publishers 2005); AG Koroma,

now expressly recognise solidarity as a guiding principle, such as the recently adopted *WHO Pandemic Agreement*.[158]

Regularly invoked by states, the UN and humanitarian organisations in disaster response, solidarity is also increasingly recognised within IDRL, as reflected in its inclusion in key binding and non-binding instruments.[159] A notable example is the Draft Articles, which highlight solidarity in their preamble: 'mindful of the fundamental value of solidarity in international relations and the importance of strengthening international cooperation in respect of all phases of a disaster'.[160] Several treaties likewise make explicit reference to solidarity. The AADMER provides: 'The Parties shall, in the spirit of solidarity and partnership and in accordance with their respective needs, capabilities and situations, strengthen co-operation and co-ordination to achieve the objectives of this Agreement.'[161] Similarly, the *Framework Convention on Civil Defence Assistance* states that 'assistance shall be undertaken in a spirit of humanity, solidarity and impartiality'.[162] The *Treaty on the Functioning of the European Union* uses comparable language in its specific provision on disaster assistance, notably titled the 'solidarity clause': 'The Union and its Member States shall act jointly in a spirit of solidarity if a Member State is . . . the victim of a natural or man-made disaster.'[163] The preamble to the *Inter-American Convention to Facilitate Disaster Assistance* underscores that its aim is to foster solidarity among states in the international response to disasters: 'AWARE that a genuine spirit of solidarity and good-neighborliness between the American states has been expressed in cases of disaster and that this spirit can be strengthened through a preparedness that makes it possible to act more efficiently.'[164]

This recognition is not surprising, given how solidarity uniquely aligns with IDRL's cooperative nature. As Koroma points out:

> Perhaps nowhere is the growing importance of the notion of solidarity more evident than in the developing international law of disaster relief. Unlike other areas of international law and international relations where States frequently act in their own

'Solidarity: Evidence of an Emerging International Legal Principle' in H Hestermeyer et al (eds), *Coexistence, Cooperation and Solidarity* (Martinus Nijhoff Publishers, 2012) 103; R Wolfrum, *Solidarity and Community Interests: Driving Forces for the Interpretation and Development of International Law* (Brill, 2021) ch 5.

158 'To achieve the objective of the WHO Pandemic Agreement and to implement its provisions, the Parties shall be guided, inter alia, by the following: . . . solidarity with all people and countries in the context of health emergencies, as well as inclusivity, transparency and accountability, to achieve the common interest of a more equitable and better prepared world to prevent, respond to and recover from pandemics, recognizing different levels of capacities and capabilities, particularly of developing countries, including landlocked developing countries, as well as the special circumstances of small island developing States and of least developed countries, in relation to pandemic prevention, preparedness and response': *WHO Pandemic Agreement* (20 May 2025) art 3(5).

159 See the examples in ch 3, section IV.

160 ILC (n 7) preamble.

161 AADMER (n 101) art 3(3).

162 Framework Convention on Civil Defence Assistance (n 69) art 3.

163 *Treaty on the Functioning of the European Union* (13 December 2007) art 222(1).

164 Inter-American Convention (n 101) preamble.

> self-interest, even if it is in cooperation – the entire premise of disaster relief is that States and other actors will endeavour to act in favour of another State, not out of self interest but rather motivated by what could only be called solidarity.[165]

Unlike other areas of international law where states often prioritise self-interest, IDRL relies on selfless collective action to protect persons affected by disasters.

Yet, despite its growing recognition and intuitive appeal, solidarity remains underexplored and underutilised in IDRL. Its meaning is still largely undefined and underconceptualised, leaving unanswered questions about how it does – or could – function within IDRL. While the literature on solidarity in international law has gained momentum in recent years and IDRL has developed as a distinct area of study, few works have sought to bring these strands together in a comprehensive way. Some studies have made valuable contributions to understanding solidarity in IDRL, but they pursue objectives distinct from the comprehensive analysis offered in this book by primarily examining solidarity in relation to specific aspects of IDRL.[166] This limited treatment reflects a wider pattern in international law, also seen in regimes such as global health law and international climate change law, where solidarity is frequently invoked yet remains underexamined and underutilised.[167]

However, without a clear understanding of its meaning, legal status and implications, solidarity risks functioning as a mere rhetorical device rather than a meaningful principle guiding international disaster response. A comprehensive examination is therefore essential – not only to clarify the role of solidarity, but also to assess its capacity to generate concrete obligations, shape the interpretation of existing norms, and influence the future development of IDRL. Such an inquiry can illuminate how solidarity might help bridge the existing framework, grounded in sovereignty and voluntarism, with a vision of international disaster response as a shared responsibility.

This book responds to this need by presenting the first comprehensive examination of solidarity in IDRL. The first part of the book explores the meaning and legal status of solidarity, analysing its current role in IDRL. Drawing on theoretical perspectives, legal instruments and scholarly work, Chapter 2 conceptualises solidarity as representing the pursuit of common objectives through differentiated international cooperation and assistance. In the context of disasters, the protection of the rights and dignity of affected persons is identified as the common goal at the core of solidarity. Chapter 3 then assesses its legal status through a systematic, evidence-based analysis of key legal documents, including

[165] Koroma (n 157) 103, 123.

[166] See, eg, Wellens (n 157) 775, 784 ff; K Wellens, 'Revisiting Solidarity as a (Re-)Emerging Constitutional Principle: Some Further Reflections' in R Wolfrum and C Kojima (eds), *Solidarity: A Structural Principle of International Law* (Springer, 2010) 3, 14 ff; Koroma (n 157) 123 ff; O'Donnell and Allan, 'A Duty of Solidarity?' (n 10); Zorzi Giustiniani (n 10) chs 8–9; Wolfrum (n 157) 428 ff; O'Donnell and Allan, 'Identifying Solidarity' (n 10).

[167] Den Heijer and van der Wilt (n 6) 4.

treaties, UN General Assembly resolutions and statements of states. It argues that although solidarity is gaining recognition as a legal principle, states still regard it as a non-binding principle – a moral aspiration rather than a legally binding obligation or a principle capable of creating, modifying or confirming rights and obligations under international law.

Despite its doctrinally non-binding status, solidarity nonetheless plays a normative role in shaping IDRL. It can influence state conduct and guide the interpretation and development of the regime, even if it does not yet operate as a binding principle of international law. Its growing recognition in treaties, soft law instruments and practice suggests that solidarity is more than a rhetorical device; it reflects an emerging sense of shared responsibility for protecting persons affected by disasters. It is therefore important to explore the transformative potential of solidarity. If treated as more than a moral aspiration, solidarity could challenge the status quo by providing a normative counterweight to a framework grounded in the principles of sovereignty and voluntarism, and by reimagining IDRL as a regime based on shared responsibility.

The second part of this book therefore examines what IDRL would look like if interpreted and developed through the lens of solidarity. Its central argument is that solidarity has transformative potential, capable of reorienting IDRL from a sovereignty-centred regime characterised by state autonomy and voluntarism towards one that prioritises the protection of disaster-affected persons through differentiated international cooperation and assistance. This shift has significant implications for IDRL without radically overhauling its established principles. Importantly, solidarity does not seek to centralise disaster response or supplant sovereignty; rather, it operates within the existing framework in which the affected state retains the primary role in disaster response.[168] Nonetheless, solidarity reconceptualises disaster response as a shared responsibility of all states, altering their respective roles and expanding the scope of cooperation. Chapters 4–7 explore these changes in detail, demonstrating the transformative potential of solidarity as a principle of IDRL.

This analysis is not a purely theoretical or intellectual exercise, but rather represents a substantive effort to demonstrate what IDRL could look like if grounded in the principle of solidarity. In doing so, the book moves beyond rhetorical affirmations, showing how solidarity can be operationalised to enhance cooperation, improve protection for disaster-affected populations and strengthen the regime's responsiveness to future disasters. At the same time, it addresses anxieties and concerns that embracing solidarity could undermine state sovereignty. By examining how solidarity can operate alongside other principles – complementing rather than displacing them – the book illustrates that, when taken seriously, solidarity can enrich IDRL without eroding its core foundations.

[168] The interaction between solidarity and sovereignty is discussed in ch 4, section II.

However, it is not enough to outline the transformative potential of solidarity in broad and abstract terms. Without a closer look at how solidarity would change concrete norms and practices, there is still a substantial risk of it remaining a rhetorical device used to underscore the importance of cooperation without leading to tangible action. To examine how solidarity can be operationalised in IDRL, Chapters 5–7 move beyond its high-level implications to explore how it can reshape three dimensions of international disaster response: the role of the affected state (Chapter 5), the role of third states and assisting actors (Chapter 6), and the scope of international cooperation (Chapter 7). These chapters analyse how specific topics within these dimensions can be interpreted through the lens of solidarity, demonstrating how it can be translated into concrete norms and practices. Rather than providing an exhaustive overview of all relevant issues shaping these dimensions, the analysis focuses on selected topics of particular interest – either because they illustrate solidarity's transformative potential or because they remain contentious or unresolved in IDRL. The purpose is of the analysis is normative: to explore how these issues could be reinterpreted through the lens of solidarity rather than descriptively analysing how solidarity is currently reflected in existing law.

This analysis is particularly timely, as states prepare to negotiate a global treaty on the protection of persons in the event of disasters. If solidarity is to be more than an aspiration, the treaty must reflect its substance in meaningful ways. This book contributes to that effort by illustrating what IDRL could look like when solidarity is treated as a key principle of international disaster response, offering a blueprint for turning words into action. Moreover, applying the lens of solidarity to contested issues provides novel perspectives, opening up new avenues for resolving them and advancing IDRL as a rounder regime.

Yet, while incorporating solidarity into IDRL can be transformative, solidarity is not a panacea. Political realities, resource constraints and limitations in states' capacity to assist present significant obstacles to its full and unreserved implementation. These barriers cannot be overlooked and will be addressed in two key ways throughout the book. First, it is acknowledged that solidarity cannot operate in isolation and must be reconciled with other principles of international law. Therefore, Chapter 4, section II examines the interaction between solidarity and the foundational principle of sovereignty that dictates IDRL. The analysis highlights that solidarity does not override state sovereignty; affected states retain control over disaster response within their territories. However, solidarity does impose limits on the discretion of states, including their right to refuse international cooperation when external aid is essential for protecting affected populations. Balancing the principles of solidarity and sovereignty offers a realistic and balanced path forward for incorporating solidarity into IDRL without eroding its foundational principles. Second, there are practical and structural barriers to implementing solidarity within IDRL. A particular concern is the extent to which states are willing to act in solidarity in practice, making sacrifices by committing to cooperation in disaster response. Indeed, practice shows that not all states might be willing to make sacrifices, trying to preserve control under the banner of sovereignty. The lack of accountability and enforcement mechanisms in IDRL compound this problem by providing few avenues to compel states to comply with their obligations. Acknowledging these limitations, the book proposes realistic strategies to overcome these challenges, offering a pragmatic roadmap for effectively incorporating solidarity into IDRL.[169]

IV. METHODOLOGY AND STRUCTURE OF THE BOOK

This book is divided into eight chapters, employing a combination of theoretical and doctrinal methodologies. The present chapter has outlined the book's objectives and approach, providing the context for the analysis that follows. Chapters 2 and 3 focus on the role of solidarity in IDRL. Chapter 2 conceptualises solidarity by drawing on theory, legal instruments and scholarship. Recognising that the concept of solidarity originates in philosophy, sociology and political theory, it engages with influential perspectives, including the work of sociologist Émile Durkheim, who popularised the conceptual study of solidarity, to help contextualise and understand the term. This theoretical foundation is complemented by an analysis of its use in international law. Chapter 3 then assesses the legal status of solidarity in IDRL through a systematic analysis of key legal documents, guided by the ILC's Draft Conclusions on General Principles of Law, which provide a methodology for identifying general principles of international law.[170]

The subsequent chapters examine the transformative potential of solidarity in IDRL. This analysis adopts a primarily doctrinal methodology, which is understood as 'research into the law and legal concepts'.[171] It involves a comprehensive and systematic review of IDRL's legal sources, including treaties, practice and soft law instruments. Through this approach, the book identifies applicable norms, as well as gaps and ambiguities within the existing framework, and then critically analyses selected issues through the lens of solidarity. This methodology aligns with the book's objectives, offering the tools necessary for a structured interpretation and analysis of IDRL.

Chapter 4 investigates how incorporating solidarity as a principle of IDRL could transform the regime, proposing five fundamental changes it could effect. It also examines the interplay between solidarity and other principles of IDRL, particularly sovereignty, demonstrating how these principles can be applied concurrently in a complementary manner. Chapters 5–7 build on this analysis

[169] The obstacles to the realisation of solidarity in IDRL are highlighted throughout its analysis of specific issues in chs 5–7. Chapter 8, section III proposes potential solutions to these obstacles.

[170] ILC, 'Draft Conclusions on General Principles of Law Adopted on First Reading' (12 May 2023) A/CN.4/L.982.

[171] T Hutchinson and N Duncan, 'Defining and Describing What We Do: Doctrinal Legal Research' (2012) 17(1) *Deakin Law Review* 83, 85.

by exploring how solidarity could reshape IDRL in relation to specific issues. Chapter 5 focuses on the role of the affected state, applying solidarity to the right of persons in disasters to receive humanitarian assistance, the state's duty to seek international assistance and the limits on its discretion regarding consent. Chapter 6 addresses the role of third states and assisting actors, including their responsibility for the protection of persons in disasters beyond their jurisdiction, the right to offer assistance, the duty to provide assistance and the accountability for alleged breaches of international obligations in the context of disasters and the prospect of enforcement. Chapter 7 turns to international cooperation, examining issues such as the exchange of information, the facilitation of international assistance and building the capacity of states to respond to disasters.

Finally, Chapter 8 summarises the findings of the book and reflects on how solidarity could transform IDRL from a system of ad hoc responses premised on state autonomy and voluntarism towards a regime that pursues the protection of persons in disasters through differentiated international cooperation and assistance. The chapter also look forwards, exploring how solidarity can be practically implemented in IDRL and how some challenges to realising solidarity, as highlighted throughout the book, can be overcome. The book ends on a note of hope, highlighting unique opportunities for achieving a solidarity-based approach to international cooperation in disaster response in a future of climate change.

2

Solidarity in International Law

I. INTRODUCTION

Solidarity is increasingly invoked in international disaster response as a call to collective action. Yet, despite its intuitive appeal and growing presence in instruments and discourse, its meaning remains elusive. As Chapter 1, section III demonstrated, solidarity is frequently referenced in IDRL, often framed as a foundational value underpinning cooperation and assistance. However, these references rarely clarify what solidarity entails, how it operates within international law or what obligations it might generate.[1] Without a clearer articulation of its conceptual contours, solidarity risks serving as little more than a rhetorical device – something states can pay lip service to without consequence – rather than a meaningful principle shaping state conduct.

This chapter seeks to address that gap by examining the meaning of solidarity in international law. It begins by tracing solidarity's conceptual origins in sociology and political and legal theory, recognising that solidarity has long been associated with notions of common goals, shared responsibility and mutual support. Drawing on influential thinkers such as Émile Durkheim, the chapter explores how solidarity has been theorised as both a social bond and a normative concept.

Building on this theoretical foundation, the chapter then turns to international law, analysing how solidarity has been conceptualised and applied across various legal regimes. While there is no settled definition of solidarity in international law, common themes and patterns emerge in its use. Solidarity is generally framed as a normative principle that binds states together in the pursuit of common goals, particularly in terms of addressing shared global needs and challenges. This framing emphasises the willingness of states to support one another in achieving these goals. Crucially, however, solidarity differs from general cooperation in that it recognises the unequal capacities and responsibilities of states, which prevent them from contributing equally to these common objectives. While all states are

[1] For instance, the ILC referred to solidarity as a 'key concept' and 'fundamental value' in the Draft Articles, but did not explain what this means or how it functions: see ILC, 'Draft Articles on the Protection of Persons in the Event of Disasters' (27 May 2016) UN Doc A/CN.4/L.871 (hereinafter 'Draft Articles') preamble; ILC, 'Commentaries on the Draft Articles on the Protection of Persons in the Event of Disasters' (2016) UN Doc A/71/10, 18.

expected to participate in the pursuit of shared goals, some may receive support while others provide it, depending on the circumstances.

The chapter then examines how solidarity can be understood in the specific context of international disaster response. This step is necessary because, despite its frequent invocation, solidarity remains conceptually underdeveloped within this regime.[2] Establishing a uniform understanding of solidarity in this context is challenging given that different actors may invoke the term with varying intentions and interpretations. Yet, without a clearer delineation of the concept's contours, it becomes difficult to assess its significance within IDRL. Establishing a shared conceptual understanding is therefore essential for analysing how solidarity operates in this regime and for guiding its interpretation in the chapters that follow.

However, it is not the intention of this chapter – or of the book more broadly – to construct a legal definition of solidarity. Rather, the aim is to establish a shared conceptual understanding that can serve as a foundation for the analysis that follows. Solidarity has proved to be, as one scholar aptly put it, 'notoriously hard to define . . . due to the fact that there exists no explicit and coherent theoretical tradition of its use as a systematic term'.[3] In light of this, the approach taken here aligns with common practice in the academic literature in which '[t]he term "solidarity" allows for narrower and wider definitions, which is why most authors do not argue for a correct, but rather for a sound, use of the term'.[4] By focusing on drafting the conceptual contours of solidarity, this chapter lays the groundwork for the book's subsequent engagement with the concept.

II. THEORIES OF SOLIDARITY

Solidarity as a cultural concept has a rich history and is expressed diversely across the world, rooted in different traditions that emphasise collective responsibility,

[2] Some scholars have discussed the role of solidarity in IDRL, but often without elaborating on its exact meaning. See K Wellens, 'Solidarity as a Constitutional Principle: Its Expanding Role and Inherent Limitations' in RStJ MacDonald and DM Johnston (eds), *Towards World Constitutionalism: Issues in the Legal Ordering of the World Community* (Martinus Nijhoff Publishers, 2005) 775, 784 ff; K Wellens, 'Revisiting Solidarity as a (Re-)Emerging Constitutional Principle: Some Further Reflections' in R Wolfrum and C Kojima (eds), *Solidarity: A Structural Principle of International Law* (Springer, 2010) 3, 14 ff; AG Koroma, 'Solidarity: Evidence of an Emerging International Legal Principle' in H Hestermeyer et al (eds), *Coexistence, Cooperation and Solidarity* (Martinus Nijhoff Publishers, 2012) 103, 123 ff; R Wolfrum, *Solidarity and Community Interests: Driving Forces for the Interpretation and Development of International Law* (Brill Nijhoff, 2021) 428 ff. That said, some scholars have examined the meaning of solidarity in the context of disasters in more detail: see F Zorzi Giustiniani, *International Law in Disaster Scenarios: Applicable Rules and Principles* (Springer, 2021) 96 ff; S Villani, *The Concept of Solidarity within EU Disaster Response Law: A Legal Assessment* (Bononia University Press, 2021) 26 ff.

[3] S Derpmann, 'Solidarity and Cosmopolitanism' (2009) 12(3) *Ethical Theory and Moral Practice* 303, 304.

[4] ibid 305.

mutual aid and interdependence. In African philosophy, for instance, the concept of *ubuntu* – often translated as 'I am because we are' – captures a sense of communal identity and moral obligation of mutual support towards others.[5] In Islamic traditions, *ummah* denotes the global community of believers, united by faith and mutual support, with practices such as *zakat* (obligatory almsgiving) embodying solidarity with the poor and vulnerable.[6] In Christian social teachings solidarity is taught through the idea of *caritas* (charity), a theological virtue calling people to love and serve others, particularly the poor and marginalised.[7] In Confucian ethics, solidarity is expressed through hierarchical yet reciprocal relationships, where social harmony depends on the fulfilment of duties to family and society.[8] Likewise, Buddhist traditions advance solidarity through *karuṇā* (compassion), framing care for others as an essential spiritual pursuit.[9]

Yet, the term 'solidarity' is connected to sociological, political and legal concepts developed mainly in Europe.[10] The linguistic roots of the term can be traced back to Roman law, where the *obligatio in solidum* made individual members of a family or community personally liable for shared debts.[11] Its modern usage, however, is most closely associated with the French word *solidarité*, which gained prominence as a political and legal concept during the French Revolution.[12] Often invoked alongside the revolutionary value of *fraternité* (fraternity), solidarity came to represent society's moral obligation to support its underprivileged members.[13]

This modern use of the term 'solidarity' typically refers to a social bond that connects individuals within a community through a shared sense of belonging and mutual responsibility, prompting them to support one another, especially in times of need or adversity.[14] Such support can take various forms: mutual assistance, where people directly help each other; burden-sharing, where responsibilities or hardships are distributed across the group; and preferential treatment, where vulnerable or disadvantaged members receive additional support. Typically, this commitment is directed inwardly, limited to those

[5] BD Ajitoni, 'Ubuntu and the Philosophy of Community in African Thought: An Exploration of Collective Identity and Social Harmony' (2024) 7(3) *Journal of African Studies and Sustainable Development* 1.

[6] Z Ali et al, 'The Role of Islamic Values in Promoting Social Justice and Community Welfare' (2024) V(1) *International Research Journal of Management and Social Sciences* 575.

[7] GJ Beyer, 'The Meaning of Solidarity in Catholic Social Teaching' (2014) 15(1) *Political Theology* 7; MJ Clark, 'Pope Francis and the Christological Dimensions of Solidarity in Catholic Social Teaching' (2019) 80(1) *Theological Studies* 102.

[8] MJ Yeh, 'Confucian Welfarism: Intellectual Origins of Solidarity for Health and Welfare Systems' (2023) 16(3) *Public Health Ethics* 232.

[9] WKD Soguilon, 'The Compassionate Buddhist: A Preliminary Reflection on the Buddhist Concept of Karuna and Its Implications' (2024) 11 *Open Access Library Journal* e12180.

[10] S Stjernø, *Solidarity in Europe: The History of an Idea* (Cambridge University Press, 2004).

[11] K Bayertz, 'Four Uses of "Solidarity"' in K Bayertz (ed), *Solidarity* (Springer, 1999) 3, 3.

[12] K Metz, 'Solidarity and History: Institutions and Social Concepts of Solidarity in 19th Century Western Europe' in K Bayertz (ed), *Solidarity* (Springer, 1999) 191, 191.

[13] Bayertz (n 11) 21.

[14] ibid 3.

recognised as part of the community. As Derpmann observes: 'It is distinctive about obligations of solidarity that they do not only *imply*, but *are essentially about* the inequality of moral concern for those who do belong to a community and those who do not.'[15] Solidarity is also fundamentally tied to the notion of sacrifice: members may provide support 'to promote the well-being of other members, even [when] incurring significant sacrifices for themselves'.[16] This willingness to bear costs without expecting reciprocity reflects a deeper sense of moral obligation and shared responsibility within the community.

Since its popularisation during and after the French Revolution, solidarity has been theorised as both a descriptive and normative concept across a range of disciplines, each offering distinct yet complementary perspectives.[17] Foremost among these is sociology, where solidarity serves as a descriptive and explanatory framework to examine how social cohesion is formed and sustained within groups or societies through shared values, mutual dependence or collective identity.[18] In the late nineteenth century, French sociologist Émile Durkheim developed a theory of solidarity that remains foundational today, explaining how social cohesion operates differently in traditional and modern societies.[19] He distinguished between two forms of solidarity. 'Mechanical solidarity' characterises pre-industrial societies, where individuals share similar work, values and lifestyles. In such contexts, cohesion arises from homogeneity, with the collective conscience dominating individual autonomy.[20] Social bonds are strong because people feel connected through shared experiences and beliefs, fostering a readiness to support one another. By contrast, 'organic solidarity' emerges in more complex, industrialised societies, where individuals perform specialised roles. Cohesion here is based on interdependence rather than similarity; people rely on one another to fulfil distinct functions within the social system. Mutual support thus becomes a necessity of interdependence: the failure of one can directly affect others and, ultimately, society as a whole.

Building on Durkheim's foundational work, sociological theorisation of solidarity has expanded to highlight its dual character as both a descriptive and normative concept. While Durkheim examined how solidarity sustains social cohesion through shared values or interdependence, later theorists have underscored its significance in addressing inequality, fostering collective identity and enabling political agency.[21] Solidarity is now understood not only as a mechanism that explains

[15] Derpmann (n 3) 305 (emphasis in original).

[16] ibid.

[17] Bayertz (n 11) 3. See also G Alpa, *Solidarity: A Normative Principle* (Kluwer, 2023).

[18] Bayertz (n 11) 3.

[19] E Durkheim, *The Division of Labour in Society* (Free Press, Collier Macmillan, 1964) (originally published in French in 1893).

[20] See also A Gofman, 'Durkheim's Theory of Social Solidarity and Social Rules' in V Jeffries (ed), *The Palgrave Handbook of Altruism, Morality, and Social Solidarity* (Palgrave Macmillan US, 2014) 45, 46.

[21] See, eg, MA Yerkes and M Bal (eds), *Solidarity and Social Justice in Contemporary Societies: An Interdisciplinary Approach to Understanding Inequalities* (Springer, 2022); K Banting and W Kymlicka (eds), *The Strains of Commitment: The Political Sources of Solidarity in Diverse Societies* (Oxford University Press, 2017).

how individuals are bound within a social structure, but also as a moral and political commitment to mutual support, particularly in diverse or fragmented societies. Thinkers such as Jürgen Habermas have linked solidarity to democratic discourse and communicative action,[22] while Pierre Bourdieu has demonstrated how it is shaped by power relations and social capital.[23] This broadened understanding recognises that solidarity is dynamic rather than static, adapting to shifting social conditions and serving as a key concept for analysing both how societies function and how they ought to respond to injustice and vulnerability.

Alongside its development in sociology, solidarity has also been theorised as a political and legal concept, where it denotes a normative commitment amongst members of a community to support one another, particularly the vulnerable or marginalised.[24] Politically, it has been closely tied to the idea of social justice, often serving as a foundation for movements advocating rights, equality and inclusion.[25] At the international level, expressions of solidarity have historically played a prominent role in mobilising support for suppressed groups across borders, for example, in global protests against South Africa's apartheid regime and in support of the plight of Palestinians.[26] In these contexts, solidarity operates not merely as an abstract ideal but also as a performative gesture that seeks to translate moral commitment into political action.

As a legal concept, solidarity refers to the principle that members of a community have obligations to support one another, particularly in situations of vulnerability, inequality or collective risk.[27] While not always explicitly codified as such, solidarity has been linked to legal frameworks that reflect mutual assistance, burden-sharing and collective responsibility.[28] Scholars have especially noted its institutionalisation in modern welfare states, which provide social safety nets for citizens who need it.[29] In this sense, solidarity is not only theorised as a moral ideal or political aspiration but also serves as a foundation for institutional and legal frameworks designed to operationalise mutual support within and across communities.

Solidarity also lies at the centre of the political and legal theory of solidarism, which emphasises the social obligations individuals and states owe to one another, grounded in shared humanity.[30] Emerging in late nineteenth- and early twenti-

[22] M Pensky, 'Solidarity' in A Allen and E Mendieta (eds), *The Cambridge Habermas Lexicon* (Cambridge University Press, 2019) 427.

[23] P Bourdieu, *On the State: Lectures at the Collège de France, 1989–1992* (Polity, 2014). See also D Riley, 'The New Durkheim: Bourdieu and the State' (2015) 2(2) *Critical Historical Studies* 261.

[24] See generally Alpa (n 17); R Forst, 'Solidarity: Concept, Conceptions, and Contexts' in A Sangiovanni and J Viehoff (eds), *The Virtue of Solidarity* (Oxford University Press, 2024) 35.

[25] Hannah Arendt, for instance, highlights the importance of solidarity as an antidote against totalitarianism; see H Arendt, *On Revolution* (Faber, 1963) 88 ff. See also DD Kim, *Arendt's Solidarity: Anti-Semitism and Racism in the Atlantic World* (Stanford University Press, 2024).

[26] CC Gould, 'Transnational Solidarities' (2007) 38(1) *Journal of Social Philosophy* 148.

[27] Bayertz (n 11) 21.

[28] ibid.

[29] Metz (n 12).

[30] M Koskenniemi, *The Gentle Civilizer of Nations: The Rise and Fall of International Law, 1870–1960* (Cambridge University Press, 2002) ch 4.

eth-century Europe, solidarism was a school of thought developed as a response to both liberal individualism and Marxist collectivism, offering a middle path that prioritises the mutual obligations of individuals and the state within society as 'a social-democratic modernization of "liberty, equality, and fraternity"' through a 'general aversion to the absolutism of individual rights and an emotional preference for social responsibility'.[31] Solidarist thinkers such as Léon Bourgeois argued that the division of labour creates a 'social debt' owed by the privileged to the less fortunate, which must be repaid through social policies and international cooperation.[32] Léon Duguit argued that law derives its legitimacy not from the will of a sovereign, but from its capacity to fulfil social needs and promote cohesion.[33] Duguit's concept of solidarity emphasised that individuals are inherently interdependent and that law should reflect this by prioritising duties over rights.

Notably, the solidarist movement also used its theory of solidarity as a basis for reconstructing international law, rejecting traditional notions of state sovereignty and legal positivism.[34] Georges Scelle advanced these ideas by proposing a 'solidarist post-sovereignty' model of international law.[35] He viewed states not as isolated sovereign entities, but as participants in a global legal order rooted in solidarity.[36] He envisioned international law as a system of objective norms arising from the social interdependence of peoples, advocating for federative arrangements and global institutions that reflect shared human values and responsibilities. In this system, diplomats would simultaneously serve national and international interests, thereby institutionalising solidarity across borders. Yet solidarist theory never fully materialised as a foundation for reimagining international law; its normative appeal often overshadowed by the realist prioritisation of state interests and the positivist emphasis on consent-based obligations.[37]

III. SOLIDARITY IN INTERNATIONAL LAW

Although the solidarist theory of international law never gained widespread traction, solidarity nonetheless entered the discourse on international law as a normative principle embodying the notions of shared responsibility and mutual

[31] ibid 288–89.

[32] JES Hayward, 'The Official Social Philosophy of the French Third Republic: Léon Bourgeois and Solidarism' (1961) 6(1) *International Review of Social History* 19.

[33] Koskenniemi (n 30) 297 ff; A Paul, 'An Analysis of Leon Duguit's Theory of "Social Solidarity"' (2021) 3(1) *Indian Journal of Law and Legal Research* 1.

[34] Koskenniemi (n 30) 288; C Tixier, 'The Legacy of Léon Bourgeois: From the Solidarist Doctrine to the Emergence of International Arbitration' in JQ Olmstead (ed), *Reconsidering Peace and Patriotism during the First World War* (Springer, 2017) 33. See also C Eggett, 'Solidarity as an International Legal Norm' in E Kassoti and N Idriz (eds), *The Principle of Solidarity: The Principle of Solidarity: International and EU Law Perspectives* (TMC Asser Press, 2023) 29, 33.

[35] H Thierry, 'The Thought of Georges Scelle' (1990) 1(1) *European Journal of International Law* 193.

[36] See also Tixier (n 34).

[37] Koskenniemi (n 30) ch 4.

support among states.[38] As early as the eighteenth century, Emer de Vattel positioned solidarity as a foundational principle of international law, suggesting that states should assist one another in times of need, particularly during humanitarian crises.[39] Today, solidarity is a concept invoked across various regimes of international law,[40] including international environmental law,[41] international climate change law,[42] international trade law,[43] international development law,[44] international refugee law,[45] IHRL[46] and IHL.[47] Yet it remains conceptually vague and elusive.

Despite its growing presence in treaties, UN resolutions and other statements, solidarity is often left undefined.[48] When definitions are provided, they tend to be broad and indeterminate, offering little clarity about its concrete meaning or implications. For example, the Millennium Declaration, adopted by the UN General Assembly in 2000, identified solidarity as one of the 'fundamental values essential to international relations in the twenty-first century', meaning that '[g]lobal challenges must be managed in a way that distributes the costs and burdens fairly in accordance with basic principles of equity and social justice. Those who suffer or who benefit least deserve help from those who

[38] Eggett (n 34) 33.

[39] E de Vattel, *Le Droit des Gens, ou Principes de la Loi Naturelle, Appliqués à la Conduite et aux Affaires des Nations et des Souverains* (1758) 11–20.

[40] For general overviews of the development of solidarity as a principle of international law, see Wellens, 'Solidarity as a Constitutional Principle' (n 2); Koroma (n 2); Wolfrum (n 2) ch 5. For a critique on tracing solidarity across international law, see D Tladi, 'In Search of Solidarity in International Law' in Kassoti and Idriz (n 34) 17.

[41] A Williams, 'Solidarity, Justice and Climate Change Law' (2009) 10 *Melbourne Journal of International Law* 493; H Hestermeyer, 'Reality or Aspiration? Solidarity in International Environmental and World Trade Law' (Max Planck Institute, 2012) 9 ff; Wellens, 'Solidarity as a Constitutional Principle' (n 2) 789–790; D Campanelli, 'Principle of Solidarity', *Max Planck Encyclopedia of International Law* (Oxford University Press, March 2011) para 6; Koroma (n 2) 110–13; Wolfrum (n 2) 406.

[42] Williams (n 41); Wolfrum (n 2) 413–14.

[43] Hestermeyer (n 41) 14; Wolfrum (n 2) 446.

[44] Koroma (n 2) 113–17; Wellens, 'Solidarity as a Constitutional Principle' (n 2) 790–794; Hestermeyer (n 41) 13–18; P Dann, 'Solidarity and the Law of Development Cooperation' in Wolfrum and Kojima (n 2) 55; RStJ MacDonald, 'Solidarity in the Practice and Discourse of Public International Law' (1996) 8 *Pace International Law Review* 259.

[45] Koroma (n 2) 117–19; Wolfrum (n 2) 450; G Martin, 'International Solidarity and Co-operation in Assistance to African Refugees: Burden-Sharing or Burden-Shifting?' (1995) 7 *International Journal of Refugee Law* 250.

[46] C Wellman, 'Solidarity, the Individual and Human Rights' (2000) 22 *Human Rights Quarterly* 639; Koroma (n 2) 108–10; R Wolfrum, 'Solidarity' in D Shelton (ed), *The Oxford Handbook of International Human Rights Law* (Oxford University Press 2013) 410.

[47] Koroma (n 2) 105–07; Campanelli (n 41) para 15; Wellens, 'Solidarity as a Constitutional Principle' (n 2) 783–784; Wolfrum (n 2) 427.

[48] L Boisson de Chazournes, 'Responsibility to Protect: Reflecting Solidarity?' in Wolfrum and Kojima (n 2) 93, 93–94. International courts have not had or taken the opportunity to clarify the meaning (or legal status) of solidarity in international law either. For instance, the International Court of Justice (ICJ) mentioned the term 'solidarity' several times in one case, but did not discuss its meaning; see *Maritime Dispute (Peru v Chile)* (Judgment) [2014] ICJ Rep 3, paras 125, 150–51.

benefit most'.[49] More recently, the *WHO Pandemic Agreement* listed solidarity as one of its guiding principles, providing that parties shall be guided by:

> [S]olidarity with all people and countries in the context of health emergencies, as well as inclusivity, transparency and accountability, to achieve the common interest of a more equitable and better prepared world to prevent, respond to and recover from pandemics, recognizing different levels of capacities and capabilities, particularly of developing countries, including landlocked developing countries, as well as the special circumstances of small island developing States and of least developed countries, in relation to pandemic prevention, preparedness and response.[50]

Solidarity has also been developed as a legal concept at the regional level within EU law.[51] Solidarity was envisioned as the foundation for European integration and has, over time, become embedded in the EU treaties, where it is invoked across diverse policy areas such as asylum, energy and disaster response.[52] While solidarity is not defined and remains context-dependent and somewhat ambiguous in EU law, it aligns closely with the notions of shared responsibility and mutual support, often requiring Member States to consider the interests of others, even at the expense of national interests.

Despite the absence of a clear, unifying definition, certain common themes and patterns can be identified in terms of how solidarity is used across international law. Broadly, legal scholarship conceptualises solidarity as the pursuit of common goals by a community of states that support one another through differentiated cooperation and assistance.[53] The term 'common' denotes that the achievement of the goal(s) in question is a collective task rather than a one-sided effort.[54] Examples include the protection of democratic values, the eradication of extreme poverty and the preservation of the environment. This understanding

[49] UN General Assembly Res 55/2 (8 September 2000) UN Doc A/RES/55/2 para 6. See also UN General Assembly Res 56/151 (19 December 2001) UN Doc A/RES/56/151 para 3(f); UN General Assembly Res 57/213 (18 December 2002) UN Doc A/RES/57/213 para 4(f).

[50] *WHO Pandemic Agreement* (20 May 2025) art 3(5).

[51] See generally Villani (n 2); J Czuczai, 'The Principle of Solidarity in the EU Legal Order – Some Practical Examples after Lisbon' in J Czuczai and F Naert (eds), *The EU as a Global Actor: Bridging Legal Theory and Practice* (Brill Nijhoff, 2017) 145; A Biondi, E Dagilytė and E Küçük (eds), *Solidarity in EU Law: Legal Principle in the Making* (Edward Elgar Publishing, 2018); Kassoti and Idriz (n 34); S Saracino, 'Understanding Solidarity in the European Union: An Analytical Framework' (2024) 53(5) *Theory and Society* 1093.

[52] See, eg, *Treaty on the European Union* (13 December 2007) arts 2, 3, 21, 24, 31–32; *Treaty on the Functioning of the European Union* (13 December 2007) arts 67, 80, 122,194, 222.

[53] See generally Wolfrum (n 2) 396; MacDonald (n 44) 259–60; Wellens, 'Solidarity as a Constitutional Principle' (n 2) 775; Koroma (n 2) 103; Campanelli (n 41) para 5; Dann (n 44) 57; Williams (n 41) 498; Hestermeyer (n 41) 8; KP Sommermann, 'Some Reflections on the Concept of Solidarity and its Transformation into a Legal Principle' (2014) 52(1) *Archiv des Völkerrechts* 10, 10; H Neuhold, 'Common Security: The Litmus Test of International Solidarity' in Wolfrum and Kojima (n 2) 193, 193–94; L Casini, 'Solidarity between States in the Global Legal Space' (2013) https://papers.ssrn.com/sol3/papers.cfm?abstract_id=2368209, 3; I Badanova, 'Making Sense of Solidarity in International Law: Input from the Integration of the European Gas Market' (2019) 11(2) *European Journal of Legal Studies* 105.

[54] Dann (n 53) 61.

frames solidarity as a normative principle that underpins cooperative behaviour among states, particularly in contexts where collective action is necessary to address global need as challenges.

Solidarity, when conceptualised as the pursuit of common goals by a community, reflects a relational dynamic rooted in shared values, goals or vulnerabilities.[55] It can be used to express 'a spirit of unity among individuals, peoples, States and international organizations, encompassing the union of interests, purposes and actions and the recognition of different needs and rights to achieve common goals'.[56] Echoing sociological theories, solidarity emerges within groups that perceive themselves as interconnected, whether through historical ties, similar worldviews or mutual dependencies. These groups may encompass the 'international community',[57] but more commonly consist of smaller coalitions of states and others united by regional proximity, ideological alignment or common objectives. The strength and coherence of solidarity depend on the degree of group identification and commitment to mutually support one another – the stronger the social bonds, the greater the solidarity.[58]

However, solidarity extends beyond describing cohesion among states to add a normative dimension to their relationships within a community.[59] It builds on the presupposition that states are committed to working collaboratively towards common goals and are willing to assist one another in that pursuit.[60] This understanding of solidarity implies a dual structure of responsibility: each state bears individual obligations to contribute its share, while the community as a whole carries a collective responsibility to support its members in fulfilling those obligations, particularly those less able to do so.[61]

Importantly, this conception of solidarity does not suggest a transfer of responsibility from individual states to the collective. Rather, it preserves the individual responsibility of each state to contribute to common goals while introducing a shared responsibility among the community of states to assist members facing difficulties in meeting their commitments.[62] In this way, solidarity has a

[55] Wellens, 'Solidarity as a Constitutional Principle' (n 2) 775; Koroma (n 2) 103; Hestermeyer (n 41) 8.

[56] Draft Declaration on the Right to International Solidarity in UN Human Rights Council, 'Report of the Independent Expert on Human Rights and International Solidarity' (25 April 2017) UN Doc A/HRC/35/35 annex, art 1(1).

[57] Much has been written on the concept of the 'international community' in the academic literature, see, eg, H Bull, *The Anarchical Society: A Study of Order in World Politics,* 2nd edn (Macmillan, 1995); E Benvenisti and G Nolte (eds), *Community Interests across International Law* (Oxford University Press, 2018). See also Tladi (n 40) 25.

[58] Williams (n 41) 498; Neuhold (n 53) 194.

[59] Williams (n 41) 498; R Wolfrum, 'International Law of Cooperation' in *Max Planck Encyclopedia of International Law* (Oxford University Press, 2010) para 3; Neuhold (n 53) 193–194; Koroma (n 2) 103; MacDonald (n 44) 259–260; Sommermann (n 53) 10.

[60] Neuhold (n 53) 193–94; Campanelli (n 41) para 9; Boisson de Chazournes (n 48) 96.

[61] RM Rizki, 'Promotion and Protection of All Human Rights, Civil, Political, Economic, Social and Cultural Rights, Including the Right to Development' (15 August 2008) UN Doc A/HRC/9/10 para 6; Dann (n 53) 57; Williams (n 41) 500.

[62] Williams (n 41) 498; Sommermann (n 53) 10.

complementary effect: it reinforces the autonomy and duties of individual states while embedding them within a broader system of mutual support. This dual structure of responsibility reflects Durkheim's theory of organic solidarity, which emphasises the interdependence of individuals – or, in this context, states – performing distinct functions within a complex society. Just as members of a society support one another in fulfilling their roles, particularly when some struggle, states are expected to uphold their own commitments while assisting others in achieving shared goals.

This understanding of solidarity also implies that states' contributions are not equal but differentiated according to their respective capacities.[63] In essence, solidarity recognises that although all states are expected to contribute to common goals, some may require support while others do not, depending on their circumstances.[64] As Wolfrum explains:

> The principle of solidarity is aware and takes into account that there is for one or other reason *de facto* an inequality between the actors involved and that the benefits to be achieved from the common action as well as the contributions of each participant in the common action differ. This means that when trying to achieve a common goal the contributions of some may exceed those of others. Although the benefits achieved should accrue to the community, in particular cases solidarity-based actions may be designed to benefit some States or even only one.[65]

The justification for differentiation varies across contexts, but is typically rooted in the recognition of existing inequalities between states that make support for some necessary or appropriate.[66] In some cases, differentiation is grounded in socio-economic disparities that constrain the capacities and capabilities of certain states to contribute to shared objectives. This is reflected, for instance, in the *WHO Pandemic Agreement*, which grounds the need for solidarity in the recognition of 'different levels of capacities and capabilities, particularly of developing countries, including landlocked developing countries, as well as the special circumstances of small island developing States and of least developed countries, in relation to pandemic prevention, preparedness and response'.[67] In other instances, differentiation is justified by historical factors – such as the enduring effects of colonisation – or other structural inequalities. In the context of climate change, for example, solidarity with less developed states is based on the disproportionate contributions of economically developed states to global warming.[68] However, whatever the reason, solidarity acquires a deeper normative dimension through the differentiation of contributions that goes beyond

[63] Wolfrum (n 2) 90.
[64] Williams (n 41) 498–500.
[65] Wolfrum (n 2) 396.
[66] ibid.
[67] WHO Pandemic Agreement (n 50) art 3(5).
[68] *United Nations Framework Convention on Climate Change* (9 May 1992) (UNFCCC) art 3(1).

pragmatism: it demands not only cooperation but also acknowledgement of unequal burdens and a commitment to equitable support.[69]

Another defining characteristic of solidarity is the notion of sacrifice: support is in principle provided without the expectation of receiving anything in return.[70] This element distinguishes solidarity from more traditional forms of international cooperation, which are often transactional in nature: states engage in exchanges designed to yield mutual benefits, even if not in strictly equal terms.[71] Solidarity, by contrast, embodies a model of cooperation that transcends self-interest, allowing some states to benefit directly while others contribute primarily through support.[72] That said, although the costs and benefits of solidarity may be distributed unevenly, all members of the community ultimately benefit in an indirect way.[73] This is because international cooperation and assistance help to advance common goals, serving the interests of the community as a whole.

Through its differentiating nature and the underlying notion of sacrifice, solidarity is fundamentally about advancing social justice. It seeks to address and reduce structural inequalities between states by promoting differentiated international cooperation and assistance in pursuit of common objectives. As Wolfrum argued, solidarity seeks to 'fulfil a certain mission, namely the promotion of international social justice among States. This is because at its heart the principle of solidarity strives for the amelioration, at least a gradual one, of inequalities among States'.[74] This is also reflected in the earlier-cited Millennium Declaration, which emphasises that the costs and burdens in addressing global needs and challenges must be distributed fairly 'in accordance with basic principles of equity and social justice' as '[t]hose who suffer or who benefit least deserve help from those who benefit most'.[75] Differentiation ensures that states contribute according to their capacities, while sacrifice allows some states to support others without expecting direct returns. Together, these elements reflect a commitment to fairness and equity, recognising that socio-economic, historical and other structural disparities shape the ability of states to participate in collective action to address global needs and challenges. Solidarity thus becomes a vehicle for redistributive justice, enabling the international community to work collectively towards a more balanced and inclusive global order where all states, regardless of their position, have the opportunity to contribute to and benefit from the pursuit of shared goals.

Solidarity is expressed in diverse ways across international law through varying methods of support, reflecting its flexible and context-dependent

[69] Wolfrum (n 2) 396.

[70] Neuhold (n 53) 193–94. See also Campanelli (n 41) para 9; Boisson de Chazournes (n 48) 96.

[71] Wolfrum (n 59) paras 2–3.

[72] Koroma (n 2) 103.

[73] Boisson de Chazournes (n 48) 95.

[74] Wolfrum (n 2) 87.

[75] UN General Assembly Res 55/2 (n 49) para 6. See also UN General Assembly Res 56/151 (n 49) para 3(f); UN General Assembly Res 57/213 (n 49) para 4(f).

nature. Wolfrum has identified three distinct levels of intervention through which solidarity operates.[76] The first involves the pursuit of common objectives through collective action, where members of the international community work together in a coordinated manner towards shared goals. Examples include global health initiatives such as COVAX, the COVID-19 vaccines-sharing initiative that supplied vaccines to lower-income countries led by the World Health Organization (WHO).[77]

The second level involves achieving common objectives through the principle of common but differentiated responsibilities. Under this principle, states agree to pursue shared goals by allocating responsibilities and obligations in a differentiated manner, with some states accepting greater burdens to alleviate those of others,[78] thereby 'translating notions of solidarity and equity into legal obligations'.[79] This principle is embedded, for example, in the *United Nations Framework Convention on Climate Change* (UNFCCC), where developed states committed to taking the lead in combating climate change 'on the basis of equity and in accordance with their common but differentiated responsibilities and respective capabilities'.[80] Here, solidarity manifests not through collective action or direct assistance, but through burden-sharing, achieving a differentiation in the collective pursuit of common objectives.

The third level consists of actions taken specifically to benefit particular states.[81] This may include humanitarian aid, technical assistance or financial support.[82] In some instances, such support is provided directly, with one state assisting another. In these cases, the contributions to and benefits of international cooperation are clearly differentiated between providers and beneficiaries.

[76] R Wolfrum, 'Solidarity amongst States: An Emerging Structural Principle of International Law' (2009) 49(1) *Indian Journal of International Law* 8. Some have taken an even more expansive view on solidarity. For instance, the UN Human Rights Council has stated that 'international solidarity is not limited to international assistance and cooperation, aid, charity or humanitarian assistance; it is a broader concept and principle that includes sustainability in international relations, especially international economic relations, the peaceful coexistence of all members of the international community, equal partnerships and the equitable sharing of benefits and burdens': UN Human Rights Council Res 41/5 (11 July 2019) UN Doc A/HRC/RES/41/5 para 2.

[77] Established during the COVID-19 pandemic in 2020, COVAX was a global initiative co-led by the WHO, Gavi and the Coalition for Epidemic Preparedness Innovations (CEPI), aimed at ensuring equitable access to COVID-19 vaccines worldwide. It sought to pool resources from wealthier nations to fund vaccine procurement and distribution for lower-income countries, thereby countering vaccine nationalism and promoting global health equity. COVAX ended on 31 December 2023. For more information, see WHO, 'COVAX' www.who.int/initiatives/act-accelerator/covax.

[78] E Hey, 'Common But Differentiated Responsibilities' in *Max Planck Encyclopedia of International Law* (Oxford University Press, 2011) para 1.

[79] M den Heijer and H van der Wilt, 'Global Solidarity and Common But Differentiated Responsibilities' in M den Heijer and H an der Wilt (eds), *Netherlands Yearbook of International Law 2020* (TMC Asser Press, 2022) 3, 5. See also Wolfrum (n 46) 404.

[80] UNFCCC (n 68) art 3(1).

[81] See also A Ud Din, 'Differential Treatment for Developing Countries as a Manifestation of Solidarity: Overcoming New Challenges by Going Back to the Basics' in Kassoti and Idriz (n 34) 129, 134.

[82] Campanelli (n 41) paras 9–10.

In other situations, support is offered through collective schemes, such as funds or programmes, run by international organisations, NGOs, the private sector or others. Support can also take more indirect forms, such as through systems of preferential treatment that grant certain privileges or benefits to specific states.[83] This approach is common in international trade agreements which may grant states reduced tariff rates or lower import and export standards.[84] Such privileges and benefits also constitute a form of support, as they intentionally differentiate benefits in favour of certain states only.

Finally, there are competing theories about what motivates states to support one another in a spirit of solidarity. One explanation suggests that solidarity is an act of altruism 'whereby members of a community act out of good faith or a sense of philanthropy',[85] grounded in a 'genuine concern for the well-being of others'.[86] However, this view is not entirely convincing in the context of international law, as practice shows that states are generally less inclined to provide support out of charity only.[87] In contrast, states have demonstrated a greater willingness to cooperate in a spirit of solidarity to address problems that also affect them, such as the depletion of the ozone layer, than in areas where altruistic action provides them with no benefit, as seen in global efforts to eradicate extreme poverty.[88] A more persuasive explanation therefore proposes that states act in solidarity out of recognition of the deep global interdependencies that make mutual support necessary to safeguard both collective and individual interests.[89] Echoing Durkheim's theory of organic solidarity, this view holds that globalisation has created intricate networks of interdependence among states, making them, to some extent, reliant on one another's actions.[90] Climate change exemplifies this interconnectedness, illustrating that all states must cooperate to achieve shared goals such as reducing CO_2 emissions and mitigating global warming. In the face of existing inequalities that hinder some states from contributing equally or otherwise justify differentiated responsibilities, mutual support becomes a condition for collective success rather than an expression of altruism. Another motivation for solidarity could lie in the acknowledgement of historical injustices that have produced enduring structural inequalities.

[83] Wolfrum (n 79) 404.

[84] E Tempone, 'Special and Differential Treatment' in *Max Planck Encyclopedia of International Law* (Oxford University Press, 2014).

[85] Williams (n 41) 502. See also Hestermeyer (n 41) 8; E Küçük, 'Solidarity in EU Law: An Elusive Political Statement or a Legal Principle with Substance?' in A Biondi, E Dagilytė and E Küçük (eds), *Solidarity in EU Law* (Edward Elgar, 2018) 38, 40; C Arnsperger and Y Varoufakis, 'Toward a Theory of Solidarity' (2003) 59(2) *Erkenntnis* 157, 157.

[86] Küçük (n 85) 41.

[87] Williams (n 41) 501; Hestermeyer (n 41) 19.

[88] Hestermeyer (n 41) 19.

[89] Durkheim (n 19).

[90] Williams (n 41) 501; Hestermeyer (n 41) 8; Campanelli (n 41) para 4; Wellens, 'Solidarity as a Constitutional Principle' (n 2) 776; Koroma (n 2) 103; Rizki (n 61) para 4; PM Dupuy, 'International Law: Torn between Coexistence, Cooperation and Globalization. General Conclusions' (1998) 9(2) *European Journal of International Law* 278, 284.

Colonial legacies, exploitative economic arrangements and disproportionate contributions to environmental degradation – such as the historically higher CO_2 emissions of industrialised states – have created asymmetries in vulnerability and capacity that need to be addressed through differentiated cooperation. Solidarity, in this sense, is not merely an expression of goodwill, but a corrective principle aimed at addressing these imbalances and promoting equity.

The question of what motivates states to act in solidarity is highly relevant to their compliance with obligations of support under international law. When solidarity is framed as a responsibility rather than an act of charity, states are more likely to engage in sustained, solidarity-based cooperation.[91] This framing positions solidarity as a normative duty rather than as a philanthropic gesture. Conversely, where states perceive solidarity as merely a moral virtue or an expression of goodwill, compliance tends to be weaker, inconsistent and vulnerable to shifting political priorities. In the context of international disaster response, this distinction is critical: solidarity is likely to be more effective when understood as a shared responsibility rather than as an altruistic act that can be deferred or withdrawn at will.

IV. SOLIDARITY IN THE CONTEXT OF INTERNATIONAL DISASTER RESPONSE

Building on the previous section's analysis of how solidarity is broadly conceptualised within international law, this section turns to the specific context of international disaster response to explore how solidarity is understood. As discussed, solidarity generally refers to the pursuit of common goals by a community of states through differentiated forms of cooperation and assistance. Applied to the context of international disaster response, solidarity centres on the shared goal of protecting people affected by disasters. In disaster response, the protection of disaster-affected populations is increasingly viewed not as the sole responsibility of the state(s) in which the disaster occurs, but as a collective concern of the international community.[92] This understanding is reflected in numerous treaties, UN General Assembly resolutions and patterns of practice, all of which indicate that states recognise a shared responsibility in responding to disasters.

Evidence of this growing recognition can be seen in instruments, which affirm that while the primary responsibility for disaster response lies with the affected state(s), the protection of disaster-affected populations is a matter of international concern, particularly where cooperation is needed to avert or alleviate human suffering. The AADMER, for instance, responds to concerns over 'the increasing frequency and scale of disasters in the ASEAN region and their

[91] Hestermeyer (n 41) 18–19.

[92] ILC, 'Fourth Report on the Protection of Persons in the Event of Disasters, by Mr. Eduardo Valencia-Ospina, Special Rapporteur' (11 May 2011) UN Doc A/CN.4/643 para 81.

damaging impacts both short-term and long-term',[93] and expresses a shared commitment of state parties:

> [T]o provide effective mechanisms to achieve substantial reduction of disaster losses in lives and in the social, economic and environmental assets of the Parties, and to jointly respond to disaster emergencies through concerted national efforts and intensified regional and international cooperation.[94]

Similarly, the *Inter-American Convention to Facilitate Disaster Assistance* recognises in its preamble that 'the human suffering caused by such disasters can be relieved more effectively and swiftly' through coordinated international assistance, and that 'a genuine spirit of solidarity and good-neighbourliness between the American states has been expressed in cases of disaster and that this spirit can be strengthened through preparedness that makes it possible to act more efficiently'.[95]

At the UN, General Assembly resolutions have consistently emphasised the international community's concern for the well-being of people affected by disasters and the need for cooperation to prevent or alleviate unnecessary suffering. Resolution 46/182, which sets out guiding principles for humanitarian emergency assistance, expresses deep concern 'about the suffering of the victims of disasters and emergency situations, the loss in human lives, the flow of refugees, the mass displacement of people and the material destruction'.[96] It acknowledges that '[h]umanitarian assistance is of cardinal importance for the victims of natural disasters and other emergencies' and that, although '[e]ach State has the responsibility first and foremost to take care of the victims of natural disasters and other emergencies occurring on its territory', it is possible that 'the magnitude and duration of many emergencies may be beyond the response capacity of many affected countries' and affirms that international cooperation is therefore 'of great importance'.[97] More recently, Resolution 79/128, which initiated negotiations on a global treaty on the protection of persons in the event of disasters, reiterates concern over the growing frequency and severity of disasters and affirms that protecting affected populations is 'of major importance in the relations of States'.[98]

The long-standing and widespread practice of international cooperation in disaster response further demonstrates that the protection of persons affected

[93] *ASEAN Agreement on Disaster Management and Emergency Response* (26 July 2005) (AADMER) preamble.

[94] ibid art 2. Some treaties also cite other interests necessitating international cooperation in disaster response, such as the protection of the environment or mitigating spill-over effects or transboundary harm. See, eg, *Tampere Convention on the Provision of Telecommunication Resources for Disaster Mitigation and Relief Operations* (18 June 1998) preamble.

[95] *Inter-American Convention to Facilitate Disaster Assistance* (6 July 1991) preamble.

[96] UN General Assembly Res 46/182 (19 December 1991) UN Doc A/RES/46/182 preamble. Earlier resolutions also expressed these concerns; see, eg, UN General Assembly Res 43/131 (8 December 1988) UN Doc A/RES/43/131 preamble.

[97] UN General Assembly Res 46/182 (n 96) paras 1, 4 and 5.

[98] UN General Assembly Res 79/128 (4 December 2024) UN Doc A/RES/79/128 preamble.

by disasters is not regarded as the exclusive responsibility of the affected state, but rather as a shared concern of the international community. For decades – if not centuries[99] – states have consistently provided assistance in the aftermath of disasters, even when not affected themselves. This consistent pattern of behaviour reflects a collective recognition of the importance of alleviating human suffering wherever it occurs. The regularity and formalisation of such cooperative efforts – through regional and bilateral agreements – illustrate that the protection of persons affected by disasters is considered a shared interest of all states.

Taken together, this evidence points to the conclusion that the protection of persons affected by disasters is increasingly recognised as a common objective of the international community and lies at the centre of solidarity in this context. This shared concern does not displace the primary responsibility of the affected state but complements it by affirming the legitimate role of non-affected states in supporting disaster response efforts.[100] As the ILC's Special Rapporteur on the Protection of Persons in the Event of Disasters, Eduardo Valencia-Ospina, observed:

> Non-affected States, as members of the international community, have an interest in the protection of persons in the event of disasters not occurring within their territory. This interest needs to be understood in the context of the primary responsibility of the affected State in the protection of persons in its territory, as it also is an expression of the principle of humanity, underpinned by solidarity. Furthermore, recognition of such interest is instrumental to the preservation of human dignity in the event of disasters, and the protection of human rights.[101]

Solidarity implies that the common goal of protecting persons affected by disasters is pursued by a community of states willing to support one another. In this context, this community should be understood in broad terms: the consistent pattern of global cooperation suggests that it encompasses a wide and diverse range of states.[102] The protection of persons affected by disasters appears to be

[99] The provision of humanitarian aid after disasters has a long history pre-dating the formation of nation-states. The literature often refers to the English humanitarian mission sent to Portugal after the 1755 Lisbon earthquake as an early example of 'modern' international cooperation in disaster response. See ILC, 'Preliminary Report on the Protection of Persons in the Event of Disasters, by Mr. Eduardo Valencia-Ospina, Special Rapporteur' (5 May 2008) UN Doc A/CN.4/598 para 14 ff; P Macalister-Smith, *International Humanitarian Assistance: Disaster Relief Actions in International Law and Organization* (Kluwer, 1985) 17, 53–55.

[100] See ch 5, section II on the role of the affected state in light of solidarity.

[101] ILC (n 92) para 81.

[102] Eggett argues that 'it is conceivable that a broad principle of solidarity could applied to a diverse range of actors': Eggett (n 34) 43. Tladi, on the other hand, pushes back on the idea that there exists an international community from which solidarity can originate. He argues that: 'It is easy to speak of an international community but it is not at all clear that an international community truly exists. There is, of course, a collection of States committed to particular objectives and willing to cooperate and coordinate to achieve these objectives. But how and which of these objectives are prioritised, how they are to be achieved and at what cost, are all products of bargain, of *quid pro quo* and of influence, which is itself dependent on power': Tladi (n 40) 26.

recognised as a shared goal of *all* states, not only those linked by geography or political alignment. Indeed, disaster assistance usually transcends traditional political, ideological and regional divides, with states providing aid to others with whom they may have limited diplomatic ties or even strained relations.[103] It is also important to recognise that this community extends beyond states themselves. Assisting non-state actors – such as international organisations and humanitarian organisations like Red Cross and Red Crescent societies – also share the common goal of protecting persons affected by disasters and are often among the first to mobilise in their aftermath.[104] At the same time, there is a clear trend towards regionalisation, as states increasingly formalise and intensify their cooperation through regional agreements and institutional frameworks.[105] These regional efforts show that solidarity can occur on multiple levels of international partnership.

Solidarity in the context of international disaster response is most commonly expressed through forms of cooperation and assistance that benefit the affected state(s) rather than through coordinated collective action. International cooperation typically takes the form of targeted support that complements and strengthens national efforts. This corresponds to Wolfrum's third level of solidarity-based action: measures taken by states to assist others in achieving shared objectives.[106] Such support can take many forms, depending on the nature and scale of the disaster and the specific needs of the affected state and its population.[107] The Draft Articles, for example, list various forms of cooperation, including 'humanitarian assistance, coordination of international relief actions and communications, and making available relief personnel, equipment and goods, and scientific, medical and technical resources'.[108] While humanitarian aid is the most visible and immediate form of support, other forms such as technical and financial assistance also play a crucial role in helping states reduce risks, enhance preparedness and build resilience.[109]

As explained in the previous section, a defining feature of solidarity is that states are willing to support one another through *differentiated* cooperation and assistance. In the context of international disaster response, this differentiation

[103] I Kelman, *Disaster Diplomacy* (Routledge, 2012).

[104] UN General Assembly Res 46/182 (n 96) recognises the important role of non-state actors in international disaster response: 'Intergovernmental and non- governmental organizations working impartially and with strictly humanitarian motives should continue to make a significant contribution in supplementing national efforts' (para 5).

[105] Examples of increased cooperation on regional level include the EU in Europe, ASEAN in Southeast Asia and the Caribbean Disaster Emergency Management Agency (CDEMA) in the Caribbean.

[106] Wolfrum (n 76).

[107] ILC, 'Commentaries' (n 1) 41.

[108] Draft Articles (n 1) art 8. The Commentaries also highlight other forms of cooperation, including 'financial support; technology transfer covering, among others, technology relating to satellite imagery; training; information sharing; joint simulation exercises and planning; and undertaking needs assessments and situation overview': ILC, 'Commentaries' (n 1) 41.

[109] Draft Articles (n 1) art 9. See also ILC, 'Commentaries' (n 1) 40.

reflects the understanding that while affected states hold primary responsibility for protecting disaster-affected populations, they may require support from others. Disaster aid is therefore not automatic but provided according to need. This differentiation is rooted in the recognition of structural inequalities between states, which can affect their ability to respond effectively to disasters. In this context, inequality is not solely – or even primarily – about socio-economic disparities among states. Not all economically disadvantaged states require international assistance and, conversely, some highly developed states may need external support when confronted with large-scale or complex disasters.[110] Rather, it reflects the understanding that states' national response capacities are unequal (see Chapter 7, section III.C).[111] States with limited capacities may require more support than those whose response systems are less easily overwhelmed. While socio-economic factors play a role since resources are essential for building effective disaster response systems,[112] inequality in this context is broader than economic status alone. It also encompasses disparities in preparedness, institutional strength, technical expertise and logistical infrastructure.

Beyond disparities in national response capacities, other factors may also justify differentiated cooperation and assistance in the spirit of solidarity. One compelling example is the expectation that industrialised states provide support to states disproportionately affected by climate change, increasing their vulnerability to disasters. This expectation is grounded in the recognition that wealthier, historically high-emitting states bear a greater responsibility for the global climate crisis due to their disproportionate contributions to greenhouse gas emissions. This line of reasoning underpins the negotiations and implementation of the global loss and damage fund,[113] which aims to compensate states for the harm they suffer as a result of climate-related disasters.[114] In this context, solidarity is not only about addressing immediate needs but also about acknowledging historical responsibility and promoting fairness in the distribution of burdens and support.

[110] As illustrated by disasters such as 2005 Hurricane Katrina in the US, the 2015 Christchurch earthquake in New Zealand and the 2011 Tōhoku earthquake and tsunami in Japan, in which developed states all required and accepted international aid.

[111] European Commission, 'INFORM Report 2024' (2024) 21–22.

[112] Studies show that low-income countries are more vulnerable to the effects of disasters due to their reduced capacity to cope with and recover from disastrous events: S Hallegatte et al, 'From Poverty to Disaster and Back: A Review of the Literature' (2020) 4(1) *Economics of Disasters and Climate Change* 223.

[113] M Pill, 'Towards a Funding Mechanism for Loss and Damage from Climate Change Impacts' (2022) 35 *Climate Risk Management* 100391, 4.

[114] In 2022, the Conference of the Parties of the UNFCCC agreed on a loss and damage fund for the first time. The loss and damage fund is an agreement to provide funding to countries that are most vulnerable and affected by climate change. See UNFCCC Secretariat, 'COP27 Reaches Breakthrough Agreement on New "Loss and Damage" Fund for Vulnerable Countries' (20 November 2022) https://unfccc.int/news/cop27-reaches-breakthrough-agreement-on-new-loss-and-damage-fund-for-vulnerable-countries. Yet, the implementation of the fund is still ongoing, with states negotiating their respective contributions to the fund as well as procedures on how to distribute the money.

Solidarity is therefore fundamentally about social justice. Differentiated cooperation recognises that some states are less able to protect their populations in the face of disasters or suffer disproportionate damage due to the (in)actions of others. Providing assistance to these states is not merely a humanitarian gesture or a means of achieving common goals; it is a way of addressing structural inequalities that affect states' ability to respond effectively. Solidarity thus involves a commitment to bridging these gaps by supporting states that are less equipped to respond, promoting a more equitable distribution of protection and resilience across the international community.

V. CONCLUSION

This chapter has examined the conceptual contours of solidarity by tracing its origins in sociology, political and legal theory, and analysing its use across international law. It established that solidarity is framed both as a relational concept, describing the social bond that connects members of a community, and a normative commitment to mutual support within that community. Although often left undefined, solidarity is generally understood in international law as the pursuit of common goals by a community of states (and others) that support one another through differentiated cooperation and assistance. This model of solidarity departs from traditional notions of transactional cooperation, instead embracing an approach that acknowledges and responds to existing inequalities between states. It recognises that contributions to collective efforts are not equal, but should be differentiated according to capacity and responsibility. On top of this, solidarity entails a willingness to provide support without expectation of reciprocity, even when benefits are unevenly distributed. This understanding positions solidarity not merely as altruism, but also as a response to the realities of an interdependent world, where mutual support is increasingly essential to achieving shared objectives, and a correction to existing inequalities.

In the context of international disaster response, solidarity is about the protection of persons affected by disasters. While states retain primary responsibility for disaster response within their jurisdictions, solidarity acknowledges that national response capacities of states are unequal. It is in response to these disparities that states offer aid to those whose response capacities are overwhelmed – not to supplant national efforts, but to complement and reinforce them. Viewed through this lens, solidarity reframes international disaster response as a project of social justice. Cooperation and assistance become an expression of shared responsibility grounded in interdependence and a recognition of structural inequality. Solidarity, in this sense, is not only about achieving common goals; it is also about addressing the systemic conditions that shape states' ability to respond effectively. It reflects a deeper normative commitment to ensuring that all persons affected by disasters receive protection, regardless of where they are and regardless of the capacities of the state in which they reside.

Having established the conceptual contours of solidarity, the next chapter turns to examine its legal status. Although solidarity is frequently invoked in treaties, resolutions and practice, its status as a *legal* principle remains contested. The following chapter will therefore assess whether – and to what extent – solidarity has been translated from a conceptual notion into a legal norm capable of creating, modifying or confirming rights and obligations of states.

3

Solidarity as a Legal Principle

I. INTRODUCTION

OFTEN PORTRAYED AS A foundational principle of international law guiding collective action in addressing global needs and challenges,[1] solidarity is increasingly invoked in IDRL. It features in treaties,[2] in the ILC's Draft Articles[3] and in statements by states and non-state actors alike.[4] Yet despite its intuitive appeal and frequent invocation in disaster contexts, the legal status of solidarity remains unclear.[5] The ILC, for instance, described solidarity as a 'key concept' or 'fundamental value' in the Draft Articles without clarifying its legal standing.[6] Likewise, where solidarity is discussed in the academic literature, its precise legal status is rarely examined.[7] This uncertainty raises important questions about whether solidarity functions merely as a moral appeal or has evolved into a legal principle, or anything in between. A detailed,

[1] M den Heijer and H van der Wilt, 'Global Solidarity and Common But Differentiated Responsibilities' in M den Heijer and H van der Wilt (eds), *Netherlands Yearbook of International Law 2020* (TMC Asser Press, 2022) 3, 4.

[2] See examples in section IV.A.

[3] '*Mindful* of the fundamental value of solidarity in international relations and the importance of strengthening international cooperation in respect of all phases of a disaster': ILC, 'Draft Articles on the Protection of Persons in the Event of Disasters' (27 May 2016) UN Doc A/CN.4/L.871 (hereinafter 'Draft Articles') preamble.

[4] See examples in section IV.C.

[5] C Eggett, 'Solidarity as an International Legal Norm' in E Kassoti and N Idriz (eds), *The Principle of Solidarity: The Principle of Solidarity: International and EU Law Perspectives* (TMC Asser Press, 2023) 29, 30.

[6] Draft Articles (n 3) preamble; ILC, 'Commentaries on the Draft Articles on the Protection of Persons in the Event of Disasters' (2016) UN Doc A/71/10, 18.

[7] See, eg, K Wellens, 'Solidarity as a Constitutional Principle: Its Expanding Role and Inherent Limitations' in RStJ MacDonald and DM Johnston (eds), *Towards World Constitutionalism: Issues in the Legal Ordering of the World Community* (Martinus Nijhoff Publishers, 2005) 775, 784 ff; K Wellens, 'Revisiting Solidarity as a (Re-)Emerging Constitutional Principle: Some Further Reflections' in R Wolfrum and C Kojima (eds), *Solidarity: A Structural Principle of International Law* (Springer, 2010) 3, 14 ff; AG Koroma, 'Solidarity: Evidence of an Emerging International Legal Principle' in H Hestermeyer et al (eds), *Coexistence, Cooperation and Solidarity* (Martinus Nijhoff Publishers, 2012) 103, 123 ff; F Zorzi Giustiniani, *International Law in Disaster Scenarios: Applicable Rules and Principles* (Springer, 2021) 96 ff; R Wolfrum, *Solidarity and Community Interests: Driving Forces for the Interpretation and Development of International Law* (Brill Nijhoff, 2021) 428 ff. Exceptions are S Villani, *The Concept of Solidarity within EU Disaster Response Law: A Legal Assessment* (Bononia University Press, 2021) 26 ff; Eggett (n 5).

evidence-based analysis of its legal status is therefore essential to understanding solidarity's potential role in IDRL. This chapter provides that analysis.[8]

Uncertainty about the legal status of solidarity is not unique to IDRL. What solidarity is and what it does remain debated across international law more broadly. While its presence in international law is generally acknowledged, its status as a *legal* principle continues to be contested.[9] Scholarly views on this range from optimism to scepticism. Some regard solidarity as a legal principle that 'has given rise to the creation, modification or confirmation of rights and obligations',[10] whereas others doubt this, arguing that solidarity 'is too abstract and too indefinite in contours and contents to become a normative concept that produces steering effects on states' behaviour in international relations'.[11]

In examining the legal status of solidarity, it is important to be precise with terminology, particularly when describing solidarity as a 'principle'. Terms such as 'principle', 'general principle', 'general principle of law', 'general principle of international law' and 'principle of international law' are often used interchangeably in case law, practice and scholarship, usually without clarification of their respective legal status or function.[12] This chapter asks specifically whether solidarity has emerged as a general principle of law within the meaning of article 38(1)(c) of the *Statute of the International Court of Justice* (ICJ Statute), which recognises general principles of law are a formal source of international law, distinct from treaty and customary law.[13]

Focusing on whether solidarity qualifies as a general principle is justified by the potentially far-reaching implications this status could have for IDRL.[14] If recognised as a general principle under Article 38(1)(c) of the ICJ Statute, solidarity would presumably serve two key functions within IDRL. First, it could form the source of primary rights and obligations of states,[15] although there is general

[8] This analysis is largely based on T Mulder, '"In the Spirit of Solidarity": An Analysis of Solidarity as a Principle of International Disaster Response Law' (2023) 6(1) *Yearbook of International Disaster Law* 301.

[9] RStJ MacDonald, 'Solidarity in the Practice and Discourse of Public International Law' (1996) 8 *Pace International Law Review* 259, 262; A Williams, 'Solidarity, Justice and Climate Change Law' (2009) 10 *Melbourne Journal of International Law* 493, 504; Eggett (n 5) 33.

[10] Wellens, 'Solidarity as a Constitutional Principle' (n 7) 776.

[11] U Beyerlin, 'Discussion Following the Presentation by Karel Wellens' in R Wolfrum and C Kojima (eds), *Solidarity: A Structural Principle of International Law* (Springer, 2010) 42.

[12] ILC, 'First Report on General Principles of Law by Marcelo Vázquez-Bermúdez, Special Rapporteur' (5 April 2019) UN Doc A/CN.4/732, para 254. On the meaning of the term 'principle' in relation to solidarity, see Eggett (n 5) 36.

[13] 'The Court, whose function is to decide in accordance with international law such disputes as are submitted to it, shall apply: . . . c. the general principles of law recognized by civilized nations': *Statute of the International Court of Justice* (26 June 1945) art 38(1).

[14] On the role of general principles in IDRL generally, see I Saunders, 'International Disaster Relief Law and Article 38(1)(c) of the Statute of the International Court of Justice: The Forgotten Source of International Law' in DD Caron, MJ Kelly and A Telesetsky (eds), *The International Law of Disaster Relief* (Cambridge University Press, 2014) 29; D Cubie, 'Sources of IDL: Focus on General Principles of Law' (2024) 5 *Yearbook of International Disaster Law* 493.

[15] ILC, 'Draft Conclusions on General Principles of Law Adopted on First Reading' (12 May 2023) A/CN.4/L.982 (hereinafter 'Draft Conclusions') concl 10(2)(b).

agreement that general principles mainly act as 'gap fillers' to prevent situations of *non liquet* where no applicable treaty or customary rule exists.[16] Second, solidarity could guide the interpretation of treaty and customary international law as a general principle.[17] Both functions could profoundly influence IDRL by creating, modifying or confirming states' rights and obligations in response to disasters.

To address its central question, this chapter first traces the development of solidarity's legal standing in international law, focusing on whether it has evolved from a purely political notion into a binding legal principle. It then turns to the specific context of IDRL to consider whether solidarity has emerged as a general principle of law within this regime. While solidarity may have gained broader recognition across international law, it is not uncommon to assess general principles within particular regimes.[18] In doing so, this chapter adopts the methodology for identifying general principles developed by the ILC in its Draft Conclusions on General Principles of International Law (Draft Conclusions).[19] Through a comprehensive, systematic and evidence-based analysis, it examines key legal sources – including treaties, UN General Assembly resolutions and statements by states – to assess the legal status of solidarity in IDRL.[20] The chapter concludes that although solidarity enjoys widespread support among states, it remains largely understood as a moral aspiration rather than a general principle capable of creating binding rights and obligations.[21] Nonetheless, the evidence shows that solidarity holds considerable normative value and could play a pivotal role in shaping the interpretation and future development of IDRL.

II. FROM POLITICAL NOTION TO LEGAL PRINCIPLE?

Legal scholars have long advocated for the recognition of solidarity as a principle of international law. As discussed in the previous chapter, one of the earliest expressions of solidarity in legal thought can be traced to de Vattel in the eighteenth century, who described it as a foundational principle governing relations among states.[22] This early conception presented solidarity as a principle of

[16] ibid concl 10(1). See also ILC, 'Third Report on General Principles of Law by Marcelo Vázquez-Bermúdez, Special Rapporteur' (18 April 2022) UN Doc A/CN.4/753, paras 39 ff; I Saunders, *General Principles as a Source of International Law: Art 38(1)(c) of the Statute of the International Court of Justice* (Hart Publishing, 2020) 48, 89, 173; G Gaja, 'General Principles of Law' in *Max Planck Encyclopedia of International Law* (Oxford University Press, 2013) para 21; HWA Thirlway, *The Sources of International Law*, 2nd edn (Oxford University Press, 2019) 106.

[17] Draft Conclusions (n 15) concl 10(2)(a).

[18] See, for example, a discussion of the precautionary principle as a general principle within international environmental law in *Pulp Mills on the River Uruguay (Argentina v Uruguay)* (Judgment) [2010] ICJ Rep 14, Separate Opinion of Judge Cançado Trindade, para 48.

[19] Draft Conclusions (n 15).

[20] Mulder (n 8).

[21] ibid 318.

[22] E de Vattel, *Le Droit des Gens, ou Principes de la Loi Naturelle, Appliqués à la Conduite et aux Affaires des Nations et des Souverains* (1758).

mutual support and cooperation, particularly in times of humanitarian crisis.[23] The idea gained further momentum in the early twentieth century through the legal-political solidarist movement, which advanced a reformist vision of international law grounded in solidarity and challenged traditional notions of state sovereignty and legal positivism.[24]

Despite these early efforts to elevate solidarity, it has never firmly established itself as a mainstream principle of international law. It is not widely recognised as a legal principle in treaties or UN resolutions, nor has it been affirmed as such by (international) courts or consistently upheld in state practice.[25] Instead, solidarity has largely remained a political notion, invoked in diplomatic rhetoric and normative arguments about what international law ought to be.

As a political notion, solidarity has on several occasions been invoked to promote collective action and international cooperation in addressing global needs and challenges.[26] A notable example is its use during the debates on the New International Economic Order (NIEO) in the 1970s.[27] The NIEO comprised proposals to eliminate global economic and social inequalities by establishing a new international framework based on 'equity, sovereign equality, interdependence, common interest and cooperation among all states'.[28] Although the UN General Assembly's resolutions on the NIEO did not explicitly refer to solidarity,[29] records of the debates show that states invoked it as a political argument in support of the initiative.[30] However, solidarity was presented not as a legal principle, but as a normative political notion.

Solidarity played a similar role in the adoption of the UN Millennium Declaration in 2000.[31] In that Declaration, states unanimously committed to

[23] MacDonald (n 9) 260.

[24] M Koskenniemi, *The Gentle Civilizer of Nations: The Rise and Fall of International Law, 1870–1960* (Cambridge University Press, 2002) ch 4; C Tixier, 'The Legacy of Léon Bourgeois: From the Solidarist Doctrine to the Emergence of International Arbitration' in JQ Olmstead (ed), *Reconsidering Peace and Patriotism during the First World War* (Springer, 2017) 33; H Thierry, 'The Thought of Georges Scelle' (1990) 1(1) *European Journal of International Law* 193.

[25] The ICJ referred to 'solidarity' several times in one case, but did not discuss its meaning or legal status as a principle; see *Maritime Dispute (Peru v Chile)* (Judgment) [2014] ICJ Rep 3 paras 125, 150–51.

[26] I Badanova, 'Making Sense of Solidarity in International Law: Input from the Integration of the European Gas Market' (2019) 11(2) *European Journal of Legal Studies* 105, 109.

[27] ibid 109; MacDonald (n 9) 263.

[28] UN General Assembly Res 3201 (S-VI) (1 May 1974) UN Doc A/Res/S-6/3201.

[29] ibid.

[30] UN General Assembly, '6th Special Session: Plenary Meeting - Verbatim Records (No A/PV.2208-2223, 2226-2231' (1974). See also MacDonald (n 9) 263; W Verwey, 'The Principle of Solidarity as a Legal Cornerstone of a New International Economic Order' in *North-South Dialogue: A New International Economic Order* (Institute of International Public Law and International Relations of Thessaloniki, 1982) 487, 489.

[31] UN General Assembly Res 55/2 (8 September 2000) UN Doc A/RES/55/2, para 6. See also Badanova (n 26) 109; Koroma (n 7) 114; P Dann, 'Solidarity and the Law of Development Cooperation' in Wolfrum and Kojima (n 11) 55, 62 ff; D Campanelli, 'Principle of Solidarity' in *Max Planck Encyclopedia of International Law* (Oxford University Press, 2011) para 17; A Szpak, 'International Solidarity as the Basis for Millennium/Sustainable Development Goals' (2017) 26(1) *Polish Quarterly of International Affairs* 106.

a broad range of development goals relating to peace, development, human rights, poverty, hunger, disease and environmental degradation. The Declaration describes solidarity as a 'fundamental value' that is 'essential to international relations in the twenty-first century', but stops short of recognising it as a principle of international law.[32] In both instances, solidarity was framed as a normative ideal – an expression of shared responsibility and global partnership – rather than a legal principle with binding effect.[33]

However, in recent decades, solidarity has gradually evolved, becoming increasingly embedded across international law. Scholars have observed that various regimes of international law increasingly reflect solidarity,[34] including international environmental law,[35] international climate change law,[36] international trade law,[37] international development law,[38] international refugee law,[39] IHRL[40] and IHL.[41] Yet, the development of solidarity as a principle has not been uniform across these regimes. As Wellens observes, 'the principle of solidarity has reached different stages of development in various branches of international law'.[42] Moreover, given its particular nature, solidarity role may be more meaningful in some regimes of international law than in others, particularly in those that seek to address global needs and challenges. Therefore, as Wolfrum notes, it is not likely or necessarily desirable that 'the principle of solidarity should or will govern international law in its totality'.[43]

However, in many regimes of international law, solidarity is still not explicitly recognised as a legal principle per se in treaties or soft law instruments. Rather than formally codifying solidarity as a principle, these regimes often 'give expression' to its underlying concept – the pursuit of common goals through differentiated cooperation and assistance – through existing norms and

[32] UN General Assembly Res 55/2 (n 31) para 6.

[33] Badanova (n 26) 109.

[34] For overviews of the principle of solidarity in international law, see Wellens, 'Solidarity as a Constitutional Principle' (n 7); Koroma (n 7); Wolfrum (n 7) ch 5.

[35] Williams (n 9); Wellens, 'Solidarity as a Constitutional Principle' (n 7) 789–90; Campanelli (n 31) para 6; Koroma (n 7) 110–13; Wolfrum (n 7) 406; H Hestermeyer, 'Reality or Aspiration? Solidarity in International Environmental and World Trade Law' (Max Planck Institute, 2012) 9 ff. However, for a critique, see D Tladi, 'In Search of Solidarity in International Law' in E Kassoti and N Idriz (eds), *The Principle of Solidarity: The Principle of Solidarity: International and EU Law Perspectives* (TMC Asser Press, 2023) 17.

[36] Williams (n 9); Wolfrum (n 7) 413–414.

[37] Hestermeyer (n 35) 14; Wolfrum (n 7) 446.

[38] Koroma (n 7) 113–17; Wellens, 'Solidarity as a Constitutional Principle' (n 7) 790–94; Hestermeyer (n 35) 13–18; MacDonald (n 9); Dann (n 31).

[39] Koroma (n 7) 117–19; Wolfrum (n 7) 450; G Martin, 'International Solidarity and Co-operation in Assistance to African Refugees: Burden-Sharing or Burden-Shifting?' (1995) 7 *International Journal of Refugee Law* 250.

[40] Koroma (n 7) 108110; C Wellman, 'Solidarity, the Individual and Human Rights' (2000) 22(3) *Human Rights Quarterly* 639; R Wolfrum, 'Solidarity' in D Shelton (ed), *The Oxford Handbook of International Human Rights Law* (Oxford University Press, 2013) 401, 410.

[41] Koroma (n 7) 105–07; Campanelli (n 31) para 15; Wellens, 'Solidarity as a Constitutional Principle' (n 7) 783–84; Wolfrum (n 7) 427.

[42] Wellens, 'Solidarity as a Constitutional Principle' (n 7) 778.

[43] Wolfrum (n 7) 92.

mechanisms.[44] For example, the *UN Framework Convention on Climate Change* (UNFCCC) reflects solidarity through the principle of common but differentiated responsibilities, whereby states with greater historical contributions to climate change and more resources accept greater obligations to alleviate the burden on other states.[45] Similarly, the system of Special and Differential Treatment in World Trade Organization agreements embodies solidarity by seeking to address global economic inequalities through redistributive measures that favour developing countries.[46] Although these legal regimes do not explicitly refer to solidarity as a principle, they nonetheless give legal expression to its normative core, embedding it within binding legal frameworks.

At the same time, there is a trend towards explicitly codifying solidarity in both binding and non-binding instruments across international law. As discussed earlier, the UN Millennium Declaration of 2000 identifies solidarity as one of the fundamental values of international relations in the twenty-first century.[47] Solidarity is now also expressly referenced in several treaties, including the *African Charter on Human and Peoples' Rights* and the *United Nations Convention to Combat Desertification*.[48] The *WHO Pandemic Agreement* codifies solidarity as a guiding principle in pandemic prevention, preparedness and response, marking a significant step towards embedding solidarity in global health governance.[49] These developments indicate a growing readiness among states to recognise solidarity not only as a political ideal but also as a normative principle with potential legal significance.

Some efforts have also been made to develop solidarity as a legal principle – or even as a right – within IHRL. These efforts are most evident in the advocacy surrounding so-called third-generation rights, often referred to as 'solidarity rights'.[50] These include the rights to development, peace, a healthy environment

[44] L Boisson de Chazournes, 'Responsibility to Protect: Reflecting Solidarity?' in Wolfrum and Kojima (n 11) 93, 95, 104,109. See also MacDonald (n 9) 301; Williams (n 9) 502; Wolfrum (n 40) 403; Koroma (n 7); Wellens, 'Solidarity as a Constitutional Principle' (n 7) 778; Dann (n 31) 61; Campanelli (n 31) para 22.

[45] *United Nations Framework Convention on Climate Change* (9 May 1992) (UNFCCC) art 3(1). See also Williams (n 9) 506; Koroma (n 7) 111; Hestermeyer (n 35) 10; Campanelli (n 31) para 6; Wolfrum (n 40) 408.

[46] World Trade Organization, 'Differential and More Favourable Treatment Reciprocity and Fuller Participation of Developing Countries' (28 November 1979); E Tempone, 'Special and Differential Treatment' in *Max Planck Encyclopedia of International Law* (Oxford University Press, 2014). See also Wolfrum (n 7) 449; Koroma (n 7) 116.

[47] UN General Assembly Res 55/2 (n 31) para 6.

[48] *African Charter on Human and Peoples' Rights* (27 June 1981) arts 10(2), 21(4), 23(1), 23(2), 29(3); *United Nations Convention to Combat Desertification in those Countries Experiencing Serious Drought and/or Desertification, Particularly in Africa* (14 October 1994) arts 3(b), 4(1)(b).

[49] *WHO Pandemic Agreement* (20 May 2025) art 3(5).

[50] Wellman (n 40); P Minnerop, N Roht-Arriaza and S Aminzadeh, 'Solidarity Rights (Development, Peace, Environment, Humanitarian Assistance)' in *Max Planck Encyclopedia of International Law* (Oxford University Press, 2018); P Alston, 'A Third Generation of Solidarity Rights: Progressive Development or Obfuscation of International Human Rights Law?' (1982) 29(3) *Netherlands International Law Review* 307.

and humanitarian assistance, all of which are premised on the understanding that their realisation depends on solidarity among states and peoples. These rights reflect a shift from individual entitlements to collective responsibilities, recognising that global challenges require cooperative responses grounded in mutual support. In addition, the UN Human Rights Council has appointed an Independent Expert on human rights and international solidarity.[51] Successive mandate holders have worked towards drafting a Declaration on Human Rights and International Solidarity, recognising a 'right to international solidarity' encompassing the 'right of individuals and peoples to participate meaningfully in, contribute to and enjoy a social and international order in which all human rights and fundamental freedoms can be realized'.[52] Any draft is yet to be adopted.

Of all regimes of international law, solidarity has arguably been developed most extensively as a legal principle within EU law.[53] It is explicitly recognised and codified in several provisions of the EU treaties, where it serves as a principle across diverse policy areas, including asylum, energy and disaster response.[54] The European Court of Justice has also affirmed solidarity as a binding legal principle of EU law.[55] Yet, despite this formal recognition, the precise meaning of solidarity and the legal consequences that stem from it remain somewhat ambiguous.[56] The principle is frequently invoked to justify collective action and burden-sharing, but its practical application varies across contexts and its enforceability is not always clear.

Taken together, these developments suggest that solidarity has evolved over time into more than a merely political notion. Eggett argues that: 'Convincing claims can be made that solidarity is not a mere rhetorical device, but sets expectations and provides reasons for certain action by states.'[57] Koroma observes that 'solidarity often began as an oblique reference – to community, neighbourliness, or the common good – but has since given way to concrete, interrelated

[51] The Independent Expert on human rights and international solidarity was first appointed in 2005.

[52] UN Human Rights Council, 'Revised Draft Declaration on Human Rights and International Solidarity' (2 May 2023) A/HRC/53/32 annex art 4(1).

[53] See generally Villani (n 7); SM Giang and A Grimmel (eds), *Solidarity in the European Union* (Springer, 2017); J Czuczai, 'The Principle of Solidarity in the EU Legal Order: Some Practical Examples after Lisbon' in J Czuczai and F Naert (eds), *The EU as a Global Actor: Bridging Legal Theory and Practice* (Brill Nijhoff, 2017) 145; A Biondi, E Dagilytė and E Küçük (eds), *Solidarity in EU Law: Legal Principle in the Making* (Edward Elgar, 2018); D Saracino, 'Understanding Solidarity in the European Union: An Analytical Framework' (2024) 53(5) *Theory and Society* 1093; E Kassoti and N Idriz (eds), *The Principle of Solidarity: International and EU Law Perspectives* (TMC Asser Press, 2023).

[54] *Treaty on the European Union* (13 December 2007) arts 2, 3, 21, 24, 31–32; *Treaty on the Functioning of the European Union* (13 December 2007) arts 67, 80, 122,194, 222.

[55] Cases C-6/69 and 11/69 *Commission v France* ECLI:EU:C:1969:68, para 16; Case 39/72 *Commission v Italy* ECLI:EU:C:1973:13, para 25.

[56] A Grimmel, 'Solidarity in the European Union: Fundamental Value or "Empty Signifier"' in A Grimmel and SM Giang (eds), *Solidarity in the European Union* (Springer, 2017) 161.

[57] Eggett (n 5) 50.

negative and even positive state obligations'.[58] Wellens describes this trajectory as a gradual evolution of solidarity's legal status: 'first as a notion, then as a political and finally as a legal principle of international law'.[59] Although its legal consolidation remains uneven and contested, the increasing codification and incorporation of solidarity across various regimes indeed point to a broader trend towards its recognition as a principle capable of creating, modifying or confirming states' rights and obligations.

However, caution is warranted. While these developments are compelling, they do not necessarily indicate that solidarity has attained the status of a legal principle in international law. In contrast to optimistic interpretations, a more sceptical school of thought acknowledges the presence of solidarity in international law as a normative notion but asserts that '[i]t would be hardly sustainable that solidarity is today a fully acknowledged legal principle governing international law and from which it would be possible to draw a clear set of duties and obligations for international subjects'.[60]

Rather than making sweeping generalised claims about its legal status, it is necessary to examine solidarity's legal development more closely. If it has evolved into a binding principle, in what capacity would this have occurred? It is unlikely that solidarity has emerged as a principle of treaty law, given its sporadic and inconsistent recognition in treaty texts despite an early trend towards codification.[61] Nor has it emerged as a principle of customary international law;[62] although Neuhold argues that 'solidarity between subjects of international law could also evolve into a rule of customary international law if practised repeatedly and with the necessary *opinio juris*'.[63] The progressive invocation of solidarity in international law could be seen as state practice, or at least as a potential generator of it. However, den Heijer and van der Wilt observe that 'there is a huge gap between the language of solidarity and state practice'.[64] They highlight, for example, the general failure of implementation and oversight in international cooperation and assistance on climate change, and the 'disappointing rollout' of COVAX, the WHO-led COVID-19 vaccine-sharing initiative, which 'could not prevent growing discrepancies in vaccination coverage between the rich and poor countries'.[65] In addition, there is a persistent lack of *opinio juris*. References to solidarity tend to be political rhetoric aimed at

[58] Koroma (n 7) 129.

[59] Wellens, 'Revisiting Solidarity as a (Re-)Emerging Constitutional Principle' (n 7) 4.

[60] Campanelli (n 31) para 21. See also Boisson de Chazournes (n 44) 95; MacDonald (n 9) 301; Williams (n 9) 502; Wolfrum (n 40) 403; Koroma (n 7); Wellens, 'Solidarity as a Constitutional Principle' (n 7) 778; Dann (n 31) 61; Campanelli (n 31) para 22; JP Cot in 'Discussion Following the Presentation by Philipp Dann' in Wolfrum and Kojima (n 11) 81.

[61] Eggett (n 5) 47.

[62] ibid 48.

[63] H Neuhold, 'Common Security: The Litmus Test of International Solidarity' in Wolfrum and Kojima (n 11) 193, 196.

[64] Den Heijer and van der Wilt (n 1) 4.

[65] ibid.

promoting international cooperation and assistance rather than expressions of a recognised legal norm.[66]

This leaves the question of whether solidarity has emerged as a general principle of international law in terms of Article 38(1)(c) of the ICJ Statute. Given its broad and abstract character, this remains a possibility. To assess it, the next section turns to the methodology for identifying general principles of international law.

III. METHODOLOGY: IDENTIFYING GENERAL PRINCIPLES OF INTERNATIONAL LAW

The process of identifying general principles in international law is far from straightforward. Although international courts have applied general principles on numerous occasions, their identification has often lacked 'methodological clarity'.[67] Some courts have articulated specific methodologies for identifying general principles, while others have simply affirmed their existence without explaining the underlying reasoning. Recognising this ambiguity, the ILC undertook a study to clarify the concept of general principles and provide practical guidance on how to identify them. Nearing completion, the ILC adopted the Draft Conclusions on General Principles of Law (Draft Conclusions) on first reading in 2023.[68] In the absence of a universally accepted methodology, these Draft Conclusions, which are grounded in state practice, judicial decisions and scholarship, offer a useful starting point for assessing whether solidarity may constitute a general principle of international law.

According to the Draft Conclusions, the central element in identifying a general principle is its recognition by states and, in some cases, international organisations.[69] This recognition must be established through a careful and comprehensive examination of all available evidence demonstrating that such recognition has taken place.[70] Importantly, the methodology for determining recognition varies depending on the category of general principle under consideration.

[66] See, eg, A Rahman-Shepherd et al, 'Solidarity in Response to the COVID-19 Pandemic' (Chatham House, 2021).

[67] M Biddulph and D Newman, 'A Contextualized Account of General Principles of International Law' (2014) 26(2) *Pace International Law Review* 286, 301.

[68] Draft Conclusions (n 15).

[69] ibid concl 2. Following discussions on the Draft Conclusions adopted on the first reading in the UN General Assembly's Sixth Committee, the ILC Special Rapporteur proposed to amend the text to clarify that while '[i]t is primarily the recognition by States that contributes to the formation of general principles of law', '[i]n certain cases, the recognition by international organizations may also contribute to the formation of general principles of law': ILC, 'Fourth Report on General Principles of Law by Marcelo Vázquez-Bermúdez, Special Rapporteur' (18 February 2025) UN Doc A/CN.4/785, 13.

[70] ILC, 'Commentaries on the Draft Conclusions on General Principles of Law Adopted on First Reading' (2023) UN Doc A/78/10, 14.

The Draft Conclusions distinguish between two categories of general principles: those derived from domestic legal systems and those formed independently within the international legal system.[71] The first category includes principles developed *in foro domestico* and later transposed into international law, such as good faith, *res judicata* and due process.[72] Identifying a general principle from this category involves a two-step process: first, a comparative analysis of domestic legal systems to establish its widespread recognition; and, second, an assessment of its compatibility with or transposition into international law.[73] However, this methodology is of limited relevance here. There is little evidence to suggest that solidarity falls within this category, as it is not widely recognised as a legal principle in domestic legal systems.[74] The focus must therefore be on the second category: principles formed within the international legal system itself.

However, this second category remains contested. The *travaux préparatoires* of the ICJ Statute suggest that the drafters considered only principles developed *in foro domestico* in the context of Article 38(1)(c), leaving some states, scholars and ILC members sceptical of the existence of principles formed independently within the international legal system.[75] Nevertheless, the Draft Conclusions acknowledge that certain general principles of law do not originate in domestic legal systems, but instead develop within the international legal order itself. This view is persuasive, as not all principles relevant to international law can emerge from domestic contexts, given the unique nature of international relations.[76] Principles such as sovereign equality, territorial integrity, *uti possidetis* and non-intervention exemplify this category: they are foundational to the structure and functioning of the international legal system, yet lack clear analogues in most domestic legal systems.[77] It is within this category that solidarity may plausibly be situated, warranting closer examination of whether it meets the criteria for recognition as a general principle formed within the international legal system.

For general principles formed within the international legal system, the Draft Conclusions propose a methodology focused on determining whether the international community recognises the principle as binding.[78] Such recognition must be 'wide and representative, reflecting a common understanding of the

[71] Draft Conclusions (n 15) concl 3.

[72] ILC (n 12) paras 101, 199.

[73] Draft Conclusions (n 15) concl 4.

[74] However, scholars note that some constitutional systems have incorporated (a form of) solidarity; see MacDonald (n 9) 290 ff; KP Sommermann, 'Some Reflections on the Concept of Solidarity and its Transformation into a Legal Principle' (2014) 52(1) *Archiv des Völkerrechts* 10, 16.

[75] ILC (n 70) 16; ILC (n 69) paras 69–70, 73–76; Saunders (n 16) 236; O Pomson, 'General Principles of Law Formed within the International Legal System?' *EJIL: Talk!* (12 July 2022) www.ejiltalk.org/general-principles-of-law-formed-within-the-international-legal-system.

[76] ILC (n 12) paras 231–53. See also MC Bassiouni, 'A Functional Approach to General Principles of International Law' (1990) 11(3) *Michigan Journal of International Law* 768, 772.

[77] ILC (n 70) 22.

[78] Draft Conclusions (n 15) concl 7(1).

community of nations',[79] and may be evidenced through a variety of sources, 'such as international instruments reflecting the principle, resolutions adopted by international organizations or at intergovernmental conferences, and statements made by States'.[80] While the Draft Conclusions do not prescribe a rigid methodology, the accompanying commentaries clarify that recognition may be established in different ways.[81]

In some instances, states have expressly recognised general principles in treaties, resolutions and official statements, providing clear evidence of their legal status. One prominent example is the principle of humanity, which is acknowledged in the Martens Clause within IHL treaties.[82] Similarly, in international environmental law, the polluter pays principle has been explicitly recognised in both treaties and resolutions.[83] For example, the preamble to the *International Convention on Oil Pollution Preparedness, Response and Cooperation* notes: 'taking account of the "polluter pays" principle as a general principle of international environmental law'.[84] Recognition may also be found in statements made by states, as illustrated in the *Frontier Dispute (Burkina Faso/Mali)* case, where the ICJ considered references to the principle of *uti possidetis* in statements by African leaders as evidence of its recognition as a general principle formed within the international legal system.[85]

Where recognition is not express, it may nonetheless be inferred from existing rules of international law through an inductive analysis of relevant materials, including treaties, resolutions and statements of states.[86] The purpose of this analysis is to determine whether a general principle is reflected in existing rules or implicitly underlies them as a normative foundation.[87] If such a connection can be established, recognition of the principle may be inferred from the acceptance of those rules. Case law supports this inductive approach. For instance, in the *Corfu Channel* case, the ICJ inferred certain 'general and well-recognised principles', including 'elementary considerations of humanity', from existing treaty and customary rules.[88] Likewise, in its *Reservations Advisory Opinion*, the ICJ

[79] ILC, 'Second Report on General Principles of Law by Marcelo Vázquez-Bermúdez, Special Rapporteur' (9 April 2020) UN Doc A/CN.4/741, para 123.

[80] ILC (n 70) 23.

[81] ibid 22 ff.

[82] ILC (n 79) paras 131-134. The Martens clause refers to 'principles of international law derived from established custom, from the principles of humanity and from the dictates of public conscience': *Protocol Additional (I) to the Geneva Conventions of 12 August 1949, and Relating to the Protection of Victims of International Armed Conflicts* (8 June 1977) art 1(2).

[83] ILC (n 79) paras 135–36.

[84] *International Convention on Oil Pollution Preparedness, Response and Cooperation* (30 November 1990) preamble.

[85] *Frontier Dispute (Burkina Faso v Mali)* (Judgment) [1986] ICJ Rep 554, para 22. See also ILC (n 70) 24.

[86] ILC (n 70) 23.

[87] ibid.

[88] *Corfu Channel Case (United Kingdom of Great Britain and Northern Ireland v Albania)* (Merits) [1949] ICJ Rep 4, 22

held that 'the principles underlying the [Genocide] Convention are principles which are recognised by civilized nations as binding on States, even without any conventional obligation', implying that general principles can be deduced from the normative structure and content of the Genocide Convention itself.[89]

However, there is no one-size-fits-all approach to the inductive analysis required to infer general principles from existing rules. Rather, the process entails a case-by-case assessment of relevant materials, interpreted within their specific context and in light of the text and intentions of the parties.[90] The analysis is inherently interpretative, seeking to uncover the normative principles that underpin these rules. This approach mirrors the methodology used to determine the object and purpose of treaties, which similarly involves deducing implicit normative foundations from a treaty's terms.[91] In that context, the object and purpose are identified through an inductive analysis of the treaty's text, title, preamble and overall structure, and, where appropriate, supplemented by its preparatory works and the subsequent practice of the parties.[92]

At the same time, the inductive methodology for identifying general principles differs from that used to determine customary international law, even though the boundaries between the two are blurred.[93] Simma and Alston have argued that these methodologies have converged in case law, largely due to the overemphasis placed on *opinio juris* in the identification of custom.[94] International courts often rely on resolutions, declarations and other expressions of state views to establish customary norms, thereby sidestepping the more complex task of assessing actual – and often ambivalent or inconsistent – state practice.[95] This approach creates ambiguity about what courts are in fact identifying: the acceptance of a practice as customary law or recognition of a general principle underlying that practice. As a result, it is sometimes unclear whether a court has recognised customary international law or a general principle of law.

Despite this convergence in practice, it is crucial to underscore the fundamentally different purposes of the two methodologies. The identification of customary international law seeks to determine whether a practice has crystallised into a legally binding norm through consistent state practice accompanied by *opinio juris*.[96] By contrast, the identification of general principles involves

[89] *Reservations to the Convention on Genocide* (Advisory Opinion) [1951] ICJ Rep 15, 23.
[90] ILC (n 79) para 165.
[91] In its project on reservations to treaties, the ILC addressed the question of how to identify the object and purpose of treaties: ILC, 'Guide to Practice on Reservations to Treaties' (2011) UN Doc A/65/10 guideline 3.1.5.1.
[92] ibid.
[93] ILC (n 79) para 166.
[94] B Simma and P Alston, 'The Sources of Human Rights Law: Custom, Jus Cogens, and General Principles' (1988) 12 *Australian Year Book of International Law* 82, 96–97.
[95] See, eg, *Military and Paramilitary Activities in and against Nicaragua (Nicaragua v United States of America)* (Judgment) [1986] ICJ Rep 14 paras 187–201 on the use of force.
[96] See generally ILC, 'Draft Conclusions on Identification of Customary International Law' (2018) UN Doc A/73/10.

inferring recognition from a principle's reflection in, or its normative underpinning of, existing rules of international law.[97] Whereas the former asks whether states act in a certain way out of a sense of legal obligation, the latter asks whether existing rules affirm a broader principle that is recognised as a legally binding norm.

It is not always possible to pinpoint the precise reasoning that supports the inference of general principles, as they often reflect implicit and abstract normative foundations underlying existing rules. The interpretative nature of the inductive methodology is also evident in case law. In the *Furundžija* case, for instance, the Trial Chamber of the International Criminal Tribunal for the Former Yugoslavia (ICTY) identified the general principle of respect for human dignity as intrinsic to international law.[98] The Trial Chamber observed that '[t]he essence of the whole corpus of international humanitarian law as well as human rights law lies in the protection of the human dignity of every person' and that this principle constitutes 'the basic underpinning and indeed the very *raison d'être* of international humanitarian law and human rights law'.[99] Yet, the Trial Chamber did not articulate the precise analytical steps leading to this conclusion. This illustrates that a certain degree of subjectivity is inherent and acceptable in inductive reasoning, allowing for interpretative flexibility so long as the resulting interpretation is coherent and not contradicted by other legal understandings.[100] Such flexibility is particularly important when dealing with principles like solidarity, which are not always conceptually defined as clearly as other principles.

However, merely inferring a normative underpinning from existing rules is insufficient to identify a general principle. Normative underpinnings may reflect moral or political values that states do not necessarily recognise as *legal* principles capable of creating, modifying or confirming norms. While existing rules may be inspired by underlying moral or political considerations, their legitimacy or binding force does not necessarily derive from those considerations. Furthermore, an underpinning principle may be specific to a particular set of rules and not intended to extend beyond them, which could prevent its recognition as a *general* principle. This suggests that the identification of a general principle also requires some indication that states acknowledge that the existing rules must be grounded in the principle in question *as a matter of law*. Although this aspect is not explicitly addressed by the ILC, it could align with their requirement that general principles must possess autonomous status, meaning that they can be applied independently of the rules from which they are deduced.[101]

[97] ILC (n 79) paras 166–70.
[98] *Prosecutor v Furundžija* (Judgment) ICTY-95-17/1 (10 December 1998)
[99] ibid para 183. See also ILC (n 70) 24.
[100] A degree of subjectivity is not uncommon in international law; virtually all interpretative exercises are inherently subjective. See ILC, 'Guide to Practice on Reservations to Treaties with Commentaries' (2011) UN Doc A/65/10, 216.
[101] ILC (n 70) 23; ILC (n 79) para 145.

The autonomous status aspect of general principles appears to be affirmed in international jurisprudence. In the *Reservations Advisory Opinion*, the ICJ emphasised that the general principles underlying the Genocide Convention bind all states 'even without any conventional obligation'.[102] This statement implies that such principles possess an autonomous legal character, capable of application independently of the treaty provisions from which they are derived. However, determining whether a principle enjoys autonomous status is methodologically challenging. There is a risk of circular reasoning: a principle must be applied independently to demonstrate autonomy, yet its autonomy is often inferred from instances of independent application. To avoid this circularity, it is better to seek evidence that states recognise the principle as capable of operating independently of specific rules and of generating, modifying or confirming legal norms in its own right. Such evidence may be found in various sources, including treaty preparatory works, as well as in resolutions and statements of states, which may indicate a shared understanding of the principle's normative authority.

IV. IDENTIFYING SOLIDARITY IN INTERNATIONAL DISASTER RESPONSE LAW

The central question of this chapter is whether solidarity has emerged as a general principle within IDRL. If solidarity constitutes a general principle, it could serve as a source of law from which rights and obligations could be drawn. To address this question, this section undertakes an inductive analysis of treaties, resolutions and statements of states to assess whether solidarity has attained widespread recognition as a general principle with binding force. The inquiry focuses on how states appear to understand when they invoke solidarity in the context of disaster response.

At first glance, there appears to be considerable evidence supporting the recognition of solidarity as a general principle within IDRL. The regime is fundamentally premised on the notion that international cooperation and assistance may be necessary to protect persons affected by disasters, particularly when national capacities are overwhelmed.[103] As Koroma observed, 'the entire premise of disaster relief is that States and other actors will endeavor to act in favor of another State, not out of self-interest but rather motivated by what could only be called solidarity'.[104]

[102] *Reservations Advisory Opinion* (n 89) 23.

[103] 'The magnitude and duration of many emergencies may be beyond the response capacity of many affected countries. International cooperation to address emergency situations and to strengthen the response capacity of affected countries is thus of great importance': UN General Assembly Res 46/182 (19 December 1991) UN Doc A/RES/46/182, para 5.

[104] Koroma (n 7) 123.

Today, solidarity indeed appears to be embedded in most international frameworks governing disaster response, including both binding treaties and non-binding soft law instruments (see section IV.A). While these instruments do not typically recognise solidarity explicitly as a general principle, it can be inferred as a normative underpinning from the frameworks they establish for international cooperation and assistance. These frameworks consistently reflect the expectation that states will support one another in responding to disasters, often without anticipation of reciprocal benefit. Practice appears to confirm this general readiness of states to assist other states. International cooperation has been consistently observed in the aftermath of virtually all major disasters and can be traced through centuries of humanitarian response,[105] indicating a deeply rooted normative orientation of the regime that may support the emergence of solidarity as a general principle. Explicit references to solidarity in treaties, resolutions and statements of states further underscore its centrality in the practice of international disaster response. Such references reinforce the presumption that solidarity is widely recognised by states as a general principle of IDRL.

Yet, upon closer examination, it becomes clear that states tend to recognise solidarity more as a moral aspiration than as a principle capable of creating, modifying or confirming rights and obligations. The following subsections analyse three categories of evidence that may indicate recognition of solidarity: treaties and soft law, UN resolutions and statements made by states. While solidarity is indeed widely acknowledged as a cornerstone of international disaster response, it has not yet achieved the status of a general principle. The primary reason for this conclusion lies in the voluntary nature of international cooperation in disaster response. Although solidarity is reflected in established frameworks for assistance, states rarely assume binding obligations to act in a spirit of solidarity with affected states. This suggests that, despite its normative prominence, solidarity is generally perceived not as a legal norm with autonomous binding force, but rather as morally 'the right thing to do' in times of disasters.

A. Solidarity in Treaties and Soft Law

As discussed in Chapter 1, section II.B, IDRL is a fragmented regime within international law. Unlike areas governed by a comprehensive flagship treaty, IDRL consists of a patchwork of global, regional and bilateral treaties and soft law. These treaties vary significantly in terms of both material scope – covering different types of disasters and aspects of disaster response – and geographical

[105] ILC, 'Preliminary Report on the Protection of Persons in the Event of Disasters, by Mr. Eduardo Valencia-Ospina, Special Rapporteur' (5 May 2008) UN Doc A/CN.4/598 paras 14 ff; P Macalister-Smith, *International Humanitarian Assistance: Disaster Relief Actions in International Law and Organization* (Kluwer, 1985) 53–55.

coverage. Nonetheless, an analysis of global and regional disaster response treaties shows that solidarity is reflected in their provisions, even if it is seldom mentioned explicitly. Despite variations in scope and modalities of cooperation – ranging from technical support to logistical aid – they all establish frameworks for international cooperation and assistance in disaster situations. The common thread is the facilitation of assistance to disaster-affected states. Notably, IDRL treaties depart from traditional models of international cooperation premised on mutual benefit; instead, they emphasise a form of solidarity-based cooperation, in which states provide assistance without expecting anything in return. This spirit of solidarity is particularly evident in provisions setting out rules and procedures for offering, accepting and delivering assistance, suggesting that solidarity is a foundational, albeit implicit, underpinning principle of IDRL treaties.

A clear example of how solidarity is reflected in IDRL treaties is the *Tampere Convention on the Provision of Telecommunication Resources for Disaster Mitigation and Relief Operations* (Tampere Convention).[106] As its title indicates, the Tampere Convention focuses on facilitating international cooperation in the use of telecommunications during disaster response. Open to all states and among the most widely ratified global treaties in IDRL,[107] the Tampere Convention does not explicitly refer to solidarity. Nonetheless, solidarity can be inferred as a normative underpinning of its framework. The Tampere Convention's stated objective to 'facilitate international cooperation to mitigate the impact of disasters' signals a cooperative purpose grounded in solidarity.[108] Article 3 establishes a general duty to cooperate in deploying telecommunication resources in disaster settings, while subsequent provisions elaborate on the modalities of such cooperation. Notably, Article 4 allows affected states to request assistance, and if assistance is offered and accepted, the Tampere Convention sets out procedures for its provision, including coordination mechanisms, privileges and immunities for assisting personnel, and termination protocols.[109] Importantly, the Tampere Convention anticipates that assistance will be provided without expectation of reimbursement, unless agreed otherwise.[110] This approach thus departs from traditional models of international cooperation based on mutual benefit and instead reflects a solidarity-based framework, in which states demonstrate a willingness to assist others in times of need without expecting anything in return. Accordingly, solidarity can reasonably be inferred as a principle underpinning the Tampere Convention.

The Tampere Convention is only one example illustrating how solidarity is reflected in IDRL treaties. This underlying theme can be observed across virtually all treaties in the field. Global treaties such as the *Convention on Assistance*

[106] *Tampere Convention on the Provision of Telecommunication Resources for Disaster Mitigation and Relief Operations* (18 June 1998).
[107] As of December 2025, 50 states have ratified the Tampere Convention.
[108] Tampere Convention (n 106) preamble.
[109] ibid arts 4–9.
[110] ibid art 7(5).

in the Case of a Nuclear Accident or Radiological Emergency (Nuclear Accident Convention)[111] and the *Framework Convention on Civil Defence Assistance*,[112] as well as various treaties addressing environmental disasters and industrial accidents,[113] all establish mechanisms for international cooperation and assistance that support affected states without expectation of anything in return. These treaties consistently promote cooperation that prioritises humanitarian assistance over reciprocal benefit. In addition, regional treaties on disaster response reflect this spirit of solidarity among their parties in a similar manner.[114] While the modalities of cooperation differ, the overarching objective of facilitating assistance to disaster-affected states remains constant, reinforcing the view that solidarity is a normative underpinning of IDRL treaties.

States have also consistently demonstrated a readiness to cooperate with and provide assistance to disaster-affected states without a treaty basis. This practice is evident in the international responses to numerous major disasters. Following the 2025 Myanmar earthquake, states and humanitarian organisations mobilised rapidly, providing humanitarian aid without a formal agreement in place to facilitate this assistance.[115] Similarly, the 2023 Turkey-Syria earthquake prompted assistance from over 100 countries without a basis in a IDRL treaty.[116] Historical precedents reinforce this pattern: the 2022 Pakistan floods likewise elicited widespread international support; the 2015 Nepal earthquake triggered a massive global response; the 2011 Christchurch earthquake saw foreign governments and organisations offer assistance to support New Zealand's recovery; and the

[111] *Convention on Assistance in the Case of a Nuclear Accident or Radiological Emergency* (26 September 1986).

[112] *Framework Convention on Civil Defence Assistance* (22 May 2000).

[113] See, eg, Oil Pollution Convention (n 84); *Desertification Convention* (n 48); *Convention on the Protection and Use of Transboundary Watercourses and International Lakes* (17 March 1992); *Convention on the Transboundary Effects of Industrial Accidents* (17 March 1992).

[114] *ASEAN Agreement on Disaster Management and Emergency Response* (26 July 2005) (AADMER); *Inter-American Convention to Facilitate Disaster Assistance* (6 July 1991); *Arab Cooperation Agreement on Regulating and Facilitating Relief Operations 1987* (3 September 1987) (Arab League Agreement); *Agreement among the Governments of the Participating States of the Black Sea Economic Cooperation (BSEC) on Collaboration in Emergency Assistance and Emergency Response to Natural and Manmade Disasters* (15 April 1998) (BSEC Agreement); *Agreement Establishing the Caribbean Disaster Emergency Management Agency* (4 July 2008) (CDEMA Agreement); *SAARC Agreement on Rapid Response to Natural Disasters, 2011* (26 May 2011); *Agreement between Governments of Member States of Shanghai Cooperation Organization on Cooperation in Delivery of Assistance for Emergency Liquidation* (26 October 2005) (Shanghai Agreement). While not a formal treaty, the EU has also developed rules for regional cooperation in disaster response: *Decision No 1313/2013/EU of the European Parliament and of the Council of 17 December 2013 on a Union Civil Protection Mechanism* (20 December 2013) (last amended in 2023) (hereinafter 'EU Civil Protection Mechanism').

[115] 'Myanmar Quake Toll Passes 1,000 as Rescuers Dig for Survivors' *The Japan Times* (29 March 2025) www.japantimes.co.jp/news/2025/03/29/asia-pacific/myanmar-earthquake-junta-aid-toll. However, the AADMER (n 114) did provide a legal framework for cooperation between state parties.

[116] H Atay Alam, 'Turkey Receives Offers of Quake Aid from Nearly 100 Countries' *CNN* (10 February 2023) https://edition.cnn.com/middleeast/live-news/turkey-syria-earthquake-updates-2-9-23-intl#h_2700d06892d3c9707c61820e6d21ab22.

2004 Indian Ocean tsunami prompted an unprecedented outpouring of global solidarity.

In addition to treaties, solidarity can be inferred from key soft law instruments, including the Draft Articles and the IDRL Guidelines.[117] Although non-binding, these instruments carry considerable authority, drawing on existing treaty law and practice and enjoying broad support among states.[118] Like treaties, both instruments seek to facilitate international cooperation and assistance in disaster response based on solidarity. They operate on the expectation that states will assist affected states without anticipating anything in return, reinforcing the normative role of solidarity in IDRL.

While solidarity is clearly reflected in the frameworks for international cooperation and assistance in disaster response, inferring its recognition as a general principle of IDRL from these treaties and other international instruments remains challenging. These instruments are designed to facilitate cooperation among states to support disaster-affected populations, yet they typically do so on a voluntary basis. In other words, although they establish mechanisms for solidarity-based cooperation, they do not generally impose binding obligations on states to act in solidarity. For instance, the Tampere Convention includes a general duty to cooperate,[119] but its provisions on providing assistance leave states with the discretion to determine whether and how they will assist.[120] The Tampere Convention does also not confer a corresponding right to receive assistance on affected states. Similar approaches are evident in other treaties and soft law instruments, where cooperation is encouraged and even facilitated, but is not obligatory.[121] While some bilateral treaties contain binding obligations to assist, such commitments are rare and largely absent from multilateral treaties.[122] This voluntary character of international cooperation under IDRL complicates the recognition of solidarity as a general principle, suggesting that states view it more as a commendable aspiration than a binding legal norm. In practice, states often provide assistance out of humanitarian concern or because 'it is the right thing to do', but they are not legally obligated to do so under a general principle of solidarity.

Notwithstanding the voluntary nature of international cooperation, some IDRL treaties and other instruments explicitly refer to solidarity in their texts.

[117] Draft Articles (n 3); IFRC, 'Guidelines for the Domestic Facilitation and Regulation of International Disaster Relief and Initial Recovery Assistance' (2007) (hereinafter 'IDRL Guidelines').

[118] S Sivakumaran, 'Techniques in International Law-Making: Extrapolation, Analogy, Form and the Emergence of an International Law of Disaster Relief' (2017) 28(4) *European Journal of International Law* 1097.

[119] Tampere Convention (n 106) art 3(1).

[120] ibid art 4.

[121] See, eg, Nuclear Accident Convention (n 111) art 2; Civil Defence Assistance Convention (n 112) art 3; AADMER (n 114) art 11; Inter-American Convention (n 114) art II; BSEC Agreement (n 114) art 4; Draft Articles (n 3) arts 7, 12; IDRL Guidelines (n 117) arts 10–12.

[122] ILC, 'Memorandum by the Secretariat on the Protection of Persons in the Event of Disasters' (11 December 2007) UN Doc A/CN.4/590, para 63.

A common formulation is that states should act 'in the spirit of solidarity' when responding to disasters. For example, the *ASEAN Agreement on Disaster Management and Emergency Response* (AADMER) provides that: 'The Parties shall, in the spirit of solidarity and partnership and in accordance with their respective needs, capabilities and situations, strengthen co-operation and co-ordination to achieve the objectives of this Agreement.'[123] Similarly, the *Framework Convention on Civil Defence Assistance* stipulates that 'assistance shall be undertaken in a spirit of humanity, solidarity and impartiality'.[124] The *Treaty on the Functioning of the European Union* goes further, including a provision titled 'solidarity clause', which provides that 'the Union and its Member States shall act jointly in a spirit of solidarity if a Member State is . . . the victim of a natural or man-made disaster'.[125] Even where solidarity is not mentioned in operative provisions, it often appears in preambular language, as in the *Inter-American Convention to Facilitate Disaster Assistance*, which acknowledges 'a genuine spirit of solidarity and good-neighborliness' among state parties in disaster settings.[126] Soft law instruments reflect this same pattern. The Draft Articles, for instance, refer in the preamble to being 'mindful of the fundamental value of solidarity in international relations'.[127]

However, it is important to note that none of these references explicitly recognises solidarity as a general principle. The absence of such recognition could suggest that solidarity has not yet attained the status of a legally binding principle within IDRL. For instance, although solidarity featured prominently in the drafting of the Draft Articles and is expressly mentioned in the preamble, it is described as a 'fundamental value' rather than as a legal principle.[128] This wording could indicate that while solidarity is viewed as an important normative underpinning, it has not been elevated to the level of a principle capable of generating binding obligations. This interpretation is reinforced by the Draft Articles' explicit inclusion of other principles, such as the humanitarian principles of humanity, neutrality and impartiality.[129] The contrast in how solidarity is treated relative to these principles could signal its current standing as a normative aspiration rather than a general principle of law.

Whether explicit references to solidarity in treaties and other instruments imply recognition of a binding principle ultimately turns on a fundamental doctrinal question: what is the legal character of these references? The central question here is whether these references to solidarity are aspirational or possess a 'fundamentally norm-creating character', which is a prerequisite for a rule or

[123] AADMER (n 114) art 3(3).
[124] Civil Defence Assistance Convention (n 112) art 3(d).
[125] Treaty on the Functioning of the European Union (n 54) art 222(1).
[126] Inter-American Convention (n 114) preamble.
[127] Draft Articles (n 3) preamble.
[128] ILC (n 6) 18.
[129] Draft Articles (n 3) art 6.

principle to be considered binding law according to the ICJ.[130] Some scholars argue that for a norm to have binding force in international law, it must prescribe specific conduct with sufficient precision.[131] Solidarity does not prescribe specific conduct in the way that more concrete legal norms do; rather, it establishes primers for conduct or general expectations that guide state behaviour.[132] Moreover, the obligations that arise from solidarity are not uniform; they depend on the specific circumstances, particularly with respect to how cooperation and assistance are differentiated and which states bear the greatest burdens. By its nature, solidarity generates uneven obligations: some states are expected to contribute more to the collective effort than others.[133] Accordingly, solidarity may lack the precision traditionally associated with 'hard' law.

However, as Raustiala argues, while a lack of precision may affect how treaty norms are interpreted, it does not undermine their legality or legal status; norms acquire binding force through their incorporation into treaties.[134] Indeed, many norms in international law lack precision in the sense that they do not prescribe specific conduct. While these norms do not always neatly conform to the misconception that international law must be specific enough to apply more or less the same in each similar situation – a misunderstanding that Hakimi refers to as 'the rulebook conception' – they are accepted as law nonetheless.[135] This suggests that references to solidarity in treaties may amount to more than aspirational rhetoric; they could be understood as binding legal norms that commit states to act 'in the spirit of solidarity' in disaster response, albeit as open norms subject to further interpretation to determine the specific obligations they entail.

This doctrinal question is relevant because if references to solidarity are interpreted as legally binding, they suggest that acting in solidarity in response to disasters is not merely voluntary but also a legal obligation under international law. In this light, such references move beyond the general frameworks for voluntary cooperation established in IDRL treaties and soft law instruments. They imply that states may indeed bear legal obligations to act in solidarity, even if the precise content and scope of those obligations remain indeterminate and open to interpretation. It is this engagement with solidarity that may support the inference that solidarity is recognised as a general principle underpinning IDRL. While these obligations may not prescribe specific conduct, their inclusion in treaty texts and other authoritative instruments reflects a shared

[130] *North Sea Continental Shelf (Germany v Denmark; Germany v Netherlands)* (Judgment) [1969] ICJ Rep 3, para 72.

[131] See, eg, C Chinkin, 'The Challenge of Soft Law: Development and Change in International Law' (1989) 38(4) *International and Comparative Law Quarterly* 850, 851. See also Eggett (n 5) 36–41.

[132] Other more abstract principles operate similarly by establishing primers to conduct rather than prescribing specific (in)actions. See R Dworkin, *Taking Rights Seriously* (Duckworth, 1977) 40–42.

[133] Wolfrum (n 7) 396.

[134] K Raustiala, 'Form and Substance in International Agreements' (2005) 99(3) *American Journal of International Law* 581, 58–589.

[135] M Hakimi, 'Making Sense of Customary International Law' (2020) 118(8) *Michigan Law Review* 1487, 1497.

understanding among states that solidarity can form the basis for legal obligations in disaster response.

However, it is important to place this argument in perspective and exercise caution when drawing broad conclusions from these explicit references to solidarity. Such references remain relatively uncommon and are generally confined to treaties with limited scope and participation, rendering them insufficiently representative of widespread recognition among states. As discussed earlier, inferring recognition of solidarity as a general principle of IDRL remains difficult, given that most treaties and soft law instruments continue to emphasise voluntary cooperation. This prevailing emphasis indicates that solidarity is still regarded more as a moral aspiration than as a binding legal principle capable of creating, modifying and confirming rights and obligations. Nonetheless, the inclusion of solidarity in binding treaty texts – even as an open norm – may signal a gradual evolution in terms of how states understand their obligations in disaster response. Should future instruments, including the forthcoming treaty on the protection of persons in the event of disasters, increasingly incorporate solidarity, stronger evidence could emerge to support its recognition as a general principle of IDRL.

B. Solidarity in UN Resolutions

Potential evidence for the recognition of solidarity as a general principle of IDRL can also be found in resolutions adopted by international organisations. Resolutions of the UN General Assembly are particularly significant in this regard, as they have repeatedly addressed international cooperation in disaster response. These resolutions often underscore the importance of solidarity in facilitating disaster relief and promoting international assistance. Yet, the analysis of these resolutions follows a similar pattern to that of the treaties and soft law instruments discussed above: although solidarity may be inferred as a normative underpinning, resolutions stop short of evidencing its recognition as a general principle.

Like IDRL treaties, several UN General Assembly resolutions seek to facilitate international cooperation and assistance in disaster response on the basis of solidarity. A particularly illustrative example is Resolution 46/182, which articulates the fundamental principles of international disaster response and establishes a general framework for cooperation.[136] It emphasises the critical importance of humanitarian assistance to affected communities and recognises that international cooperation may be indispensable, particularly when the affected state's capacity is overwhelmed.[137] While less detailed in procedural and operational terms than most IDRL treaties and soft law instruments, Resolution

[136] UN General Assembly Res 46/182 (n 103).
[137] ibid paras 1, 5.

46/182 outlines a cooperative framework grounded in the consent of the affected state.[138] Importantly, it presumes that states will offer assistance without expectation of reciprocity, reflecting a solidarity-based approach. This emphasis is reinforced by subsequent UN resolutions, which encourage states to implement the solidarity-oriented frameworks established in treaties and soft law instruments.[139] Additionally, many resolutions call for the provision of humanitarian assistance in response to specific disasters without expectation of reciprocal benefit.[140]

While UN General Assembly resolutions endorse solidarity-based international cooperation in disaster response, they do not necessarily demonstrate that solidarity is recognised as a general principle of IDRL. Like treaties and soft law instruments, these resolutions envisage cooperation on a voluntary basis and do not impose a legal obligation on states to act in solidarity. For instance, neither Resolution 46/182 nor any other resolution indicates or implies that states must cooperate with or provide assistance to affected states as a matter of international law. Instead, they leave it to each state's discretion to decide whether and how to assist. Although these resolutions affirm that solidarity is a cornerstone of international disaster response and reflect a shared moral commitment to cooperation and assistance, they fall short of recognising it as a general principle.

Furthermore, unlike IDRL treaties, recognition of solidarity as a general principle cannot be inferred from explicit references in UN resolutions. While some resolutions mention solidarity, these references typically highlight that international cooperation and assistance in response to disasters are acts of solidarity rather than asserting the legal status of solidarity.[141] For example, the UN General Assembly acknowledged the 'spirit of solidarity' in the context of the 2022 Pakistan floods:

> Welcoming the assistance and contributions of the international community, including Governments, international organizations, civil society and the private sector, in the relief and rehabilitation efforts, *which reflect the spirit of international solidarity and cooperation*, to address and meet the challenges of the disaster, and in this context also appreciating the role of the people and Government of Pakistan.[142]

[138] ibid para 3.

[139] See, eg, UN General Assembly Res 78/120 (8 December 2023) UN Doc A/RES/78/120, paras 21–22.

[140] See, eg, UN General Assembly Res 45/100 (14 December 1990) UN Doc A/RES/45/100, para 5; UN General Assembly Res 77/1 (7 October 2022) UN Doc A/RES/77/1, preamble.

[141] See, eg, UN General Assembly Res 34/56 (29 November 1979) UN Doc A/RES/34/56, preamble; UN General Assembly Res 40/231 (17 December 1985) UN Doc A/RES/40/231, preamble; UN General Assembly Res 55/240 (26 January 2001) UN Doc A/RES/55/240, preamble; UN General Assembly Res 60/13 (14 November 2005) UN Doc A/RES/60/13, preamble; UN General Assembly Res 60/220 (2 December 2005) UN Doc A/RES/60/220, para 1; UN General Assembly Res 63/137 (11 December 2008) UN Doc A/RES/63/137, preamble; UN General Assembly Res 74/270 (2 April 2020) UN Doc A/RES/74/270, para 6.

[142] UN General Assembly Res 77/1 (n 140) (emphasis added).

This language functions as a descriptive observation about the response rather than a normative statement on legal obligations.[143] The resolution does not suggest that states were required to act in solidarity, nor does it imply that solidarity carries binding legal force. Consequently, while such references support the view that solidarity underpins international cooperation and assistance in disaster response, they do not indicate recognition of solidarity as a general principle of IDRL. This could have been different if the resolutions explicitly stated that rights and obligations derive from solidarity, but in their current form, they reinforce its status as a moral aspiration rather than a legally binding norm.

It is also noteworthy that explicit references to solidarity are absent in some of the key UN resolutions. For instance, even though Resolution 46/182 establishes a cooperative framework that is clearly grounded in solidarity, it does not explicitly mention the term in either its preambular or operative clauses.[144] Similarly, the annual UN General Assembly resolutions on international cooperation in disaster response do not reference solidarity, despite being a comprehensive resolution reaffirming the fundamental principles of international disaster law and urging states to collaborate on disaster prevention and response.[145] While the absence of explicit mentions does not rule out the possibility that solidarity is recognised as a general principle, this omission suggests that states do not yet conceive of solidarity as a legal principle from which the rules of IDRL rules may derive.

C. Solidarity in Statements of States

The recognition of general principles of international law may be inferred not only from treaties and UN resolutions but also from statements made by individual states. Such statements can serve as evidence of a principle's acceptance. In the case of solidarity, this mode of recognition is especially relevant, given its prominent invocation in the context of disasters and international relations overall in recent years.[146] However, while these expressions may indicate a growing normative appeal, they fall short of establishing solidarity as a general principle of IDRL.

Among the various statements issued in the context of disasters, three types can be distinguished for the purposes of analysing potential evidence of the

[143] Similar statements were made by the ILC, which called offers of international disaster assistance 'the practical manifestation of the principle of solidarity': ILC (n 6) 56, 57. Similarly, the IFRC noted that 'relief actions are an expression of international solidarity': IFRC, 'Res. XVIII International Relief Actions – Revision of Principles' (1965) 47(563) *International Review of the Red Cross* 581, 582.

[144] UN General Assembly Res 46/182 (n 103).

[145] The UN General Assembly traditionally adopts a resolution reaffirming commitments regarding international cooperation in disaster response every year. The latest resolution is UN General Assembly Res 80/113 (10 December 2025) UN Doc A/RES/80/113.

[146] Den Heijer and van der Wilt (n 1) 4.

recognition of solidarity: statements expressing condolences and sympathy; statements appealing for or announcing international assistance; and statements made in the UN General Assembly's Sixth Committee regarding the role of solidarity in the development of IDRL. However, none of these categories of statements provides unequivocal evidence that solidarity is recognised as a general principle yet.

First, states often use the language of solidarity to express condolences and sympathy towards disaster victims and affected states. These expressions serve a primarily rhetoric function, but are often formulaic and lack substance. Phrases such as 'we stand in solidarity with the victims' have become commonplace in diplomatic responses to disasters. For example, following the 2023 Moroccan earthquake, the Spanish Prime Minister conveyed his 'solidarity and support to the people of Morocco in the wake of this terrible earthquake . . . Spain stands with the victims of this tragedy'.[147] Similarly, the US Secretary of State tweeted: 'We are deeply saddened by the loss of life from yesterday's earthquake in Morocco and extend our heartfelt condolences to the families of those affected. We offer our support and solidarity to our Moroccan partners at this tragic time.'[148] However, recognition of solidarity as a general principle cannot clearly be inferred from these statements. Such statements highlight the sociological dimension of solidarity, emphasising feelings of sympathy, belonging and kinship that arise from a sense of feeling connected in times of tragedy. While such statements evoke the emotional resonance of solidarity, they do not necessarily engage with its normative dimension – that is, the idea that solidarity entails obligations of mutual assistance and cooperation.

More relevant, perhaps, are those statements in which expressions of solidarity are explicitly linked to international assistance, aligning with a second category: appeals for or offers of aid in the aftermath of disasters. These statements may indicate recognition of a general principle by suggesting that solidarity prompts or should prompt states to offer assistance to the affected state. For instance, in the wake of the devastating 2022 floods, Pakistan appealed to the international community for 'full support and solidarity with the people of Pakistan . . . in alleviating their suffering and in helping to rebuild their lives and communities'.[149] Here, solidarity is invoked not only as a sentiment but also as a basis for requesting concrete assistance. Conversely, expressions of solidarity often accompany offers of aid. Following the 2023 Turkey-Syria earthquake, Belgium's Foreign Minister stated: 'We stand in solidarity with the

[147] 'World Leaders Offer Solidarity after Devastating Morocco Earthquake' *France24* (10 September 2023) www.france24.com/en/africa/20230910-world-leaders-offer-solidarity-after-devastating-morocco-earthquake.

[148] A Blinken, *Twitter* (9 September 2023) twitter.com/SecBlinken/status/1700499840357089405.

[149] Government of Pakistan, 'Joint Launch of 2022 Pakistan Floods Response Plan by Government of Pakistan and the United Nations' (30 August 2022) https://reliefweb.int/report/pakistan/joint-launch-2022-pakistan-floods-response-plan-government-pakistan-and-united-nations.

people of Türkiye and are ready to offer assistance.'[150] After the 2020 Beirut port explosion, Qatar expressed 'solidarity with brotherly Lebanon and its willingness to provide all kinds of assistance'.[151] Even where the term 'solidarity' is not explicitly used, the sentiment may be inferred from the context. For example, the President of the European Commission, responding to the 2023 Turkey-Syria earthquake, declared:

> We are all shaken by the devastating effects of the earthquakes that have hit Türkiye and Syria this week. The priority now is to work around the clock to save as many lives as possible . . . But we are already sending now a message to the people of Türkiye and Syria: the EU will support your communities. Because no one should be left alone when a tragedy like this hits a people.[152]

Although the statement does not explicitly use the term, it is possible to deduce solidarity from it in that it signals a readiness to support the affected states and communities.

While statements appealing for or announcing assistance may suggest that states view solidarity as a cornerstone of international disaster response, and that such assistance constitutes an act of solidarity, they do not necessarily evidence recognition of solidarity as a general principle of IDRL. This is so for two main reasons. First, it is not always clear that assistance is offered without the expectation of reciprocal benefits. Donor states may negotiate conditions or pursue strategic interests at a later stage, casting doubt on whether the assistance was genuinely grounded in solidarity or motivated by other considerations.[153] Moreover, offers of assistance do not always materialise into actual support, leaving uncertainty as to whether the expressions of solidarity were sincere or merely symbolic. Second, as with treaty texts and resolutions, solidarity in these statements is typically framed as a moral aspiration rather than a legal norm. Appeals for solidarity-based cooperation are often couched in ethical language, suggesting that states should assist because it is morally the right thing to do rather than because they are legally obligated to do so. Affected states rarely assert a right to receive assistance grounded in solidarity and donor states seldom imply that they are under a legal duty to provide it.

[150] BB Donmez, 'World Leaders Voice Solidarity after Powerful Earthquake Strikes Türkiye' *AA* (6 February 2023) www.aa.com.tr/en/world/world-leaders-voice-solidarity-after-powerful-earthquake-strikes-turkiye/2807597.

[151] 'Beirut Explosion: World Reacts to Deadly Blast in Lebanon Capital' *Al Jazeera* (5 August 2020) www.aljazeera.com/news/2020/8/5/beirut-explosion-world-reacts-to-deadly-blast-in-lebanon-capital.

[152] European Commission, 'European Commission and Swedish Presidency of the Council Will Organise a Donors' Conference for the People of Türkiye and Syria Affected by the Earthquake' (8 February 2023) https://ec.europa.eu/commission/presscorner/detail/en/ip_23_708.

[153] For instance, after Hurricane Irma left a trail of destruction in the Caribbean in 2017, the Netherlands pledged millions in relief and recovery aid to Dutch Saint Martin, but only under strict conditions relating to oversight and anti-corruption measures, leading to a political crisis and significant delays in the provision of aid to affected communities: 'St. Martin's Leader Quits over Irma Aid Spat' *DW* (25 November 2017) www.dw.com/en/dutch-saint-martins-leader-quits-over-hurricane-irma-aid-controversy/a-41525021.

Perhaps the most convincing evidence for the recognition of solidarity can be found in a third category of statements: those made by states in the UN General Assembly's Sixth Committee during discussions on the Draft Articles. As cited in section IV.A, the Draft Articles explicitly refer to solidarity in its preamble, endorsing it as one of the 'key concepts underlying the [Draft Articles]'.[154] Several states supported this approach in the Sixth Committee.[155] Some went further by commenting directly on solidarity. For example, the delegation of Haiti described 'international solidarity [as] a fundamental principle, especially in the context of natural disasters'.[156] Other states were less explicit, but nonetheless implied a normative understanding of solidarity. Turkey, for instance, stated that 'close cooperation and solidarity on the part of the international community was paramount for efficient disaster relief'.[157]

These statements could indeed suggest that solidarity is viewed as more than merely a moral or political value by at least some states. However, two key issues complicate any definitive conclusion that solidarity has been recognised as a general principle of IDRL. First, the statements in question are not representative of the broader international community; only a limited number of states have explicitly addressed the legal status of solidarity in this context. Second, while these statements emphasise the importance of solidarity in international disaster response, they do not necessarily imply its recognition as a general principle. Instead, most appear to highlight that solidarity is a principle with the *potential* to become legally binding in the future rather than an already-established general principle. This view was clearly articulated by Spain, which described solidarity as not yet a legal principle of IDRL, but rather an 'emerging concept on which any system for the protection of persons in the event of disasters should eventually be built'.[158] Similarly, China indicated that it does not consider solidarity to be a legal principle yet:

> Solidarity and cooperation could be included [in the Draft Articles] as moral values, provided that their inclusion could in no way be construed as an obligation on the part of disaster-affected States to accept relief or on the part of States providing relief to satisfy requests for assistance, since that depended on their capacity.[159]

[154] ILC (n 6) 18.
[155] For example, China and Spain in UN General Assembly Sixth Committee, 'Summary Record of the 20th Meeting' (17 December 2009) UN Doc A/C.6/64/SR.20, paras 24, 50; Ecuador in UN General Assembly Sixth Committee, 'Summary Record of the 24th Meeting' (29 November 2016) UN Doc A/C.6/71/SR.24, para 12; Sudan in UN General Assembly Sixth Committee, 'Summary Record of the 31st Meeting' (31 January 2019) UN Doc A/C.6/73/SR.31, para 40; El Salvador in UN General Assembly Sixth Committee, 'Summary Record of the 17th Meeting' (30 November 2020) UN Doc A/C.6/75/SR.17, para 64; Vietnam in UN General Assembly Sixth Committee, 'Summary Record of the 18th Meeting' (16 December 2020) UN Doc A/C.6/75/SR.18, para 14. See also UN General Assembly Sixth Committee, 'Oral Report of the Chair of the Working Group on Protection of Persons in the Event of Disasters' (8 November 2023).
[156] UN General Assembly Sixth Committee, 'Summary Record of the 18th Meeting' (n 155) para 17.
[157] UN General Assembly Sixth Committee, 'Summary Record of the 27th Meeting' (24 November 2014) UN Doc A/C.6/69/SR.27 para 30.
[158] UN General Assembly Sixth Committee, 'Summary Record of the 20th Meeting' (n 155) para 9.
[159] ibid para 24.

These positions reflect a broader trend across treaties and soft law: solidarity is widely endorsed as a normative principle, but it has not yet crystallised into a general principle of law capable of creating, modifying and confirming rights and obligations within IDRL.

V. CONCLUSION

This chapter examined the legal status of solidarity in IDRL, demonstrating that while the principle appears to have evolved beyond a purely political notion within international law, it has not yet attained the status of a general principle in terms of Article 38(1)(c) of the ICJ Statute. Through a comprehensive, systematic and evidence-based analysis of treaties, soft law instruments, UN General Assembly resolutions and statements of states, this chapter has explored whether solidarity has been recognised by states as a general principle capable of creating, modifying and confirming rights and obligations. The analysis has revealed that although solidarity is embedded in the frameworks facilitating international cooperation and assistance, it is predominantly treated as a moral aspiration rather than a legally binding principle. This is reflected in the voluntary nature of cooperation envisaged by these instruments, which encourage but do not obligate states to act in solidarity. Some treaties and soft law instruments do incorporate explicit commitments to act 'in the spirit of solidarity', offering stronger – though still limited – evidence of its potential legally binding character. However, such references remain rare and insufficiently representative. Similarly, resolutions and statements made by states, including those made in the UN General Assembly's Sixth Committee, often emphasise solidarity's normative importance, but stop short of recognising it as a general principle of law. Instead, the prevailing view appears to be that solidarity represents a moral imperative to assist disaster-affected states rather than a legal obligation arising from a recognised principle of IDRL.

However, this conclusion does not diminish the relevance or importance of solidarity within IDRL. While solidarity may not yet be recognised as a general principle of international law, the evidence clearly demonstrates that it holds significant normative value in the field. Treaties, soft law and resolutions consistently urge states to act in solidarity by expressing a readiness to cooperate with and assist disaster-affected states without the expectation of reciprocal benefits. In practice, states indeed demonstrate this spirit of solidarity, not only through their rhetoric but also through tangible cooperation including the provision of aid. These practices show that solidarity can and does operate within IDRL.[160]

The question then becomes what role solidarity can and should play in IDRL. While it may not yet be recognised as a general principle capable of autonomously establishing rights and obligations, solidarity could nonetheless serve

[160] A similar argument in relation to general international law is made in MacDonald (n 9) 301.

other meaningful functions. One such possibility is its use as an interpretative tool. Given that virtually all treaties and soft law instruments in the field establish frameworks for international cooperation and assistance based on solidarity and considering the consistent endorsement of solidarity by states in disaster response, it could be argued that solidarity represents one of the key purposes underpinning IDRL.[161]

In this sense, solidarity could inform the teleological interpretation of IDRL, guiding the understanding and application of its rules in a manner that promotes solidarity with disaster-affected states. A teleological interpretation is a method of interpretation that seeks to give effect to the underlying rationale or purpose of law.[162] This approach is well established and widely applied in international law. For instance, in the interpretation of treaties, Article 31(1)(a) of the *Vienna Convention on the Law of Treaties* provides that a treaty shall be interpreted 'in the light of its object and purpose'.[163] The teleological method is likewise employed in the identification and interpretation of customary international law.[164]

Applying solidarity as an interpretive lens within a teleological framework would mean that IDRL should be construed so as to give rise to differentiated international cooperation and assistance in pursuit of the common goal of protecting persons affected by disasters.[165] This interpretative function would be especially relevant in the context of treaties where states have committed to act in solidarity, suggesting that their conduct should be assessed against the background of solidarity. While not creating binding obligations on its own, solidarity in this role could help shape the interpretation and practical implementation of IDRL instruments.

However, caution is warranted in using solidarity as a teleological interpretative lens, as this function risks inflating its role and treating it as a quasi-general principle capable of altering IDRL as a binding norm. If solidarity were used to construe binding obligations of cooperation and assistance, it could effectively elevate the principle to a status it has not yet attained, despite the lack of formal recognition. Therefore, while solidarity may inform the interpretation of

[161] Wellens, 'Revisiting Solidarity as a (Re-)Emerging Constitutional Principle' (n 7) 45; Wolfrum (n 40) 403.

[162] G Letsas, 'Strasbourg's Interpretive Ethic: Lessons for the International Lawyer' (2010) 21(3) *European Journal of International Law* 509, 533; J Pauwelyn and M Elsig, 'The Politics of Treaty Interpretation: Variations and Explanations Across International Tribunals' in MA Pollack and JL Dunoff (eds), *Interdisciplinary Perspectives on International Law and International Relations: The State of the Art* (Cambridge University Press, 2011) 445, 451.

[163] *Vienna Convention on the Law of Treaties* (23 May 1969).

[164] ICJ Judge Tanaka observed that '[t]he method of logical and teleological interpretation can be applied in the case of customary law as in the case of written law': *North Sea Continental Shelf Case* (n 130) Dissenting Opinion of Judge Tanaka 182. See also O Ammann, *Domestic Courts and the Interpretation of International Law: Methods and Reasoning Based on the Swiss Example* (Brill Nijhoff, 2020) 209; P Merkouris, 'Interpreting the Customary Rules on Interpretation' (2017) 19 *International Community Law Review* 126, 141.

[165] As argued in ch 2, section IV.

existing rules, it cannot be used to fill gaps or create new rights or obligations under IDRL. Furthermore, its interpretative function is also constrained by other rules of treaty interpretation. Notably, other principles such as state sovereignty must be considered alongside solidarity, as they reflect other normative purposes underpinning the regime and also inform the teleological interpretation of IDRL.[166] Moreover, teleological interpretation is rarely applied in isolation.[167] It operates in conjunction with other interpretative methods, including the textual method (based on the ordinary meaning of treaty text),[168] the contextual method (drawing on preambles, annexes and preparatory works)[169] and the systemic method (considering other applicable rules of international law).[170] As such, the teleological interpretation of IDRL through the lens of solidarity offers a valuable starting point for interpreting the regime rather than the endpoint.

Beyond its potential function as an interpretative tool for existing rules, solidarity can also inform the future development of IDRL. Eggett argues that even if it is not recognised as a general principle, 'solidarity could play a role in the development of specific rules' and that '[t]his role is of course enhanced if solidarity is seen as a principle with significant weight in different areas and contexts'.[171] As a widely acknowledged cornerstone of international disaster response, solidarity offers a strong normative foundation upon which future treaties and soft law could be built – not as a matter of law, but because it enjoys broad support among states. Future instruments could incorporate explicit commitments to solidarity in their texts and adopt substantive rules that reflect the principle, such as obligations to cooperate with and assist affected states without expecting anything in return. In this capacity, solidarity could guide the evolution of IDRL, ensuring that international disaster response is rooted in genuine, solidarity-based cooperation rather than rhetorical affirmation alone.

If states choose to commit to solidarity more explicitly, it could pave the way for its evolution into a general principle of international law in the future. Should solidarity continue to shape IDRL normatively and if states begin to accept that solidarity entails concrete commitments to international cooperation and assistance in disaster response, this could signal a shift from viewing solidarity as a more aspiration to recognising it as a legal principle. Early signs

[166] ILC, 'Conclusions of the Work of the Study Group on the Fragmentation of International Law: Difficulties Arising from the Diversification and Expansion of International Law' (2006) UN Doc A/61/10, para 1.

[167] Ammann (n 164) 212.

[168] Vienna Convention on the Law of Treaties (n 163) art 31(1). See also R Gardiner, *Treaty Interpretation,* 2nd edn (Oxford University Press, 2015) 181; Ammann (n 164) 197; Pauwelyn and Elsig (n 162) 450.

[169] Vienna Convention on the Law of Treaties (n 163) arts 31–32. See also Gardiner (n 168) 197; Ammann (n 164) 202.

[170] Vienna Convention on the Law of Treaties (n 163) art 31(3)(c). See also Ammann (n 164) 202; Pauwelyn and Elsig (n 162) 457.

[171] Eggett (n 5) 49.

of such a development can be seen in treaties that include explicit commitments to act in solidarity in the international response to disasters.[172] Importantly, though, recognition does not depend solely on explicit references; treaties that implicitly reflect solidarity in their content also contribute to its normative consolidation. A unique opportunity to advance solidarity lies in the negotiations of the treaty on the protection of persons in the event of disasters. These negotiations give states a genuine chance to translate their support for solidarity into legal commitments by drafting a treaty grounded in solidarity. This would require more than symbolic gestures – it would necessitate the establishment of a solidarity-based framework for international cooperation, wherein states accept obligations to support one another in times of disaster.

This raises the important question of what IDRL would or should look like if interpreted and developed through the lens of solidarity. In other words, if states were to fully commit to solidarity, how would that reshape the legal framework of international disaster response? The next chapters of this book take up this question. Chapter 4 explores the transformative potential of solidarity at a high level, arguing that it could reorient IDRL from a sovereignty-centred regime characterised by state autonomy and voluntarism to one focused on the protection of disaster-affected persons through obligations of differentiated international cooperation and assistance. The chapters that follow then zoom in on specific issues within the regime, examining them through the lens of solidarity to assess how they might be reimagined. This is not a purely theoretical exercise; rather, it is a substantive effort to demonstrate what IDRL could look like if it were grounded in the principle of solidarity. In doing so, the book moves beyond rhetorical affirmations to solidarity and provides a practical roadmap for its implementation, showing how solidarity can be operationalised to enhance cooperation, improve protection for persons affected by disasters and address structural inequalities in disaster response.

[172] See discussion in section IV.A.

4

Solidarity in International Disaster Response Law

I. INTRODUCTION

WHERE THE PREVIOUS TWO chapters examined the meaning and legal status of solidarity in IDRL, this chapter turns to a forward-looking inquiry: what would IDRL look like if interpreted and developed through the lens of solidarity? In other words, if states were to fully commit to solidarity as a principle, how would that reshape the legal framework governing international disaster response? This question remains largely unexplored in legal scholarship. While some scholars have addressed specific contentious issues through the perspective of solidarity,[1] a comprehensive analysis of its transformative potential across IDRL has yet to be undertaken. This is not unique to IDRL; across international law more broadly, the transformative potential of solidarity remains largely underexamined. Much of the academic literature focuses on describing the function of solidarity and how it is expressed within specific legal regimes – for example, through the principle of common but differentiated responsibilities in international climate change law.[2] However, these discussions often stop short of exploring the full and concrete implications of applying solidarity as an interpretative lens and model for future development,

[1] See, eg, K Wellens, 'Solidarity as a Constitutional Principle: Its Expanding Role and Inherent Limitations' in RStJ MacDonald and DM Johnston (eds), *Towards World Constitutionalism: Issues in the Legal Ordering of the World Community* (Martinus Nijhoff Publishers, 2005) 775, 784 ff; K Wellens, 'Revisiting Solidarity as a (Re-)Emerging Constitutional Principle: Some Further Reflections' in R Wolfrum and C Kojima (eds), *Solidarity: A Structural Principle of International Law* (Springer, 2010) 3, 14 ff; AG Koroma, 'Solidarity: Evidence of an Emerging International Legal Principle' in H Hestermeyer et al (eds), *Coexistence, Cooperation and Solidarity* (Martinus Nijhoff Publishers, 2012) 103, 123 ff; F Zorzi Giustiniani, *International Law in Disaster Scenarios: Applicable Rules and Principles* (Springer, 2021) chs 8–9; R Wolfrum, *Solidarity and Community Interests: Driving Forces for the Interpretation and Development of International Law* (Brill Nijhoff, 2021) 428 ff; S Villani, *The Concept of Solidarity within EU Disaster Response Law: A Legal Assessment* (Bononia University Press, 2021).

[2] See, eg, Wolfrum (n 1); Wellens, 'Revisiting Solidarity as a (Re-)Emerging Constitutional Principle' (n 1); Koroma (n 1); Wolfrum and Kojima (n 1); A Williams, 'Solidarity, Justice and Climate Change Law' (2009) 10 *Melbourne Journal of International Law* 493; M den Heijer and H van der Wilt, 'Global Solidarity and Common but Differentiated Responsibilities' in M den Heijer and H van der Wilt (eds), *Netherlands Yearbook of International Law 2020* (TMC Asser Press, 2022) 3.

and its capacity to reshape regimes and challenge some of the foundational assumptions of international law. This chapter seeks to fill that gap by considering how solidarity could reorient IDRL from a sovereignty-centred regime characterised by state autonomy and voluntarism to one pursuing the protection of disaster-affected persons through differentiated international cooperation and assistance.

The aim of this chapter is not to propose a radical redraft of IDRL based solely on the principle of solidarity. Such an approach would not only be unrealistic, given the slow recognition of solidarity as a legal principle, but would also overlook the fact that solidarity does not operate in a vacuum. Any proposal to reinterpret or develop the regime through solidarity must therefore be situated alongside other foundational principles of IDRL. For this reason, the chapter begins by exploring how solidarity interacts with existing principles, with a particular focus on its relationship with state sovereignty – a principle that continues to be widely endorsed and emphasised by states. Addressing the interaction between solidarity and sovereignty is particularly necessary in light of general concerns and anxieties that a solidarity-based approach might undermine or override the sovereignty of both affected and assisting states. While solidarity and sovereignty are often portrayed as being in tension, this chapter argues that they are not inherently incompatible. Rather, solidarity can coexist with sovereignty, although it may place certain constraints on the discretion of affected states, particularly in contexts where international cooperation is essential to protect persons affected by disasters.

After examining the interaction between these two principles, this chapter proceeds to analyse how our understanding of IDRL changes if the regime is interpreted and developed through the lens of solidarity, taking into account its concurrent application alongside the principle of sovereignty. The purpose here is primarily normative: to explore how solidarity should be reflected in IDRL if embraced as something more than mere rhetoric, rather than to offer a purely descriptive account of how it is currently reflected. It is argued that implementing solidarity into IDRL would have five significant high-level implications for the regime. First, solidarity would place limits on the sovereignty of affected states by balancing national interests with the common goal of protecting persons in disasters, thereby constraining the discretion of states to delay or refuse international assistance. Second, solidarity would call for the development of rights and obligations for third states, giving substance to their shared responsibility to support affected states in disaster response. Third, interpreting IDRL through the lens of solidarity would require the regime to centre the rights of persons affected by disasters and the corresponding obligations of states to ensure the realisation of those rights. Fourth, solidarity would give rise to a binding duty to cooperate in disaster response that goes beyond voluntarism without the expectation of reciprocal benefits. Fifth, solidarity would introduce a differentiated approach to cooperation and assistance, requiring states to contribute to the common goal in accordance with their respective national response capacities.

This would mean that states with greater resources and capacities bear correspondingly greater responsibilities than those with more limited means.

This high-level analysis of the implications of interpreting and developing IDRL through the lens of solidarity sets the stage for the subsequent chapters of the book. The following chapters will examine the implementation of solidarity in IDRL more closely across three dimensions of international disaster response. In doing so, the book moves from conceptual analysis to practical application, offering a detailed exploration of how solidarity can be operationalised to address persistent challenges in IDRL and contribute to a more equitable international disaster response framework.

II. BALANCING SOLIDARITY AND SOVEREIGNTY

Like any principle of international law, solidarity does not operate in isolation. It functions within a broader context and is shaped by its interaction with other, often overlapping principles. This means that solidarity should be understood not as a standalone or overriding principle, but as one that interacts with, complements and at times challenges other foundational principles. Among these, the principle of sovereignty remains particularly significant – not only because it is widely recognised as a cornerstone of IDRL, but also because solidarity is often juxtaposed with sovereignty, giving rise to concerns that strengthening solidarity as a legal principle may encroach upon the sovereign discretion of states to determine whether, when and how to engage in international cooperation.[3] For instance, while the Draft Articles recognise solidarity as a fundamental value underpinning international disaster response,[4] the ILC felt the need to emphasise that it 'cannot be interpreted as diminishing the sovereignty of affected States and their prerogatives within the limits of international law'.[5] Accordingly, any effort to interpret or develop IDRL through the lens of solidarity must begin by examining how it relates to other principles rather than assuming its primacy or independence.

The interaction between legal principles is not a novel concern in international law. In 2006, the ILC Study Group on the Fragmentation of International Law addressed the topic of norm and regime interaction, providing a useful starting point for understanding how principles relate to one another.[6] Central to the

[3] See, eg, A-M Slaughter, 'Security, Solidarity, and Sovereignty: The Grand Themes of UN Reform' (2005) 99(3) *American Journal of International Law* 619.

[4] ILC, 'Draft Articles on the Protection of Persons in the Event of Disasters' (27 May 2016) UN Doc A/CN.4/L.871 (Draft Articles) preamble.

[5] ILC, 'Commentaries on the Draft Articles on the Protection of Persons in the Event of Disasters' (2016) UN Doc A/71/10, 18.

[6] ILC, 'Conclusions of the Work of the Study Group on the Fragmentation of International Law: Difficulties Arising from the Diversification and Expansion of International Law' (2006) UN Doc A/61/10.

Study Group's conclusions is the recognition that rules and principles of international law do not exist in isolation, but operate in relation to one another.[7]

However, the terminology in this context can lead to confusion. Whereas Chapter 3 used the term 'principle' to describe general principles of law under Article 38(1)(c) of the ICJ Statute[8] – a source of international law – the term is used differently in the context of norm interaction. Here, 'principle' refers to the content of norms rather than their legal status, describing norms in general and abstract terms, in contrast to 'rules', which denote binding norms in specific and concrete terms. [9] For example, the freedom of navigation is considered a principle due to its general nature, whereas the obligation for submarines to surface and show their flag in territorial waters is a rule because of its specificity.[10] Despite this definitional distinction, both rules and principles can apply as binding norms of international law, as clarified by the ICJ in the *Gulf of Maine* case:

> [T]he association of the terms 'rules' and 'principles' is no more than the use of a dual expression to convey one and the same idea, since in this context 'principles' clearly means principles of law, that is, it also includes rules of international law in whose case the use of the term 'principles' may be justified because of their more general and more fundamental character.[11]

In this book, the term 'norm' is used as an umbrella concept encompassing both rules and principles.[12]

As norms exist along one another, they must therefore be interpreted against the background of other applicable rules and principles.[13] The ILC Study Group emphasised that in the interpretation and application of international law, 'it is often necessary to determine the precise relationship between two or more rules and principles that are both valid and applicable in respect of a situation'.[14] To this end, they identified two primary types of normative relationships: one of interpretation, where one norm informs the meaning or scope of another; and one of conflict, where norms are incompatible and a method of resolution must be found.[15]

[7] 'International law is a legal system. Its rules and principles (i.e., its norms) act in relation to and should be interpreted against the background of other rules and principles. As a legal system, international law is not a random collection of such norms. There are meaningful relationships between them': ibid para 1.

[8] *Statute of the International Court of Justice* (26 June 1945).

[9] R Wolfrum, 'General International Law (Principles, Rules, and Standards)' in *Max Planck Encyclopedia of International Law* (Oxford University Press, 2010) para 6; ILC, 'Fragmentation of International Law: Difficulties Arising from the Diversification and Expansion of International Law' (13 April 2006) UN Doc A/CN.4/L.682, para 28.

[10] International Law Association, 'Statement of Principles Applicable to the Formation of General Customary International Law' (2000) 11.

[11] *Delimitation of the Maritime Boundary in the Gulf of Maine Area (Canada v United States of America)* (Judgment) [1982] ICJ Rep 246, para 79.

[12] In doing so, this book follows the practice of the ILC Study Group in ILC (n 6) para 1.

[13] ibid para 1.

[14] ibid.

[15] ibid.

First, a relationship of interpretation is one 'where one norm assists in the interpretation of another'.[16] In this relationship, the norms in question are compatible, meaning that states can comply with both simultaneously and that they are applied together. However, because norms have distinct meanings, those that interact through a relationship of interpretation must be read against the background of one another in a harmonious way so that they 'give rise to a single set of compatible obligations'.[17] This indicates that norms shape the interpretation of others, inter alia, by serving as an 'application, clarification, updating or modification' of the other.[18] Consequently, norms may not always be applied to their fullest extent, but must instead be balanced in a coherent and complementary manner when applied concurrently.

Alternatively, the ILC Study Group described a relationship of conflict as one 'where two norms that are both valid and applicable point to incompatible decisions so that a choice must be made between them'.[19] International law has developed rules that allow one norm to prevail over another in cases of conflict. These rules are based on a hierarchy of norms and include the principle of *lex specialis derogat legi generali* (specific norms prevail over general norms),[20] the rule that *jus cogens* (peremptory norms) overrides other norms,[21] and the rule that obligations under the *Charter of the United Nations* (UN Charter) take precedence over other conflicting obligations of international law.[22]

Based on the definitions of the two types of relationships, the deciding factor in how to determine the relationship between norms appears to be whether the norms in question are compatible. If they are compatible, norms interact through a relationship of interpretation; if they are incompatible, they interact through a relationship of conflict. The 'compatibility' of norms is defined broadly in the academic literature,[23] where norms are considered incompatible only when two (or more) norms cannot be complied with simultaneously.[24] This would occur, for example, if one norm requires certain conduct that another prohibits. However, international law operates on a strong presumption against such inconsistencies between norms.[25] It is a general rule of interpretation to assume that norms do not contradict other norms of international law.[26]

[16] ibid.

[17] ibid para 4. For a case study of norm-interaction in the context of disasters, see T Mulder, G Simm and S Williams, 'Regime Interaction and the Protection of Refugees during COVID-19' (2020) 3 *Yearbook of International Disaster Law* 92, 120.

[18] ILC (n 6) para 2.

[19] ibid.

[20] ibid paras 5–10.

[21] ibid para 32. See also *Vienna Convention on the Law of Treaties* (23 May 1969) art 53.

[22] ILC (n 6) para 34. See *Charter of the United Nations* (24 October 1945) art 103.

[23] J Pauwelyn, *Conflict of Norms in Public International Law: How WTO Law Relates to Other Rules of International Law* (Cambridge University Press, 2003) 167.

[24] ibid.

[25] ibid 240; ILC (n 9) para 37.

[26] The ICJ hinted at this interpretation in *Case Concerning Right of Passage over Indian Territory (Portugal v India)* (Preliminary Objections) [1957] ICJ Rep 125, 142. See also Pauwelyn (n 23) 240; ILC (n 9) paras 38–39.

Instead, it is common practice to resolve any apparent conflict through a harmonious interpretation of the norms in question.[27] In other words, norms should be interpreted so as to give rise to a single set of compatible obligations to the greatest extent possible,[28] which often requires a compromise whereby neither norm is applied in full. The narrow definition of conflict, combined with the presumption against incompatibility, implies that relationships of conflict are exceptional in international law.[29]

Norm interaction in international law can occur at different levels. In some cases, it involves the interplay between concrete and specific rules; in others, it concerns broader and more abstract principles. Determining the precise relationship between two or more abstract principles that are both valid and applicable in a given context may nonetheless be important for the interpretation and application of international law. The ICJ addressed such a situation in the *Jurisdictional Immunities* case, where it examined the interaction between the principles of territorial sovereignty and sovereign equality in the context of state immunity.[30] These principles stand in normative tension: territorial sovereignty suggests that a state may exercise jurisdiction over all activities within its territory, including those of foreign states, while sovereign equality implies that no state should be subject to the jurisdiction of another. As the ICJ observed: 'Exceptions to the immunity of the State represent a departure from the principle of sovereign equality. Immunity may represent a departure from the principle of territorial sovereignty and the jurisdiction which flows from it.'[31] However, rather than allowing one principle to override the other, the ICJ sought to interpret and apply both principles in a harmonious manner to the greatest extent possible so as to give rise to a single set of compatible rules on state immunity. This approach underscores the importance of reconciling abstract principles where possible, rather than treating them as inherently conflicting.

Against this background, it is clear that, according to the rules on norm interaction, it is necessary to determine the relationship between solidarity and other foundational principles of IDRL before applying it. The sovereignty of states is a – if not *the* – fundamental principle of international law. In its essence, the principle of sovereignty protects the freedom of states to determine their own destiny without external interference.[32] The principle is reflected in several corollary principles that safeguard the autonomy of states and their authority over matters within their jurisdiction, such as the principle of sovereign equality

[27] ILC (n 9) para 42.

[28] ILC (n 6) para 4. See also Pauwelyn (n 23) 240–41.

[29] Pauwelyn (n 23) 172.

[30] *Jurisdictional Immunities of the State (Germany v Italy; Greece Intervening)* (Judgment) [2012] ICJ Rep 99

[31] ibid para 57. See also *Certain Activities Carried Out by Nicaragua in the Border Area (Costa Rica v Nicaragua) and Construction of a Road in Costa Rica along the San Juan River (Nicaragua v Costa Rica)* (Judgment) [2015] ICJ Rep 665, Separate Opinion of Judge Donoghue, paras 3–6.

[32] S Besson, 'Sovereignty' in *Max Planck Encyclopedia of International Law* (Oxford University Press, 2011).

(ie, all states are equal),[33] the principle of territorial sovereignty (ie, a state has the exclusive right to exercise supreme authority within its jurisdiction)[34] and the principle of non-intervention (ie, no state shall interfere in the internal affairs of another).[35] The principle of sovereignty generates both rights and obligations for states.[36] For example, contemporary legal scholarship has linked sovereignty to the responsibility of states to protect their populations and uphold human rights within their jurisdictions, although the scope of this responsibility remains contested.[37]

As discussed in Chapter 1, section II.C.i, the principle of sovereignty is fundamental to IDRL. Both binding and non-binding instruments consistently affirm that the sovereignty of states must be respected in disaster response.[38] For example, UN General Assembly Resolution 46/182 emphasises that '[t]he sovereignty, territorial integrity and national unity of States must be fully respected in accordance with the Charter of the United Nations'.[39] The Draft Articles similarly acknowledge sovereignty in their preamble, '*stressing* the principle of the sovereignty of States and, consequently, reaffirming the primary role of the State affected by a disaster in providing disaster relief assistance'.[40] The ILC explained that sovereignty is a principle 'against which the entire set of Draft Articles is to be understood'.[41] States (and non-state actors) have endorsed this position.[42]

[33] UN Charter (n 22) art 2(1); UN General Assembly Res 2625 (XXV) (24 October 1970) UN Doc A/RES/2625 (XXV) para 1.

[34] *Island of Palmas (Netherlands v United States)* (1928) II RIAA 829, 838; *Corfu Channel Case (United Kingdom of Great Britain and Northern Ireland v Albania)* (Merits) [1949] ICJ Rep 4, 35.

[35] *UN Charter* (n 22) art 2(4); UN General Assembly Res 2625 (XXV) (n 33) para 1. See also *Military and Paramilitary Activities in and against Nicaragua (Nicaragua v United States of America)* (Judgment) [1986] ICJ Rep 14 para 202.

[36] *Corfu Channel Case* (n 34) Separate Opinion of Judge Alvarez, 43.

[37] ICISS, 'The Responsibility to Protect: Report of the International Commission on Intervention and State Sovereignty' (2001) 13; UN General Assembly Res 60/1 (16 September 2005) UN Doc A/RES/60/1, para 138. See also H Shue, 'Limiting Sovereignty' in JM Welsh (ed), *Humanitarian Intervention and International Relations* (Oxford University Press, 2004) 11; A Peters, 'Humanity as the A and Ω of Sovereignty' (2009) 20(3) *European Journal of International Law* 513.

[38] See, eg, Draft Articles (n 4) preamble, art 10; *Framework Convention on Civil Defence Assistance* (22 May 2000) art 3(a); *ASEAN Agreement on Disaster Management and Emergency Response* (26 July 2005) (AADMER) art 3(1); *Agreement between Member States and Associate Members of the Association of Caribbean States for Regional Cooperation on Natural Disasters* (16 April 1999) (ACS Agreement) art 4.

[39] UN General Assembly Res 46/182 (19 December 1991) UN Doc A/RES/46/182, para 3.

[40] Draft Articles (n 4) preamble (emphasis in original).

[41] ILC (n 5) 18.

[42] See comments of the delegations of Australia, the Czech Republic, Finland (on behalf of the Nordic countries), the EU, the OCHA, the World Food Programme and the IFRC in ILC, 'Comments and Observations Received from Governments and International Organizations' (14 March 2016) UN Doc A/CN.4/696; Finland in UN General Assembly Sixth Committee, 'Summary Record of the 20th Meeting' (10 November 2014) UN Doc A/C.6/69/SR.20, para 10; Cuba, Thailand, Venezuela and Sri Lanka in UN General Assembly Sixth Committee, 'Summary Record of the 21st Meeting' (22 December 2009) UN Doc A/C.6/64/SR.21, paras 8, 6, 42, 54; Estonia in UN General Assembly Sixth Committee, 'Summary Record of the 23rd Meeting' (1 December 2010) UN Doc A/C.6/65/SR.23, para 68; Indonesia in UN General Assembly Sixth Committee, 'Summary Record of the 24th Meeting' (1 December 2010) UN Doc A/C.6/65/SR.24, para 69; Mexico, Argentina and India in UN

For instance, the delegation of Germany in the UN General Assembly's Sixth Committee affirmed 'the general understanding of the sovereignty of States as the principle underlying the draft articles'.[43]

The principle of sovereignty is also reflected in the primary role of the affected state in disaster response, which is well established in IDRL.[44] This primary role means that the affected state has the exclusive authority to oversee and regulate all aspects of the response, including the initiation, coordination, direction, implementation and supervision of relief activities.[45] It also encompasses the prerogative of the affected state to give or withhold consent to the provision of international disaster assistance.[46] At the same time, the primary role entails responsibilities, including the affected state's duty to protect persons in disasters occurring on its territory or within areas under its jurisdiction or control.[47] According to the ILC, the primary role of the affected state is grounded in the 'core' and 'overarching' principle of sovereignty.[48]

At first sight, the principles of sovereignty and solidarity could appear antithetical in the context of IDRL because they rest on fundamentally different premises about the nature of responsibility and international cooperation. Sovereignty emphasises the primacy of the affected state's authority, framing

---

General Assembly Sixth Committee, 'Summary Record of the 25th Meeting' (1 December 2010) UN Doc A/C.6/65/SR.25, paras 6, 25, 36; Slovenia, Slovakia and South Africa in UN General Assembly Sixth Committee, 'Summary Record of the 20th Meeting', paras 40, 73, 102; Italy in UN General Assembly Sixth Committee, 'Summary Record of the 20th Meeting' (11 November 2016) UN Doc A/C.6/71/SR.20, para 88; Peru, Romania, Portugal, Spain, the Philippines and Sudan in UN General Assembly Sixth Committee, 'Summary Record of the 21st Meeting' (16 November 2016) UN Doc A/C.6/71/SR.21, paras 36, 62, 91, 105,122, 136; Colombia and Japan in UN General Assembly Sixth Committee, 'Summary Record of the 22nd Meeting' (22 November 2016) UN Doc A/C.6/71/SR.22, paras 48, 60.

[43] UN General Assembly Sixth Committee, 'Summary Record of the 21st Meeting' (n 42) para 115.

[44] The sovereignty-based primary role of the affected state is examined further in ch 5, section II.

[45] Draft Articles (n 4) art 10(2); UN General Assembly Res 46/182 (n 39) para 4; IFRC, 'Guidelines for the Domestic Facilitation and Regulation of International Disaster Relief and Initial Recovery Assistance' (2007) art 3(3) (hereinafter 'IDRL Guidelines'); *Tampere Convention on the Provision of Telecommunication Resources for Disaster Mitigation and Relief Operations* (18 June 1998) art 4(8); AADMER (n 38) art 3(2); *Inter-American Convention to Facilitate Disaster Assistance* (6 July 1991) art IV(a); *Agreement among the Governments of the Participating States of the Black Sea Economic Cooperation (BSEC) on Collaboration in Emergency Assistance and Emergency Response to Natural and Manmade Disasters* (15 April 1998) (BSEC Agreement) art 8(1); *Agreement between Governments of Member States of Shanghai Cooperation Organization on Cooperation in Delivery of Assistance for Emergency Liquidation* (26 October 2005) (Shanghai Agreement) art 6(1); *Agreement Establishing the Caribbean Disaster Emergency Management Agency* (4 July 2008) (CDEMA Agreement) art XXII(1); *Decision No 1313/2013/EU of the European Parliament and of the Council of 17 December 2013 on a Union Civil Protection Mechanism* (20 December 2013) (EU Civil Protection Mechanism) art 15(5).

[46] Draft Articles (n 4) art 13(1); IDRL Guidelines (n 45) art 10(1); UN General Assembly Res 46/182 (n 39) para 4.

[47] Draft Articles (n 4) art 10(1); IDRL Guidelines (n 45) art 3(1); UN General Assembly Res 46/182 (n 39) para 4; *Convention on Assistance in the Case of a Nuclear Accident or Radiological Emergency* (26 September 1986) art 3(a); AADMER (n 38) art 3(1); Inter-American Convention (n 45) art IV(a).

[48] ILC (n 5) 51, 64.

disaster response as a domestic matter over which the state retains exclusive control. This perspective prioritises non-interference and the right of the state to seek, accept or reject external assistance on its own accord and to regulate disaster response operations within its jurisdiction. In contrast, solidarity reimagines disaster response as a shared responsibility, where the protection of affected persons becomes a common objective of the international community.[49] These divergent starting points can lead to conflicting interpretations of IDRL: sovereignty may justify restrictive or conditional engagement with international actors, whereas solidarity may advocate for more open and cooperative approaches to disaster response.

The tension between sovereignty and solidarity in IDRL becomes particularly evident in two key areas: discretion in disaster response and international cooperation. First, sovereignty upholds the affected state's right to determine the nature and scope of its disaster response, including whether and how to engage with other states or non-state actors offering assistance. This discretion can result in delayed or restricted access for humanitarian aid, particularly where the state prioritises political or strategic considerations over external support.[50] Contrastingly, solidarity calls for more proactive and unconditional support, potentially clashing with a state's desire to retain control over the response. Second, sovereignty implies that cooperation is voluntary and rests entirely at the discretion of each state, reinforcing its autonomy. However, solidarity conveys a normative expectation that states should cooperate and assist one another, not merely as a matter of choice but as an obligation grounded in a shared responsibility for disaster response.[51] These examples illustrate how the two principles can give rise to seemingly incompatible interpretations of IDRL that appear to lead to irreconcilable outcomes.

However, as the ICJ's approach in the *Jurisdictional Immunities* case illustrates, such normative tensions need not result in zero-sum outcomes. Instead, they invite careful interpretation aimed at harmonising principles to the greatest extent possible so that they can be applied concurrently. This approach is equally relevant to the relationship between solidarity and sovereignty, which do not need to be mutually exclusive. In fact, their coexistence is supported by international instruments, such as the 2005 Hyogo Framework for Action, which preceded the Sendai Framework for Disaster Risk Reduction:

> Taking into account the importance of international cooperation and partnerships, each State has the primary responsibility for its own sustainable development and for taking effective measures to reduce disaster risk, including for the protection of people on its territory, infrastructure and other national assets from the impact of disasters. At the same time, in the context of increasing global interdependence,

[49] This argument is made in ch 2, section IV.
[50] See examples in ch 5, section III.C.
[51] On the normative nature of solidarity, see ch 2, section II.

> concerted international cooperation and an enabling international environment are required to stimulate and contribute to developing the knowledge, capacities and motivation needed for disaster risk reduction at all levels.[52]

Rather than allowing one principle to override the other, the principles of solidarity and sovereignty can be interpreted in a harmonious manner in which they are compatible, although through a compromise whereby neither principle is applied in full.

In this interpretation, solidarity does not diminish the sovereignty or primary role of the affected state; rather, it builds upon it. Solidarity presupposes that each state bears the principal responsibility for responding to disasters within its jurisdiction. As explained in Chapter 2, section III, solidarity operates through a dual structure of responsibility: each state holds individual obligations to pursue shared goals according to its respective capacities, while the international community collectively bears a responsibility to support states – particularly those with limited capacity – in fulfilling these obligations.[53] However, this does not mean that the responsibility for protecting persons affected by disasters transfers to the international community, even when a state's national response capacity is overwhelmed.[54] Instead, other states assume an auxiliary role, providing support through cooperation and assistance to help the affected state meet its obligations.[55] In this way, sovereignty remains the foundation of disaster response, while solidarity complements it by fostering a cooperative framework that enables states to meet their responsibilities and achieve common objectives.

That said, it is undeniable that the principles of sovereignty and solidarity place pressure on one another and cannot be applied in their fullest form without generating conflict, particularly in situations where international cooperation is essential to protect persons affected by disasters. Tension becomes most acute when an affected state rejects international assistance that is vital to safeguarding lives, thereby obstructing the collective objective and undermining the interests of other states committed to that goal. As will be discussed further in section III.A below, a harmonious interpretation of these principles suggests that solidarity places limits on the circumstances in which a state may legitimately reject aid, without entirely overriding sovereignty.

[52] World Conference on Disaster Reduction, 'Hyogo Framework for Action 2005–2015: Building the Resilience of Nations and Communities to Disasters' (22 January 2005) UN Doc A/CONF.206/6. See also ILC, 'Fourth Report on the Protection of Persons in the Event of Disasters, by Mr. Eduardo Valencia-Ospina, Special Rapporteur' (11 May 2011) UN Doc A/CN.4/643, para 83.

[53] Williams (n 2) 500; RM Rizki, 'Promotion and Protection of All Human Rights, Civil, Political, Economic, Social and Cultural Rights, Including the Right to Development' (15 August 2008) UN Doc A/HRC/9/10, para 6; P Dann, 'Solidarity and the Law of Development Cooperation' in Wolfrum and Kojima (n 1) 55, 57.

[54] Williams (n 2) 498; KP Sommermann, 'Some Reflections on the Concept of Solidarity and its Transformation into a Legal Principle' (2014) 52(1) *Archiv des Völkerrechts* 10, 10.

[55] On the auxiliary role of third states and assisting actors, see ch 6, section II.

Furthermore, solidarity does not override the sovereignty of the affected state in the sense that other states may intervene in pursuit of a common goal. If a state refuses international assistance in circumstances where such aid is necessary to protect affected persons and that refusal constitutes a breach of international law, consequences may indeed follow.[56] However, solidarity does not provide a legal basis for intervention or for bypassing the affected state by delivering aid directly to affected populations without its consent.[57] Thus, while solidarity may constrain a state's discretion in rejecting aid, it does so within a legal framework that continues to uphold sovereignty as a core principle of IDRL.

In addition to challenging the sovereignty of the affected state, solidarity also places pressure on the sovereignty of third states by seeking to establish obligations to cooperate and provide assistance where necessary to protect persons affected by disasters. Traditionally, states have relied on voluntarism, maintaining that it lies within their discretion to decide whether, how and to what extent they engage in disaster cooperation.[58] However, solidarity challenges this discretionary approach by suggesting that in situations where an affected state's national response capacity is overwhelmed, other states bear a legal obligation to assist in order to achieve the common goal.[59] Assistance, viewed through this lens, is not merely a moral imperative or 'the right thing to do', but a legal duty grounded in the shared responsibility of all states for the protection of persons affected by disasters. This interpretation limits the autonomy of states to opt out of disaster cooperation. Yet, importantly, solidarity also recognises that these obligations are differentiated: states are not equally bound, but are expected to contribute in proportion to their capacities. Those with greater resources and capabilities may therefore be expected to do more than others.[60]

In conclusion, while solidarity challenges and constrains sovereignty, it does not diminish or override it. These principles, though founded on different premises, are not inherently incompatible. A harmonious interpretation of IDRL aims to respect and balance both principles to the greatest extent possible. This conclusion should alleviate concerns and anxieties over the idea that a solidarity-based approach might undermine state sovereignty. At the same time, solidarity does contest the status quo in IDRL, particularly the discretion states exercise in determining whether, how and to what extent they respond to disasters. This challenge is constructive: it pushes for a reimagining of international disaster response that places shared responsibility for protecting persons affected by disasters at its centre, implemented through differentiated cooperation and assistance. In this way, solidarity seeks to enrich IDRL by fostering a cooperative

[56] The accountability for breaches and enforcement of IDRL is discussed in ch 6, section III.D.

[57] See further discussion in ch 6, section III.A.

[58] The voluntary nature of international cooperation in disaster response is discussed in ch 1, section II.C.iv and ch 3, section IV

[59] The duty to assist is examined in ch 6, section III.C.

[60] Wolfrum (n 1) 396.

framework that enables states to fulfil their responsibilities and achieve common objectives without displacing the foundational role of sovereignty.

III. IMPLICATIONS OF INCORPORATING SOLIDARITY

Having examined the relationship between solidarity and sovereignty and how they can be interpreted harmoniously, this section now considers how interpreting and developing IDRL through the lens of solidarity – while maintaining respect for state sovereignty – reshapes the regime. Implementing solidarity would represent a significant shift, reorienting IDRL from a sovereignty-centred framework characterised by state autonomy and voluntarism to one grounded in the protection of persons affected by disasters as a shared responsibility of all states.[61] This reorientation challenges the ad hoc nature of current disaster responses and the broad discretion states currently enjoy in determining whether and how to cooperate. Solidarity introduces a more cooperative framework that emphasises differentiated cooperation and assistance based on states' respective capacities. It does not seek to override sovereignty, but rather to recalibrate it in light of a common objective of protecting persons affected by disasters.

The following subsections identify five key implications of this shift, illustrating how solidarity can reshape IDRL into a regime that better reflects the imperative to protect vulnerable populations in times of emergency and the need for international cooperation and assistance.

A. Constraints on State Discretion

As argued, a solidarity-based interpretation of IDRL fundamentally redefines disaster response from an internal matter managed by the affected state to a shared responsibility of the international community. This shift does not diminish the primary role of the affected state, but does place constraints on its discretion. Viewed through the lens of solidarity, the affected state must take into account not only its own interests when determining how to respond to disasters, but also the collective interest of all states in protecting persons affected by disasters.[62] This reconceptualisation means that decisions about whether to seek or accept international assistance are no longer purely domestic prerogatives;

[61] As observed by Wolfrum, '[t]he introduction of the principle of solidarity as a structural principle of international law reorients international law from a set of rules to preserve the present state of existing international relations into a regime to fulfil a certain mission, namely the promotion of international social justice among States': ibid 87.

[62] 'Solidarity means the obligation of an individual State to take into consideration in its policy the interests of other States or their subjects or the common interests of the world community': R Wolfrum, 'International Law of Cooperation' in *Max Planck Encyclopedia of International Law* (Oxford University Press, 2010) para 3.

they must also be assessed in light of the broader objective shared by all states to protect disaster-affected persons. In doing so, solidarity introduces a normative expectation that the affected state will act in a manner consistent with this common goal, thereby narrowing the scope of its discretion in disaster response.

It should be noted that although the affected state has the primary role in responding to disasters within its jurisdiction, its discretion in determining when, how and to what extent to act is already constrained by international law – most notably by its obligations to protect persons affected by disasters.[63] These obligations require states to take appropriate measures to respond to disasters and to provide humanitarian assistance where necessary to meet people's needs and uphold their rights and dignity. Accordingly, affected states cannot invoke sovereignty to justify inaction or inadequate action that would undermine the protection of those at risk.

Solidarity introduces an additional layer of constraint by recognising that the protection of persons affected by disasters is a shared interest of all states. By committing to the common objective of protecting those affected, states should refrain from actions – or inaction – that would undermine this goal, as doing so would compromise the collective aims on which solidarity is founded. In determining its disaster response, the affected state must therefore take into account not only its own national interests but also the shared interest of all states in achieving the overarching objective of protecting persons at risk.[64] Where these interests conflict, the state cannot simply prioritise its own national interests; rather, it must balance them against the collective interest of all states. This reflects the spirit of solidarity, recognising that the state does not act alone, but is part of a community bound by common objectives. As Wolfrum notes, solidarity may, in these situations, mean that 'a State has to sacrifice, or at least to limit, its individual interests for the overarching interest of the international community'.[65]

This interpretation carries implications for the affected state's decisions about whether to seek or accept international assistance. When a state is unable or unwilling to ensure protection that adequately meets the needs of disaster-affected populations and upholds their rights, solidarity suggests that it has a duty to seek support from other states or assisting actors. In such circumstances, the affected state cannot, without compelling justification, invoke sovereignty as a reason to refuse assistance, as doing so would impede the common objective, harm the shared interests of all states in this objective and thus undermine solidarity. Instead, solidarity requires the affected state to cooperate and actively seek assistance if doing so is necessary to meet its obligations. As will be further discussed in Chapter 5, section III.B, there is precedent for a duty to seek

[63] Draft Articles (n 4) art 10(1). See also ILC (n 5) 51.

[64] Wolfrum (n 62) para 3; RStJ MacDonald, 'Solidarity in the Practice and Discourse of Public International Law' (1996) 8 *Pace International Law Review* 259, 259–260.

[65] Wolfrum (n 1) 90.

assistance in IDRL.[66] By seeking international assistance, the affected state not only fulfils its own responsibilities but also contributes to the collective goals of the international community, helping to ensure that protection of affected populations is neither delayed nor denied due to the limitations or choices of a single state.

Reconceptualising the protection of persons affected by disasters as a shared responsibility of all states also limits the discretion of affected states to refuse international assistance when it is offered. While the requirement of consent to foreign aid remains a fundamental principle of IDRL – reflecting respect for state sovereignty – this discretion is not absolute.[67] Chapter 5, section III.C explains that international law may already constrain a state's ability to withhold consent where doing so would be arbitrary.[68] Interpreting these limits through the lens of solidarity reinforces and clarifies their normative foundation: the affected state must not withhold consent when international assistance is essential to the effective protection of those in need. Refusing such assistance would not only breach the state's duty to protect its population but would also undermine the collective objective and shared interest of all states in the protection of disaster-affected people. Solidarity therefore requires that the affected state exercise its consent consistently with this common purpose, rather than solely as an assertion of unilateral control over all matters falling with their jurisdiction.

A solidarity-based interpretation thus requires that the affected state take into account the shared interest of all states in disaster response alongside its own national interests. However, this shared interest does not automatically override national interests. To suggest otherwise would hollow out the very notion of sovereignty, reducing the affected state's discretion to act only within the confines of what serves the collective interest, rather than allowing it genuine freedom to determine its response. Such an approach would also be inconsistent with the widespread support for sovereignty as a foundational principle of IDRL.[69] Instead, it is argued here that when national interests and the shared interests of all states come into conflict, the affected state must engage in a careful balancing act. It may still pursue its national interests, provided that doing so does not disproportionately undermine the collective objective of protecting affected populations. Chapter 5, section III.C develops this argument further in the context of the requirement of consent to international aid, suggesting that affected states may, in limited circumstances, withhold consent if they have compelling reasons and doing so is proportionate in light of the situation. Referring to real-world examples, such decisions might include measures to protect national security or public health, or to regulate the flow of incoming

[66] See, eg, Draft Articles (n 4) art 11; IDRL Guidelines (n 45) art 3(2).

[67] ILC (n 5) 59.

[68] Draft Articles (n 4) art 13(2).

[69] Such an interpretation would also go against the ILC's comment that solidarity 'cannot be interpreted as diminishing the sovereignty of affected States and their prerogatives within the limits of international law': ILC (n 5) 18.

aid to ensure that national authorities remain able to coordinate an effective response and prevent bottlenecks in distribution.

Furthermore, it should be reiterated that while solidarity places constraints on the discretion of the affected state, it does not provide a legal basis for intervention by other states or for bypassing the affected state by delivering aid directly to affected populations without its consent. As argued above, solidarity must operate within the framework of sovereignty and respect for territorial integrity. If a state refuses to seek or accept international assistance in circumstances where such aid is essential to protect affected persons and that refusal is not justified by acceptable reasons, consequences may indeed follow.[70] However, that refusal cannot lead to unilateral intervention or providing assistance without consent. That is, as noted above, because solidarity does not entail a transfer of responsibility for protecting disaster-affected persons to the international community; rather, it reinforces that the affected state remains primarily responsible, while other states, in turn, have a duty to support that role – not to supplant it – by providing cooperation and assistance in ways that respect the affected state's sovereignty.

B. Rights and Duties of Third States

A solidarity-based reconceptualisation of disaster response as a shared responsibility of all states has important implications not only for affected states but also for non-affected third states. If the protection of persons affected by disasters is understood as a common goal, then third states cannot remain passive or engage in cooperation solely on a voluntary basis. Solidarity implies that third states have a responsibility to support affected states when necessary, particularly where the latter lack the capacity to adequately protect their populations.[71] This represents a significant departure from the current framework of IDRL, in which cooperation and assistance are encouraged but not required, remaining largely discretionary and dependent on political will.[72] Instead, solidarity calls for a more principled approach, under which third states are expected to engage in international cooperation and assistance as part of their shared responsibility for the protection of persons affected by disasters. While this does not mean that all states must contribute equally (see section III.E), it does mean that cooperation and assistance can no longer be viewed as optional.

However, a solidarity-based interpretation of IDRL does not imply that third states are directly responsible for the protection of disaster-affected populations

[70] The consequences of breaching obligations under IDRL are explored in ch 6, section III.D.

[71] Williams (n 2) 498; Wolfrum (n 62) para 3; Koroma (n 1) 103; MacDonald (n 64) 259–260; Sommermann (n 54) 10; H Neuhold, 'Common Security: The Litmus Test of International Solidarity' in Wolfrum and Kojima (n 1) 193, 193–94.

[72] The voluntary nature of international cooperation in disaster response has been established in ch 1, section II.C.iv and ch 3, section IV.

beyond their jurisdiction.[73] Such an interpretation would suggest the existence of extraterritorial obligations that lack a clear foundation in international law and risk undermining the sovereignty of the affected state. Instead, solidarity conceives the role of third states as an auxiliary one: they share a responsibility to assist the affected state in fulfilling its primary duty to protect persons within its jurisdiction when needed.[74] This approach ensures that international cooperation is directed towards enabling the affected state to meet its responsibilities, rather than displacing them.

This interpretation of solidarity distinguishes it from other concepts that assign protection responsibilities to the international community as a whole, such as the doctrine of the Responsibility to Protect (R2P).[75] R2P provides that when a state is unable or unwilling to protect its population from serious harm, that responsibility shifts to the international community, potentially justifying intervention.[76] Solidarity, by contrast, does not envisage such a transfer of responsibility. However, what solidarity adds is a complementary layer of shared responsibility: other states are expected to support the affected state in fulfilling its obligations, particularly when its capacity is overwhelmed. In this sense, solidarity reconceptualises disaster response as a collective endeavour, but one that continues to respect and preserve the primary role of the affected state.

Viewed through the lens of solidarity, the recalibration of the role of third states carries significant implications for IDRL. To give meaningful effect to their shared responsibility, IDRL must establish clearer rights *and* duties for third states. For example, third states should have a recognised right to offer assistance to affected states. As will be discussed in Chapter 6, section III.B, this right is not yet firmly embedded as positive law in IDRL, but it should be relatively uncontroversial if it is understood as affirming the ability to extend an offer of help; it is an expression of third states' willingness to cooperate in the pursuit of the common objective. However, such a right does not mean that affected states must accept every offer, although – as discussed in the previous section – their discretion to refuse assistance is not without limits. Moreover, solidarity implies that third states also bear a legal duty to assist, particularly when an affected state lacks the capacity to protect disaster-affected populations (see Chapter 6, section III.C). This would represent a major shift in IDRL, which currently enables assistance primarily where states voluntarily agree to provide it, but does not obligate them to do so.[77] Solidarity demands more: it calls for binding commitments to cooperation and assistance in pursuit of the common objective of protecting persons affected by disasters. Yet, importantly, this duty would not apply uniformly to all states, but would be differentiated according to their relative capacities (see section III.E).

[73] The responsibilities of third states is further discussed in ch 6, section III.A.

[74] On the auxiliary role of third states and assisting actors, see ch 6, section II.

[75] The doctrine of R2P in the context of disasters is examined in ch 6, section III.A.

[76] ICISS (n 37) XI–XII. See also F Deng, 'From "Sovereignty as Responsibility" to the "Responsibility to Protect"' (2010) 2(4) *Global Responsibility to Protect* 353, 354–55.

[77] See the analysis in ch 3, section IV.

Recognising the rights and duties of third states under a solidarity-based interpretation of IDRL also raises important questions regarding the role of assisting actors, such as UN agencies, the IFRC and national Red Cross and Red Crescent societies. These actors play a crucial role in the delivery of aid on the ground and are often among the first to respond in disaster situations. Viewed through the lens of solidarity, there is a strong argument that these actors form part of the broader international community committed to the common objective of protecting persons affected by disasters. On that basis, it could be argued that they should possess a right to offer assistance. Indeed, some precedent exists for such a right under IHL and in certain non-binding instruments of IDRL.[78] However, extending a complementary duty to assist to non-state actors is more complex and contentious. It raises doctrinal questions concerning the legal personality and subjecthood of non-state actors in international law,[79] as well as practical concerns about how such obligations could be defined, implemented and enforced. For the time being, a duty to assist for non-state actors may remain primarily a moral obligation, reflecting their essential role in disaster response without imposing formal legal responsibilities.

Furthermore, reconceptualising the protection of persons affected by disasters as a shared interest of all states also has important implications for the legal character of the obligations involved. Specifically, it suggests that the obligations of the affected state in disaster response – particularly those relating to the protection of persons – should be understood as obligations *erga omnes*, owed to the international community as a whole.[80] Unlike bilateral obligations, which are owed by one state to another, obligations *erga omnes* are owed towards 'the international community as a whole'.[81] As such, these obligations are 'the concern of all States' and 'all States can be held to have a legal interest in their protection'.[82] This is significant in the context of IDRL because it implies that any state may take action under the law of state responsibility in response to a breach of such obligations (see Chapter 6, section III.D).[83]

[78] These precedents are detailed in ch 6, section III.B.

[79] International organisations may possess international legal personality, capable of holding rights and duties under international law, to the extent necessary to fulfil the functions assigned to them under their constituent instruments. However, the legal personality of NGOs is far more complex. Traditionally, NGOs lack international legal personality, but there is a trend towards assigning specific legal status in certain circumstances. See C Walter, 'Subjects of International Law' in *Max Planck Encyclopedia of International Law* (Oxford University Press, 2007) paras 5–6.

[80] See also F Romanin Jacur, 'Solidarity and Differentiation: Moral and Legal Obligations of States in Addressing Global Challenges: The Case of Climate Change' in den Heijer and van der Wilt (eds) (n 2) 75, 89.

[81] *Barcelona Traction, Light and Power Company, Limited (Belgium v Spain)* (Judgment) [1970] ICJ Rep 3, para 33. See also JA Frowein, 'Obligations Erga Omnes' in *Max Planck Encyclopedia of International Law* (Oxford University Press, 2008).

[82] *Barcelona Traction Case* (n 81) para 33.

[83] ILC, 'Articles on Responsibility of States for Internationally Wrongful Acts' (31 May 2001) UN Doc A/56/10, arts 42, 48(1). See also Institut de Droit International, 'Obligations and Rights Erga Omnes in International Law' (2005) art 2.

C. Centring the Rights of Persons in Disasters

The third major implication of interpreting IDRL through the lens of solidarity is that it calls for the centring of the rights of persons affected by disasters. International law in this field has traditionally been state-centric, focusing on the relationships between states while largely neglecting the vertical dimension of disaster response – that is, the relationship between states and individuals.[84] Although scholars have long advocated for a rights-based approach to disaster response, the rights of disaster-affected persons remain underdeveloped and insufficiently theorised.[85] The Draft Articles affirm, in relatively uncontroversial terms, that '[p]ersons affected by disasters are entitled to the respect for and protection of their human rights in accordance with international law'.[86]

Although solidarity, as conceptualised in this book, primarily emphasises cooperation between states in pursuit of common objectives, this state-centric orientation must not obscure the central importance of the rights of affected individuals. A solidarity-based approach that focuses solely on inter-state cooperation risks reducing individuals to passive objects of assistance rather than recognising them as rights-holders entitled to protection. If IDRL is interpreted through the lens of solidarity, then the protection of persons affected by disasters becomes its chief objective. This should place the respect of individual rights at the very core of the regime alongside the rights and obligations of states. As Tladi has argued similarly in relation to the Draft Articles, 'if the overriding consideration is the protection of persons, then rather than create rights for third States, the emphasis ought to have been placed more on strengthening the rights of affected persons rather than creating rights for third States'.[87] This imperative is reinforced by the intrinsic connection between the rights of affected people and the obligations of states in disaster response. For instance, the duty to seek assistance when necessary and the limits on a state's right to withhold consent to international aid are both shaped by the obligations to respect and uphold the human rights of those affected. Solidarity should therefore not only guide how states cooperate with one another, but also reinforce the legal entitlements of individuals whose protection is the very purpose of that cooperation.

The need to protect human rights and dignity places particular emphasis on whether persons affected by disasters have a right to receive humanitarian assistance. As will be discussed further in Chapter 5, section III.A, international

[84] On the horizontal and vertical dimensions of IDRL, see ch 1, section II.A.

[85] See, eg, W Kälin, 'Protection of Victims of Disasters: The "Vertical" Dimension of the Draft Articles on the Protection of Persons in the Event of Disasters' (2019) 1(1) *Yearbook of International Disaster Law* 28; D Cubie, *The International Legal Protection of Persons in Humanitarian Crises: Exploring the Acquis Humanitaire* (Hart Publishing, 2017) 109.

[86] Draft Articles (n 4) art 5.

[87] D Tladi, 'The International Law Commission's Draft Articles on the Protection of Persons in the Event of Disasters: Codification, Progressive Development or Creation of Law from Thin Air?' (2017) 16(3) *Chinese Journal of International Law* 425, 450.

law has not yet recognised a standalone right to humanitarian assistance. Nonetheless, such a right is arguably implied in the realisation of other well-established rights that are typically disrupted during disasters, such as the rights to life, food, water, health and housing.[88] Humanitarian assistance is often indispensable to the fulfilment of these rights in disaster contexts. The affected state is the primary duty-bearer, responsible for ensuring the provision of adequate humanitarian assistance to those affected. Where the affected state is unable to fulfil this obligation, it has a duty to seek international assistance.[89] While third states do not bear direct obligations to ensure the provision of humanitarian assistance to individuals outside their jurisdiction, they have a duty to cooperate in supporting the affected state to realise this right.[90] Interpreted through the lens of solidarity, this right thus becomes situated within a framework of shared responsibility, wherein states must cooperate to ensure its effective realisation.

If IDRL is to embrace a genuinely rights-based approach – one that centres on the protection of affected people and remains attentive to human rights – it must also be supported by institutional frameworks capable of ensuring effective oversight and accountability.[91] This includes sustained attention to the application of human rights in disaster settings within established IHRL monitoring mechanisms. As Hesselman observes, these mechanisms already 'engage rather extensively and in considerable detail with efforts of international (disaster) assistance, and their monitoring outputs include clear instructions on the types and levels of assistance needed and what needs to be provided by international actors'.[92] This represents an important development that must be continued and strengthened to ensure that the protection of persons remains front and centre in disaster response.

[88] R Hardcastle and A Chua, 'Victims of Natural Disasters: The Right to Receive Humanitarian Assistance' (1997) 1(4) *International Journal of Human Rights* 35, 39; MG Pietropaolo, 'A Human Rights-Based Approach to Humanitarian Assistance: Current and Prospective Scenarios' (2016) 7(2) *Journal of International Humanitarian Legal Studies* 257, 267; W Kälin, 'The Human Rights Dimension of Natural or Human-Made Disasters' (2012) 55 *German Yearbook of International Law* 119, 140; D Fisher, 'The Right to Humanitarian Assistance' (2010) 41 *Studies in Transnational Legal Policy* 47, 53; A Creta, 'A (Human) Right to Humanitarian Assistance in Disaster Situations? Surveying Public International Law' in A de Guttry, M Gestri and G Venturini (eds), *International Disaster Response Law* (TMC Asser Press, 2012) 353, 360; K Cedervall Lauta, 'Human Rights and Natural Disasters' in S Breau and K Samuel (eds), *Research Handbook on Disasters and International Law* (Edward Elgar, 2016) 91, 104; Cubie (n 85) 321; J Benton Heath, 'Disasters, Relief, and Neglect: The Duty to Accept Humanitarian Assistance and the Work of the International Law Commission' (2011) 43 *NYU Journal for International Law & Politics* 419, 438.

[89] The duty to seek assistance is discussed in ch 5, section III.B.

[90] The extraterritorial obligations of third states are examined in ch 6, section III.A.

[91] D Cubie and M Hesselman, 'Accountability for the Human Rights Implications of Natural Disasters: A Proposal for Systemic International Oversight' (2015) 33(1) *Netherlands Quarterly of Human Rights* 9.

[92] M Hesselman, 'A Right to International (Humanitarian) Assistance in Times of Disaster' in F Zorzi Giustiniani et al (eds), *Routledge Handbook of Human Rights and Disasters* (Routledge, 2018) 65, 78.

D. The Duty to Cooperate

The fourth implication is that solidarity gives rise to a binding duty to cooperate in disaster response. There is already broad support for a duty to cooperate in disaster response.[93] The Draft Articles codify this duty, stating: 'In the application of the present draft articles, States shall, as appropriate, cooperate among themselves, with the United Nations, with the components of the Red Cross and Red Crescent Movement, and with other assisting actors.'[94] States have long engaged in cooperation following disasters, showing a particular willingness to assist when another state's national response capacity has been overwhelmed. This practice reflects a shared understanding that disaster response often requires concerted efforts of the international community to ensure adequate protection for those affected. UN General Assembly Resolution 46/128 affirms, in this light, that: 'The magnitude and duration of many emergencies may be beyond the response capacity of many affected countries. International cooperation to address emergency situations and to strengthen the response capacity of affected countries is thus of great importance.'[95] Similarly, most IDRL treaties identify cooperation as a core objective.[96] States also widely endorsed the importance of international cooperation for protecting persons in disasters during debates in the UN General Assembly's Sixth Committee.[97]

[93] See ch 1, section II.C.iv on the duty to cooperate in IDRL.
[94] Draft Articles (n 4) art 7.
[95] UN General Assembly Res 46/182 (n 39) para 5.
[96] See, eg, Tampere Convention (n 45) preamble; Nuclear Accident Convention (n 47) preamble; Civil Defence Assistance Convention (n 38) preamble; AADMER (n 38) art 2; Inter-American Convention (n 45) preamble; BSEC Agreement (n 45) preamble; Shanghai Agreement (n 45) preamble; ACS Agreement (n 38) art 2; *Arab Cooperation Agreement on Regulating and Facilitating Relief Operations 1987* (3 September 1987) (Arab League Agreement) preamble. See also Draft Articles (n 4) preamble; UN General Assembly Res 75/124 (11 December 2020) UN Doc A/RES/75/124, preamble.
[97] See, eg, Finland (on behalf of the Nordic countries) and the IFRC in ILC, 'Comments and Observations Received from Governments and International Organizations' (n 42); China in UN General Assembly Sixth Committee, 'Summary Record of the 20th Meeting' (17 December 2009) UN Doc A/C.6/64/SR.20, para 24; Poland in UN General Assembly Sixth Committee, 'Summary Record of the 21st Meeting' (n 42) para 77; Romania in UN General Assembly Sixth Committee, 'Summary Record of the 22nd Meeting' (8 February 2009) UN Doc A/C.6/64/SR.22, para 25; New Zealand in UN General Assembly Sixth Committee, 'Summary Record of the 22nd Meeting' (1 December 2010) UN Doc A/C.6/65/SR.22, para 71; Monaco in UN General Assembly Sixth Committee, 'Summary Record of the 23rd Meeting' (n 42) para 88; Ireland in UN General Assembly Sixth Committee, 'Summary Record of the 19th Meeting' (17 November 2014) UN Doc A/C.6/69/SR.19, para 172; South Africa in UN General Assembly Sixth Committee, 'Summary Record of the 20th Meeting' (n 42) para 104; Hungary in UN General Assembly Sixth Committee, 'Summary Record of the 24th Meeting' (3 December 2014) UN Doc A/C.6/69/SR.24, para 39; Trinidad and Tobago in UN General Assembly Sixth Committee, 'Summary Record of the 26th Meeting' (20 November 2014) UN Doc A/C.6/69/SR.26, para 116; Turkey in UN General Assembly Sixth Committee, 'Summary Record of the 27th Meeting' (24 November 2014) UN Doc A/C.6/69/SR.27, para 30; Ecuador and the IFRC in UN General Assembly Sixth Committee, 'Summary Record of the 24th Meeting' (29 November 2016) UN Doc A/C.6/71/SR.24, paras 12, 27.

Cooperation lies at the very core of what solidarity entails. Indeed, solidarity can be understood as a specialised form of cooperation – one grounded in social cohesion and a shared commitment to common objectives through mutual support.[98] Cooperation is essential to fulfilling the shared responsibility to assist states that lack the capacity to meet their obligations in pursuit of common goals.[99] Without cooperation, solidarity cannot be meaningfully realised. In this sense, cooperation becomes the operational expression of solidarity: it is the 'core vehicle' through which a community advances its collective goals.[100] Accordingly, implementing solidarity in IDRL should necessarily entail a corresponding duty to cooperate among states and other relevant actors involved in disaster response.

However, solidarity changes the duty to cooperate in three key ways. First, it fundamentally challenges the prevailing voluntarist understanding of the duty to cooperate by asserting that cooperation should be treated as a legal obligation that is grounded in a shared responsibility for the protection of persons affected by disasters.[101] Despite broad support for the duty to cooperate, many states continue to interpret it as fundamentally voluntary, especially for non-affected third states. During discussions on the Draft Articles in the UN General Assembly's Sixth Committee, several states expressed general support for the duty to cooperate, but opposed the imposition of specific binding obligations to partake in cooperation.[102] The UK, for instance, rejected 'the recourse to "duties"' on the grounds that it would be 'at odds with existing State practice and with the essentially voluntary nature of the principle of cooperation'.[103] As discussed in Chapter 3, section IV.A, states generally do not frame cooperation in disaster response as a legal obligation under international law, but rather as a moral imperative that is the right thing to do.

Despite this resistance, if states are genuine about their commitment to solidarity, the duty to cooperate must ultimately give rise to specific binding obligations to engage in international cooperation. Without such obligations, solidarity risks becoming merely rhetorical and conditional on states' goodwill rather than a reliable promise of support grounded in mutual trust and reliance. In this sense, the duty to cooperate provides the foundation for an affected state's duty to seek and accept international assistance when its national response

[98] Wolfrum (n 62) para 3.

[99] 'In the specific context of disaster relief, the principle of cooperation is a *conditio sine qua non* to successful relief actions': ILC, 'Memorandum by the Secretariat on the Protection of Persons in the Event of Disasters' (11 December 2007) UN Doc A/CN.4/590, para 18.

[100] Rizki (n 53) para 6.

[101] Williams (n 2) 498; Wolfrum (n 62) para 3; Neuhold (n 71) 193–194; Koroma (n 1) 103; MacDonald (n 64) 259–260; Sommermann (n 54) 10.

[102] ILC, 'Eight Report on the Protection of Persons in the Event of Disasters, by Mr. Eduardo Valencia-Ospina, Special Rapporteur' (17 March 2016) UN Doc A/CN.4/697, para 146.

[103] UK in UN General Assembly Sixth Committee, 'Summary Record of the 19th Meeting' (4 December 2012) UN Doc A/C.6/67/SR.19 para 65.

capacity is overwhelmed,[104] and for a corresponding duty of third states to provide such assistance.[105] The latter represents a significant departure from past practice, where assistance has traditionally been voluntary. However, solidarity requires more than aspirational commitments: affected states must be able to rely on the support of others when necessary. Therefore, third states should bear a binding duty to assist. This does not mean that states are required to cooperate in all circumstances or at all times; rather, solidarity qualifies the duty to cooperate, applying only when the affected state is unable to ensure the protection of persons affected by disasters for which it holds primary responsibility.

Second, solidarity also reshapes the nature of cooperation itself, marking a departure from traditional transactional models towards a form of cooperation grounded in a shared commitment to common objectives through mutual support. International cooperation often hinges on mutual benefit: each participating state expects to gain something, even if those benefits are unevenly distributed.[106] Solidarity-based cooperation, by contrast, is not driven by self-interest, but by a shared commitment to advancing collective goals.[107] This means that states are not expected to reciprocate, repay or reimburse any received benefits – embedding an element of sacrifice into cooperation.[108] As a result, some states are expected to contribute more to the common interests, while only some may benefit from international cooperation and assistance.[109] Yet all states ultimately gain from the achievement of the common objective.[110] Solidarity thus calls for a different form of cooperation – one that transcends direct reciprocal benefits and embodies a shared responsibility for collective goals through mutual support.

This raises the question of why states would engage in solidarity-based cooperation in disaster response even when they do not benefit directly. As explained in Chapter 2, section III, there may be different motivations for states to act in solidarity with one another, but when it is framed as a responsibility rather than an act of charity, states are more likely to engage in solidarity-based cooperation.[111] In addition, the expectation that states may one day rely on others when their own capacities are overwhelmed can also play a factor. While such

[104] The topics are explored further in ch 5, sections III.B and III.C.

[105] The duty to assist is examined in ch 6, section III.C.

[106] L Boisson de Chazournes, 'Responsibility to Protect: Reflecting Solidarity?' in Wolfrum and Kojima (n 1) 93, 95–96.

[107] Koroma (n 1) 103.

[108] Neuhold (n 71) 193–94; D Campanelli, 'Principle of Solidarity' in *Max Planck Encyclopedia of International Law* (Oxford University Press, 2011) para 9; Boisson de Chazournes (n 106) 96. Several treaties also affirm this principle, stating that disaster assistance is generally offered without the expectation of repayment, 'unless agreed otherwise'. See, eg, Tampere Convention (n 45) art 7(5); Inter-American Convention (n 45) art XIV; Nuclear Accident Convention (n 47) art 7(1); Shanghai Agreement (n 45) art 11(1); BSEC Agreement (n 45) art 3(3).

[109] Wolfrum (n 1) 396.

[110] Boisson de Chazournes (n 106) 95.

[111] H Hestermeyer, 'Reality or Aspiration? Solidarity in International Environmental and World Trade Law' (Max Planck Institute, 2012) 18–19.

expectations may seem transactional, they do not amount to a quid pro quo: there is no guarantee of reciprocity, nor is future assistance treated as repayment for previously provided aid. Cooperation in this sense is not contingent on a state's previous contributions to disaster response, but is instead grounded in a principled commitment to mutual support and shared responsibility.

Third, solidarity challenges the ad hoc and reactive nature of cooperation in disaster response by reframing it as a proactive and continuous process that spans all stages of disaster management.[112] Rather than viewing cooperation as something that begins only after disaster strikes, solidarity pushes for an expanded understanding of cooperation as a long-term process. This approach calls for structured and systematic collaboration between states and assisting actors, emphasising protection as an ongoing commitment. It prioritises efforts to reduce vulnerabilities and build resilience alongside cooperation in the immediate aftermath of disasters, shifting focus towards minimising the need for humanitarian assistance when hazards occur.[113] Part of this cooperation should be a commitment to collaborate in building states' national response capacities, making them more resilient to disasters. Ultimately, this broader and more systematic understanding of cooperation enables solidarity to achieve its true purpose: addressing structural inequalities that leave some states better equipped than others, thereby advancing international social justice.

E. Differentiated Cooperation

Finally, solidarity implies that cooperation among states is not equal, but differentiated according to their respective capacities.[114] As discussed in Chapter 2, section III, a defining feature of solidarity is the equitable distribution of responsibilities in pursuing common goals, guided by the principle that those with greater capacity should bear a greater share of the burden. That chapter explained that solidarity presupposes a collective commitment among states to work together towards shared objectives and to assist one another in that pursuit.[115] At the same time, solidarity recognises that while all states are expected to contribute, some may require support while others are in a position to provide it.[116] This recognition stems from an acknowledgement of the structural inequalities that

[112] This reframing is further elaborated in ch 7, section II.

[113] States have made commitments to work on reducing risks under the Sendai Framework for Disaster Risk Reduction, which recognises that 'reduction of disaster risk is a common concern for all States and the extent to which developing countries are able to effectively enhance and implement national disaster risk reduction policies and measures in the context of their respective circumstances and capabilities can be further enhanced through the provision of sustainable international cooperation': World Conference on Disaster Risk Reduction, 'Sendai Framework for Disaster Risk Reduction 2015–2030' (18 March 2015) UN Doc A/CONF.224/L.2, para 19(a).

[114] Wolfrum (n 62) para 3; Boisson de Chazournes (n 106) 95; Campanelli (n 108) para 12.

[115] Neuhold (n 71) 193–94; Campanelli (n 108) para 9; Boisson de Chazournes (n 106) 96.

[116] Williams (n 2) 498–500.

shape the capacities of states to act.[117] In response to this reality, solidarity calls for differentiated contributions towards common goals, taking these inequalities into account. Consequently, Wolfrum explains that 'when trying to achieve a common goal, the contributions of some may exceed those of others' and, in some cases, 'solidarity-based actions may be designed to benefit some States or even only one'.[118] In this way, solidarity addresses inequality not by imposing equal obligations, but by ensuring that responsibilities are distributed fairly and equitably among states.

Differentiation of responsibilities operates on two levels in IDRL: between affected states and third states, and among third states. As previously discussed, solidarity implies a dual structure of responsibility, whereby each state bears an individual duty to contribute to common goals to the extent that it is capable of doing so.[119] Hence, the affected state is expected to respond to disasters within its own territory and should seek international assistance only when its national capacities are overwhelmed or insufficient to ensure the protection of affected persons. States with sufficient response capacities are thus expected to manage their own disasters. This interpretation qualifies the duty to cooperate, preserving the affected state's discretion to manage disaster response when it is both able and willing to provide adequate protection to those affected. It also calibrates expectations placed on third states, recognising that their (binding) duty to assist arises only in response to the affected state's needs. In this way, disaster response is not framed as a universal collective endeavour requiring joint action by all states in every instance, but as a differentiated system of responsibilities based on need and capacity.

However, this is not to suggest that states with sufficient response capacities should refrain from engaging in international cooperation and assistance. While such states may not be under a legal obligation to do so, they are nonetheless encouraged to cooperate with other states and assisting actors where such cooperation could enhance the effectiveness of disaster response. As the ILC has observed:

> Cooperation in the provision of assistance at all stages of disaster relief is central to facilitating an adequate and effective response to disasters and constitutes a practical manifestation of the principle of solidarity. Even if an affected State is capable and willing to provide the required assistance, cooperation and assistance by international actors will in many cases ensure a more adequate, rapid and extensive response to disasters and an enhanced protection of affected persons.[120]

Differentiation of responsibilities in IDRL also occurs among third states themselves. While all states share a responsibility to support affected states,

[117] Wolfrum (n 1) 396.
[118] ibid.
[119] This argument was developed in ch 2, section III.
[120] ILC (n 5) 56.

this responsibility is not uniform; rather, it is differentiated according to each state's capacity to assist. States with greater resources are expected to contribute more to international disaster response efforts than those with more limited capacities. This differentiation reflects an acknowledgement of the structural inequalities that prevent states from contributing equally and affirms that those with greater capacity should bear a correspondingly greater share of the burden in the pursuit of common goals.

By differentiating responsibility, solidarity reframes cooperation in international disaster response as fundamentally a matter of social justice. It acknowledges and seeks to address the structural inequalities that leave some states better equipped than others to protect their populations in the event of disaster. Rather than imposing uniform obligations, solidarity directs assistance towards those states that need it most, while expecting states with sufficient capacities to manage their own responses. At the same time, it places greater expectations on those with the resources and capability to contribute more substantially to international efforts, thereby easing the burden on states with limited capacities. In this way, solidarity operates as a mechanism of redistributive justice, striving for 'the amelioration, at least a gradual one, of inequalities among States'.[121] It thus reframes international cooperation in disaster response as both equitable and responsive to real-world disparities.

IV. CONCLUSION

This chapter set out to explore what IDRL would look like if interpreted and developed through the lens of solidarity. It has demonstrated that solidarity has the potential to become a transformative principle, reorienting IDRL from a sovereignty-centred regime characterised by state autonomy and voluntarism to one that prioritises the protection of disaster-affected persons through differentiated international cooperation and assistance. While solidarity does not seek to radically reform IDRL, it recasts its central principles in a different light: disaster response is no longer viewed as a purely domestic matter of the affected state, but as a shared responsibility of all states. This reconceptualisation, while upholding the core tenets of international disaster response, nonetheless changes IDRL by reinterpreting the rights of affected states, the duties of third states and the scope and nature of international cooperation. This analysis is also relevant beyond IDRL as the implications discussed in this chapter could also apply to other regimes where solidarity plays or could play a key role, such as international climate change law and global health law, provided that solidarity should be interpreted within the specific context of each regime.

[121] Wolfrum (n 1) 87.

Examining the implications of using solidarity as an interpretative lens and model for future development was undertaken within the broader context of norm interaction. Because solidarity does not exist in isolation, it was necessary to assess its relationship with other foundational principles of IDRL, particularly the principle of sovereignty. Despite points of normative tension, these principles are not antithetical and can be applied concurrently through a harmonious interpretation that recognises the protection of persons in disasters as a shared responsibility of all states. In this interpretation, the affected state retains the primary role in disaster response, while other states assume an auxiliary role in supporting the affected state when necessary. Solidarity does not diminish or override sovereignty in this interpretation, but it recalibrates its application: sovereignty remains the foundation of disaster response, but is exercised in harmony with solidarity, ensuring that national interests do not undermine the shared responsibility for the protection of affected persons.

Building on this interpretation, the chapter has identified five significant implications of implementing solidarity as a principle of IDRL. First, solidarity constrains the affected state's discretion by requiring decisions to reflect the common interest of all states in protecting persons in disasters rather than solely national priorities. Second, solidarity calls for clearer rights and duties of third states, moving beyond voluntarism to give substance to their shared responsibility to assist. Third, solidarity centres the rights of persons affected by disasters – and corresponding state obligations to ensure those rights are realised – as the ultimate objective. Fourth, it gives rise to a binding duty to cooperate in disaster response, shifting cooperation from an ad hoc and reactive practice to a proactive and sustained process grounded in shared responsibility. Fifth, solidarity introduces differentiation: states' obligations to contribute are calibrated according to their capacities, placing greater responsibilities on those with more resources.

Taken together, these implications challenge the status quo in IDRL by embedding solidarity as a normative principle that complements – rather than supplants – sovereignty, fostering a more equitable and rights-centred framework for international disaster response. This analysis lays the foundation for the following chapters, which move from examining the transformative potential of solidarity on a high level to how it can shape three key dimensions of IDRL in more detail.

5

The Role of the Affected State

I. INTRODUCTION

BUILDING ON THE PREVIOUS chapter's exploration of the high-level implications of implementing solidarity as a principle in IDRL, the next three chapters examine in greater detail how this principle could reshape core dimensions of this regime. They focus specifically on the role of the affected state (Chapter 5), the role of third states and assisting actors (Chapter 6) and the scope of international cooperation (Chapter 7), considering how these might be reimagined through the lens of solidarity. These chapters move beyond exploring the transformative potential of solidarity on a high level and engage with specific contested or unsettled issues within these dimensions, asking how they should be interpreted in light of solidarity.

This shift from general theorisation to a more granular analysis of solidarity's implementation is important for several reasons. First, while high-level observations about how solidarity might reorient IDRL are valuable in terms of understanding its transformative potential, they risk remaining abstract and aspirational unless they are grounded in concrete legal norms and practices. Without such detail, the practical implementation of solidarity may be undermined. Scrutinising how solidarity can be operationalised provides clearer guidance on translating it into concrete norms and practices. This is particularly relevant for practitioners and policy makers, including those involved in negotiating the treaty on the protection of persons in disasters. Moreover, as discussed in Chapter 3, section III, the recognition of solidarity as a general principle of IDRL may be inferred from norms that reflect it as a normative underpinning. Analysing what such norms would look like could therefore contribute to the future identification of solidarity as a general principle. Finally, a detailed analysis allows for a more refined and nuanced understanding of how solidarity would reimagine IDRL, including its interaction with other foundational principles such as sovereignty and the challenges that may arise in its implementation. This level of scrutiny is essential for moving from theory to practice in a meaningful and credible way.

The present chapter examines how solidarity reimagines the role of the affected state in IDRL. It begins by reviewing how IDRL currently conceives this role before considering how it should be reconceptualised through the lens of solidarity (section II). Building on the arguments developed in Chapter 4, it argues that solidarity affirms the primacy of the affected state while also placing limits on its discretion and imposing a duty to cooperate when it is unable or unwilling to ensure adequate protection for those affected. The chapter then addresses three issues central to the role of the affected state: the right to receive humanitarian assistance, the duty to seek international assistance and the principle of consent. Rather than merely describing how solidarity is currently reflected in these topics, it adopts a normative approach, exploring how these issues should be interpreted and developed through the lens of solidarity. While the analysis demonstrates the transformative potential of solidarity, it also recognises that significant obstacles to its full implementation remain, including the absence of accountability and enforcement mechanisms to ensure that states fulfil their solidarity-based obligations. These limitations are not overlooked; the chapter engages with them directly and considers realistic strategies for addressing them.

II. SOLIDARITY AND THE PRIMARY ROLE OF THE AFFECTED STATE

It is well established that the affected state holds the primary role in responding to disasters within its jurisdiction.[1] This primary role encompasses both the responsibility to protect persons affected by disasters[2] and the exclusive authority to direct, control, coordinate and supervise all disaster response efforts on its territory.[3] Rooted in the principle of sovereignty,[4] this primary role positions disaster response as a matter falling squarely within the domestic domain of

[1] ILC, 'Draft Articles on the Protection of Persons in the Event of Disasters' (27 May 2016) UN Doc A/CN.4/L.871, art 10(2); UN General Assembly Res 46/182 (19 December 1991) UN Doc A/RES/46/182, para 4; IFRC, 'Guidelines for the Domestic Facilitation and Regulation of International Disaster Relief and Initial Recovery Assistance' (2007) art 3(3); *Tampere Convention on the Provision of Telecommunication Resources for Disaster Mitigation and Relief Operations* (18 June 1998) art 4(8); *ASEAN Agreement on Disaster Management and Emergency Response* (26 July 2005) (AADMER) art 3(2); *Inter-American Convention to Facilitate Disaster Assistance* (6 July 1991) art IV(a); *Agreement among the Governments of the Participating States of the Black Sea Economic Cooperation (BSEC) on Collaboration in Emergency Assistance and Emergency Response to Natural and Manmade Disasters* (15 April 1998) (BSEC Agreement) art 8(1); *Agreement between Governments of Member States of Shanghai Cooperation Organization on Cooperation in Delivery of Assistance for Emergency Liquidation* (26 October 2005) art 6(1); *Agreement Establishing the Caribbean Disaster Emergency Management Agency* (4 July 2008) (CDEMA Agreement) art XXII(1); *Decision No 1313/2013/EU of the European Parliament and of the Council of 17 December 2013 on a Union Civil Protection Mechanism* (20 December 2013) (EU Civil Protection Mechanism) art 15(5).

[2] Draft Articles (n 1) art 10(1); UN General Assembly Res 46/182 (n 1) para 4; IDRL Guidelines (n 1) art 3(1).

[3] Draft Articles (n 1) art 10(2); IDRL Guidelines (n 1) art 3(3); UN General Assembly Res 46/182 (n 1) para 4; Tampere Convention (n 1) art 4(8); Inter-American Convention (n 1) art IV(a); BSEC Agreement (n 1) art 8(1); Shanghai Agreement (n 1) art 6(1); CDEMA Agreement (n 1) art XXII(1); EU Civil Protection Mechanism (n 1) art 15(5).

[4] 'Stressing the principle of the sovereignty of States and, consequently, reaffirming the primary role of the State affected by a disaster in providing disaster relief assistance': Draft Articles (n 1) preamble. See also ILC, 'Commentaries on the Draft Articles on the Protection of Persons in the Event of Disasters' (2016) UN Doc A/71/10, 51.

the affected state. While this does not preclude international cooperation, such engagement remains – in principle – at the discretion of the affected state, which retains full control over whether, how and to what extent external actors may participate in response efforts. A central element of the affected state's control over disaster response is the principle that it must give consent before any external actors – whether third states, international organisations or NGOs – can provide disaster assistance within its territory (see section III.C).[5] This principle of consent is fundamental to the state's primary role, as it safeguards the affected state's sovereignty and territorial integrity by enabling the regulation of access by foreign relief personnel and resources.[6]

While the primary role implies a broad discretion to determine how to respond to disasters and to adopt measures it deems appropriate,[7] this discretion is not absolute.[8] International law imposes clear limitations, particularly through the state's duty to protect persons affected by disasters.[9] This duty arises not only from the principle of sovereignty itself – understood as a responsibility to protect the population within a state's territory – but also from IHRL, which requires states to uphold the human rights and dignity of people, even in the event of disaster.[10] This duty is further affirmed in key instruments such as UN General Assembly Resolution 46/182, which declares that: 'Each State has the responsibility first and foremost to take care of the victims of natural disasters and other emergencies occurring on its territory.'[11] As such, the affected state's discretion in exercising its primary role is constrained by the need to ensure adequate protection for disaster-affected populations.

The discretion of the affected state narrows significantly in situations where it is unable or unwilling to ensure adequate protection for disaster-affected populations. In such cases, the state may be under a duty to seek international assistance, even if it would prefer not to engage with external actors. While there is precedent for recognising such a duty,[12] it remains contested by states, some of which view it as a potential encroachment on their sovereignty (see section III.B). After all, a duty to seek assistance challenges the notion that states

[5] Draft Articles (n 1) art 13(1); IDRL Guidelines (n 1) art 10(1); UN General Assembly Res 46/182 (n 1) para 4; *Tampere Convention* (n 1) art 4(5); *AADMER* (n 1) art 3(1); *Framework Convention on Civil Defence Assistance* (22 May 2000) art 3(a).

[6] G Bartolini, 'A Universal Treaty for Disasters? Remarks on the International Law Commission's Draft Articles on the Protection of Persons in the Event of Disasters' (2017) 99(906) *International Review of the Red Cross* 1103, 1125.

[7] ILC, 'Third Report on the Protection of Persons in the Event of Disasters, by Mr. Eduardo Valencia-Ospina, Special Rapporteur' (31 March 2010) UN Doc A/CN.4/629, para 74.

[8] ILC (n 4) 59.

[9] Draft Articles (n 1) art 10(1); UN General Assembly Res 46/182 (n 1) para 4; IDRL Guidelines (n 1) art 3(1).

[10] ILC (n 4) 51.

[11] UN General Assembly Res 46/182 (n 1) para 4.

[12] Draft Articles (n 1) art 11; IDRL Guidelines (n 1) art 3(2); Institute de Droit International (IDI), 'Resolution on Humanitarian Assistance' (2003) 86(856) *International Review of the Red Cross* 874, art III(3).

are free to determine how to manage disasters within their territory. Similarly controversial are proposed limitations on the principle of consent (see section III.C). It has been suggested that states must not arbitrarily withhold consent from external actors willing to provide disaster assistance.[13] This could mean that an affected state should not withhold consent when international assistance is necessary to ensure adequate protection for its population.[14] Yet this interpretation is contentious, as it may be seen to undermine the state's control over who and what enters its territory.

Reimagining this role through the lens of solidarity does not entail a radical overhaul of the affected state's current position within IDRL. Rather, it preserves the state's primary role, but grounds it in a different logic. Whereas the current conception of the affected state's role is deeply rooted in the principle of sovereignty and frames disaster response as a matter within the domestic sphere, solidarity reframes disaster response – and more specifically the protection of affected populations – as a shared responsibility of the international community.[15] However, this does not mean that disaster response becomes a collective endeavour in which all states jointly manage disasters at a central level. Instead, solidarity operates through dual structure of responsibility: affected states bear an individual responsibility to protect disaster-affected persons within their jurisdiction, while other states have a collective responsibility to support the affected state when needed.[16] Under a solidarity-based interpretation of IDRL, the affected state therefore retains its primary role, including both the duty to protect and the exclusive authority to direct, control, coordinate and supervise disaster response efforts on its territory. This interpretation remains consistent with the current conception of the affected state's role in IDRL and preserves its sovereignty.

While not radically reforming the affected state's primary role, placing it within a framework of shared responsibility is crucial for understanding the constraints on its discretion in disaster response. As argued in Chapter 4, section III.A, reimagining disaster response as a shared responsibility of the international community has direct implications for how the affected state must act. While the primary role suggests that the state is free to determine its response within the context of its international obligations, solidarity requires that it also consider the shared interest of other states in protecting persons affected by disasters. When the actions – or inactions – of the affected state undermine this protection, they not only harm those directly impacted but also impair community interests and the very spirit of solidarity. Accordingly, in determining its disaster response, the affected state must weigh up not only its own national interests but also the broader, shared interest underpinning solidarity in IDRL.

[13] Draft Articles (n 1) art 13(2). See also IDI (n 12) art VIII(1).
[14] ILC (n 4) 62.
[15] On this reframing, see ch 4, section III.A.
[16] This argument was developed in ch 2, section III.

Where these interests conflict, the state cannot simply prioritise its own preferences; rather, it must balance them against the protection of affected persons, recognising that its decisions have implications for community interests too.[17]

This reinterpretation becomes particularly significant when the affected state is unable or unwilling to ensure adequate protection for disaster-affected populations. In such circumstances, solidarity implies that the state has a duty to seek support from other states or assisting actors. Sovereignty cannot be invoked as a reason to refuse assistance, since doing so would undermine the shared interests of all states. Similarly, solidarity limits the affected state's discretion to refuse international assistance when it is offered. Where such assistance is essential to the protection of those in need, the state must not withhold consent. Refusing aid in these circumstances would not only breach the state's duty to safeguard its population but would also go against the premise of solidarity by disregarding the shared responsibility to protect disaster-affected people. While these constraints arguably already exist under international law,[18] solidarity adds an important dimension: it frames the state's obligations not only as duties owed to its own population but also as duties owed to other states that share an interest in the protection of those at risk.

This reimagined understanding of the affected state's role underpins the obligations examined throughout the remainder of this chapter. On the surface, implementing solidarity may not appear to radically transform IDRL, but its true impact lies in reorienting disaster response from a sovereign matter of the affected state to a shared responsibility of the international community. Within this understanding of IDRL, the affected state continues to occupy the primary role, but it does so as part of a cooperative structure of shared responsibilities in which other states and assisting actors support its efforts through international cooperation and assistance. This shift does not dismantle the foundations of IDRL as it currently stands; rather, it recasts the obligations of the affected state in a framework where all states share responsibility for protecting persons affected by disasters.

III. SELECTED ISSUES

Building on the solidarity-based interpretation of the affected state's role, this section examines how solidarity reshapes three specific facets of that role within IDRL. It focuses on the right to receive humanitarian assistance in the context of disasters and the corresponding obligations of the affected state (section III.A); the affected state's duty to seek international assistance when it is unable

[17] R Wolfrum, *Solidarity and Community Interests: Driving Forces for the Interpretation and Development of International Law* (Brill Nijhoff, 2021) 90.

[18] Such constraints are discussed further in sections III.B and III.C in relation to the duty to seek assistance and the principle of consent respectively.

or unwilling to ensure adequate protection (section III.B); and the principle of consent governing the provision of international assistance (section III.C). Each subsection begins by outlining how IDRL currently addresses these issues, before turning to a normative analysis of how solidarity would reimagine them. Through this approach, the chapter demonstrates the potential of solidarity to transform the role of the affected state in IDRL.

A. The Right to Humanitarian Assistance in Disasters

This subsection delves further into the responsibility of the affected state to protect persons affected by disasters within its jurisdiction, focusing specifically on the right to receive humanitarian assistance and the corresponding obligations of states. According to the UN General Assembly, humanitarian assistance is 'of cardinal importance for the victims of natural disasters and other emergencies', particularly those who are unable to access resources and services critical to their survival and the fulfilment of their essential needs.[19] As highlighted in Chapter 1, section I, the IFRC estimates that each year more than 130 million people affected by disasters require humanitarian assistance.[20] If current trends continue, this number is projected to rise to over 200 million by 2050, driven largely by the increasing frequency and intensity of disasters linked to climate change.[21] Against this backdrop, the right to humanitarian assistance and the corresponding obligations of states is a central facet of the role of the affected state in disaster response.

Traditionally, the provision of humanitarian assistance in disasters has often been framed as a duty of states and as a means of meeting the essential needs of affected populations, rather than as a right held by those individuals. This state-centric approach highlights the obligations of states, but overlooks the position of disaster-affected persons, risking their reduction to passive objects of disaster response rather than active rights-holders. Scholars have therefore advocated for a rights-based approach to IDRL – one that centres the agency and entitlements of those impacted by disasters.[22] Examining the responsibilities of the affected state must therefore also involve considering the rights of those affected. This raises the question of whether people affected by disasters are entitled to a right to receive humanitarian assistance.

[19] UN General Assembly Res 46/182 (n 1) para 1.

[20] This figure is based on data gathered between 2010 and 2019: IFRC, 'World Disasters Report 2020: Come Heat or High Water' (2020) www.ifrc.org/document/world-disasters-report-2020, 153.

[21] IFRC, 'The Cost of Doing Nothing' (2019) www.ifrc.org/document/cost-doing-nothing, 3.

[22] W Kälin, 'The Human Rights Dimension of Natural or Human-Made Disasters' (2012) 55 *German Yearbook of International Law* 119; D Cubie, *The International Legal Protection of Persons in Humanitarian Crises: Exploring the Acquis Humanitaire* (Hart Publishing, 2017) 109. See also ILC (n 4) 20.

Despite its growing relevance, the right to receive humanitarian assistance in the context of disasters has not yet materialised as a matter of positive international law.[23] No treaty codifies such a right and while there is widespread practice of providing humanitarian assistance to disaster-affected populations – by both states and non-state actors – this practice has not been accompanied by sufficient *opinio juris* to support the emergence of a right under customary law.[24] The right has not been formally endorsed by states, UN General Assembly resolutions have not recognised it as a legal entitlement and neither the Draft Articles nor the IDRL Guidelines explicitly affirm it. However, the ILC, while choosing not to cite potentially applicable human rights in the Draft Articles themselves,[25] refers to the right to receive humanitarian assistance as an example of a relevant right in disaster contexts in the accompanying commentaries.[26]

The right to receive humanitarian assistance finds growing support in a range of soft law instruments, which reflect an emerging recognition of this right.[27] For example, the Resolution on Humanitarian Assistance adopted by the Institut de Droit International (IDI) affirms that:

> The victims of disaster are entitled to request and receive humanitarian assistance. Assistance may be sought on behalf of the victims, by the members of the group, by local and regional authorities, the government of the affected State, and national or international organizations.[28]

Similarly, the Mohonk Criteria for Humanitarian Assistance in Complex Emergencies declare that 'everyone has the right to request and receive humanitarian aid necessary to sustain life and dignity from competent authorities or local, national or international governmental and non-governmental organizations'.[29] The IFRC also supports this view in its Principles and Rules for Red Cross and Red Crescent in Disaster Relief, stating that: 'The Red Cross and Red Crescent in its endeavour to prevent and alleviate human suffering, considers

[23] ILC, 'Memorandum by the Secretariat on the Protection of Persons in the Event of Disasters' (11 December 2007) UN Doc A/CN.4/590, para 257.

[24] R Hardcastle and A Chua, 'Victims of Natural Disasters: The Right to Receive Humanitarian Assistance' (1997) 1(4) *International Journal of Human Rights* 35, 39; MG Pietropaolo, 'A Human Rights-Based Approach to Humanitarian Assistance: Current and Prospective Scenarios' (2016) 7(2) *Journal of International Humanitarian Legal Studies* 257, 265.

[25] 'The Commission did not consider it feasible to draw up an exhaustive list of all potentially applicable [human] rights and was concerned that such a list could lead to an a contrario interpretation that rights not mentioned therein were not applicable': ILC (n 4) 32.

[26] ibid.

[27] A Creta, 'A (Human) Right to Humanitarian Assistance in Disaster Situations? Surveying Public International Law' in A de Guttry, M Gestri and G Venturini (eds), *International Disaster Response Law* (TMC Asser Press, 2012) 353, 363.

[28] IDI (n 12) art II(2).

[29] Task Force on Ethical and Legal Issues in Humanitarian Assistance, 'The Mohonk Criteria for Humanitarian Assistance in Complex Emergencies' (1994) JM Ebersole, 'Mohonk Criteria for Humanitarian Assistance in Complex Emergencies' (1995) 4(3) *Disaster Prevention and Management* 14, 16.

it a fundamental right of all people to both offer and receive humanitarian assistance.'[30]

Even if there is currently insufficient evidence to support the emergence of an *autonomous* right to humanitarian assistance in international law,[31] several scholars argue that such a right is implied within IHRL.[32] As discussed in Chapter 1, section II.C.iii, human rights continue to apply in disaster settings.[33] Disasters often disrupt the enjoyment of fundamental rights, including the rights to life, food, water, health and housing. In these circumstances, humanitarian assistance is indispensable to meeting the basic needs of affected populations and upholding their human rights. This connection implies that there is an indirect or implied right to receive humanitarian assistance in disaster contexts, derived from the necessity of upholding other human rights.

Support for an implied right to humanitarian assistance is further reinforced by several instruments. The Guiding Principles on the Right to Humanitarian Assistance adopted by the International Institute of Humanitarian Law (IIHL), for instance, explicitly build on the notion that:

> Every human being has the right to humanitarian assistance in order to ensure respect for the human rights to life, health, protection against cruel and degrading treatment and other human rights which are essential to survival, well-being and protection in public emergencies.[34]

In a similar vein, the UN General Assembly has stated that the failure to provide humanitarian assistance in disaster contexts threatens human rights, noting that 'the abandonment of the victims of natural disasters and similar emergency situations without humanitarian assistance constitutes a threat to human life and

[30] IFRC, 'The Principles and Rules for Red Cross and Red Crescent in Disaster Relief' (1996) 36(310) *International Review of the Red Cross* 102, principle 2.1. IFRC and ICRC, 'Code of Conduct for the International Red Cross and Red Crescent Movement and Non-Governmental Organisations (NGOs) in Disaster Relief' (1994) principle 1 similarly states: 'The right to receive humanitarian assistance, and to offer it, is a fundamental humanitarian principle which should be enjoyed by all citizens of all countries. As members of the international community, we recognise our obligation to provide humanitarian assistance wherever it is needed.'

[31] Hardcastle and Chua (n 24) 39; Cubie (n 22) 326; Y Dinstein, 'The Right to Humanitarian Assistance' (2000) 53(4) *Naval War College Review* 77, 77; H Spieker, 'The Right to Give and Receive Humanitarian Assistance' in HJ Heintze and A Zwitter (eds), *International Law and Humanitarian Assistance: A Crosscut through Legal Issues Pertaining to Humanitarianism* (Springer, 2011) 7, 29.

[32] Hardcastle and Chua (n 24) 39; Pietropaolo (n 24) 267; Kälin (n 22) 140; Creta (n 27) 360; Cubie (n 22) 321; D Fisher, 'The Right to Humanitarian Assistance' (2010) 41 *Studies in Transnational Legal Policy* 47, 53; K Cedervall Lauta, 'Human Rights and Natural Disasters' in S Breau and K Samuel (eds), *Research Handbook on Disasters and International Law* (Edward Elgar, 2016) 91, 104; J Benton Heath, 'Disasters, Relief, and Neglect: The Duty to Accept Humanitarian Assistance and the Work of the International Law Commission' (2011) 43 *NYU Journal for International Law & Politics* 419, 438.

[33] Draft Articles (n 1) art 5. See also Kälin (n 22); E Sommario, 'Limitation and Derogation Provisions in International Human Rights Law Treaties and Their Use in Disaster Settings' in F Zorzi Giustiniani et al (eds), *Routledge Handbook of Human Rights and Disasters* (Routledge, 2018) 98.

[34] IIHL, 'Guiding Principles on the Right to Humanitarian Assistance' (1993) 33(297) *International Review of the Red Cross* 519, principle 1.

an offence to human dignity'.[35] Echoing this language, the IDI's Resolution on Humanitarian Assistance emphasises that '[l]eaving the victims of disaster without humanitarian assistance constitutes a threat to human life and an offence to human dignity and therefore a violation of fundamental human rights'.[36] These instruments thus suggest that the absence of assistance may constitute a breach of IHRL.

Additionally, practice by UN human rights treaty bodies suggests tentative support for this interpretation. While the right to humanitarian assistance is not explicitly codified in human rights treaties, treaty bodies have, on several occasions, reviewed and commented on state obligations relating to the provision of humanitarian assistance in disaster situations in the realisation of human rights.[37] This practice reveals a growing recognition of the relevance of humanitarian assistance in upholding human rights in disaster settings, and may signal support for the development of this right.

If recognised, the right to humanitarian assistance would encompass the provision of goods and services that are needed for survival and to uphold human rights and dignity. While not defined in international law, humanitarian assistance typically refers to 'activities and the human and material resources for the provision of goods and services of an exclusively humanitarian character, indispensable for the survival and the fulfilment of the essential needs of the victims of disasters'.[38] Humanitarian assistance may include 'food items, medical supplies, clothing, shelter, seeds and tools, as well as the provision of infrastructure, such as schools and roads'.[39] Based on this understanding, individuals would be entitled to receive aid necessary to meet their essential needs during or in the aftermath of a disaster. The content and scope of this assistance must be determined by the specific circumstances and needs of each person.

As the primary duty-bearer of this right, the affected state is responsible for ensuring the provision of humanitarian assistance within its jurisdiction.[40] This assistance must be sufficient to meet the essential needs of affected individuals and must be delivered in accordance with the humanitarian principles of humanity, neutrality, impartiality and independence.[41] These principles require, among other things, that assistance be provided solely on the basis of need, prioritising the most urgent cases of distress without discrimination based on

[35] UN General Assembly Res 43/131 (8 December 1988) UN Doc A/RES/43/131, preamble.

[36] IDI (n 12) art 2(1).

[37] See generally M Hesselman, 'A Right to International (Humanitarian) Assistance in Times of Disaster' in Zorzi Giustiniani et al (n 33) 65.

[38] IDI (n 12) art I(1). See also IIHL (n 34) principle 9; Creta (n 27) 356; Cubie (n 22) 19.

[39] ReliefWeb Project, 'Glossary of Humanitarian Terms' (2008) https://reliefweb.int/report/world/reliefweb-glossary-humanitarian-terms-enko, 10.

[40] IIHL (n 34) principle 4.

[41] Draft Articles (n 1) art 6; IDRL Guidelines (n 1) art 4(2); UN General Assembly Res 46/182 (n 1) para 2.

nationality, race, gender, religious belief, class or political opinion.[42] Moreover, humanitarian assistance must be quantitatively and qualitatively adequate. Practice has shown that inappropriate or inadequate aid remains a recurring issue in disaster response.[43] Examples include the delivery of goods unsuited to local conditions such as winter clothing in tropical climates or culturally inappropriate items like thong underwear and high-heeled boots.[44] In some cases, relief workers have arrived unprepared and become dependent on aid themselves.[45] To address these challenges, international humanitarian organisations have developed guidelines, such as the Sphere Handbook,[46] which set general standards for the appropriateness and adequacy of humanitarian assistance, helping to ensure that aid is both effective and respectful of local needs and contexts.

The implementation of solidarity in IDRL would reinforce the right to humanitarian assistance in the context of disasters. As argued in Chapter 4, section III.C, the rights of individuals affected by disasters need to be centred, placing their protection at the heart of solidarity in IDRL. Solidarity is not merely a principle guiding inter-state cooperation; at its core, it reflects a common goal that prioritises the human rights and dignity of those impacted by disasters. Accordingly, the provision of humanitarian assistance should not be seen merely as an outcome of solidarity, but framed as a right of those affected, placing people at the centre of what solidarity seeks to achieve. Solidarity then becomes a vehicle for protecting rights.

While solidarity does not substantially alter the content of the right to humanitarian assistance per se, it fundamentally reframes its fulfilment as a shared – but differentiated – responsibility of all states. The affected state remains the duty-bearer, affirming its primary role in disaster response and its duty to protect persons within its jurisdiction. However, when viewed through the lens of solidarity, this duty is to be situated within a broader context that treats the protection of disaster-affected populations as a common concern of all states.[47] Accordingly, fulfilling the right to humanitarian assistance is not solely the responsibility of the affected state, but also of other states that have a duty to support it in ensuring this right is realised. As discussed in Chapter 4, section III.E, the differentiating nature of solidarity means that affected states are expected to mobilise their own resources first to ensure the provision of sufficient and adequate humanitarian

[42] ILC (n 4) 33–36.

[43] D Fisher, 'Law and Legal Issues in International Disaster Response: A Desk Study' (IFRC, 2007) 133 ff; D Fisher, 'The Future of International Disaster Response Law' (2012) 55 *German Yearbook of International Law* 87, 94; I Granger, 'IDRL in Haiti: A Study on the Legal Framework for the Facilitation and Regulation of International Disaster Response in Haiti' (IFRC, 2012) 44 ff.

[44] Fisher (n 43) 137.

[45] Granger (n 43) 45.

[46] Sphere Project, 'The Sphere Handbook: Humanitarian Charter and Minimum Standards in Humanitarian Response' (2018) https://spherestandards.org/handbook.

[47] This argument is made in ch 4, section III.A.

assistance in accordance with humanitarian principles.[48] However, when those resources prove insufficient, international cooperation becomes essential to guarantee the continued enjoyment of this right. This is particularly important for states with limited capacities to provide humanitarian assistance, which may rely on external assistance in fulfilling their obligations and protecting those affected by disasters. In this way, solidarity reinforces the affected state's primary role while also assigning a shared responsibility to other states, embedding the right to humanitarian assistance within a framework of international cooperation and assistance.

Solidarity also reshapes the understanding of to whom the affected state owes its duties. While the affected state unquestionably owes a duty to persons affected by disasters who are the rights-holders, it also owes a duty to fulfil the right to humanitarian assistance to other states. As argued previously, if the protection of persons affected by disasters is reconceived as a matter of shared responsibility among all states, the obligations that contribute to this protection should be understood as obligations *erga omnes*, or duties owed to the international community as a whole.[49] This understanding means that compliance with the right to humanitarian assistance becomes a legitimate concern of all states.[50] Chapter 6, section III.D further explores the options for third states to respond to breaches of protective obligations by the affected state.

Finally, situating the right to humanitarian assistance within a framework of shared responsibility also has implications for the duty to cooperate of the affected state. When a state is unable to fulfil this right on its own due to overwhelmed response capacities, it must engage in international cooperation to ensure that affected populations receive the assistance to which they are entitled. The next subsection turns to this issue, examining the duty to seek international assistance in IDRL.

B. The Duty to Seek International Assistance

The duty to seek international assistance remains a contested issue within IDRL. While it is widely acknowledged that 'the magnitude and duration of many emergencies may be beyond the response capacity of many affected countries', making international cooperation 'of great importance',[51] the legal status of a duty to seek assistance is far from settled. In situations where

[48] However, states are free to engage in international cooperation in fulfilling their obligations if they wish to do so. See ILC (n 4) 56.

[49] See ch 4, section III.B.

[50] *Barcelona Traction, Light and Power Company, Limited (Belgium v Spain)* (Judgment) [1970] ICJ Rep 3, para 33.

[51] UN General Assembly Res 46/182 (n 1) para 5.

national response capacities are overwhelmed, several soft law instruments suggest that affected states have an obligation to request external assistance.[52] Notably, the Draft Articles provide that: 'To the extent that a disaster manifestly exceeds its national response capacity, the affected State has the duty to seek assistance from, as appropriate, other States, the United Nations, and other potential assisting actors.'[53] However, the emergence of this duty as a binding norm under international law remains controversial. It has not crystallised into a legal obligation under treaty law or customary international law.[54] Although the inclusion of this duty in the Draft Articles has received support from several states and international organisations,[55] that support is far from universal, and significant resistance remains, particularly from states concerned about potential encroachments on their sovereignty.[56] It is therefore expected to become a contentious topic in the negotiations of a treaty on the protection of persons in the event of disasters.

While an autonomous duty to seek international assistance has not yet crystallised in IDRL, there is a strong basis for recognising such a duty under IHRL. The logic is straightforward: even when a disaster is overwhelming, states continue to hold core obligations to ensure the minimum essential levels of human rights, including the rights to life, food, water, health and shelter.[57] As discussed in the previous section, this includes an implied obligation to ensure the provision of sufficient and adequate humanitarian assistance necessary for the survival and the fulfilment of the essential needs of those affected. When a state's capacity is overwhelmed and it is unable to meet these

[52] Draft Articles (n 1) art 11; IDRL Guidelines (n 1) art 3(2); IDI (n 12) art III(3).

[53] Draft Articles (n 1) art 11.

[54] ILC (n 23) para 57.

[55] See the EU and Finland (on behalf of the Nordic States) in UN General Assembly Sixth Committee, 'Summary Record of the 21st Meeting' (2 December 2011) UN Doc A/C.6/66/SR.21, paras 56, 60; Czech Republic and Spain in UN General Assembly Sixth Committee, 'Summary Record of the 23rd Meeting' (14 November 2011) UN Doc A/C.6/66/SR.23, paras 19, 50; India and Romania in UN General Assembly Sixth Committee, 'Summary Record of the 25th Meeting' (9 December 2011) UN Doc A/C.6/66/SR.25, paras 13, 18; Tonga (on behalf of the 12 Pacific Small Island Developing States) in UN General Assembly Sixth Committee, 'Summary Record of the 20th Meeting' (10 November 2014) UN Doc A/C.6/69/SR.20, para 6.

[56] For a discussion of states' views on the duty to seek international assistance in the Draft Articles, see SD Murphy, 'Protection of Persons in the Event of Disasters and Other Topics: The Sixty-Eighth Session of the International Law Commission' (2016) 110(4) *American Journal of International Law* 718, 723.

[57] Although states' obligations may be temporarily limited, derogated or reduced, states retain core non-derogable obligations to ensure the minimum essential levels of enjoyment of human rights that 'continue to exist in situations of conflict, emergency and natural disaster': CESCR, 'Poverty and the International Covenant on Economic, Social and Cultural Rights' (10 May 2001) UN Doc E/C.12/2001/10, para 18; CESCR, 'General Comment No. 3: The Nature of States Parties' Obligations (Art. 2, Para. 1, of the Covenant)' (14 December 1990) UN Doc E/1991/23, para 10. See also E Sommario, 'Derogation from Human Rights Treaties in Situations of Natural or Man-Made Disasters' in de Guttry, Gestri and Venturini (n 27) 323, 348.

core obligations on its own, states must seek assistance from other states or assisting actors.[58]

Human rights treaties indeed provide a basis for a positive duty to seek international assistance. States have a general duty to cooperate in the realisation of human rights and may be expected to engage in international cooperation to meet their obligations.[59] The *International Covenant on Economic, Social and Cultural Rights* (ICESCR), for example, affirms that in realising the right to adequate food, 'States Parties will take appropriate steps to ensure the realization of this right, recognizing to this effect the essential importance of international co-operation based on free consent'.[60] The Committee on Economic, Social and Cultural Rights (CESCR), in interpreting this provision, has clarified that if a state claims resource constraints prevent it from ensuring access to food, it must demonstrate that it has made every effort to use all available resources and has 'unsuccessfully sought to obtain international support to ensure the availability and accessibility of the necessary food'.[61]

Similarly, the *Convention on the Rights of the Child* (CRC) obliges states to 'undertake all appropriate legislative, administrative, and other measures for the implementation of the rights recognized in the present Convention' and that they 'shall undertake such measures to the maximum extent of their available resources and, where needed, within the framework of international co-operation'.[62] The Committee on the Rights of the Child has interpreted this provision to mean that:

> States parties have an obligation to cooperate with one another in the promotion of universal respect for, and observance of, human rights, including the rights of the child. States that lack the resources needed to implement the rights enshrined in the [Convention on the Rights of the Child] and its Optional Protocols are obliged to seek international cooperation, be it bilateral, regional, interregional, global or multilateral.[63]

These interpretations support the view that when a state cannot meet its human rights obligations using its own resources, it has a positive duty to seek international assistance to uphold those rights.

[58] ILC (n 4) 53–54; S Jansen-Wilhelm, *Accepting Assistance in the Aftermath of Disasters: Standards for States under International Law* (Intersentia, 2015) 164. See also ETO Consortium, 'Maastricht Principles on Extraterritorial Obligations of States in the Area of Economic, Social and Cultural Rights' (2011) principle 34. A positive duty to seek international assistance may also derive from the implied right to humanitarian assistance under IHRL; see Hardcastle and Chua (n 24) 42; Pietropaolo (n 24) 273.

[59] See, eg, *Charter of the United Nations* (24 October 1945) arts 55–56; *International Covenant on Economic, Social and Cultural Rights* (16 December 1966) (ICESCR) art 2(1).

[60] ICESCR (n 59) art 11(1).

[61] CESCR, 'General Comment No. 12: The Right to Adequate Food (Art. 11)' (12 May 1999) UN Doc E/C.12/1999/5, para 17.

[62] *Convention on the Rights of the Child* (20 November 1989) (CRC) art 4.

[63] Committee on the Rights of the Child, 'General Comment No. 19 on Public Budgeting for the Realization of Children's Rights (Art. 4)' (20 July 2016) UN Doc CRC/C/GC/19, para 35.

The duty to seek international assistance should be understood as a qualified obligation that applies only when a disaster manifestly exceeds the affected state's national response capacity. This condition is recognised in several soft law instruments,[64] including the Draft Articles,[65] and aligns with the interpretations provided by human rights treaty bodies. The concept of national response capacity must be interpreted broadly to encompass the combination of all the strengths and resources available within a state that can reduce the effects of a disaster.[66] Capacity can include 'infrastructure, institutions, human knowledge and skills, and collective attributes such as social relationships, leadership and management'.[67] As the ILC rightly notes:

> [T]he national response capacity of an affected State may not always be sufficient or insufficient in absolute terms. An affected State's national capacity may be manifestly exceeded in relation to one aspect of disaster relief operations, although the State remains capable of undertaking other operations.[68]

For example, a state may face critical shortages of food, water or medical supplies, triggering a duty to seek assistance specifically in relation to those needs, rather than for the entirety of the disaster response. Nonetheless, the affected state is still free to seek international assistance in other areas where its response capacity is sufficient if it chooses to do so.[69]

The Draft Articles further clarify that the affected state may seek assistance from a range of actors, including other states, the UN and other assisting actors such as Red Cross or Red Crescent societies and NGOs.[70] The affected state retains the sovereign discretion to determine from whom it seeks assistance.[71] This flexibility is part of its primary role in disaster response and reflects its authority to direct, control, coordinate and supervise relief efforts within its territory. Typically, states issue a general appeal for assistance, inviting support from

[64] For example: '*If an affected State determines that a disaster situation exceeds national coping capacities*, it should seek international and/or regional assistance to address the needs of affected persons': IDRL Guidelines (n 1) art 3(2) (emphasis added); '*Whenever the affected State is unable to provide sufficient humanitarian assistance to the victims placed under its jurisdiction or de facto control*, it shall seek assistance from competent international organizations and/or from third States': IDI (n 12) art III(3) (emphasis added).

[65] '*To the extent that a disaster manifestly exceeds its national response capacity*, the affected State has the duty to seek assistance from, as appropriate, other States, the United Nations, and other potential assisting actors': Draft Articles (n 1) art 11 (emphasis added).

[66] UNDRR, 'Definition: Capacity' www.undrr.org/terminology/capacity.

[67] ibid.

[68] ILC (n 4) 53.

[69] ibid 56.

[70] Draft Articles (n 1) art 11. Other soft law instruments also indicate that assistance can be sought from both state and non-state actors willing to assist – see IDRL Guidelines (n 1) art 3(2); IDI (n 12) art III(3).

[71] ILC (n 4) 56.

any willing actors.[72] However, they may also choose to solicit aid from specific actors only,[73] provided that the assistance sought is sufficient to meet the needs of affected populations.[74] This discretion allows states to control the response to disasters within their jurisdiction while still fulfilling their obligations. However, it is relevant to note that a formal appeal or request for international assistance by the affected state is not always necessary in practice; third states and assisting actors often proactively offer support before an official request is made. The right to make such unsolicited offers of assistance is discussed in Chapter 6, section III.B.

It should come as no surprise that if solidarity is given effect in IDRL, the affected state should bear a duty to seek international assistance when its national response capacity is overwhelmed. In fact, this duty is foundational to the model of shared responsibility that solidarity presupposes. The act of requesting assistance should be understood as the critical link that activates this shared responsibility, enabling other states to support the affected state in the protection of people affected by disasters. In this way, the affected state's duty to seek help is not a relinquishment of responsibility, but rather the first and necessary step in operationalising solidarity in disaster response.

Interpreted through this lens, the duty of an affected state to seek assistance should be qualified, applying only to the extent that its national response capacities are overwhelmed. This interpretation thus aligns with the scope envisaged in soft law instruments and the commentary of UN human rights treaty bodies. A qualified duty fits squarely within solidarity's framework of dual responsibilities: it reinforces that the affected state retains primary responsibility for the protection of disaster-affected populations and should exhaust its own resources before turning to international aid. This interpretation therefore also has a differentiating purpose: it differentiates responsibilities among states based on their capacities, placing greater expectations on those with greater capacities to manage disasters independently, while enabling states with more limited capacities to seek and receive international support earlier. In this way, solidarity functions as a mechanism for equitable burden-sharing, responding to structural inequalities between states.

At first glance, the implementation of solidarity may seem to leave the duty to seek assistance unchanged from its current formulation under IDRL. However, solidarity adds a crucial dimension: it reframes the duty not only as a consequence

[72] For example, in the aftermath of the catastrophic floods in 2022, Pakistan issued, in collaboration with the UN, a general appeal for international aid; see Government of Pakistan, 'Joint Launch of 2022 Pakistan Floods Response Plan by Government of Pakistan and the United Nations' (30 August 2022) https://reliefweb.int/report/pakistan/joint-launch-2022-pakistan-floods-response-plan-government-pakistan-and-united-nations.

[73] For example, from states with whom the affected state has agreed to cooperate in disaster response bilateral or regional agreements, including AADMER (n 1).

[74] ILC (n 4) 56.

of obligations owed to disaster-affected individuals under IHRL, but also as a duty owed to other states who share an interest in protection. Solidarity therefore situates the duty to seek assistance within a cooperative framework of shared responsibilities, in which other states support the efforts of the affected state through international cooperation and assistance, united by a common goal. As a duty owed to other states, the failure to seek assistance when it is under a duty to so directly affects other states, which may take appropriate action in response.[75]

Yet, the implementation of a solidarity-based duty to seek international assistance is likely to encounter resistance from at least some states concerned about the implications for their sovereignty.[76] The duty necessarily limits the discretion of the affected state in determining how to respond to disasters, creating tension with the principle of sovereignty. Indonesia articulated this concern during discussions in the UN General Assembly's Sixth Committee on the Draft Articles, where it argued that such a duty undermines 'the principles of non-intervention and the sovereign right of that State to use its own judgement and keep all options open'.[77] These objections highlight a potential challenge to the realisation of solidarity in IDRL: if states perceive the duty to seek assistance as an encroachment on their sovereign prerogatives, they may be reluctant to endorse, accept or comply with it. Offering an alternative, opposing states have suggested that the duty to seek international assistance should be understood hortatory rather than obligatory.[78]

However, if states are committed to solidarity in IDRL, the duty to seek international assistance should be understood not as a discretionary act, but as a binding legal obligation. As argued in Chapter 4, section III.D, cooperation lies at the heart of solidarity and must go beyond voluntarism.[79] Accordingly, when a state's national response capacities are overwhelmed, seeking international assistance cannot be viewed as merely encouraged or optional – it must be a legal duty. Failure to seek assistance in such circumstances not only risks violating the rights of those affected, but also harms the common interest of all states to ensure their protection, thereby undermining solidarity.

[75] Which actions can be taken in response to the failure to seek assistance are explored in ch 6, section III.D.

[76] Austria, France and the UK in UN General Assembly Sixth Committee, 'Summary Record of the 23rd Meeting' (n 55) paras 23, 38, 45; Russia and Malaysia in UN General Assembly Sixth Committee, 'Summary Record of the 24th Meeting' (1 December 2011) UN Doc A/C.6/66/SR.24, paras 37, 114.

[77] UN General Assembly Sixth Committee, 'Summary Record of the 24th Meeting' (n 76) para 70.

[78] Austria, Israel, France, China, the UK and the Netherlands in UN General Assembly Sixth Committee, 'Summary Record of the 23rd Meeting' (n 55) paras 23, 33, 38, 42, 45, 48; Greece, Cuba, Russia, Iran, Portugal, Indonesia, South Korea, Thailand and Malaysia in UN General Assembly Sixth Committee, 'Summary Record of the 24th Meeting' (n 76) paras 25, 26, 37, 50, 66, 70, 82, 90, 114; Pakistan, Argentina and Algeria in UN General Assembly Sixth Committee, 'Summary Record of the 25th Meeting' (n 55) paras 7, 10, 33; Sri Lanka in UN General Assembly Sixth Committee, 'Summary Record of the 27th Meeting' (8 December 2011) UN Doc A/C.6/66/SR.27, para 19.

[79] The ILC has noted that in addition to IHRL, the duty to seek international assistance is also rooted in the duty to cooperate: ILC (n 4) 53.

While the duty to seek international assistance does indeed introduce a degree of constraint on the affected state's discretion in disaster response, it does not override or diminish state sovereignty. The obligation applies only in situations where national response capacities are overwhelmed, meaning that in all other circumstances, the affected state retains full autonomy in deciding whether to engage external actors. Even when the duty is triggered, sovereignty remains intact: seeking assistance is not an invitation for external actors to take over, but a call for cooperation under the direction of the affected state, which retains the right to direct, control, coordinate and supervise all disaster response efforts within its territory.[80] This retention of the primary role is further reinforced by the affected state's discretion in choosing from whom to seek assistance.[81] Furthermore, the duty to seek assistance does not equate to a duty to *accept* it.[82] The principle of consent remains applicable, preserving the state's control over access to its territory.[83] However, its freedom to withhold consent may be limited when the state is unable or unwilling to ensure protection on its own (see section III.C).

For these reasons, a harmonious balance can be found between solidarity and sovereignty in a way that applies both principles without allowing either one to dominate. This balance necessarily involves a compromise in which neither can be applied in their fullest, most absolute forms. What therefore may be needed is a reframing of the duty to seek assistance: Rather than viewing it negatively as an encroachment on sovereignty, it should be understood positively as a mechanism through which states can access the support they need to protect disaster-affected populations. In this light, the duty becomes a tool of empowerment rather than intervention, enabling states to fulfil their responsibilities with the support of others when their own capacities fall short. Seen in this way, the duty also becomes a key element in the differentiation of responsibilities in disaster response, reflecting the striving for social justice that underpins solidarity.[84] By allowing states with smaller response capacities to seek support from others, the duty contributes to narrowing global inequalities and fostering a more equitable and fair international disaster response system.

Even if concerns over sovereignty were eased, another significant challenge to the implementation of the duty to seek international assistance – and by extension to the realisation of solidarity in IDRL – is the determination of when a state's national response capacity is genuinely overwhelmed. This determination

[80] Draft Articles (n 1) art 10(2); IDRL Guidelines (n 1) art 3(3); UN General Assembly Res 46/182 (n 1) para 4; Tampere Convention (n 1) art 4(8); Inter-American Convention (n 1) art IV(a); BSEC Agreement (n 1) art 8(1); Shanghai Agreement (n 1) art 6(1); CDEMA Agreement (n 1) art XXII(1); EU Civil Protection Mechanism (n 1) art 15(5).

[81] ILC (n 4) 56.

[82] ibid 55.

[83] Draft Articles (n 1) art 13(1); IDRL Guidelines (n 1) art 10(1); UN General Assembly Res 46/182 (n 1) para 4.

[84] Wolfrum (n 17) 87.

would usually involve a needs assessment, which maps the needs of the persons affected by the disaster and assesses them against the available capacity to address those needs.[85] The ILC has noted that 'the affected State will be in the best position, in principle, to determine the severity of a disaster situation and the limits of its national response capacity'.[86] While this makes sense from a practical standpoint, past experiences reveal that such determinations can be politically sensitive and subject to contestation.[87] For instance, following the 2004 Indian Ocean Tsunami, India declined to seek or accept international assistance, asserting that it could manage the response independently. Although India mounted substantial domestic relief efforts, critics questioned whether international assistance could have accelerated recovery or reached underserved areas more effectively.[88] Similarly, in the aftermath of Hurricane Katrina in 2005, the US initially declined international assistance, claiming its response capacity was sufficient.[89] Only after mounting pressure and worsening conditions did the federal government revise its assessment and accept international aid.[90] These examples illustrate how states may understate the severity of a disaster or overestimate their response capacity, potentially delaying critical international support, impeding on the protection of affected people and undermining the spirit of solidarity.

The ILC acknowledges that while it is the affected state's prerogative to assess both the severity of a disaster and the limits of its national response capacity, this assessment 'must be carried out in good faith'.[91] This requirement stems from general international law, which obligates states to fulfil their duties in good faith.[92] The principle of good faith is intended to prevent states from deliberately manipulating assessments to avoid triggering the duty to seek international assistance, whether motivated by political purposes, reputational

[85] See IFRC, 'Model Act for the Facilitation and Regulation of International Disaster Relief and Initial Recovery Assistance' (March 2013) art 5(a). See also Fisher (n 43) 94; Jansen-Wilhelm (n 58) 78.

[86] ILC (n 4) 56. See also IDRL Guidelines (n 1) art 10(1): 'The affected State should decide in a timely manner whether or not to request disaster relief or initial recovery assistance and communicate its decision promptly. In order to make this decision, the affected State should promptly assess needs.'

[87] These concerns have been expressed by the EU in ILC, 'Eighth Report on the Protection of Persons in the Event of Disasters, by Mr. Eduardo Valencia-Ospina, Special Rapporteur' (17 March 2016) UN Doc A/CN.4/697, para 244. See also Benton Heath (n 32) 464–65; M Costas Trascasas, 'Access to the Territory of a Disaster-Affected State' in de Guttry, Gestri and Venturini (n 27) 221, 229; D Fisher, 'The Law of International Disaster Response: Overview and Ramifications for Military Actors' (2007) 83 *International Law Studies Series. US Naval War College* 293, 303; P Harvey, *Towards Good Humanitarian Government: The Role of the Affected State in Disaster Response* (Overseas Development Institute, 2009) 15.

[88] A Carnegie and LR Dolan, 'The Effects of Rejecting Aid on Recipients' Reputations: Evidence from Natural Disaster Responses' (2021) 16(3) *Review of International Organizations* 495, 503.

[89] I Kelman, 'Hurricane Katrina Disaster Diplomacy' (2007) 31(3) *Disasters* 288, 298.

[90] ibid.

[91] ILC (n 4) 56.

[92] ibid.

concerns or strategic interests. However, good faith alone cannot eliminate the risk of states mistakenly understating the severity of a disaster or overestimating their response capacity.

One way to address this challenge is to improve the transparency and quality of disaster assessments. A key part of this effort would be the development and use of objective indicators that help states assess both the needs of affected populations and their own capacity to meet those needs. Progress is already being made in this area; for example, the IFRC provides guidance on conducting emergency needs assessments.[93] Furthermore, assessments can be improved through cooperation. Where appropriate, states should conduct joint needs assessments, leveraging the expertise of international actors, especially in cases where the scale or complexity of the disaster makes independent assessment difficult. Some soft law instruments already foresee such cooperation; the IDRL Guidelines, for instance, recommend that states consider 'undertaking joint needs assessments with the United Nations and other assisting humanitarian organisations'.[94] In practice, various organisations typically offer support in this area. For example, the UN Office for the Coordination of Humanitarian Affairs (OCHA) can, upon request by the affected state, activate its Disaster Assessment and Coordination (UNDAC) system, deploying a team within 24–48 hours that can assist with needs assessments.[95] UNDAC has been activated in many disasters, including in Grenada and Saint Vincent and the Grenadines following Hurricane Beryl in 2024,[96] Turkey following the earthquake in 2023[97] and Peru following heavy floods and landslides in 2023.[98] The Global Facility for Disaster Reduction and Recovery (GFDRR), a multi-donor partnership administered by the World Bank, also assists states with assessing their needs, usually for recovery and reconstruction.[99] The GFDRR has cooperated with states including

[93] IFRC, 'Emergency Needs Assessments' www.ifrc.org/our-work/disasters-climate-and-crises/supporting-local-humanitarian-action/emergency-needs.

[94] IDRL Guidelines (n 1) art 10(1). See also UN General Assembly Res 46/182 (n 1) para 35(c); ILC (n 4) 56; Fisher (n 43) 94; Jansen-Wilhelm (n 58) 79.

[95] OCHA, 'Needs Assessment and Analysis' www.unocha.org/es/themes/needs-assessment-and-analysis.

[96] CDEMA and OCHA, 'Grenada and Saint Vincent and the Grenadines: CDEMA and UNDAC Deployment' (2024) https://reliefweb.int/report/grenada/grenada-and-saint-vincent-and-grenadines-cdema-and-undac-deployment-13072024.

[97] OCHA, 'End of Mission Report: United Nations Disaster Assessment & Coordination (UNDAC) 7.8 Earthquake (February 6, 2023)' (2023) https://reliefweb.int/report/turkiye/end-mission-report-united-nations-disaster-assessment-coordination-undac-78-earthquake-february-6-2023-turkiye-undac-mission-february-6-may-17-2023.

[98] OCHA, 'Informe de Misión: United Nations Disaster Assessment & Coordination (UNDAC) Lluvias, Inundaciones y Deslizamientos de Tierra en el Norte del Perú' (2023) https://reliefweb.int/report/peru/informe-de-mision-united-nations-disaster-assessment-coordination-undac-lluvias-inundaciones-y-deslizamientos-de-tierra-en-el-norte-del-peru-peru-fecha-de-mision-11-30-de-abril-de-2023.

[99] GFDRR, 'Post Disaster Needs Assessments' www.gfdrr.org/en/post-disaster-needs-assessments.

Libya following heavy floods in 2023,[100] Albania following an earthquake in 2019[101] and Tonga following Cyclone Gita in 2018.[102] Joint assessments could not only enhance the accuracy of determining whether national capacities are overwhelmed, but could also introduce checks and balances that could reduce the risk of flawed assessments and avoid unnecessary delays in mobilising international assistance.

In addition to improving the quality of needs assessments, a further challenge lies in the lack of oversight and accountability. Currently, the determination of whether national response capacities are overwhelmed falls entirely within the sovereign domain of the affected state, with no formal mechanisms for external review or verification. This absence of oversight becomes particularly problematic when there are credible doubts about a state's refusal to seek or accept aid, despite apparent need. In such cases, other states and assisting actors, such as the UN and NGOs, may publicly or privately contest the decision, exerting pressure on the affected state to reconsider and seek (and accept) assistance. However, these efforts remain informal, leaving the international community with limited recourse when a state's assessment appears to conflict with the realities on the ground. This accountability gap undermines the reliability of the duty to seek assistance and poses a potential barrier to the realisation of solidarity in IDRL.

If viewed through the lens of solidarity, some degree of oversight over the affected state's determination of whether its national response capacity is overwhelmed is not only appropriate but also necessary. Incorrect assessments can directly undermine the common goal of protecting persons affected by disasters and thus solidarity among states. While the affected state should retain the primary role in making this determination – ideally in collaboration with experts – solidarity means that other states have a legitimate interest in ensuring that these assessments are accurate and timely. This is especially important in situations where the refusal to seek assistance may jeopardise lives or hinder the distribution of humanitarian assistance. Oversight in this context is not antithetical to solidarity. While solidarity is grounded in trust that states will pursue common objectives together, oversight should not be seen as a lack of trust, but rather as a reflection of the shared responsibility of the international community and a mechanism for other states to safeguard the pursuit of common goals, ensuring that decisions align with the overarching commitment to protect those affected.

[100] World Bank, European Union and UN, 'Libya Storm and Flooding 2023: Rapid Damage and Needs Assessment' (2024) www.gfdrr.org/en/publication/libya-storm-and-flooding-2023-rapid-damage-and-needs-assessment.

[101] Government of Albania et al, 'Albania: Post-Disaster Needs Assessment' (2019) https://enlargement.ec.europa.eu/document/download/0909ed0e-222c-43a4-a11e-17bf9fb193e8_en.

[102] Government of Tonga, 'Post Disaster Rapid Assessment: Tropical Cyclone Gita' (2018) www.gfdrr.org/sites/default/files/publication/WB_Tonga_Report_FA02_Medium.pdf.

If solidarity and the duty to seek assistance are to be meaningfully operationalised, appropriate oversight and accountability mechanisms are therefore essential. However, such mechanisms do not yet exist. While there are established systems for monitoring human rights obligations, these are not well suited to this context because they are not designed to respond to real-time decisions made during disasters. What is needed is an international body or institution with a mandate to oversee the application of IDRL and raise concerns when credible doubts arise about a state's refusal to seek or accept aid. Although organisations such as the UN and the Red Cross Movement can exert institutional influence, they lack any formal mandate to perform this role. Chapter 8, section III will revisit this issue and explore ways to address this potential obstacle to the full realisation of solidarity.

C. The Principle of Consent

Even when states must seek assistance, the provision of international assistance is ultimately subject to the consent of the affected state. This principle is a cornerstone of IDRL as it currently stands. Rooted in the concept of state sovereignty, consent represents 'the expression of the will of the sovereign who permits activities on its territory that may otherwise constitute violations of the principle of non-intervention'.[103] As such, consent serves as a safeguard against unwanted intervention and a critical tool through which states maintain control over access to their territory.[104]

Originally developed in IHL,[105] the principle is now well established in IDRL. For instance, UN General Assembly Resolution 46/182 affirms that:

> [T]he sovereignty, territorial integrity and national unity of States must be fully respected in accordance with the Charter of the United Nations. In this context, humanitarian assistance should be provided with the consent of the affected country and in principle on the basis of an appeal by the affected country.[106]

Similarly, the Draft Articles stipulate that '[t]he provision of external assistance requires the consent of the affected State'.[107] Many IDRL treaties reaffirm this

[103] ILC, 'Fourth Report on the Protection of Persons in the Event of Disasters, by Mr. Eduardo Valencia-Ospina, Special Rapporteur' (11 May 2011) UN Doc A/CN.4/643, para 52.

[104] Bartolini (n 6) 1125.

[105] See *Protocol Additional (I) to the Geneva Conventions of 12 August 1949, and Relating to the Protection of Victims of Non-international Armed Conflicts* (8 June 1977) art 70(1). See also C Ryngaert, 'Humanitarian Assistance and the Conundrum of Consent: A Legal Perspective' (2013) 5(2) *Amsterdam Law Forum* 5.

[106] UN General Assembly Res 46/182 (n 1) para 3.

[107] Draft Articles (n 1) art 13(1).

principle explicitly,[108] while others imply it by allowing international assistance only upon the request of the affected state.[109]

While the principle is largely uncontroversial, the scope of the state's discretion to withhold such consent remains contested. Consent, by definition, is a discretionary power.[110] However, this discretion is not absolute but constrained by international law, particularly by the state's duty to protect persons affected by disasters.[111] The logic follows from earlier discussions: the affected state bears the primary responsibility to ensure adequate protection for those impacted. If it is unable or unwilling to fulfil this duty – such as when its national response capacity is overwhelmed – it must not only seek assistance but also accept it. In such circumstances, withholding consent to external aid that is essential for protecting lives and alleviating suffering would constitute a failure to meet international obligations.[112]

Limitations to the principle of consent are not merely theoretical; they are of critical importance in practice. Experience shows that affected states have, at times, refused or delayed acceptance of international assistance even when their national response capacities were clearly overwhelmed.[113] One study suggests that international assistance is rejected or delayed in approximately one in four major disasters.[114] A stark example is the Myanmar government's blanket refusal of international aid following Cyclone Nargis in 2008, despite the disaster's devastating impact on millions of people.[115] Although it was evident that Myanmar's response capacity was overwhelmed, the government declined assistance, reportedly due to fears of foreign interference in domestic affairs.[116] This

[108] See, eg, Tampere Convention (n 1) art 4(5); Civil Defence Assistance Convention (n 5) art 3(a); AADMER (n 1) art 3(1); *SAARC Agreement on Rapid Response to Natural Disasters, 2011* (26 May 2011) art III(1). See also IDRL Guidelines (n 1) art 10(1).

[109] See, eg, *Inter-American Convention* (n 1) art 2; *BSEC Agreement* (n 1) art 3(2); *Shanghai Agreement* (n 1) art 2(2); *Convention on Assistance in the Case of a Nuclear Accident or Radiological Emergency* (26 September 1986) art 2; *Agreement between Member States and Associate Members of the Association of Caribbean States for Regional Cooperation on Natural Disasters* (16 April 1999) (ACS Agreement) art 4.

[110] ILC (n 23) para 65.

[111] Benton Heath (n 32); Costas Trascasas (n 87); Ryngaert (n 105); Jansen-Wilhelm (n 58); A Telec, 'Challenges to State Sovereignty in the Provision of International Natural Disaster Relief' in DD Caron, MJ Kelly and A Telesetsky (eds), *The International Law of Disaster Relief* (Cambridge University Press, 2014) 270; M Thomson, 'The Obligation Not to Arbitrarily Refuse International Disaster Relief: A Question of Sovereignty' (2015) 16 *Melbourne Journal of International Law* 1; S Sivakumaran, 'Arbitrary Withholding of Consent to Humanitarian Assistance in Situations of Disaster' (2015) 64(3) *International and Comparative Law Quarterly* 501. On the principle of consent in relation to the right to humanitarian assistance, see Hardcastle and Chua (n 24) 43; Pietropaolo (n 24) 275; Kälin (n 22) 143.

[112] ILC (n 4) 60.

[113] Some examples are discussed in Costas Trascasas (n 87) 226–27.

[114] T Nelson, 'Rejecting the Gift Horse: International Politics of Disaster Aid Refusal' (2010) 10(3) *Conflict, Security & Development* 379, 391.

[115] For an overview of events, see A Selth, 'Even Paranoids Have Enemies: Cyclone Nargis and Myanmar's Fears of Invasion' (2008) 30(3) *Contemporary Southeast Asia* 379, 386 ff.

[116] ibid 390 ff.

refusal exacerbated human suffering and provoked widespread international criticism,[117] until diplomatic mediation by ASEAN led to Myanmar accepting aid from neighbouring states.[118] Other examples include Iran after the 2003 Bam earthquake,[119] India following the 2004 Indian Ocean Tsunami and the 2005 Kashmir earthquake,[120] and Italy after the 2009 L'Aquila earthquake.[121] Common underlying reasons for withholding consent include concerns over foreign interference, overconfidence in domestic capabilities, national pride and the desire to project strength and control to both domestic and international audiences.[122]

The ILC extensively debated the principle of consent and proposed in the Draft Articles that while states retain the prerogative to grant or withhold consent to external assistance,[123] '[c]onsent to external assistance shall not be withheld arbitrarily'.[124] This proposal will be the starting point for negotiations on this subject in the forthcoming treaty on the protection of persons in the event of disasters. The proposed limitation draws from established principles in IHL and IHRL, suggesting that in some circumstances, states must accept international assistance.[125] For example, *Additional Protocol I to the Geneva Conventions* obligates parties to a conflict to 'allow and facilitate rapid and unimpeded passage of all relief consignments, equipment and personnel' necessary to meet the basic needs of civilians in occupied territories.[126] Similarly, the Guiding Principles on Internal Displacement stipulate that consent to humanitarian assistance provided by international organisations and other actors 'shall not be arbitrarily withheld, particularly when authorities concerned are unable or unwilling to provide the required humanitarian assistance'.[127]

However, the concept of arbitrariness in this context remains ambiguous. When is withholding consent to external assistance 'arbitrary'? International law offers varying interpretations of what constitutes 'arbitrary' conduct. In IHRL, the Human Rights Committee has stated that arbitrariness 'is not to be equated with "against the law", but must be interpreted more broadly to include elements of inappropriateness, injustice, lack of predictability and due process

[117] S Mydans, 'Myanmar Faces Pressure to Allow Major Aid Effort' *New York Times* (8 May 2008) www.nytimes.com/2008/05/08/world/asia/08myanmar.html.

[118] K Loevy, 'The Legal Politics of Jurisdiction: Understanding ASEAN's Role in Myanmar's Disaster, Cyclone Nargis (2008)' (2015) 5(1) *Asian Journal of International Law* 55.

[119] I Kelman, *Disaster Diplomacy* (Routledge, 2012) 21.

[120] Costas Trascasas (n 87) 226.

[121] Jansen-Wilhelm (n 58) 80–81.

[122] Costas Trascasas (n 87) 226; Thomson (n 111) 16 ff; Carnegie and Dolan (n 88); F Zorzi Giustiniani, *International Law in Disaster Scenarios: Applicable Rules and Principles* (Springer, 2021) 71. See also Kelman (n 119).

[123] Draft Articles (n 1) art 13(1).

[124] ibid art 13(2).

[125] ILC (n 4) 60.

[126] Additional Protocol I (n 105) art 70(2).

[127] UN Economic and Social Council, 'Guiding Principles on Internal Displacement' (11 February 1998) UN Doc E/CN.4/1998/53/Add.2, principle 25(2). See also IDI (n 12) art VIII(1).

of law, as well as elements of reasonableness, necessity and proportionality'.[128] In IHL, the standard is applied to the requirement of consent for humanitarian relief operations in armed conflict, where consent may only be withheld 'for valid reasons, not for arbitrary or capricious ones'.[129] The Oxford Guidance on the Law Relating to Humanitarian Relief Operations in Situations of Armed Conflict, a non-binding interpretation of this area of IHL, elaborates further, stating that consent is withheld arbitrarily if:

> (i) it is withheld in circumstances that result in the violation by a state of its obligations under international law with respect to the civilian population in question; or (ii) the withholding of consent violates the principles of necessity and proportionality; or (iii) consent is withheld in a manner that is unreasonable, unjust, lacking in predictability or that is otherwise inappropriate.[130]

The ILC did not provide a precise definition of arbitrariness in the Draft Articles.[131] Instead, it offered three illustrative examples in the accompanying commentaries to clarify what would prima facie constitute valid reasons for withholding consent.[132] First, consent may be withheld if the affected state is both willing and able to protect persons affected by disasters in accordance with international law. Second, refusal is not arbitrary if the state has already accepted sufficient assistance from other actors. Third, withholding consent is justified if the offer of assistance violates international law, including the humanitarian principles of humanity, neutrality, impartiality and independence. By extension, the affected state may also reject assistance that is inappropriate or inadequate.[133] These examples imply *a contrario* that withholding consent to bona fide offers of international assistance is arbitrary when such assistance is necessary to protect disaster-affected persons and fulfil the state's protective obligations.[134]

If interpreted through the lens of solidarity, the affected state's discretion to withhold consent to international assistance must be understood as limited. As discussed in Chapter 4, section III.A, solidarity requires that states consider not only their own national interests but also the shared interest of all states in protecting persons affected by disasters. When these interests conflict, the affected state cannot simply prioritise its own sovereignty or domestic concerns; it must balance them against the common goal. Accordingly, the affected state must not, without justification, withhold consent to assistance that is essential

[128] UN Human Rights Committee, 'General Comment No. 35 on Article 9, Liberty and Security of Person' (16 December 2014) UN Doc CCPR/C/GC/35, para 12.

[129] Y Sandoz, C Swinarski and B Zimmermann (eds), *Commentary on the Additional Protocols* (ICRC, 1987) para 2805.

[130] D Akande and EC Gillard, 'Oxford Guidance on the Law Relating to Humanitarian Relief Operations in Situations of Armed Conflict' (OCHA, 2016), 22.

[131] Sivakumaran (n 111).

[132] ILC (n 4) 62.

[133] ibid 65.

[134] See also IDI (n 12) art VIII(1).

for the protection of those in need. Refusing such assistance would not only breach the state's duty to protect the rights and dignity of affected populations, but would also undermine the shared interest of the international community in disaster response. Solidarity thus demands that the principle of consent be exercised in a manner consistent with this collective purpose, rather than exclusively as a unilateral assertion of control over all matters within the state's jurisdiction.

The solidarity-based duty to cooperate further reinforces the limitations on the affected state's discretion to withhold consent. While the affected state retains the primary role in disaster response, this role is conditioned by the duty to cooperate with other states and assisting non-state actors when it is unable to ensure adequate protection on its own.[135] Withholding consent in such circumstances would effectively obstruct this duty to cooperate, preventing third states and assisting actors from providing the necessary support in the spirit of solidarity. In this way, the principle of consent must be interpreted not as a barrier to cooperation, but as a gateway to it – one that must remain open when international assistance is essential to fulfilling the shared responsibility of protecting disaster-affected people.

Viewed through the lens of solidarity, the restrictions on the affected state's discretion to withhold consent largely overlap with those proposed by the ILC. Solidarity does not demand that the affected state accept all or any offers of international assistance; in principle, the state retains the sovereign right to reject assistance, provided it is both willing and able to ensure adequate protection. This respects the primary role of the affected state and its authority over access to its territory. However, this discretion narrows significantly when the state is unable or unwilling to meet its protective obligations. This interpretation aligns with the ILC's position that consent must not be withheld arbitrarily, particularly when assistance is necessary to safeguard those affected. However, what solidarity adds is a deeper normative foundation: the restriction is not only grounded in the state's duty to protect its own population, but also in its duty to other states to pursue the common objective that binds them through solidarity.

It is not unlikely that some states will resist a solidarity-based interpretation of the principle of consent, particularly where it implies limitations on their discretion to withhold consent. Discussions in the UN General Assembly's Sixth Committee on the Draft Articles revealed that the scope of this discretion remains highly contentious. Some states welcomed limitations that reflect 'a balanced conception of the modern concept of sovereignty as having a dual nature entailing both rights and obligations',[136] although many called for further clarification

[135] The solidarity-based duty to cooperate was discussed in ch 4, section III.D.

[136] Chile in UN General Assembly Sixth Committee, 'Summary Record of the 24th Meeting' (n 76) para 9. See also Finland in UN General Assembly Sixth Committee, 'Summary Record of the 21st Meeting' (n 55) para 60; El Salvador in UN General Assembly Sixth Committee, 'Summary Record of the 22nd Meeting' (1 December 2011) UN Doc A/C.6/66/SR.22, para 13; Spain in UN General Assembly Sixth Committee, 'Summary Record of the 23rd Meeting' (n 55) para 50.

on what constitutes arbitrary withholding of consent.[137] However, a number of states fundamentally and uncompromisingly opposed any restrictions, arguing that there is no basis in customary international law or state practice for limiting the affected state's discretion to grant or withhold consent.[138] These states view such limitations as an unacceptable encroachment on sovereignty.

Indeed, any limitations on the affected state's discretion to withhold consent inevitably constrain its sovereignty. However, the proposed limitations do not hollow out or undermine sovereignty. In fact, sovereignty in this context has a dual nature: on the one hand, it safeguards the affected state's freedom to determine how to respond to disasters, including whether to accept international assistance; on the other hand, it entails the responsibility to protect the population within its territory.[139] This responsibility necessarily limits the state's discretion to withhold consent when external assistance is needed to fulfil its protective obligations. Importantly, these limitations only apply when the state is unable or unwilling to ensure adequate protection. Outside such circumstances, the affected state retains full discretion to reject assistance as it sees fit. Moreover, when multiple offers of assistance are made, the state retains the right to choose from whom to accept aid and what kind of aid to accept, provided that the assistance is sufficient to meet the needs of affected persons.[140] Furthermore, even after giving consent, the affected state maintains exclusive authority to direct, control, coordinate and supervise the provision of assistance within its territory.[141] Therefore, consent does not equate to relinquishing control; it is a necessary and principled limitation that enables the state to fulfil its responsibility to protect its population in times of disaster.

It is also important to emphasise that the affected state need not always prioritise the collective interest when it is in tension with national interests. Suggesting otherwise would undermine the affected state's sovereignty and primary responsibility for the response to disasters. Rather, solidarity calls for a balancing of interests. In the context of consent, this means that there may be exceptional circumstances in which it is justified for the affected state to withhold consent to international assistance, even when such assistance is needed. However, such

[137] Israel, France, China, the UK and the Netherlands in UN General Assembly Sixth Committee, 'Summary Record of the 23rd Meeting' (n 55) paras 33, 39, 42, 45, 48; Malaysia in UN General Assembly Sixth Committee, 'Summary Record of the 24th Meeting' (n 76) paras 117–19; Argentina, Ireland and Algeria in UN General Assembly Sixth Committee, 'Summary Record of the 25th Meeting' (n 55) paras 10, 22, 33; Sri Lanka in UN General Assembly Sixth Committee, 'Summary Record of the 27th Meeting' (n 78) para 20.

[138] Cuba, Russia and Indonesia in UN General Assembly Sixth Committee, 'Summary Record of the 24th Meeting' (n 76) paras 27, 37, 70; China in UN General Assembly Sixth Committee, 'Summary Record of the 23rd Meeting' (n 55) para 42.

[139] ILC (n 4) 59–60.

[140] ibid 62.

[141] Draft Articles (n 1) art 10(2); UN General Assembly Res 46/182 (n 1) para 4; IDRL Guidelines (n 1) art 3(3).

justification must be narrowly construed and only accepted where the reason for withholding consent is proportionate to the consequences of delaying or denying necessary aid. This approach respects the affected state's sovereignty while ensuring that its discretion is exercised in alignment with the overarching common objective that solidarity seeks to promote.

Proportionality is a well-established principle in international law used to balance competing interests, ensuring that the pursuit of a legitimate objective does not excessively interfere with other protected interests.[142] It is reflected across various legal regimes, including IHL in assessing the permissibility of attacks in armed conflict,[143] the law of the sea in maritime delimitation,[144] World Trade Organization law in the application of general exceptions,[145] the law on state responsibility in the use of countermeasures,[146] and IHRL in the restriction of human rights.[147] Generally, a proportionality test comprises three elements: suitability, necessity and proportionality *stricto sensu*.[148] First, the measure in question must be suitable to achieve a legitimate aim.[149] Second, it must be the least intrusive means available to achieve that aim (necessity).[150] Third, the measure must not excessively interfere with other interests (proportionality *stricto sensu*), meaning there must be 'a reasonable and proportional relationship between the interference and the importance of reasons underlying the interference itself'.[151] The application of this test is inherently context-dependent.

Applying a proportionality test offers a pragmatic, nuanced and context-sensitive means of balancing the affected state's national interests with the common goal underpinning solidarity. The three elements of the proportionality test must be applied to assess whether consent may be withheld. First, the affected state must demonstrate that withholding consent is a suitable means to achieve the cited aim. If withholding consent does not meaningfully contribute to achieving the aim, it is not suitable. Second, the affected state must show that withholding consent is the least intrusive option available to pursue that aim, meaning that no less restrictive alternative could achieve the same result. This includes imposing conditions on consent or restricting access in specific

[142] E Crawford, 'Proportionality' in *Max Planck Encyclopedia of International Law* (Oxford University Press, 2011) para 1.

[143] ibid para 19.

[144] R Wolfrum, 'Proportionality: Reconsidering the Application of an Established Principle in International Law' (2022) 99 *International Law Studies* 676, 681 ff.

[145] ibid 680.

[146] ILC, 'Articles on Responsibility of States for Internationally Wrongful Acts' (31 May 2001) UN Doc A/56/10, art 51.

[147] Crawford (n 142) para 20.

[148] ibid para 2.

[149] P de Sena and L Acconciamessa, 'Balancing Test' in *Max Planck Encyclopedia of International Law* (Oxford University Press, 2021) paras 24–25.

[150] ibid para 26.

[151] ibid para 27.

cases only,[152] rather than withholding consent blanketly. Third, the state must assess proportionality *stricto sensu* by weighing up the reason for withholding consent against the common goal of protecting persons affected by disasters. This requires a careful evaluation of whether the interference with international assistance is excessive in light of the humanitarian needs at stake. In essence, the affected state must establish a reasonable and proportionate relationship between its national interests and the potential impact of rejecting aid on disaster-affected populations.

In practice, very few reasons for withholding consent to international assistance are likely to satisfy the proportionality test, especially when the needs of disaster-affected populations are severe. Fundamentally, the greater the humanitarian need, the less likely it is that withholding consent can be considered proportionate. Purely (geo)political motivations such as national pride, over-confidence in domestic capacities or the desire to project strength and control would not be sufficient justification to delay or reject assistance. Nonetheless, there are exceptional cases where justification may exist. For example, following the strongest recorded earthquake in 2023, Morocco delayed consent to certain offers of international aid while accepting others.[153] Although it was evident that Morocco's national response capacity was overwhelmed and external assistance was urgently needed, the government argued that accepting too much aid would overwhelm its ability to coordinate and manage the influx effectively, creating bottlenecks in the distribution that would delay the provision of assistance to those affected.[154] This justification was not broadly challenged by states and organisations who had offered aid, claiming that it was not driven by politics.[155] Crucially, Morocco did not reject all assistance, but selectively accepted aid, thereby mitigating adverse effects on those in need. If it had rejected all assistance, it is unlikely that that decision would have satisfied the proportionality test, given the great humanitarian needs of those affected.

Other reasons may also meet the proportionality test in certain circumstances. For instance, where granting access would expose critical infrastructure essential to national security, it may be justified for the affected state to withhold consent. However, such a decision does not absolve the state of its responsibility to protect disaster-affected populations; the state must instead identify alternative means of securing the resources necessary to ensure their adequate protection. Public health concerns may likewise justify a (temporary) refusal of assistance. The cholera outbreak in Haiti, linked to UN peacekeepers, and the COVID-19 pandemic illustrate that preventing the spread of contagious

[152] The Draft Articles permit states to 'place conditions on the provision of external assistance ... in accordance with the present draft articles, applicable rules of international law and the national law of the affected State': Draft Articles (n 1) art 14.

[153] 'Why Has Morocco Accepted Limited Foreign Aid so Far?' *Al Jazeera* (12 September 2023) www.aljazeera.com/news/2023/9/12/is-morocco-accepting-aid-certain-countries-political-reasons.

[154] ibid.

[155] ibid.

disease can constitute a legitimate reason for restricting entry to certain areas or communities.[156] Yet even in these cases, the affected state must assess whether less intrusive measures are available to achieve the same aim, ensuring that any restriction remains proportionate to the objective pursued.

The determination of whether withholding consent to external assistance is proportionate should rest with the affected state, as part of its primary role in disaster response. This mirrors the responsibility states have to assess whether their national capacities are overwhelmed. However, as with that determination, there are no oversight mechanisms to ensure objectivity or accountability, or any procedures to raise concerns about delays or rejections of international aid, even though practice suggests that states cannot always be relied upon to balance national interests with community interests, particularly when sovereignty concerns dominate their decision making.[157]

Where there are concerns over decisions to withhold consent, other states and non-state actors may contest these decisions and exert diplomatic or public pressure to secure consent, as occurred during Cyclone Nargis, when Myanmar's blanket refusal of aid drew widespread criticism.[158] However, such contestation is informal and ad hoc, reflecting the fragile institutional framework of IDRL, which lacks any procedures to review or challenge these determinations. From the perspective of solidarity, some degree of oversight and accountability is desirable because decisions to withhold consent for international assistance directly affect the collective interests of all states. For solidarity to not become a mere rhetorical commitment, mechanisms that ensure states do not prioritise narrow national interests at the expense of common objectives are required. This does not call for rigid, quasi-judicial procedures that review state decisions, as such processes could discourage participation and cooperation. Instead, what is needed is an independent body empowered to raise concerns on behalf of the international community when consent is withheld and to facilitate dialogue aimed at negotiating access to affected communities. Such a mechanism would help translate solidarity into meaningful practice, reinforcing trust among states and reducing the risk that political considerations undermine timely and effective disaster response. Chapter 8, section III elaborates further on this idea.

A further question concerns the consequences when an affected state wrongfully withholds consent to external assistance. As argued earlier, when viewed

[156] For example, in the aftermath of the Hunga Tonga–Hunga Ha'apai volcano eruption in 2022, the authorities were concerned that foreign relief workers could spread the COVID-19 virus in Tonga: D Cave, I Kwai and E Nagourney, 'An Island Nation Covered in Ash Now Worries about a Covid Intrusion' *New York Times* (18 January 2022) www.nytimes.com/2022/01/18/world/australia/tonga-volcano-covid.html. However, these concerns did not result in the rejection of much-needed international assistance: 'Tonga Eruption, Tsunami: Images Appear to Show Most of Atatā Island Wiped out' *Radio New Zealand* (19 January 2022) www.rnz.co.nz/news/world/459845/tonga-eruption-tsunami-images-appear-to-show-most-of-atata-island-wiped-out.

[157] Nelson (n 114) 391.

[158] Selth (n 115) 388.

through the lens of solidarity, the obligations of the affected state should be understood as obligations *erga omnes*,[159] meaning that all states have a legal interest in their fulfilment and may act in response to breaches. However, the critical question is what such action could entail. For example, could other states circumvent the affected state's refusal or even intervene coercively if consent is wrongfully withheld? This is not merely theoretical: during Cyclone Nargis, the possibility of invoking R2P to justify intervention was openly discussed.[160] Although Myanmar ultimately consented to assistance following ASEAN-led diplomatic mediation,[161] the episode underscores the unresolved question of how IDRL can be enforced and how states might be compelled to grant consent when necessary. The range of options available to states in responding to wrongful withholding of consent is examined in detail in Chapter 6, section III.D.

IV. CONCLUSION

This chapter began the analysis of how solidarity could reshape core dimensions of international disaster response, beginning with the role of the affected state. This inquiry is essential to ensure that solidarity moves beyond abstract and aspirational rhetoric, and becomes embedded in concrete legal norms and practices. The discussion began by outlining the affected state's role under IDRL, emphasising that, even when viewed through the lens of solidarity, the state retains its primary responsibility for disaster response (section II). However, solidarity reframes this role within a framework of shared responsibilities, wherein the affected state bears the primary responsibility for the protection of those impacted by disaster. This reinterpretation aligns broadly with existing IDRL principles; yet, as highlighted throughout this chapter, situating the affected state's role within a framework of shared responsibility is critical for understanding the constraints on its discretion and the duty to cooperate.

The affected state's discretion is first constrained by the right of disaster-affected persons to humanitarian assistance. As argued in section III.A, solidarity reinforces the recognition and development of this right in the disaster context, placing affected people at the centre of solidarity in IDRL. As the primary duty-bearer, the affected state must ensure that adequate assistance is delivered in accordance with humanitarian principles. Where its national capacities are overwhelmed, it has a corresponding duty to seek international assistance so that affected populations receive the aid to which they are entitled. Section III.B identified this duty as the critical link between the affected state's primary duty to protect and other states' shared responsibility to support that protection when necessary. Seeking help does not relinquish responsibility; it is the first and

[159] See ch 4, section III.B.
[160] Selth (n 115) 389.
[161] Loevy (n 118).

necessary step in operationalising solidarity – inviting cooperation in pursuit of common goals. Consequently, where international assistance is essential to provide adequate protection, the affected state must not withhold consent without justification. As section III.C argued, solidarity requires states to weigh their own interests against the shared interest of all states in protection. When these interests conflict, the affected state cannot simply prioritise national interests under the banner of sovereignty; it must balance them against the collective goal. While legitimate reasons to withhold consent may exist, the state must ensure that the impact on affected persons is proportionate to the objective pursued. Solidarity therefore demands that consent be exercised in service of this common purpose, rather than exclusively as a unilateral assertion of control over all matters within the state's jurisdiction.

This solidarity-based interpretation of the affected state's role may encounter resistance from states concerned about potential encroachments on sovereignty. However, as this chapter has demonstrated, while constraints on discretion inevitably limit aspects of sovereignty, they do not override or diminish sovereignty itself. The affected state continues to hold the primary role in disaster response, including exclusive authority to direct, control, coordinate and supervise all response efforts within its jurisdiction. Seeking and accepting assistance in the spirit of solidarity is not an invitation for other states to take over disaster response; rather, it is an invitation to work alongside local authorities to ensure that affected populations receive necessary humanitarian assistance. The affected state retains the right to determine from whom to seek and accept assistance, and all external aid remains subject to its direction. Solidarity thus operates through cooperation and differentiated responsibility, not through a collective takeover of disaster response. Clarifying this point should help alleviate concerns among states that solidarity could entail a loss of sovereign control.

This chapter has also highlighted potential obstacles to the successful implementation of solidarity. A key concern is that states may prioritise national interests over solidarity without facing any consequences. While practice shows that most states cooperate in disaster response, there have been instances where states delayed or refused to seek or accept assistance even when their national capacities were overwhelmed. In most cases, these decisions were politically motivated rather than based on credible justifications. This underscores the need for oversight and accountability mechanisms capable of raising concerns when credible doubts arise about such decisions. Currently, no such mechanisms exist, leaving it to individual states or non-state actors to voice concerns, which can be fragmented and ineffective. One way of addressing this problem is by mandating an international body to raise concerns on behalf of the international community. This could strengthen oversight and accountability, thereby addressing concerns over national interests trumping common interests and helping to realise the principle of solidarity in IDRL. A possible way forward on this solution will be discussed further in Chapter 8, section III.

Yet, what is perhaps most needed to make solidarity a success is a fundamental reframing of the meaning of international cooperation in disaster response. Rather than viewing engagement with third states and assisting actors negatively as a potential risk of foreign interference or an encroachment on sovereignty, it should be recast positively as a mechanism through which states can access the support they need. In this light, solidarity becomes a tool of empowerment rather than intervention, enabling states to fulfil their responsibilities with the backing of others when their own capacities fall short. Seen this way, solidarity is not about control or influence, but about creating a safety net for moments when extreme events overwhelm a state's ability to protect its population. Taking this further, solidarity is ultimately about providing support where it is most needed, acknowledging that national response capacities are unequal, but that these structural inequalities should never undermine the protection of people affected by disasters.

6

The Role of Third States and Assisting Actors

I. INTRODUCTION

WHILE THE PRIMARY RESPONSIBILITY for disaster response lies with the affected state, other states and assisting actors such as the UN, the Red Cross Movement and NGOs play an indispensable role in providing support and assistance where needed. This chapter therefore turns to their role and examines how this role can be reimagined through the lens of solidarity. This inquiry is especially important because IDRL has traditionally focused on the rights and duties of the affected state, leaving the legal position of third states – let alone assisting actors[1] – largely underexplored.[2] Yet, given solidarity's emphasis on cooperation, it is essential to consider the rights and obligations of those who provide assistance in order to understand how solidarity can be implemented in practice and how it can transform IDRL.

This chapter will follow the same structure as the previous one. It begins by examining how IDRL conceptually conceives the role of third states and assisting actors before considering how this role should be reconceptualised through the lens of solidarity (section II). It demonstrates that they are generally understood to have an auxiliary role, providing support only when the affected state's response capacities are overwhelmed. This chapter argues that solidarity reinforces this auxiliary role, but as an expression of the shared responsibility for protecting persons affected by disasters rather than a consequence of the sovereignty of the affected state.

[1] 'Assisting actors' refers to 'competent intergovernmental organization, or a relevant non-governmental organization or entity, providing assistance to an affected State with its consent': ILC, 'Draft Articles on the Protection of Persons in the Event of Disasters' (27 May 2016) UN Doc A/CN.4/L.871 (hereinafter 'Draft Articles'), art 3(d). See also the definition of 'assisting humanitarian organization' in the IDRL Guidelines, referring to 'a foreign, regional, intergovernmental or international non-profit entity whose mandate and activities are primarily focused on humanitarian relief, recovery or development': IFRC, 'Guidelines for the Domestic Facilitation and Regulation of International Disaster Relief and Initial Recovery Assistance' (2007) art 2(12).

[2] D Tladi, 'The International Law Commission's Draft Articles on the Protection of Persons in the Event of Disasters: Codification, Progressive Development or Creation of Law from Thin Air?' (2017) 16(3) *Chinese Journal of International Law* 425, 450.

This interpretation provides the basis for analysing four key issues that shape the role of third states and assisting actors in practice. Section III addresses these issues in turn: the responsibility for the protection of persons affected by disasters outside one's jurisdiction; the right to offer international assistance; the duty to provide such assistance; and the consequences of breaching obligations under IDRL, including the options available to respond to those breaches. Like the previous chapter, the aim is to adopt a normative approach, exploring how these issues should be understood if solidarity were used as an interpretative tool and model for the future development of IDRL, while also acknowledging potential obstacles to its full implementation. As emphasised in the previous chapter, this more granular analysis is necessary to move beyond abstract and aspirational claims about solidarity's transformative potential and to demonstrate how this transformation can be translated into concrete norms and practices.

II. SOLIDARITY AND THE AUXILIARY ROLE OF THIRD STATES AND ASSISTING ACTORS

Whereas the primary role of affected states is clearly articulated in both binding and non-binding instruments of IDRL,[3] the same cannot be said of third states and assisting actors. Other than the IDRL Guidelines, no instrument directly addresses their role.[4] Nevertheless, it can be inferred from IDRL that assisting actors are intended to have an auxiliary function, supplementing the affected state's primary role when necessary.[5]

[3] Draft Articles (n 1) art 10(2); UN General Assembly Res 46/182 (19 December 1991) UN Doc A/RES/46/182, para 4; IDRL Guidelines (n 1) art 3(3); *Tampere Convention on the Provision of Telecommunication Resources for Disaster Mitigation and Relief Operations* (18 June 1998) art 4(8); *ASEAN Agreement on Disaster Management and Emergency Response* (26 July 2005) (AADMER) art 3(2); *Inter-American Convention to Facilitate Disaster Assistance* (6 July 1991) art IV(a); *Agreement among the Governments of the Participating States of the Black Sea Economic Cooperation (BSEC) on Collaboration in Emergency Assistance and Emergency Response to Natural and Manmade Disasters* (15 April 1998) (hereinafter 'BSEC Agreement') art 8(1); *Agreement between Governments of Member States of Shanghai Cooperation Organization on Cooperation in Delivery of Assistance for Emergency Liquidation* (26 October 2005) (hereinafter 'Shanghai Agreement') art 6(1); *Agreement Establishing the Caribbean Disaster Emergency Management Agency* (4 July 2008) (hereinafter 'CDEMA Agreement') art XXII(1); *Decision No 1313/2013/EU of the European Parliament and of the Council of 17 December 2013 on a Union Civil Protection Mechanism* (20 December 2013) (hereinafter 'EU Civil Protection Mechanism') art 15(5).

[4] IDRL Guidelines (n 1) art 4.

[5] The word 'auxiliary' is not a standard term used in relation to the role of assisting actors, but is used by the IFRC to emphasise that the role of the Red Cross Movement is considered 'auxiliary' to the affected state's primary responsibility for disaster response. For example: 'Prevention of disasters, assistance to victims and reconstruction are first and foremost the responsibility of the public authorities. The International Federation of Red Cross and Red Crescent Societies will actively offer assistance to disaster victims through the agency of the National Society in a spirit of cooperation with the public authorities. In principle, Red Cross and Red Crescent help is of a complementary and auxiliary nature and is given primarily in the emergency and reconstruction phase': IFRC, 'The Principles and Rules for Red Cross and Red Crescent in Disaster Relief' (1996) 36(310) *International*

This auxiliary role can be drawn from the overall structure of IDRL. It stems from the principle that the affected state holds the primary responsibility for disaster response,[6] suggesting that assisting actors are expected to merely play a complementary, supportive role rather than a leading one. They bear no direct responsibility for responding to disasters outside their jurisdiction;[7] that responsibility rests squarely with the affected state alone. Instead, states have a duty to cooperate with affected states.[8] This auxiliary role is further reinforced by the qualified nature of the affected state's duty to seek assistance, which is only triggered to the extent that its national response capacities are overwhelmed.[9] Likewise, several treaties stipulate that assistance may only be provided upon the affected state's request.[10] These provisions thus suggest that third states and assisting actors only become involved when they are needed. This is also consistent with practice, where affected states manage disasters independently in most cases and typically seek external assistance only in exceptional circumstances where disasters have exceeded their capacities.[11] The principle of consent[12] and the right of the affected state to hold exclusive authority to direct, control, coordinate and supervise all response efforts within its jurisdiction further affirm this auxiliary role,[13] as the provision of assistance is subject to approval by the affected state and ultimately falls under its direction.[14] This framing too

Review of the Red Cross 102, principle 3.1. See also IDRL Guidelines (n 1) art 3(1): 'Affected States have the primary responsibility to ensure disaster risk reduction, relief and recovery assistance in their territory. National Red Cross and Red Crescent Societies, as auxiliaries to the public authorities in the humanitarian field, and domestic civil society actors play a key supporting role at the domestic level.'

[6] Draft Articles (n 1) art 10(1); UN General Assembly Res 46/182 (n 3) para 4; IDRL Guidelines (n 1) art 3(1).

[7] However, it could be argued that other states bear an indirect or secondary responsibility for the protection of persons affected by disasters under the doctrine of Responsibility to Protect (R2P). This argument is discussed further in section III.A.

[8] See, eg, Draft Articles (n 1) art 7; AADMER (n 3) art 4(a); Shanghai Agreement (n 3) art 2(1); Tampere Convention (n 3) art 3(1); *Convention on Assistance in the Case of a Nuclear Accident or Radiological Emergency* (26 September 1986) art 1(1).

[9] Draft Articles (n 1) art 11; IDRL Guidelines (n 1) art 3(2); IDI, 'Resolution on Humanitarian Assistance' (2003) 86(856) *International Review of the Red Cross* 874, art III(3).

[10] See, eg, Nuclear Accident Convention (n 8) art 2; Inter-American Convention (n 3) art 2; BSEC Agreement (n 3) art 3(2); Shanghai Agreement (n 3) art 2(2); *Agreement between Member States and Associate Members of the Association of Caribbean States for Regional Cooperation on Natural Disasters* (16 April 1999) (hereinafter 'ACS Agreement') art 4.

[11] D Fisher, *Law and Legal Issues in International Disaster Response: A Desk Study* (IFRC, 2007) 89.

[12] See, eg, Tampere Convention (n 3) art 4(5); Framework Convention on Civil Defence Assistance (22 May 2000) art 3(a); AADMER (n 3) art 3(1); *SAARC Agreement on Rapid Response to Natural Disasters, 2011* (26 May 2011) art III(1). See also IDRL Guidelines (n 1) art 10(1).

[13] Draft Articles (n 1) art 10(2); UN General Assembly Res 46/182 (n 3) para 4; IDRL Guidelines (n 1) art 3(3); Tampere Convention (n 3) art 4(8); Inter-American Convention (n 3) art IV(a); BSEC Agreement (n 3) art 8(1); Shanghai Agreement (n 3) art 6(1); CDEMA Agreement (n 3) art XXII(1); EU Civil Protection Mechanism (n 3) art 15(5).

[14] However, this does not mean that all assistance is handed over to local authorities; in most cases, assisting actors distribute aid themselves on the ground, in accordance with local laws, the humanitarian principles and directives issued by local authorities.

reinforces the idea that third states and assisting actors play a supportive rather than a leading role.

This auxiliary role also fits logically within the current framework of IDRL, which places strong emphasis on state sovereignty. This framework underscores that international assistance is not a default arrangement, but a contingency mechanism and reinforces the structural logic of IDRL, which positions assisting actors as complementary partners rather than substitutes for the affected state's primary responsibility. This framing also serves as a safeguard against unwanted interference by other states or non-state actors. This protective function is reinforced by the repeated provisions in IDRL instruments emphasising that states and assisting actors must respect the sovereignty, territorial integrity and national unity of the affected state, and to provide assistance only with its consent.[15] These rules ensure that international cooperation does not undermine state sovereignty, but rather operates within parameters set by the affected state, preserving its control over disaster response while enabling external support when necessary.

While third states and assisting actors have a duty to cooperate, their auxiliary role has traditionally been characterised by its voluntary nature.[16] States may choose to provide assistance but have no binding legal obligation to do so unless agreed otherwise in multilateral or bilateral agreements.[17] In practice, states often demonstrate a willingness to provide assistance, but the decision to engage remains theirs alone, typically influenced by humanitarian considerations and geopolitical interests. As demonstrated in Chapter 3, section IV, while third states and assisting actors are encouraged to support affected states when needed, they generally do so because it is morally the right thing to do rather than out of a perceived legal obligation. This interpretation further reinforces the central premise of IDRL: responsibility for disaster response lies with the affected state, with third states and assisting actors playing a supportive and complementary role only.

If interpreted through the lens of solidarity, the role of third states and assisting actors would remain auxiliary to the primary role of the affected state. As argued in Chapter 5, section II, solidarity upholds the affected state's primary role in disaster response, which leaves a complementary, supporting role to all others. However, solidarity embeds this auxiliary role in a fundamentally different logic, altering the interpretation of what it entails. Whereas the auxiliary role currently fits within the prevailing structural logic of IDRL as a consequence of state sovereignty and the corresponding primacy of the affected state, when understood against the background of solidarity, this role becomes an expression of the shared responsibility of all states for the protection of persons affected by

[15] 'The sovereignty, territorial integrity and national unity of States must be fully respected in accordance with the Charter of the United Nations. In this context, humanitarian assistance should be provided with the consent of the affected country and in principle on the basis of an appeal by the affected country': UN General Assembly Res 46/182 (n 3) para 3. See also Draft Articles (n 1) preamble; IDRL Guidelines (n 1) art 3(3); AADMER (n 3) art 3(1); Civil Defence Assistance Convention (n 12) art 3(b).

[16] On the duty to cooperate in IDRL, see ch 1, section II.C.iv.

[17] For further discussion, see section III.C.

disasters. Solidarity builds on the premise that while all states pursue the common objective of protecting persons affected by disasters, it is the affected state that carries the primary responsibility; others have a responsibility to support the affected state when needed.[18]

Reimagining the auxiliary role of third states and assisting actors as a reflection of shared responsibility is important because it shifts the conception of disaster response from one that falls under the responsibility of solely the affected state to one that is shared by all states, albeit with differentiated responsibilities. Under this interpretation, their role changes from something that must be curbed and controlled to prevent unwanted interference into a role where states and assisting actors stand ready to provide essential assistance when required by the affected state. Rather than centring state sovereignty as the organising principle of IDRL, this understanding takes the duty to cooperate as the starting point for defining roles in international disaster response.

Critically, however, the implementation of solidarity does not mean that the responsibility for protecting persons affected by disasters shifts from the affected state to the international community at any point. When the affected state is unable or unwilling to fulfil its protective responsibilities, it has a duty to cooperate with other states, which in turn have a duty to support the affected state. However, this support is provided through cooperation; the primary responsibility for disaster response remains at all times with the affected state and does not transfer to the international community.[19]

While responsibility for disaster response does not transfer, reimagining the role of third states and assisting actors through solidarity does call for a clearer and more precise articulation of their legal position. If the protection of persons affected by disasters is understood as a shared responsibility, states cannot remain passive or engage in cooperation solely on a voluntary basis. On the contrary, their role should come with rights and obligations that align with their auxiliary function. While states are not directly responsible for the protection of disaster-affected populations outside their jurisdiction, they do have a duty to cooperate (see section III.A). However, operationalising this duty to cooperate requires a significant departure from the prevailing principle of voluntarism in IDRL.[20] Instead, solidarity calls for a more principled approach to cooperation,

[18] This dual structure of solidarity has been established in ch 2, section III.

[19] This has been argued previously in ch 4, section III.B.

[20] A Williams, 'Solidarity, Justice and Climate Change Law' (2009) 10 *Melbourne Journal of International Law* 493, 498; R Wolfrum, 'International Law of Cooperation' in *Max Planck Encyclopedia of International Law* (Oxford University Press, 2010) para 3; H Neuhold, 'Common Security: The Litmus Test of International Solidarity' in R Wolfrum and C Kojima (eds), *Solidarity: A Structural Principle of International Law* (Springer, 2010) 193, 193–94; AG Koroma, 'Solidarity: Evidence of an Emerging International Legal Principle' in H Hestermeyer et al (eds), *Coexistence, Cooperation and Solidarity* (Martinus Nijhoff Publishers, 2012) 103, 103; RStJ MacDonald, 'Solidarity in the Practice and Discourse of Public International Law' (1996) 8 *Pace International Law Review* 259, 259–60; KP Sommermann, 'Some Reflections on the Concept of Solidarity and its Transformation into a Legal Principle' (2014) 52(1) *Archiv des Völkerrechts* 10, 10.

where third states and assisting actors are expected to provide assistance as part of their shared responsibility for the protection of persons affected by disasters. These obligations should be qualified: they apply only when the affected state's national response capacities are overwhelmed and must be differentiated, meaning that states contribute commensurate to their respective capacities rather than equally.[21]

Solidarity also reshapes the legal interest of third states in IDRL. Sharing the responsibility, all states have a legitimate legal interest in ensuring the protection of persons affected by disasters. When an affected state fails to meet its obligations to ensure the adequate protection of those affected, this harms not only the interests of the individuals whose rights are violated but also the interests of the international community as a whole. Consequently, third states may invoke the responsibility of the non-compliant state and take appropriate measures to compel compliance with its obligations under international law (see section III.D). In this context, third states do not seek to police other states, but rather to protect their own (shared) interests in the protection of persons affected by disasters.

Taken together, these two changes – recognising binding duties to cooperate and acknowledging their legal interest in IDRL – fundamentally transform the auxiliary role of third states and assisting actors. They are no longer mere Good Samaritans acting out of humanitarian concern but active participants in disaster response, albeit in a supporting capacity. Where the affected state is unable or unwilling to ensure adequate protection for its population, third states and assisting actors must step up and step in, closing critical protection gaps through cooperation and assistance in the spirit of solidarity.

III. SELECTED ISSUES

This section of the chapter explores how solidarity shapes four core aspects that shape the role of third states and assisting actors roles within IDRL. It begins by examining their responsibility for the protection of disaster-affected populations outside their jurisdiction (section III.A), followed by the right of to offer such assistance (section III.B). It then shows how solidarity reframes the duty to provide assistance (section III.C) and concludes by addressing the consequences of breaches of IDRL, including the means available for responding to such breaches (section III.D). Each subsection first outlines the current legal position under IDRL before turning to a normative analysis of how solidarity would reshape these issues.

[21] R Wolfrum, *Solidarity and Community Interests: Driving Forces for the Interpretation and Development of International Law* (Brill Nijhoff, 2021) 396.

A. Responsibility to Ensure Protection beyond Borders

International law firmly establishes that the affected state bears the primary responsibility for protecting persons within its jurisdiction during disasters.[22] While this principle is clear, far less settled is the question of whether states have obligations to ensure adequate protection beyond their own borders. This issue becomes particularly acute when an affected state is either unable or unwilling to meet its responsibilities under international law and refuses to seek or accept international assistance. In these cases, do other states have a responsibility to fill the protection gap? Such scenarios expose a critical gap in the current legal framework and raise questions about the extent to which international law might demand extraterritorial responsibilities to prevent harm and uphold fundamental rights.

There is no clear foundation in international law for an obligation requiring states to ensure the protection of persons affected by disasters beyond their own jurisdiction. Neither treaty law nor customary international law supports such a responsibility, which would also stand in tension with general principles of international law on state responsibilities.[23] Although states have long engaged in the practice of providing humanitarian assistance – with the consent of the affected state – this conduct does not amount to evidence of *opinio juris* indicating a legal duty to act, let alone a responsibility to guarantee protection for affected persons beyond borders.[24]

Despite the absence of a clear legal basis, the idea of extraterritorial responsibilities in specific situations has gained some traction in international law, particularly in relation to protecting individuals at risk of grave harm. A key development in this regard is the doctrine of Responsibility to Protect (R2P), introduced by the International Commission on Intervention and State Sovereignty (ICISS) in response to the international community's failure to prevent or halt mass atrocities in Somalia, Srebrenica and Rwanda during the 1990s.[25] R2P reframes both individual and collective state responsibilities for safeguarding populations from mass atrocity crimes and severe human rights violations. It rests on the premise that sovereignty entails a primary duty to protect populations from 'conscience-shocking situations' such as genocide, war crimes, crimes against humanity, mass starvation, civil war and other catastrophic events.[26] When a state fails to fulfil this duty, responsibility shifts to the

[22] Draft Articles (n 1) art 10(1); UN General Assembly Res 46/182 (n 3) para 4; IDRL Guidelines (n 1) art 3(1).

[23] MT Kamminga, 'Extraterritoriality', *Max Planck Encyclopedia of International Law* (Oxford University Press, 2020).

[24] R Hardcastle and A Chua, 'Victims of Natural Disasters: The Right to Receive Humanitarian Assistance' (1997) 1(4) *International Journal of Human Rights* 35, 39.

[25] ICISS, 'The Responsibility to Protect: Report of the International Commission on Intervention and State Sovereignty' (2001).

[26] ibid 33.

international community, which, under R2P, holds not only a right but also a legal *obligation* to intervene, using all necessary means, including force as a last resort.[27] Endorsed unanimously by the UN General Assembly and invoked by the UN Security Council on multiple occasions,[28] R2P represents a significant normative shift towards recognising state obligations beyond borders. That said, scholars have expressed doubts over the legal status of the doctrine, referring to it as a political doctrine rather than a legally binding one.[29]

However, it remains contested whether the doctrine of R2P applies in the context of disasters.[30] The ICISS initially included disasters within its scope, referring to 'overwhelming natural or environmental catastrophes, where the state concerned is either unwilling or unable to cope or call for assistance, and significant loss of life is occurring or threatened'.[31] Yet, the UN General Assembly's endorsement of R2P restricted its application to four mass-atrocity crimes: genocide, war crimes, ethnic cleansing and crimes against humanity.[32] This limitation was later reinforced by then UN Secretary-General Ban Ki-moon, who explicitly excluded disasters from R2P's ambit:

> The responsibility to protect applies, until Member States decide otherwise, only to the four specified crimes and violations: genocide, war crimes, ethnic cleansing and crimes against humanity. To try to extend it to cover other calamities, such as HIV/AIDS, climate change or the response to natural disasters, would undermine the 2005 consensus and stretch the concept beyond recognition or operational utility.[33]

[27] ibid xi–xii. See also F Deng, 'From "Sovereignty as Responsibility" to the "Responsibility to Protect"' (2010) 2(4) *Global Responsibility to Protect* 353, 354–55. Any intervention based on the doctrine of R2P must be authorised by the UN Security Council, see ICISS (n 25) 50.

[28] UN General Assembly Res 60/1 (16 September 2005) UN Doc A/RES/60/1, paras 138–39. See also UN Security Council Res 1674 (28 April 2006) UN Doc S/RES/1674, para 4. For example, the UN Security Council alluded to the doctrine in the authorisation of the military intervention in Libya in 2011; see UN Security Council Res 1973 (17 March 2011) UN Doc S/RES/1973, preamble.

[29] R VanLandingham, 'Politics or Law: The Dual Nature of the Responsibility to Protect' (2012) 41(1) *Denver Journal of International Law and Policy* 63; S Bernstein, 'The Responsibility to Protect after Libya: Humanitarian Prevention as Customary International Law' (2012) 38(1) *Brooklyn Journal of International Law* 305.

[30] K Da Costa, 'R.I.P. R2P: On the Controversial "Responsibility to Protect" Doctrine and Why it Adds No Value to Disasters' in F Zorzi Giustiniani et al (eds), *Routledge Handbook of Human Rights and Disasters* (Routledge, 2018) 27; J Junk, 'Testing Boundaries: Cyclone Nargis in Myanmar and the Scope of R2P' (2016) 30(1) *Global Society* 78; SE Davies, 'Natural Disasters and the Responsibility to Protect' (2012) 55 *German Yearbook of International Law* 149; M Costas Trascasas, 'Access to the Territory of a Disaster-Affected State' in A de Guttry, M Gestri and G Venturini (eds), *International Disaster Response Law* (TMC Asser Press, 2012) 221; C Allan and T O'Donnell, 'A Call to Alms? Natural Disasters, R2P, Duties of Cooperation and Uncharted Consequences' (2012) 17(3) *Journal of Conflict and Security Law* 337; J Wong, 'Reconstructing the Responsibility to Protect in the Wake of Cyclones and Separatism' (2009) 84(2) *Tulane Law Review* 219; R Barber, 'The Responsibility to Protect the Survivors of Natural Disaster: Cyclone Nargis, a Case Study' (2009) 14(1) *Journal of Conflict and Security Law* 3.

[31] ICISS (n 25) 33.

[32] UN General Assembly Res 60/1 (n 28) paras 138–39.

[33] UN Secretary General, 'Integrated and Coordinated Implementation of and Follow-up to the Outcomes of the Major United Nations Conferences and Summits in the Economic, Social and Related Fields' (12 January 2009) UN Doc A/63/677, para 10(b).

However, scholars point out that even if disasters do not fall within the scope of R2P, the doctrine could become relevant if the affected state's refusal to seek or accept international assistance meets the definition of a crime against humanity.[34]

Despite questions about the scope of the doctrine, the aftermath of Cyclone Nargis in Myanmar saw some states allude to the invocation of R2P, suggesting that international intervention might be warranted if Myanmar persisted in rejecting much-needed external assistance.[35] France's Foreign Minister Bernard Kouchner stated publicly that France would explore 'whether we can implement the Responsibility to Protect [principle], given that food, boats and relief teams are there, and obtain a United Nations [Security Council] resolution which authorises the delivery [of aid] and imposes this on the Burmese government'.[36] Although these remarks did not culminate in intervention, the threat of invoking R2P exerted significant pressure on Myanmar's government to accept a diplomatic solution,[37] underscoring the doctrine's potential influence even beyond its formal scope.

Increased attention to extraterritorial obligations under IHRL is also relevant to the question of whether states bear responsibility for protecting disaster-affected persons beyond their borders. Traditionally, IHRL emphasised the relationship between a state and individuals within its territory, but globalisation, transnational activities and the cross-border effects of state conduct have challenged this territorial paradigm. While most human rights treaties limit obligations to individuals within a state's territory or jurisdiction,[38] the interpretation of 'jurisdiction' has expanded through case law and scholarly debate,[39] now recognising that states owe human rights obligations to persons outside their territory where they exercise 'effective control'.[40]

Building on these developments, some scholars argue that states may have extraterritorial obligations to provide humanitarian assistance wherever this is

[34] Barber (n 30) 18; Wong (n 30) 249; Davies (n 30) 162; da Costa (n 30) 32; S Ford, 'Is the Failure to Respond Appropriately to a Natural Disaster a Crime against Humanity? The Responsibility to Protect and Individual Criminal Responsibility in the Aftermath of Cyclone Nargis' (2010) 38(2) *Denver Journal of International Law and Policy* 227, 237; D Cubie, *The International Legal Protection of Persons in Humanitarian Crises: Exploring the Acquis Humanitaire* (Hart Publishing, 2017) 238.

[35] A Selth, 'Even Paranoids Have Enemies: Cyclone Nargis and Myanmar's Fears of Invasion' (2008) 30(3) *Contemporary Southeast Asia* 379, 390.

[36] As cited in ibid 390.

[37] ibid 391.

[38] See, eg, *International Covenant on Civil and Political Rights* (16 December 1966) art 2.

[39] See, eg, ETO Consortium, 'Maastricht Principles on Extraterritorial Obligations of States in the Area of Economic, Social and Cultural Rights' (2011) www.etoconsortium.org/en/the-maastricht-principles.

[40] UN Human Rights Committee, 'General Comment No. 31: The Nature of the General Legal Obligation Imposed on States Parties to the Covenant' (29 March 2004) CCPR/C/21/Rev.1/Add. 13, para 10; *Loizidou v Turkey* (1996) 21 EHRR 188, para 52; *Legal Consequences of the Construction of a Wall in the Occupied Palestinian Territory* (Advisory Opinion) [2004] ICJ Rep 136, para 112.

necessary to safeguard rights, including in disaster contexts. For example, Creta contends that:

> State obligations under [the right to humanitarian assistance] include not only obligations of individual action with regard to individuals within the affected State's jurisdiction (classical nexus rights/duties under human rights law), but also obligations of individual action with regard to individuals outside of the State's jurisdiction (role of third States in humanitarian emergency situations) and in certain cases also obligations of collective action at regional/global level.[41]

Others, such as Pietropaolo, refute this interpretation, asserting that: 'The only duty-bearer in relation to the right to humanitarian assistance would be affected States which would have the obligation to provide assistance to disaster-affected people.'[42]

However, despite these developments, accepting the notion that states have a responsibility to provide humanitarian assistance or protect persons affected by disasters outside their jurisdiction would be premature. Such a claim remains aspirational, lacking convincing legal authority under IHRL. Instead, the prevailing interpretation is that states are not directly responsible for the protection of disaster-affected populations beyond their borders – except for where they exercise effective control – but do have a duty to cooperate with affected states to uphold human rights and dignity. This interpretation is reflected in the comments of the CESCR, which does not impose extraterritorial obligations on states, but instead emphasises that:

> States parties have a joint and individual responsibility, in accordance with the Charter of the United Nations and relevant resolutions of the United Nations General Assembly and of the World Health Assembly, to cooperate in providing disaster relief and humanitarian assistance in times of emergency, including assistance to refugees and internally displaced persons. [43]

This interpretation accords with the auxiliary role of third states and assisting actors, placing the responsibility for protecting affected persons with the

[41] A Creta, 'A (Human) Right to Humanitarian Assistance in Disaster Situations? Surveying Public International Law' in A de Guttry, M Gestri and G Venturini (eds), *International Disaster Response Law* (TMC Asser Press, 2012) 353, 368. It should also be noted that the Guiding Principles on the Right to Humanitarian Assistance provide: 'The right to humanitarian assistance implies the right to request and to receive such assistance, as well as to participate in its practical implementation. Persons affected by an emergency may address themselves to competent national or international organizations and other potential donors to request humanitarian assistance': IIHL, 'Guiding Principles on the Right to Humanitarian Assistance' (1993) 33(297) *International Review of the Red Cross* 519 principle 2. See also principles 5–7.

[42] MG Pietropaolo, 'A Human Rights-Based Approach to Humanitarian Assistance: Current and Prospective Scenarios' (2016) 7(2) *Journal of International Humanitarian Legal Studies* 257, 287.

[43] CESCR, 'General Comment No. 14: The Right to the Highest Attainable Standard of Health' (11 May 2000) UN Doc E/C.12/2000/4, para 40. See also CESCR, 'General Comment No. 12: The Right to Adequate Food (Art. 11)' (12 May 1999) UN Doc E/C.12/1999/5, para 38.

affected state only; others play a complementary role in this framework by supporting affected states through consent-based cooperation.

This interpretation is consistent with the principle of solidarity. As argued, while solidarity envisages a shared responsibility, it does not entail that third states assume direct responsibility for the protection of persons affected by disasters beyond their jurisdiction.[44] Third states carry neither a primary nor a secondary responsibility for protection of those affected, even when the affected state is unable or unwilling to provide adequate protection. Instead, their role is limited to supporting the affected state through cooperation, respecting its primary role in disaster response. Imposing extraterritorial responsibilities on third states would dismantle this dual structure of responsibilities and fundamentally alter IDRL by rewriting the meaning of sovereignty in disaster response. The notion that third states carry direct or indirect responsibility for protection introduces a layer of conditionality: the affected state retains authority only so long as it is able and willing to fulfil its obligations. If it fails, responsibility may shift to other states. While such responsibility could, in theory, be exercised through cooperation rather than coercion, it opens the door to potential foreign intervention, particularly where the affected state resists external assistance. This interpretation would radically depart from the well-established principle of consent, undermine the principle of non-intervention and disregard consistent state practice that emphasises the primary role of affected states and the respect for state sovereignty and territorial integrity. For these reasons, it is likely to encounter strong resistance from states.

While third states are not directly responsible for the protection of disaster-affected populations, there is nonetheless a clear need to strengthen and expand the duty to cooperate so as to give effect to their shared responsibility. As argued, this requires developing both rights and duties for third states that enable and compel them to engage in cooperation with affected states where necessary.[45] The following two subsections examine two such elements: first, the right of to offer unsolicited assistance as a means of initiating cooperation (section III.B), and second, the duty to provide such assistance when needed (section III.C).

B. The Right to Offer Assistance

Many treaties and soft law instruments prescribe a formal process whereby states affected by disasters request assistance, typically once it becomes clear that their national response capacity is overwhelmed.[46] This approach aims to structure

[44] This argument has been developed in ch 2, section III.
[45] See ch 4, section III.B.
[46] See, eg, Tampere Convention (n 3) art 4; Nuclear Accident Convention (n 8) art 2; AADMER (n 3) art 11; Inter-American Convention (n 3) art II; BSEC Agreement (n 3) art 4; Shanghai Agreement (n 3) art 3; SAARC Agreement (n 12) art VIII; EU Civil Protection Mechanism (n 3) art 15.

and facilitate international disaster response, moving away from unpredictable and chaotic ad hoc practices. In reality, however, the practice is often less orderly: time pressure, media coverage and geopolitical interests can create dynamics in which states and assisting actors offer help before any formal request has been made.[47] Notably, such offers are frequently accompanied by declarations of solidarity with affected populations.[48] This subsection examines the extent to which IDRL recognises a right to offer unsolicited assistance and argues that such a right would constitute an expression of solidarity – a means for states and assisting actors to initiate cooperation.

Despite the widespread practice of states and assisting actors offering unsolicited assistance, the legal status of a right to offer remains unsettled under IDRL.[49] Unlike IHL, which expressly recognises the humanitarian initiative of the International Committee of the Red Cross (ICRC) and other impartial humanitarian organisations in armed conflicts,[50] IDRL has not developed an equivalent right as a matter of positive law. No treaty explicitly codifies a right to offer assistance and such a right has not crystallised as a norm of customary international law either. Although offers of assistance are common, there is no evidence of *opinio juris* indicating that states perceive making such offers as a legal entitlement; instead, states and assisting actors appear to do so out of humanitarian concern.[51]

In fact, a number of treaties and soft law instruments suggest that assistance may only be offered following a formal request made by the affected state.[52] For instance, UN General Assembly Resolution 46/182 notes that 'humanitarian assistance should be provided with the consent of the affected country and in principle on the basis of an appeal by the affected country'.[53] The IDRL Guidelines also indicate that: 'Disaster relief or initial recovery assistance should

[47] Fisher (n 11) 91; S Jansen-Wilhelm, *Accepting Assistance in the Aftermath of Disasters: Standards for States under International Law* (Intersentia, 2015) 88.

[48] See examples in ch 3, section IV.B.

[49] ILC, 'Memorandum by the Secretariat on the Protection of Persons in the Event of Disasters' (11 December 2007) UN Doc A/CN.4/590, para 64.

[50] Common art 3 in *Geneva Convention for the Amelioration of the Condition of the Wounded in Armies in the Field* (12 August 1949); *Geneva Convention for the Amelioration of the Condition of Wounded, Sick and Shipwrecked Members of Armed Forces at Sea* (12 August 1949); *Geneva Convention Relative to the Protection of Civilian Persons in Time of War* (12 August 1949); *Geneva Convention Relative to the Treatment of Prisoners of War* (12 August 1949). See also *Protocol Additional (I) to the Geneva Conventions of 12 August 1949, and Relating to the Protection of Victims of International Armed Conflicts* (8 June 1977) art 81; *Protocol additional (II) to the Geneva Conventions of 12 August 1949, and Relating to the Protection of Victims of Non-international Armed Conflicts* (8 June 1977) art 18.

[51] This impression can be inferred from statements made by states, such as discussed in ch 3, section IV.

[52] See, eg, Nuclear Accident Convention (n 8) art 2; Inter-American Convention (n 3) art 2; ACS Agreement (n 10) art 4; BSEC Agreement (n 3) art 3(2); Shanghai Agreement (n 3) art 2(2).

[53] UN General Assembly Res 46/182 (n 3) para 3.

be initiated only with the consent of the affected State and in principle, on the basis of an appeal.'[54]

That said, most treaties and soft law instruments leave open the option for states and assisting actors to make unsolicited offers of assistance on their own initiative.[55] For instance, the AADMER specifies that '[a]ssistance can only be deployed at the request, and with the consent, of the Requesting Party, or, *when offered by another Party or Parties*, with the consent of the Receiving Party',[56] suggesting that state parties may offer assistance even in the absence of a formal request. It could also be argued that a right to offer assistance can be inferred from the modalities for requesting and offering assistance set up in certain treaties.[57] For example, the *Inter-American Convention to Facilitate Disaster Assistance* stipulates that: 'Requests for and offers and acceptance of assistance from one state party to another shall be communicated via diplomatic channels or the National Coordinating Authority, as the circumstances may warrant.'[58] While this language does not create an explicit right, it suggests that state parties are free to make offers if they choose.

The ILC chose to explicitly recognise the possibility of offering assistance in its Draft Articles as an acknowledgement of 'the interest of the international community in the protection of persons in the event of disasters, which is to be viewed as complementary to the primary role of the affected State enshrined in draft article 10'.[59] Draft Article 12(1) provides: 'In the event of disasters, States, the United Nations, and other potential assisting actors may offer assistance to the affected State.'[60] However, earlier drafts of this provision which framed extending offers as a right were contentious. While some states supported this framing,[61] others objected, viewing offers of assistance as

[54] IDRL Guidelines (n 1) art 10(1).

[55] ILC (n 49) para 64. See, eg, Draft Articles (n 1) art 12(1); UN Economic and Social Council, 'Guiding Principles on Internal Displacement' (11 February 1998) UN Doc E/CN.4/1998/53/Add.2, principle 25(2); IDI (n 9) art IV(1); JM Ebersole, 'Mohonk Criteria for Humanitarian Assistance in Complex Emergencies' (1995) 4(3) *Disaster Prevention and Management* 14, 19.

[56] AADMER (n 3) art 11(2) (emphasis added).

[57] ILC, 'Fourth Report on the Protection of Persons in the Event of Disasters, by Mr. Eduardo Valencia-Ospina, Special Rapporteur' (11 May 2011) UN Doc A/CN.4/643, paras 88–91.

[58] Inter-American Convention (n 3) art II(a).

[59] ILC, 'Commentaries on the Draft Articles on the Protection of Persons in the Event of Disasters' (2016) UN Doc A/71/10, 57.

[60] Draft Articles (n 1) art 12(1).

[61] Slovenia in UN General Assembly Sixth Committee, 'Summary Record of the 20th Meeting' (23 November 2011) UN Doc A/C.6/66/SR.20, para 12; Finland (on behalf of the Nordic states) in UN General Assembly Sixth Committee, 'Summary Record of the 21st Meeting' (2 December 2011) UN Doc A/C.6/66/SR.21, para 60; the Czech Republic and Austria in UN General Assembly Sixth Committee, 'Summary Record of the 23rd Meeting' (14 November 2011) UN Doc A/C.6/66/SR.23 paras 19, 25; Russia in UN General Assembly Sixth Committee, 'Summary Record of the 24th Meeting' (1 December 2011) UN Doc A/C.6/66/SR.24, para 37; Romania in UN General Assembly Sixth Committee, 'Summary Record of the 25th Meeting' (9 December 2011) UN Doc A/C.6/66/SR.25, para 19; France in UN General Assembly Sixth Committee, 'Summary Record of the 19th Meeting' (4 December 2012) UN Doc A/C.6/67/SR.19, para 95; Poland in UN General Assembly Sixth Committee, 'Summary Record of the 24th Meeting' (20 November 2013) UN Doc A/C.6/68/SR.24, para 107.

an aspect of international cooperation rather than an assertion of rights.[62] For example, Israel argued that: 'The role of third parties in offering assistance to affected States should be defined on the basis of international cooperation, not as an assertion of rights.'[63] Ultimately, the ILC removed the term 'right' and adopted more neutral language, stating that states and other actors 'may offer' assistance. According to Special Rapporteur Valencia-Ospina, this formulation ensures that states and others can offer assistance regardless of the legal grounds for doing so.[64]

Notably, the Draft Articles extend the possibility of offering assistance beyond states to include 'the United Nations, and other potential assisting actors',[65] such as (regional) international organisations, the Red Cross Movement and NGOs, provided they are mandated to do so under their respective constitutive instruments.[66] This approach is relatively unique compared to most treaties and soft law instruments, but reflects common practice, where non-state actors play a central role in delivering assistance to affected states.[67] The ILC further emphasises that 'the position of non-governmental organizations or entities in carrying out relief operations is not a novelty in international law', drawing parallels to the recognised right of humanitarian organisations to offer aid under IHL.[68] Similarly, the UN General Assembly has consistently acknowledged the vital role of non-state actors in disaster response, urging states to 'facilitate the work of [such] organizations in implementing humanitarian assistance, in particular the supply of food, medicines and health care, for which access to victims is essential'.[69] Yet, some states remained sceptical, resisting the ILC's approach

[62] Singapore and Poland in UN General Assembly Sixth Committee, 'Summary Record of the 21st Meeting' (n 61) paras 75, 86; Pakistan in UN General Assembly Sixth Committee, 'Summary Record of the 25th Meeting' (n 61) para 7.

[63] Israel in UN General Assembly Sixth Committee, 'Summary Record of the 23rd Meeting' (n 61) para 33.

[64] ILC, 'Eighth Report on the Protection of Persons in the Event of Disasters, by Mr. Eduardo Valencia-Ospina, Special Rapporteur' (17 March 2016) UN Doc A/CN.4/697, para 315.

[65] Draft Articles (n 1) art 12(1).

[66] ILC (n 59) 57.

[67] However, some instruments permit international organisations to offer assistance. For example, when it receives information of an event that may constitute a public health emergency of international concern, the World Health Organization (WHO) 'shall offer to collaborate with the State Party concerned in assessing the potential for international disease spread, possible interference with international traffic and the adequacy of control measures': *International Health Regulations (2005)* (23 May 2005) art 10(3). Some soft law instruments also extend the right to offer assistance to non-state actors. For example: 'National authorities, national and international organizations whose statutory mandates provide for the possibility of rendering humanitarian assistance, such as the ICRC, UNHCR, other organizations of the UN system, and professional humanitarian organizations, have the right to offer such assistance when the conditions laid down in the present Principles are fulfilled': IIHL (n 41) principle 5. Similarly: 'International humanitarian organizations and other appropriate actors have the right to offer their services in support of the internally displaced': UN Economic and Social Council (n 55) principle 25(2). See also Cubie (n 34) 323.

[68] ILC (n 59) 57.

[69] UN General Assembly Res 43/131 (8 December 1988) UN Doc A/RES/43/131, para 4; UN General Assembly Res 46/182 (n 3) para 6.

of treating states, international organisations and NGOs on the same juridical footing.[70] Germany, for example, raised the point that 'the draft article's formulation gave the impression that it conferred international rights directly on non-governmental organizations'.[71]

Furthermore, it must be stressed that the right to offer assistance does not equate to a duty to provide assistance. As the ILC clarified in its commentaries, 'offers, whether made unilaterally or in response to a request, are essentially voluntary and should not be construed as recognition of the existence of a legal duty to assist'.[72] Equally, an offer of assistance does not impose on the affected state a corresponding obligation to accept it.[73] In line with the principle of consent, the affected state retains discretion to accept offers in whole or in part or to decline them entirely,[74] allowing states to selectively accept assistance based on their needs and priorities.[75]

However, offers of assistance ought not be regarded as an unfriendly act or interference in the affected state's internal affairs when they are made in accordance with the humanitarian principles of humanity, neutrality and impartiality.[76] This position aligns with the ICJ's judgment in the *Nicaragua* case, where it held that:

> There can be no doubt that the provision of strictly humanitarian aid to persons or forces in another country, whatever their political affiliations or objectives, cannot be regarded as unlawful intervention, or as in any other way contrary to international law.[77]

By extension, an offer of strictly humanitarian aid cannot be considered unlawful interference. Consequently, the affected state must consider such offers in good faith, communicating its response in a timely manner.[78] It should also be recalled that the affected state must not withhold consent arbitrarily.[79]

While the right to offer assistance has not yet crystallised as a matter of positive law, it should be recognised if IDRL is developed against the background of solidarity. In many ways, the right to offer assistance is the counterpart to the affected state's duty to seek international assistance (see Chapter 5, section III.B).

[70] ILC (n 64) para 306.
[71] ibid.
[72] ILC (n 59) 57.
[73] ibid.
[74] Provided that withholding consent is not arbitrary; see ch 5, section III.C.
[75] For example, Morocco chose to accept some offers of international assistance while rejecting others, claiming that this was necessary to control a manageable influx of aid: 'Morocco Earthquake: Why Authorities Accepted Limited Foreign Aid' *Al Jazeera* (12 September 2023) www.aljazeera.com/news/2023/9/12/is-morocco-accepting-aid-certain-countries-political-reasons.
[76] Civil Defence Assistance Convention (n 12) art 3(b); UN Economic and Social Council (n 55) principle 25(2); IIHL (n 41) principle 5; ILC (n 59) 57.
[77] *Military and Paramilitary Activities in and against Nicaragua (Nicaragua v United States of America)* (Judgment) [1986] ICJ Rep 14, para 242.
[78] Draft Articles (n 1) art 13(3).
[79] ibid art 13(2).

Just as the duty to seek assistance is a critical link that activates the shared responsibility of all states – enabling others to support the affected state when needed – the right to offer should be understood as a means for states to initiate solidarity-based cooperation.[80] Therefore, an offer is 'an expression of the principles of solidarity and cooperation',[81] signalling a willingness to cooperate in protecting disaster-affected populations. Special Rapporteur Valencia-Ospina underscored this interpretation by describing offers of assistance as 'the practical manifestation of solidarity'.[82] Beyond this symbolic significance, the right to offer assistance also fits logically within a solidarity-based reinterpretation of IDRL, providing states and assisting actors with an instrument to take initiative in commencing cooperation. Where a state or assisting actor believes that support is needed, it should be able to offer it as an expression of its shared responsibility for the protection of those affected by disaster. However, this does not imply that the affected state must accept such offers; consent remains essential, though states' discretion to withhold consent may be subject to certain limitations.[83]

Further, the right to offer assistance should indeed extend beyond states to include non-state actors such as competent (regional) international organisations, the Red Cross Movement and NGOs active in disaster response as proposed in the Draft Articles. These actors share the common goal of protecting persons affected by disasters and are often among the first to mobilise in their aftermath. To enable them to express solidarity effectively, they should be able to offer assistance to affected states on the same terms as states. Such offers must adhere to humanitarian principles and remain subject to the consent of the affected state. Extending the right to offer assistance to non-state actors also follows precedent established in IHL and can therefore be done without prejudice to established principles regarding the legal personality of non-state actors, in particular that of NGOs that are, in principle, not capable of possessing rights under international law.[84] Granting non-state actors the ability to offer assistance in disaster contexts does not need to confer full legal personality, but rather acknowledges their practical role in expressing solidarity and initiating cooperation with affected states.[85]

[80] T O'Donnell and C Allan, 'A Duty of Solidarity? The International Law Commission's Draft Articles and the Right to Offer Assistance in Disasters' in S Breau and K Samuel (eds), *Research Handbook on Disasters and International Law* (Edward Elgar, 2016) 453.

[81] ILC (n 59) 57.

[82] ILC (n 57) para 84. See also ILC (n 59) 57.

[83] As discussed in ch 5, section III.C.

[84] C Walter, 'Subjects of International Law' in *Max Planck Encyclopedia of International Law* (Oxford University Press, 2007) para 6.

[85] Walter (ibid) also describes that the NGOs are increasingly granted rights to be consulted under international law, suggesting that there is room to include NGOs in consultative processes without granting them full international legal personality.

C. The Duty to Assist

If states and assisting actors have a right to offer assistance, the logical question that follows is: to what extent may they have a duty to provide such assistance? However, the duty to assist under IDRL is highly controversial and has 'not yet definitively materialized as a matter of positive law at the global level'.[86] While some states have agreed to mutual obligations to provide assistance through bilateral and multilateral disaster response agreements,[87] no such duty exists in global treaties or soft law instruments, including the Draft Articles and the IDRL Guidelines.[88] Nor has it emerged as a norm of customary international law, given the absence of both consistent state practice and *opinio juris*.[89] In fact, a binding duty to assist runs counter to the principle of voluntarism that has long dominated international cooperation in disaster response. As demonstrated in Chapter 3, section IV, the provision of assistance is typically understood as a voluntary act by states, motivated by humanitarian concern or a moral sense of doing what is right rather than by any perceived legal obligation.

The ILC ultimately decided not to include a duty to assist in its Draft Articles, as the topic proved highly contentious.[90] A few states and ILC members expressed sympathy towards recognising a positive duty to provide assistance as a complementary counterpart to the duty of the affected state to seek assistance.[91] One ILC member also highlighted the apparent asymmetry under the Draft Articles: the affected state's position is primarily characterised by obligations, whereas third states enjoy rights, such as the right to offer assistance,

[86] ILC (n 49) para 61.

[87] See, eg, BSEC Agreement (n 3) art 3(3); *Convention on Mutual Assistance between French and Spanish Fire and Emergency Services* (14 July 1959) art I(2); *Agreement between Denmark, Finland, Norway and Sweden on Cooperation across State Frontiers to Prevent or Limit Damage to Persons or Property or to the Environment in the Case of Accidents* (20 January 1989) art 2; *Convention between the Government of the French Republic and the Government of the Kingdom of Belgium on Mutual Assistance in the Event of Disasters or Serious Accidents* (21 April 1981) art 1(1); *Agreement on Cooperation between the Kingdom of Spain and the Argentine Republic on Disaster Preparedness and Prevention and Mutual Assistance in the Event of Disasters* (3 June 1988) art IX; *Convention between the Kingdom of Denmark and the Federal Republic of Germany on Mutual Assistance in the Event of Disasters or Serious Accidents* (16 May 1985) art 1(1). See also ILC (n 49) para 63.

[88] ILC (n 49) para 61.

[89] E Valencia-Ospina, 'The Work of the International Law Commission on the "Protection of Persons in the Event of Disasters"' (2019) 1(1) *Yearbook of International Disaster Law* 5, 14; M Eburn, 'International Law and Disaster Response' (2010) 36 *Monash University Law Review* 162, 167,170.

[90] ILC (n 59) 57; Valencia-Ospina (n 89) 14.

[91] See, eg, Poland in UN General Assembly Sixth Committee, 'Summary Record of the 21st Meeting' (n 61) para 86; Hungary in UN General Assembly Sixth Committee, 'Summary Record of the 24th Meeting' (n 61) para 59; Sri Lanka in UN General Assembly Sixth Committee, 'Summary Record of the 27th Meeting' (8 December 2011) UN Doc A/C.6/66/SR.27, para 20; Thailand in UN General Assembly Sixth Committee, 'Summary Record of the 19th Meeting' (n 61) para 40.

without corresponding duties.[92] He critiqued this lack of parallelism, noting that 'affected States have duties while third States have rights, but the reverse is not true'.[93] He argued that this gap could be rectified 'by also providing duties on third States and rights for the affected States'.[94]

Yet, the majority of ILC members as well as states – and some non-state actors – opposed this idea, seeking to preserve the principle of voluntarism traditionally guiding international cooperation in disaster response.[95] Opponents argued that such a duty lacks any foundation in treaty law or customary international law and is inconsistent with the historically voluntary nature of international cooperation in disaster response.[96] States also rejected the interpretation that a duty to assist flows from the broader duty to cooperate.[97] For example, Mexico asserted that 'the duty to cooperate should generally not be construed as an obligation to provide assistance but rather as an obligation to consider requests for assistance from the affected State, without there being a duty to accede to such requests'.[98]

Despite this opposition, the notion of a duty to assist those in need is not foreign to international law. Certain regimes recognise obligations to provide assistance to individuals in distress when actors are in a position to help. For example, the law of the sea imposes a duty on shipmasters to render assistance to vessels or persons in distress at sea,[99] and international space law establishes a duty to assist astronauts who land in foreign territory or otherwise find themselves in peril.[100]

[92] Tladi (n 2) 450.

[93] ibid.

[94] ibid 451.

[95] See generally ILC (n 64) paras 304–05. Comments by individual states include Slovenia in UN General Assembly Sixth Committee, 'Summary Record of the 20th Meeting' (n 61) para 12; Singapore and Italy in UN General Assembly Sixth Committee, 'Summary Record of the 21st Meeting' (n 61) paras 76, 91; Mexico and Colombia in UN General Assembly Sixth Committee, 'Summary Record of the 22nd Meeting' (1 December 2011) UN Doc A/C.6/66/SR.22, paras 21, 28; Austria, Germany, United Kingdom, the Netherlands and Spain in UN General Assembly Sixth Committee, 'Summary Record of the 23rd Meeting' (n 61) paras 23, 28, 45, 48, 50; Hungary and Malaysia in UN General Assembly Sixth Committee, 'Summary Record of the 24th Meeting' (n 61) paras 59, 120–21; Ireland in UN General Assembly Sixth Committee, 'Summary Record of the 25th Meeting' (n 61) para 21; Greece in UN General Assembly Sixth Committee, 'Summary Record of the 19th Meeting' (n 61) para 56. The Food and Agriculture Organization (FAO) submitted the view that the 'obligation to cooperate did not amount to a general duty to provide assistance': ILC (n 64) para 154.

[96] ILC, 'Fifth Report on the Protection of Persons in the Event of Disasters, by Mr. Eduardo Valencia-Ospina, Special Rapporteur' (9 April 2012) UN Doc A/CN.4/652, para 52.

[97] ibid paras 44–45.

[98] Mexico in UN General Assembly Sixth Committee, 'Summary Record of the 22nd Meeting' (n 95) para 21.

[99] *United Nations Convention on the Law of the Sea* (10 December 1982) art 98; *International Convention for the Safety of Life at Sea* (1 November 1974) reg V-33. See also I Papanicolopulu, 'The Duty to Rescue at Sea, in Peacetime and in War: A General Overview' (2016) 98(202) *International Review of the Red Cross* 491, 494.

[100] *Agreement on the Rescue of Astronauts, the Return of Astronauts and the Return of Objects Launched into Outer Space* (19 December 1967) art 2.

A duty to assist is not far-fetched under IHRL either. Core human rights – such as the right to life, the right to health and the right to an adequate standard of living – impose positive obligations on states to take measures to protect individuals from foreseeable threats, including disasters.[101] The ICESCR requires states to act 'individually and through international assistance and cooperation' to realise these rights,[102] creating a duty to cooperate.[103] When an affected state lacks the capacity to fulfil these obligations alone, international cooperation becomes essential. The CESCR has explained that in these situations, it is not only for the affected state to take action by seeking international assistance, but that all states have 'a joint and individual responsibility . . . to cooperate in providing disaster relief and humanitarian assistance in times of emergency, including assistance to refugees and internally displaced persons'.[104] Although the CESCR stops short of recognising a binding duty to assist, this interpretation suggests that providing assistance is not merely voluntary, but should be understood as a means of fulfilling obligations under IHRL. This interpretation is sensible, as leaving cooperation entirely voluntary would effectively undermine the duty to cooperate and could possibly threaten the realisation of human rights.

While it may be premature to conclude that a duty to assist exists under IHRL – given the lack of convincing legal authority – the CESCR's interpretation nonetheless challenges the traditional emphasis on voluntarism in IDRL. Rather than framing international assistance as a purely humanitarian gesture, it situates the provision of assistance within a framework of human rights, shared responsibilities and international cooperation. This perspective also nuances the criticism that a duty to assist would lack any foundation in law,[105] as such a duty is not entirely far-fetched and finds a normative basis in international law. These precedents demonstrate that international law can and does impose positive obligations to assist in situations of urgent need, opening the door for meaningfully considering a duty to assist in the context of disasters.

A duty to assist would be critical for implementing the principle of solidarity within IDRL. As argued in Chapter 4, section III.D, solidarity envisages a binding duty to cooperate for all states, which lies at its very core: states have a shared responsibility to support those unable to fulfil their own obligations in pursuit of common objectives. Providing assistance when the affected state cannot adequately protect disaster-affected populations is essential to realising

[101] *Budayeva and Others v Russia* App Nos 15339/02, 21166/02, 20058/02, 11673/02 and 15343/02 (European Court of Human Rights, 20 March 2008), para 128; UN Human Rights Committee, 'General Comment No. 36 on Article 6: Right to Life' (3 September 2019) UN Doc CCPR/C/GC/36, para 26.

[102] *International Covenant on Economic, Social and Cultural Rights* (16 December 1966) art 2(1).

[103] CESCR, 'General Comment No. 3: The Nature of States Parties' Obligations (Art. 2, Para. 1, of the C[illegible] '14 December 1990) UN Doc E/1991/23, para 14.

[illegible] neral Comment No. 14' (n 43) para 40. See also CESCR, 'General Comment No. 12'

[illegible] ra 52.

this shared responsibility; without such cooperation, solidarity cannot be meaningfully realised. In this context, the provision of assistance cannot be treated as exclusively voluntary, but needs to be understood as an obligation grounded in a shared responsibility of all states for the protection of people affected by disasters.

The duty to assist should be understood primarily as an obligation to make an offer of assistance to the affected state.[106] These offers remain subject to the consent of the affected state, although its discretion to withhold consent is limited when its national response capacities are overwhelmed.[107] Interpreted in this way, the duty to assist operates as an elaboration of the broader duty to cooperate and must not be misconstrued as a veiled mandate to intervene. Offers of assistance should further be strictly humanitarian in character and states must ensure that the proposed assistance is appropriate, adequate and delivered in accordance with international law standards, including the humanitarian principles.[108] Furthermore, offers must be non-transactional: the affected state should not be expected to reciprocate, reimburse or compensate for assistance received, unless agreed otherwise.[109] Assistance does not create a debt; rather, it reflects solidarity among states in pursuit of the common objective of protecting disaster-affected persons.

Importantly, a solidarity-based duty to assist in international disaster response should be understood as a qualified obligation, applying only to the extent that the affected state's national response capacities are overwhelmed. As explained in Chapter 4, section III.E, solidarity is inherently differentiating: it presumes that affected states will first mobilise their own resources to address disasters. This reinforces their primary responsibility, ensuring that the duty to assist does not transform disaster response into a collective enterprise of all states, and prevent states with sufficient capacities from seeking assistance unnecessarily. The provision of assistance thus becomes an expectation only when the state cannot ensure adequate protection within its jurisdiction. This interpretation also aligns with the corresponding duty of the affected state to seek international assistance, which likewise arises only when its national capacities prove insufficient (see Chapter 5, section III.B). This qualification to the duty to assist not only puts less pressure on states to provide assistance, but

[106] It should be noted that while assisting non-state actors can possess a right to offer assistance following precedent in international law, conferring a corresponding duty to assist is more complex given the lack of full international legal personality of non-state actors: Walter (n 84) paras 5–6. For this reason, ch 4, section III.B argued that, for the time being, a duty to assist for non-state actors may remain a non-binding obligation, reflecting their essential role in disaster response without imposing formal legal responsibilities under international law.

[107] As discussed in ch 5, section III.C.

[108] Draft Articles (n 1) art 6; IDRL Guidelines (n 1) art 4(2); UN General Assembly Res 46/182 (n 3) para 2. See also ILC (n 59) 57.

[109] Neuhold (n 20) 193–94; D Campanelli, 'Principle of Solidarity' in *Max Planck Encyclopedia of International Law* (Oxford University Press, 2011) para 9; L Boisson de Chazournes, 'Responsibility to Protect: Reflecting Solidarity?' in Wolfrum and Kojima (n 20) 93, 96.

it also ensures that cooperation and assistance come first and foremost to the benefit of states that need additional support. In doing so, the solidarity-based duty to assist fulfils its true purpose of addressing structural inequalities that leave some states better equipped than others to protect their populations in the event of disaster, ultimately advancing the cause of international social justice.[110]

Solidarity also differentiates the expectations placed on assisting states by recognising that states possess varying capacities to provide assistance.[111] In light of these de facto inequalities, solidarity requires that assistance be provided commensurate to each state's ability to do so.[112] Consequently, some states will inevitably contribute more than others: those with greater resources and capabilities are expected to shoulder a larger share of responsibility.[113] This differentiated approach not only reflects practical realities but also advances social justice among states by ameliorating structural inequalities that leave certain states better positioned to assist.[114] In this way, solidarity operates as both a principle of cooperation and a mechanism for redistributive justice and equity in international disaster response.

This differentiation also finds precedent in international law. The few agreements that explicitly impose a duty to assist consistently link that obligation to the respective capacities of states.[115] For example, the BSEC Agreement stipulates that '[t]he Parties shall render one another assistance according [to] their possibilities'.[116] Similarly, UN human rights treaty bodies have affirmed that the levels of cooperation are differentiated among states under IHRL. The CESCR, for instance, has repeatedly observed that while all states share a joint responsibility to cooperate in providing disaster relief and humanitarian assistance during emergencies, 'each State should contribute to this task to the maximum of its capacities' and that 'the economically developed States parties have a special responsibility and interest to assist the poorer developing States in this regard'.[117] These interpretations underscore that states with greater resources and capabilities are expected to shoulder a larger share of responsibility, consistent with solidarity's purpose of reducing structural inequalities and advancing international social justice.

While the idea of differentiating the duty to assist works well as a general theory, its practical application is far more complex. It remains unclear how to

[110] Wolfrum (n 21) 87.
[111] As argued in ch 4, section III.E.
[112] Wolfrum (n 21) 396.
[113] ibid.
[114] ibid 87.
[115] See, eg, Convention on Mutual Assistance between France and Spain (n 87) art I(2); Agreement between Denmark, Finland, Norway and Sweden (n 87) art 2; Convention between France and Belgium (n 87) art 1(1); Agreement between Spain and Argentina (n 87) art IX; Convention between Denmark and Germany (n 87) art 1(1).
[116] BSEC Agreement (n 3) art 3(3).
[117] CESCR, 'General Comment No. 14' (n 43) para 40. See also CESCR, 'General Comment No. 12' (n 43) para 38.

determine which states must provide assistance and to what extent. International law offers several models for differentiating obligations, most notably under international climate change law through the principle of common but differentiated responsibilities.[118] For example, the *Kyoto Protocol to the United Nations Framework Convention on Climate Change* adopted a binary differentiation model, whereby a predetermined group of industrialised states agreed to undertake more stringent CO_2 emission reductions than others.[119] By contrast, the *Paris Agreement* introduced a mechanism of self-differentiation, allowing states to set their own nationally determined contributions.[120]

In the context of disasters, a degree of self-differentiation would be appropriate, as each state is best placed to assess whether and to what extent it can assist. This approach introduces flexibility, recognising that a state's capacity to assist may fluctuate over time; for instance, states that are themselves affected by a disaster or have recently endured one may temporarily be less able to help others. Moreover, self-differentiation aligns with the spirit of solidarity. By contrast, objectively specifying the level of assistance expected from each state would risk undermining the non-transactional nature of solidarity, effectively creating a 'scoreboard' of contributions and obligations. At the same time, self-differentiation comes with a responsibility: states must evaluate their capacity to assist in good faith, based on factual circumstances rather than political interests or convenience. This requires trust that states will honestly calibrate their obligations to cooperate, ensuring that solidarity remains genuine rather than performative.

This raises a potential obstacle to implementing a duty to assist in IDRL: the extent to which states will comply in practice. In the absence of compliance or enforcement mechanisms within IDRL, the effectiveness of such a duty depends largely on states' willingness to provide assistance. Optimists might point to the consistent practice of states and assisting actors offering generous support in the aftermath of disasters as evidence of a general readiness to assist. Indeed, history shows that even states with long-standing political or ideological differences have often set aside their disputes to cooperate in disaster response efforts.[121]

However, there remains a persistent gap between the assistance states claim they are willing to provide and what they actually deliver. The catastrophic floods in Pakistan in 2022 illustrate this disparity. Triggered by heavier-than-usual

[118] See generally E Hey, 'Common But Differentiated Responsibilities' in *Max Planck Encyclopedia of International Law* (Oxford University Press, 2011).

[119] *Kyoto Protocol to the United Nations Framework Convention on Climate Change* (11 December 1997).

[120] *Paris Agreement* (12 December 2015) art 3. See also C Voigt and F Ferreira, 'Differentiation in the Paris Agreement' (2016) 6(1–2) *Climate Law* 58, 65.

[121] T Nelson, 'Rejecting the Gift Horse: International Politics of Disaster Aid Refusal' (2010) 10(3) *Conflict, Security & Development* 379, 382; C Allan and T O'Donnell, 'An Offer You Cannot Refuse: Natural Disasters, the Politics of Aid Refusal and Potential Legal Implications' (2013) 5(1) *Amsterdam Law Forum* 36, 41. See generally I Kelman, *Disaster Diplomacy* (Routledge, 2012).

monsoon rains and melting glaciers linked to climate change,[122] the floods submerged over one-third of the country and left more than 20 million people in need of humanitarian assistance.[123] The international community quickly rallied in support. In a resolution, the UN General Assembly conveyed 'full solidarity and sympathy with the people of Pakistan' and urged the international community 'to extend full support and assistance to the Government of Pakistan in its efforts to mitigate the adverse impacts of the floods and to meet the medium- and long-term rehabilitation and reconstruction needs'.[124] Yet, initial pledges covered only about 10 per cent of the estimated funding required.[125] Even after a UN-led fundraising push, total pledges for reconstruction and recovery still fell short by nearly half of the target amount.[126] This example reflects a broader systemic problem of underfunded humanitarian assistance programmes: a record-breaking funding gap of US$29.7 billion for UN-coordinated humanitarian appeals was reported in 2023.[127] Assistance shortfalls are particularly acute for localised, 'silent' or slow-onset disasters that fail to attract the same media attention and political urgency that other major sudden-onset disasters do. Moreover, this funding gap is expected to widen drastically as top government donors – in particular, the US under the Trump administration – have cut international humanitarian funding. It is predicted that in 2025, 'the public funding available for humanitarian action could contract by between 34% and 45% by the end of the year compared to 2023 levels'.[128]

Concerns over the genuine willingness of states to assist also echo broader doubts about the promise of solidarity in international law. Den Heijer and van der Wilt highlight the fact that 'there is a huge gap between the language of solidarity and state practice'.[129] Although states like to proclaim their commitment to act in solidarity, their track records show that they often fail to follow through. States tend to retreat from their promises when fulfilling them requires significant sacrifices or a reprioritisation of national interests. Notable examples

[122] B Clarke, F Otto and L Harrington, 'Pakistan Floods: What Role Did Climate Change Play?' *The Conversation* (3 September 2022) https://theconversation.com/pakistan-floods-what-role-did-climate-change-play-189833.

[123] OCHA, 'Revised Pakistan 2022 Floods Response Plan: 01 Sep 2022–31 May 2023' (4 October 2022) 2.

[124] UN General Assembly Res 77/1 (7 October 2022) UN Doc A/RES/77/1, paras 1 and 4.

[125] A Shahzad, 'Pakistan out of Money for Flood Recovery, UN Boosts Aid Request – Minister' *Reuters* (5 October 2022) www.reuters.com/world/asia-pacific/pakistan-says-no-space-give-economy-any-stimulus-2022-10-04.

[126] 'Donors Pledge More than $9bn for Pakistan Flood Recovery' *Al Jazeera* (9 January 2023) www.aljazeera.com/news/2023/1/9/flood-hit-pakistan-hosts-climate-resilience-meet-with-un-for-aid.

[127] Active Learning Network for Accountability and Performance, 'Global Humanitarian Assistance Report 2025' (2025) https://alnap.org/help-library/resources/global-humanitarian-assistance-gha-report-2025, 13. This data also includes assistance in humanitarian crises caused by other factors than disasters, such as armed conflicts and displacement.

[128] ibid vii.

[129] M den Heijer and H van der Wilt, 'Global Solidarity and Common but Differentiated Responsibilities' in M den Heijer and H van der Wilt (eds), *Netherlands Yearbook of International Law 2020* (TMC Asser Press, 2022) 3, 4.

include the failure to realise the long-promised fund to support developing countries in adapting to climate change, despite repeated commitments,[130] and the global response to the COVID-19 pandemic, where rhetoric of solidarity was undermined by vaccine nationalism and the inability to ensure equitable distribution of vaccines and other resources.[131]

Ultimately, the question of whether states will comply with a duty to assist comes down to whether they are sufficiently incentivised to do so. The mere promise of acting in solidarity appears to be not enough. As discussed in Chapter 2, section III, states are generally less inclined to provide support purely out of altruism.[132] By contrast, framing cooperation and assistance as necessary to achieve common objectives and as a shared responsibility may offer a stronger incentive. Echoing Durkheim's theory of organic solidarity,[133] states may be willing to cooperate without expecting anything in return when they recognise the interdependence between states that makes mutual support a condition for collective success. Viewed in this light, providing assistance is not simply an act of charity or a humanitarian gesture; it is a strategic means to achieve common goals in a globalised world where states are, to varying degrees, reliant on one another's actions.

In addition, states may be incentivised to participate by the expectation that they can rely on international support themselves if ever needed in the future. Solidarity operates on a promise of reciprocity and mutuality: members of a community help one another in times of need. A state that acts as a 'good citizen' and actively participates in this community can reasonably expect assistance when it faces a disaster and finds its national response capacities overwhelmed. Conversely, if states fail to comply with the duty to assist or do so inconsistently, they risk not receiving reciprocal support later. In the worst case, persistent unwillingness to assist may even erode a state's standing within the solidarity-based community, undermining the trust and mutual reliance that make such cooperation possible.

Yet, these questions about the feasibility of a solidarity-based duty to assist naturally leads to the question of what happens when states fail to comply with their obligations in the context of disaster response. Given the lack of enforcement mechanisms in IDRL, what are the consequences when a state disregards its duty to assist or acts inconsistently with the principle of solidarity? This raises broader issues about accountability and the options available to other

[130] While states have repeatedly agreed to establish a climate change adaptation fund to financially support developing states to cope with the effects of climate change, the UN Environment Programme reports that there is a consistent funding gap. Of the estimated at $310–365 billion annual need for adaptation finance in developing countries, actual funding went down from $28 billion to $26 billion in 2023: UN Environment Programme, 'Adaptation Gap Report 2025: Running on Empty' (2025) www.unep.org/resources/adaptation-gap-report-2025.

[131] See generally A Rahman-Shepherd et al, 'Solidarity in Response to the COVID-19 Pandemic' (Chatham House, 2021) www.chathamhouse.org/2021/07/solidarity-response-covid-19-pandemic.

[132] Williams (n 20) 501; Hestermeyer et al (n 20) 19.

[133] As discussed in ch 2, section II.

states and assisting actors to respond to such breaches. The next subsection explores these questions, examining the consequences of non-compliance and the options for states seeking to enforce or compel adherence to obligations under international law.

D. Accountability and Enforcement

While most states comply with their international obligations during disasters most of the time – providing adequate protection to affected persons and seeking international assistance when necessary – practice shows that this is unfortunately not always the case. Failures in disaster response can raise serious concerns about violations of international law, in particular, the protection of human rights and dignity, and exacerbate human suffering. Chapter 5, section III.C already highlighted examples of states refusing to seek or accept international aid despite their national response capacities being overwhelmed.[134] Myanmar's blanket refusal of assistance following Cyclone Nargis in 2008 still remains one of the most notorious cases in recent history, but more recent instances, such as delays or refusals of international aid after catastrophic earthquakes in Syria and Morocco in 2023, serve as stark reminders that issues surrounding consent remain highly relevant.[135]

Leaving aside issues around cooperation, concerns may also arise regarding how states respond – or fail to respond – to disasters within their own jurisdiction in line with their obligations under international law. In some cases, states have acted promptly, but faced criticism over the distribution of assistance, with allegations of discriminatory practices that left marginalised groups underserved.[136] Concerns over discrimination based on ethnicity, socio-economic status, gender, disability and more have been raised in many instances, such as the response to the 2004 Indian Ocean Tsunami in India,[137] the 2015 Cyclone Komen in Myanmar[138] and the 2015 earthquake in Nepal.[139] In other instances, states have failed to respond in a timely or adequate manner, leaving affected populations to cope with severe hardship. For example, during extreme flooding

[134] Research shows that international assistance is rejected or delayed in approximately one in four major disasters: Nelson (n 121) 391.

[135] R Razek et al, '"Secondary Disaster" Looms as UN Aid Finally Reaches Survivors Battling Frozen Conditions in Syria' *CNN* (10 February 2023) https://edition.cnn.com/2023/02/09/middleeast/turkey-syria-earthquake-aid-bab-al-hawa-intl-hnk/index.html; 'Morocco Earthquake' (n 75).

[136] See also HA Seglah and K Blanchard, 'Sexual and Gender Minorities and the Right to Non-discrimination: A Shortfall of Disaster Risk Reduction?' (2024) 5 *Yearbook of International Disaster Law* 133.

[137] DP Aldrich, 'Separate and Unequal Post-Tsunami Aid Distribution in Southern India' (2010) 91(5) *Social Science Quarterly* 1369.

[138] I Desportes, 'Getting Relief to Marginalised Minorities: The Response to Cyclone Komen in 2015 in Myanmar' (2019) 4(1) *Journal of International Humanitarian Action* 7.

[139] Amnesty International, 'Nepal: Earthquake Recovery Must Safeguard Human Rights' https://amnestynepal.org/activities/earthquake-recovery-must-safeguard-human-rights, 10.

in Sri Lanka triggered by Cyclone Ditwah in late 2025, nearly one million people were affected, killing hundreds and leaving hundreds of thousands more displaced in overcrowded, poorly resourced shelters.[140] Although mass evacuations were carried out, authorities faced immense public pressure for their late response, squandering opportunities to save lives by evacuating people earlier.[141] Similarly, certain measures taken to protect persons from disasters have raised human rights concerns. In the response to Cyclone Idai in 2019, the Mozambican government resettled more than 80,000 people from high-risk zones with minimal consultation, raising concerns about their agency, freedom of movement and the effects of resettlement.[142] Comparable concerns have arisen in other large-scale evacuations, where failures to consult communities, ensure safe and dignified shelter and mitigate risks of long-term displacement can lead to human rights violations.[143] During the COVID-19 pandemic, emergency measures also sparked debate over their lawfulness, including discriminatory travel restrictions and sweeping restrictions on human rights.[144]

IDRL lacks formal mechanisms for holding states accountable for breaches of international obligations during disaster response. While human rights oversight mechanisms can perform an accountability function with respect to states' human rights obligations,[145] they are not designed to respond to real-time decisions made during disasters. Besides these existing processes, there are no mechanisms dedicated specifically to monitoring compliance with states' obligations in disaster response. This gap can be explained by several structural features of IDRL: the long-standing emphasis on voluntarism in international cooperation, which questions the binding character of obligations to seek, accept and provide assistance; the decentralisation of disaster response, which places it in the sovereign domain of states; and the strong respect for state sovereignty, which discourages interference by other states. Compounding these factors is

[140] V Mishra, 'Cyclone Ditwah Brings Worst Flooding in Decades to Sri Lanka, Killing Hundreds' *UN News* (30 November 2025) https://news.un.org/en/story/2025/11/1166474.

[141] M Krishnan, 'Sri Lanka Cyclone Tragedy Exposes Government Failures' *DW* (12 December 2025) www.dw.com/en/sri-lanka-cyclone-tragedy-exposes-government-failures/a-74985337. On the importance of early evacuations to save lives, see J McAdam and T Mulder, 'A Last Resort? Reframing Evacuations as an Anticipatory Disaster Risk Management Strategy' (2026) *Journal of International Humanitarian Legal Studies* (forthcoming).

[142] C Jacobs and B Almeida, 'Government-Led Resettlement after Natural Disasters as a Durable Solution? The Case of Cyclone Idai' (2021) 40(2) *Refugee Survey Quarterly* 239.

[143] J McAdam, 'Evacuations as Displacement: Conceptual and Legal Challenges' (2025) 44(2) *Refugee Survey Quarterly* 204.

[144] See L Forman and R Habibi, 'Revisiting the Legality of Travel Restrictions under International Law during COVID-19' (2022) 71(3) *International and Comparative Law Quarterly* 743; Y Won, 'Emergency Powers and COVID-19 Derogations' (2025) 23(1) *International Journal of Constitutional Law* 113.

[145] D Cubie and M Hesselman, 'Accountability for the Human Rights Implications of Natural Disasters: A Proposal for Systemic International Oversight' (2015) 33(1) *Netherlands Quarterly of Human Rights* 9, 34–39. See also M Hesselman, 'A Right to International (Humanitarian) Assistance in Times of Disaster' in Flavia Zorzi Giustiniani et al (eds), *Routledge Handbook of Human Rights and Disasters* (Routledge, 2018) 65.

IDRL's comparatively weak institutional framework, which lacks international bodies with a mandate to monitor, let alone enforce, compliance.[146] As a result, accountability is to be mainly pursued informally through diplomatic channels and public pressure. States and international organisations may raise concerns with the affected state, as occurred following Cyclone Nargis.[147] Non-state actors, particularly human rights advocacy groups, also play a critical role by reporting alleged violations, raising awareness and pressuring governments to comply with their obligations.[148]

Beyond informal efforts to resolve breaches, states could pursue legal action under the law of state responsibility. Breaches of international obligations, in principle, constitute internationally wrongful acts for which the responsible state's responsibility may be invoked,[149] enabling other states to take 'measures of a relatively formal character', such as presenting a claim, adopting countermeasures or initiating proceedings before an international court or tribunal.[150] However, under the ILC's Articles on Responsibility of States for Internationally Wrongful Acts – the leading soft law instrument on the law of state responsibility – only 'injured' states have the right to invoke the responsibility of another state.[151] According to the ILC, a state is injured 'if the obligation breached was owed to it individually'.[152] Applied to IDRL, it is difficult to identify circumstances in which third states could claim injury from breaches of obligations that are not directly owed to them, such as the duty to protect populations, the duty to cooperate and the duty to seek assistance.[153]

Yet, if interpreted through the lens of solidarity, the obligations of states in disaster response should be understood as obligations *erga omnes* – owed to the international community as a whole. As explained in Chapter 4, section III.B, this follows logically from reconceptualising disaster response – and more specifically the protection of affected populations – as a shared responsibility of all states rather than a purely domestic affair of the affected state. Consequently, every state has a legal interest in ensuring compliance with obligations relating to the protection of disaster-affected persons, including safeguarding human

[146] Other than aforementioned UN human rights bodies.

[147] Selth (n 35); K Loevy, 'The Legal Politics of Jurisdiction: Understanding ASEAN's Role in Myanmar's Disaster, Cyclone Nargis (2008)' (2015) 5(1) *Asian Journal of International Law* 55.

[148] See T Natoli, 'Non-state Humanitarian Actors and Human Rights in Disaster Scenarios' in F Zorzi Giustiniani et al (eds), *Routledge Handbook of Human Rights and Disasters* (Routledge, 2018) 149, 155.

[149] ILC, 'Articles on Responsibility of States for Internationally Wrongful Acts' (31 May 2001) UN Doc A/56/10, arts 2 and 42.

[150] ILC, 'Articles on Responsibility of States for Internationally Wrongful Acts, with Commentaries' (2001) II(2) *Yearbook of the International Law Commission* 117.

[151] ILC (n 149) art 42.

[152] ILC (n 150) 118.

[153] A state may invoke responsibility of another state for obligations owed to the international community as a whole only if the breach 'specially affects that state' or 'is of such a character as radically to change the position of all the other States to which the obligation is owed with respect to the further performance of the obligation': ILC (n 149) art 42(b).

rights and dignity, and fulfilling duties to seek and accept international assistance when necessary. Understanding these obligations as *erga omnes* allows all states – not only those directly injured – to invoke the responsibility of another state for breaches,[154] 'not in its individual capacity by reason of having suffered injury, but in its capacity as a member of a group of States to which the obligation is owed, or indeed as a member of the international community as a whole'.[155]

Under the Articles on Responsibility of States for Internationally Wrongful Acts, a state entitled to invoke responsibility may demand cessation of the wrongful act, assurances and guarantees of non-repetition, and reparations in the interest of the beneficiaries of the breached obligation.[156] These measures provide a formal framework for addressing violations and carry significant normative weight, but their practical impact can be limited, particularly where the responsible state denies wrongdoing or refuses to rectify the situation.

When disputes arise or breaches persist, states could theoretically consider bringing claims before a competent international court or tribunal and/or resorting to countermeasures.[157] However, neither option appears particularly promising in the context of disaster response. States have not conferred jurisdiction over disaster-related matters to any international court, nor does IDRL provide dedicated dispute settlement mechanisms. Consequently, claims could only be brought before the ICJ or other fora with general jurisdiction under international dispute settlement law. Even then, the prospect of litigation is unattractive: proceedings before international courts are notoriously time-consuming, while breaches in disaster response often demand urgent action to prevent harm to affected populations.

Alternatively, states could resort to countermeasures, such as sanctions against states or individuals, to compel the responsible state to cease breaches of its obligations.[158] Although the right of non-injured states to take countermeasures remains controversial under the law of state responsibility, there is widespread practice of states doing so in response to serious human rights violations.[159] Nonetheless, countermeasures appear inappropriate and potentially counterproductive in the context of disasters. Sanctions risk isolating the responsible state, obstructing diplomatic engagement and negotiations for

[154] *Barcelona Traction, Light and Power Company, Limited (Belgium v Spain)* (Judgment) [1970] ICJ Rep 3 (hereinafter '*Barcelona Traction Case*'), para 33. See also ILC (n 149) art 48(1)(b).

[155] ILC (n 150) 126.

[156] ILC (n 149) art 48(2).

[157] ILC (n 150) 117.

[158] ILC (n 149) art 49.

[159] ibid art 54. See also C Hillgruber, 'The Right of Third States to Take Countermeasures' in C Tomuschat and JM Thouvenin (eds), *The Fundamental Rules of the International Legal Order: Jus Cogens And Obligations Erga Omnes* (Martinus Nijhoff Publishers, 2006) 265; M Dawidowicz, 'Third-Party Countermeasures: A Progressive Development of International Law?' (2016) 29 *Questions of International Law* 3.

access to affected communities.[160] Worse, they could jeopardise protection by curtailing resources the state's resources and (further) reducing its capacity to respond to disasters. Moreover, countermeasures run counter to the principle of solidarity: rather than exerting pressure, solidarity emphasises cooperation and assistance to support the affected state in fulfilling its obligations.

In light of these limited enforcement options, the following question arises: what can states effectively do to ensure the protection of disaster-affected populations, particularly when a state's refusal to comply with its obligations causes or exacerbates human suffering? This leads to the controversial question of whether states may, as a last resort, intervene with force if necessary. IDRL's strong emphasis on respect for state sovereignty and the principle of non-intervention appears to categorically reject unilateral humanitarian interventions. However, the option of intervention remains open if authorised by the UN Security Council.[161] Acting under Chapter VII of the UN Charter, the Security Council may adopt binding measures 'to maintain or restore international peace and security',[162] including measures using force.[163] Whether disasters fall within this competence is unclear. In practice, the Security Council has acted in disaster contexts only rarely, for example, by extending UN peacekeeping operations in Haiti after the 2010 earthquake, though its involvement there pre-dated the disaster due to ongoing conflict.[164] Moreover, its practice is inconsistent: while it deemed the Ebola outbreaks in West Africa in 2014 and the Democratic Republic of Congo in 2018 'threats to international peace and security',[165] it did not do so for the COVID-19 pandemic.[166] Scholars also caution against the 'securitisation' of disasters, warning that framing them as security threats risks prioritising stability over the protection of affected populations.[167]

While the Security Council has not yet authorised a humanitarian intervention in the context of disasters, it is not beyond the realm of possibility that it could do so in the future. It could, for instance, act under the doctrine of R2P,

[160] Allan and O'Donnell (n 30) 368; M Thomson, 'The Obligation Not to Arbitrarily Refuse International Disaster Relief: A Question of Sovereignty' (2015) 16 *Melbourne Journal of International Law* 1, 31.

[161] Costas Trascasas (n 30) 239.

[162] *Charter of the United Nations* (24 October 1945) art 39.

[163] ibid art 42.

[164] UN Security Council Res 1944 (2010) (14 October 2010) S/RES/1944 (2010).

[165] UN Security Council Res 2177 (2014) (18 September 2014) UN Doc S/RES/2177 (2014); UN Security Council Res 2439 (2018) (30 October 2018) UN Doc S/RES/2439 (2018). See also GL Burci, 'Ebola, the Security Council and the Securitization of Public Health' (2014) 10 *Questions of International Law* 27.

[166] However, the Security Council did note that 'the unprecedented extent of the COVID-19 pandemic is likely to endanger the maintenance of international peace and security': UN Security Council Res 2532 (2020) (1 July 2020) UN Doc S/RES/2532 (2020) preamble. See also J Farrall and C Michaelsen, 'The UN Security Council's Response to COVID-19: From the Centre to the Periphery?' (2021) 39 *Australian Yearbook of International Law* 214.

[167] Burci (n 165); H Nasu, 'The Global Security Agenda: Securitization of Everything?' in R Geiß and N Melzer (eds), *The Oxford Handbook of the International Law of Global Security* (Oxford University Press, 2021) 37.

relying on a liberal interpretation of its scope.[168] It is worth recalling that some states were open to this option in the aftermath of Cyclone Nargis.[169] Moreover, Security Council practice indicates a willingness to take measures aimed at preventing human suffering, including instructing states to permit humanitarian access to populations in need.[170] These precedents suggest that, although unlikely and politically sensitive, Security Council authorisation of humanitarian intervention in disaster contexts remains a conceivable – if exceptional – response to egregious breaches of obligations and a failure to protect disaster-affected populations.

Even if the prospect of UN Security Council-authorised humanitarian interventions remains unlikely, such interventions would fundamentally conflict with the principle of solidarity.[171] They would dismantle the solidarity-based dual framework of responsibility, in which affected states retain the primary role in disaster response while other states perform an auxiliary role by assisting them where necessary.[172] Humanitarian intervention would instead shift responsibility for protecting disaster-affected populations from the affected state to the international community, overriding the affected state's sovereignty and primary role. Moreover, serious doubts persist about the appropriateness, suitability and effectiveness of humanitarian interventions in disaster settings.[173] As Barber rightly observed, 'it is very difficult to imagine a situation in which a full-scale military invasion, for the alleged purpose of rescuing the victims of disaster, could be assessed as likely to produce a surplus of good over harm'.[174] In addition, even with the best intentions, humanitarian interventions risk undermining the neutral and impartial character of disaster relief operations, further complicating their legitimacy.[175]

All of this means that even though states have a legal interest in ensuring compliance with international obligations in the context of disaster response, there is little they can effectively do when states are unwilling to cooperate in practice. This reality leaves an enforcement gap that solidarity cannot overcome. Solidarity is directed towards cooperation because it rests on the premise of a

[168] As discussed in section III.A, the R2P doctrine as adopted by the UN General Assembly does not apply to disasters as such.

[169] Selth (n 35) 390.

[170] Costas Trascasas (n 30) 240–41.

[171] For opposing views, see Boisson de Chazournes (n 109); K Wellens, 'Revisiting Solidarity as a (Re-)Emerging Constitutional Principle: Some Further Reflections' in Wolfrum and Kojima (n 20) 3, 11; F Zorzi Giustiniani, *International Law in Disaster Scenarios: Applicable Rules and Principles* (Springer, 2021) 147.

[172] This dual structure of responsibility is key to the concept of solidarity; see ch 2, section III.

[173] Barber (n 30) 32; da Costa (n 30) 33–34; Jansen-Wilhelm (n 47) 110–11; J Benton Heath, 'Disasters, Relief, and Neglect: The Duty to Accept Humanitarian Assistance and the Work of the International Law Commission' (2011) 43 *NYU Journal for International Law & Politics* 419, 434; D Fisher, 'The Law of International Disaster Response: Overview and Ramifications for Military Actors' (2007) 83 *International Law Studies Series. US Naval War College* 293, 308.

[174] Barber (n 30) 32. See also da Costa (n 30) 33; Fisher (n 173) 308.

[175] Benton Heath (n 173) 434.

community in which states feel connected through social cohesion and are willing to support one another in pursuit of common objectives. It thus presupposes a readiness to cooperate and assist in good faith. When this willingness falters or is absent altogether, solidarity offers no remedy: it cannot be enforced, as it ultimately depends on trust and mutual reliance. However, persistent failures or refusals to cooperate risk eroding a state's standing within the solidarity-based community and, in the worst case, destabilise the very sense of solidarity that underpins international disaster response.

Instead, this enforcement gap needs to be addressed through reforms of international law itself. While the effectiveness of informal means of seeking accountability and enforcement – through diplomacy, negotiation and public pressure – should not be underestimated, it is equally necessary to strengthen formal mechanisms for holding states accountable for breaches of international law in disaster response. Doing so would affirm the legal interest of all states in compliance and provide more meaningful tools to advance the common objective of protecting disaster-affected persons. Rather than introducing coercive enforcement measures, the potential solution lies in how enforcement is pursued. Given that compliance serves the interests of all states, what is needed is an international body with a mandate to oversee the application of IDRL and address complaints of alleged breaches, on behalf of the international community. Delegating this task to an independent body could relieve individual states of pressure to act and depoliticise compliance by removing national interests from the equation. Such a body need not function as a judicial authority or an enforcer; rather, its mandate could focus on promoting compliance, reviewing complaints, advocating on behalf of affected populations as well as third states and assisting actors, and compelling states to meet their obligations through institutional influence rather than binding decisions or coercive measures. The prospect of such an international body as a means of strengthening solidarity is further explored in Chapter 8, section III.

IV. CONCLUSION

This chapter has examined the role of third states and assisting actors in IDRL and explored how this role can be reconceptualised through the principle of solidarity. It began by clarifying that IDRL traditionally frames these actors as auxiliary to the affected state, whose primary responsibility for disaster response remains paramount (see section II). While solidarity preserves this division between primary and auxiliary roles, it situates them within a different underlying logic: the auxiliary role of third states and assisting actors is not just a consequence of sovereignty and the primary role of affected states, but part of the shared responsibility of all states for the protection of persons affected by disasters. Although this reinterpretation does not radically overhaul the established roles of affected and assisting states, it nonetheless introduces a crucial shift in understanding what this auxiliary role entails. Sharing responsibility for the protection of affected populations, third states and assisting actors are no longer Good Samaritans offering aid out of humanitarian concern or goodwill; they are active stakeholders in disaster response with rights and duties, and a legal interest in the compliance of IDRL.

The chapter then undertook a closer examination of how solidarity would transform this auxiliary role in more detail through an analysis of four key issues. First, it has explored to what extent third states could be considered responsible for the protection of persons affected by disasters beyond their jurisdiction (section III.A). While solidarity entails a shared responsibility for ensuring protection, third states are not directly responsible for affected populations, as this would dismantle the dual structure of responsibilities in which the affected state has the primary role in disaster response. Even when the affected state is unwilling or unable to ensure adequate protection, this responsibility does not shift to the international community. Solidarity therefore differs from the doctrine of R2P, providing no basis for humanitarian intervention; instead, it emphasises that third states must support affected states through cooperation and assistance. The subsequent sections elaborated on the rights and obligations of third states and assisting actors under the duty to cooperate. Section III.B assessed the right to offer international assistance. Although the legal status of this right remains unsettled, it argued that third states and assisting actors should have a right to offer assistance as an expression of solidarity and willingness to cooperate, reflecting their shared responsibility for ensuring protection in disaster settings. Section III.C then turned to their obligations, contending that third states must have a duty to assist when the affected state's national response capacity is overwhelmed. A binding duty to assist would fundamentally alter IDRL by moving beyond voluntarism in international cooperation but is essential for ensuring the protection of disaster-affected persons, with solidarity requiring that states with greater capacities contribute more. Finally, section III.D examined the potential consequences of breaching IDRL, explaining that all states have a legal interest in compliance and may invoke responsibility through diplomatic means, given the absence of formal enforcement mechanisms.

While this reinterpretation would not amount to a radical overhaul of IDRL, there are nonetheless significant obstacles to the successful implementation of solidarity. Chief among these is the question of whether states are genuinely willing to cooperate and provide assistance when needed. Practice reveals a persistent gap between what states claim they are prepared to do and what they actually deliver, raising a real concern that commitments to solidarity may remain rhetorical rather than genuine. This underscores the importance of framing cooperation as a shared responsibility rather than a humanitarian gesture or an act of goodwill. Solidarity is not optional; it entails mutual obligations of support that other states must be able to rely on. Another obstacle lies in the limited means for accountability and enforcement. States are not always cooperative in disaster response and may prioritise national interests over solidarity.[176] While third states have a legal interest in holding non-compliant states responsible, their options are largely confined to diplomatic measures. Solidarity alone cannot overcome this enforcement gap, and further reforms are needed to strengthen accountability in IDRL. One proposed solution is the creation of an international body mandated to raise concerns with states on behalf of the international community – a possibility explored further in Chapter 8, section III.

Finally, the solidarity-based interpretation advanced in this chapter demonstrates that solidarity's truly transformative potential lies perhaps most in its reframing of roles within a paradigm of mutual support. Rather than perceiving the involvement of international actors in disaster response as a threat to sovereignty or a vehicle for foreign interference, it should be understood as a positive expression of shared responsibility: a means of delivering assistance where it is most urgently required. This approach emphasises that such engagement is not about advancing national interests or exerting influence or control, but about fulfilling the common objective of all states to ensure the protection of persons affected by disasters. In this sense, solidarity operates as a facilitator of humanitarianism rather than intervention, enabling states and assisting actors to alleviate suffering and uphold human dignity. Moreover, solidarity redefines international cooperation and assistance as steps towards social justice, acknowledging structural disparities in national response capacities and directing resources to those most in need. This normative shift promises a more equitable international disaster response regime – one in which states can rely on each other to ensure protection of those affected by disasters, wherever they are.

[176] This issue and illustrative examples were also discussed in ch 5, sections III.B and III.C.

7

International Cooperation in Disaster Response

I. INTRODUCTION

WHEREAS CHAPTERS 5 AND 6 examined the respective roles of states and assisting actors, this chapter shifts the focus from the rights and duties of individual actors to broader questions of international cooperation in disaster response. So far, it has been firmly established that states have a duty to cooperate – a duty that would be reinforced and deepened through the implementation of the principle of solidarity in IDRL. This chapter explores what such cooperation entails, moving beyond the previously discussed duties to seek and provide assistance when needed.[1] In doing so, it examines the areas and level of cooperation expected of states; a critical issue given that, while states often express willingness to cooperate, practice reveals persistent legal, bureaucratic and administrative barriers that undermine the effectiveness of cooperation and the overall impact of disaster relief efforts.[2] By examining the scope and content of cooperation, this chapter not only addresses these issues but also contributes to a clearer understanding of the nature and forms of cooperation envisaged by solidarity.

The structure of this chapter mirrors that of the previous two. Section II begins by outlining IDRL's current approach to international cooperation before reimagining this framework through the lens of solidarity. It argues that solidarity seeks to transform cooperation in disaster response from ad hoc and reactive humanitarian efforts into a proactive and continuous process encompassing all stages of disaster management. By treating cooperation as a vehicle for fulfilling the shared responsibility to protect persons in the context of disasters, this approach calls for more structured and systematic collaboration between states and assisting actors, as well as a broader understanding of cooperation that recognises protection as an ongoing process rather than one that begins only after disaster strikes. This reframing shifts emphasis towards supporting states in reducing vulnerabilities and building resilience, with the ultimate aim of

[1] As discussed in ch 5, section III.B and ch 6, section III.C.

[2] For a comprehensive overview of legal and practical issues in the operationalisation of international disaster response, see D Fisher, *Law and Legal Issues in International Disaster Response: A Desk Study* (IFRC, 2007).

minimising the exposure to risk and, by extension, the need for humanitarian assistance when hazards occur. Through this broader and more systematic cooperation, solidarity can achieve its true purpose: addressing structural inequalities that leave some states better equipped than others, thereby advancing international social justice.

Building on this interpretation, section III examines three key issues that shape the scope, content and level of international cooperation against the background of solidarity: the exchange of information; the facilitation of international cooperation; and collaboration in strengthening national response capacities. As in the previous chapters, a normative approach is adopted, exploring how these issues should be understood if IDRL were interpreted and developed through the lens of solidarity, while also mindful to potential obstacles to its full realisation. In doing so, the chapter moves beyond abstract and aspirational claims about solidarity's transformative potential, demonstrating how it can be translated into concrete norms and practices.

II. SOLIDARITY AND COOPERATION IN DISASTER RESPONSE

International cooperation in disaster response has a long and deeply rooted history, tracing back centuries.[3] Today, it is firmly recognised as being 'of great importance' to 'address emergency situations and to strengthen the response capacity of affected countries'.[4] Most treaties and soft law instruments in IDRL acknowledge the crucial role of international cooperation, which is often made explicit in their texts.[5] For example, the *Inter-American Convention to Facilitate*

[3] ILC, 'Preliminary Report on the Protection of Persons in the Event of Disasters, by Mr. Eduardo Valencia-Ospina, Special Rapporteur' (5 May 2008) UN Doc A/CN.4/598, paras 14 ff; P Macalister-Smith, *International Humanitarian Assistance: Disaster Relief Actions in International Law and Organization* (Kluwer Academic Publishers, 1985) 53–55.

[4] UN General Assembly Res 46/182 (19 December 1991) UN Doc A/RES/46/182, para 5.

[5] See, eg, ILC, 'Draft Articles on the Protection of Persons in the Event of Disasters' (27 May 2016) UN Doc A/CN.4/L.871 (hereinafter 'Draft Articles') preamble; *ASEAN Agreement on Disaster Management and Emergency Response* (26 July 2005) (AADMER) preamble; *Convention on Assistance in the Case of a Nuclear Accident or Radiological Emergency* (26 September 1986) (hereinafter 'Nuclear Accident Convention') preamble; *Framework Convention on Civil Defence Assistance* (22 May 2000) art 2; *Agreement among the Governments of the Participating States of the Black Sea Economic Cooperation (BSEC) on Collaboration in Emergency Assistance and Emergency Response to Natural and Manmade Disasters* (15 April 1998) (BSEC Agreement) preamble; *Agreement between Governments of Member States of Shanghai Cooperation Organization on Cooperation in Delivery of Assistance for Emergency Liquidation* (26 October 2005) (hereinafter 'Shanghai Agreement') preamble; *Agreement between Member States and Associate Members of the Association of Caribbean States for Regional Cooperation on Natural Disasters* (16 April 1999) (ACS Agreement) art 2; *Arab Cooperation Agreement on Regulating and Facilitating Relief Operations 1987* (3 September 1987) (Arab League Agreement) preamble; *SAARC Agreement on Rapid Response to Natural Disasters, 2011* (26 May 2011) art II; *Tampere Convention on the Provision of Telecommunication Resources for Disaster Mitigation and Relief Operations* (18 June 1998) preamble; *Decision No 1313/2013/EU of the European Parliament and of the Council of 17 December 2013 on a Union Civil Protection Mechanism* (20 December 2013) (EU Civil Protection Mechanism) art 1(1).

Disaster Assistance explicitly links cooperation to the protection of disaster-affected persons, noting that 'the human suffering caused by such disasters can be relieved more effectively and swiftly by means of an instrument to facilitate such assistance and to regulate international procedures for providing it in such cases'.[6] To this end, many instruments establish a duty to cooperate in the context of disasters.[7]

So far, this book has discussed in detail how solidarity moves cooperation beyond voluntarism, obligating states to cooperate when necessary to protect persons affected by disasters.[8] But solidarity also changes the nature and scope of such cooperation, which is the focus here. Historically, cooperation in disaster response has been largely ad hoc, reactive and centred around the provision of humanitarian assistance.[9] Throughout centuries, states and assisting actors have typically mobilised only after disasters strike, often improvising arrangements for coordination and delivery of aid. However, this reactive approach can result in fragmented and uneven responses that are limited to the relief phase only. Solidarity, by contrast, calls for a more systematic and proactive model of cooperation.

There are clear efforts underway to systematise cooperation in disaster response. The traditionally ad hoc approach is gradually giving way to a process of formalisation, transforming case-by-case arrangements into structured frameworks through treaties and soft law instruments. As discussed in Chapter 1, section II.B, the desire for clearer rules governing disaster response dates back to the early twentieth century, when states established the International Relief Union (IRU) – an ambitious yet ultimately unsuccessful attempt to centralise disaster response under a single international organisation.[10] Following the IRU's quick demise in the 1930s, states turned to bilateral and regional agreements to systemise cooperation, committing to mutual assistance and setting out frameworks for cooperation, including the modalities for requesting and providing aid. Soft law instruments further contributed to this trend by offering states guidance on strengthening national laws, policies and procedures related to international disaster response. The IFRC's IDRL Guidelines stand out as a prominent example of these efforts, promoting predictable and coordinated cooperation among states and assisting actors.[11]

[6] *Inter-American Convention to Facilitate Disaster Assistance* (6 July 1991) preamble.

[7] Draft Articles (n 5) art 7; Tampere Convention (n 5) art 3(1); Nuclear Accident Convention (n 5) art 1(1); AADMER (n 5) art 4(a); Shanghai Agreement (n 5) art 2(1).

[8] See ch 4, section III.D, ch 5, section III.B and ch 6, section II.C.

[9] See generally R Carvosso, 'The Reactive Model of Disaster Regulation in International Law and its Shortcomings' (2021) 34(4) *Leiden Journal of International Law* 957.

[10] See generally P Macalister-Smith, 'Reflections on the Convention Establishing an International Relief Union of July 12, 1927' (1986) 54(4) *Legal History Review* 363; JF Hutchinson, 'Disasters and the International Order – II: The International Relief Union' (2001) 23(2) *International History Review* 253.

[11] IFRC, 'Guidelines for the Domestic Facilitation and Regulation of International Disaster Relief and Initial Recovery Assistance' (2007) (hereinafter 'IDRL Guidelines').

This trend of systemising cooperation is crucial to giving effect to solidarity in IDRL. While codifying terms of cooperation in agreements is not, from the perspective of solidarity, an end in itself, the transition from improvised, ad hoc responses to structured and systematic frameworks for cooperation is essential. Such frameworks make cooperation more organised and predictable, reducing uncertainty during disasters and enabling faster, more coordinated action. They also regularise the practice of states working in solidarity with one another, embedding mutual obligations into legal instruments rather than leaving them to discretionary goodwill. In this way, formal agreements serve as a practical vehicle for operationalising solidarity and ensuring that commitments translate into meaningful action.

In addition to these developments, there is also a need to rethink what cooperation entails. While the emphasis typically lies on the provision of humanitarian assistance,[12] if the ultimate goal is the protection of affected persons, cooperation must extend far beyond relief alone. This broader understanding is increasingly reflected in IDRL instruments, which expand cooperation to encompass a wider range of activities. For example, the Draft Articles provide an illustrative, non-exhaustive list of forms of cooperation, including 'coordination of international relief actions and communications, and making available relief personnel, equipment and goods, and scientific, medical and technical resources'.[13] The Commentaries go further, highlighting additional forms such as 'financial support; technology transfer covering, among others, technology relating to satellite imagery; training; information sharing; joint simulation exercises and planning; and undertaking needs assessments and situation overview'.[14] Both the Draft Articles and the IDRL Guidelines further stress that facilitating the entry and distribution of international assistance is itself a critical component of effective cooperation (see section III.B).[15] This expanded understanding acknowledges that cooperation in disaster response is not limited to humanitarian assistance, but encompasses a comprehensive set of actions aimed at ensuring timely and effective protection.

There is also a growing awareness that international cooperation must extend beyond disaster response to encompass disaster risk reduction, aiming to prevent new risks and reduce existing ones, thereby reducing the likelihood of disasters occurring in the first place and, if they come to pass, mitigating their effects. States have committed to cooperate on a range of priorities in this regard under

[12] Most treaties indeed focus on the provision of assistance rather than other aspects of disaster response or disaster management more broadly. However, notable exceptions include the Tampere Convention (n 5) and the Civil Defence Assistance Convention (n 5).

[13] Draft Articles (n 5) art 8.

[14] ILC, 'Commentaries on the Draft Articles on the Protection of Persons in the Event of Disasters' (2016) UN Doc A/71/10, 41. Chapter 5, section III.B also emphasised the importance of cooperation in conducting needs assessments.

[15] Draft Articles (n 5) art 15; IDRL Guidelines (n 11) arts 13–15.

the Sendai Framework for Disaster Risk Reduction,[16] but this trend is also progressively reflected in other instruments. For example, the Draft Articles extend the duty to cooperate to disaster risk reduction, signalling that prevention is integral to protection.[17] States should, for example, cooperate in identifying and reducing disaster risks through joint risk assessments, collecting and disseminating risk information, and installing and operating early warning systems.[18] They should also engage in preparedness activities, including training, joint simulation exercises and coordinated planning.[19] Similarly, under the AADMER, state parties have agreed 'to co-operate in developing and implementing measures to reduce disaster losses including identification of disaster risk, development of monitoring, assessment and early warning systems' and commit to 'jointly or individually develop strategies to identify, prevent and reduce risks arising from hazards'.[20]

This expanded understanding of cooperation is critical to giving effect to solidarity because it is not sufficient for states to collaborate only in the aftermath of disasters. To achieve the common objective of protecting persons affected by disasters, cooperation must encompass all relevant aspects of disaster management, including reducing risks and preparing for disasters before they occur. This shift ensures that solidarity is operationalised not as an emergency response alone, but as a continuous commitment to protection. By embedding cooperation across the entire disaster cycle – prevention, preparedness, response and recovery – solidarity becomes a proactive principle that reduces vulnerability and strengthens resilience, rather than a reactive action once harm has already occurred.

Through these changes, solidarity seeks to transform cooperation in disaster response from an ad hoc and reactive humanitarian effort into a proactive and continuous process covering all stages of disaster management. While not attempting to centralise disaster response – since doing so would undermine the sovereignty of affected states – solidarity treats cooperation as a vehicle for fulfilling the shared responsibility of all states to protect persons in the context of disasters. A broader and more expansive understanding of cooperation recognises that protection is a continuous process, not one that begins only once disaster strikes. It shifts emphasis towards supporting states in reducing vulnerabilities and building resilience, with the ultimate aim of minimising the need for humanitarian assistance when hazards occur.

Transforming cooperation in this way is also a manifestation of the deeper purpose underlying solidarity: addressing and ameliorating the structural inequalities that leave some states better equipped to respond to disasters

[16] World Conference on Disaster Risk Reduction, 'Sendai Framework for Disaster Risk Reduction 2015–2030' (18 March 2015) UN Doc A/CONF.224/L.2, para 20 (hereinafter 'Sendai Framework').

[17] Draft Articles (n 5) arts 7 and 9. See also ILC (n 14) 50.

[18] Draft Articles (n 5) art 9(2).

[19] ILC (n 14) 41.

[20] AADMER (n 5) arts 4(a) and 6(1).

than others.[21] By cooperating to reduce risks and vulnerabilities and improve resilience through enhanced preparedness, solidarity seeks not only to close protection gaps but also to correct these global disparities. In doing so, it makes cooperation a means of advancing international social justice in the context of disasters.

III. SELECTED ISSUES

The reinterpretation of what cooperation in disaster response entails through the lens of solidarity, as outlined in the previous section, provides the foundation for exploring three specific aspects of cooperation in this section in closer detail. Section III.A examines what it means to expand cooperation beyond the provision of humanitarian aid, focusing on information sharing as a key component. Section III.B addresses a recurring challenge in international disaster response – the delayed or inefficient facilitation of international assistance – underscoring the importance of advance preparation for disaster response. Finally, section III.C considers one dimension of pre-disaster cooperation, emphasising the need for structural collaboration aimed at enhancing states' national response capacities. In doing so, the focus lies on preparedness for disaster response rather than disaster risk reduction, which falls outside the scope of this book. By analysing these issues through the lens of solidarity, this chapter illustrates what transforming cooperation from an ad hoc and reactive model into a systematic and continuous process would look like in practice, while maintaining the established framework of the affected state's primary role and the auxiliary role of assisting states.

A. Exchange of Information

Communication is key to effective international cooperation in the response to disasters.[22] To achieve optimal results, states and assisting actors must exchange information on matters such as the threat or onset of disasters, their nature, scope and effects, and the needs of affected populations. However, history shows that states are not always willing to disclose complete information, often due to fears of public panic or reputational damage. There are numerous examples of authorities attempting to downplay the severity of events. Perhaps the most notorious case is the 1986 Chernobyl nuclear accident, where authorities delayed acknowledging the reactor explosion and radiation release, initially claiming

[21] R Wolfrum, *Solidarity and Community Interests: Driving Forces for the Interpretation and Development of International Law* (Brill Nijhoff, 2021) 89.

[22] ILC (n 14) 42.

that everything was under control.[23] Evacuations were postponed for hours, and international alerts came only after Sweden detected radiation. Similar patterns occurred following the 2011 Fukushima nuclear disaster, when Japanese officials initially downplayed the severity of the meltdown and withheld contamination data for days.[24] Other examples include Ethiopian authorities obstructing documentation of the 1973 drought and famine, North Korea's secrecy regarding floods and famines in the 1990s and China's decades-long denial of the 1970 Tonghai earthquake – the country's third deadliest on record.[25] More recently, China faced criticism for delaying disclosure of the COVID-19 outbreak, slowing the global response.[26] The lack of information sharing may delay an international response and jeopardise the protection of persons affected by disasters.

Most IDRL instruments address communication and information sharing, often framing it as an obligation of the affected state to facilitate communications and provide relevant information, either directly or indirectly.[27] For example, a multilateral agreement between Denmark, Finland, Norway and Sweden on cross-border disaster cooperation explicitly states that '[t]he Contracting States shall provide each other with information of importance for this Agreement'.[28] The Tampere Convention underscores in its preamble that 'the effective, timely deployment of telecommunication resources and rapid, efficient, accurate and truthful information flows are essential to reducing loss of life, human suffering and damage to property and the environment caused by disasters'.[29] In light of this, it establishes a duty to cooperate in facilitating the use of telecommunication resources, including 'the sharing of information

[23] J Vitkovskaya, 'How the Soviet Union Stayed Silent during the Chernobyl Disaster' (25 April 2016) www.washingtonpost.com/news/worldviews/wp/2016/04/25/how-the-soviet-union-stayed-silent-during-the-chernobyl-disaster.

[24] A Yamamoto, 'Fukushima Operator Admits it Didn't Reveal Meltdown for Months' *NBC News* (26 February 2016) www.nbcnews.com/news/world/fukushima-operator-admits-it-didn-t-reveal-meltdown-months-n525431.

[25] Z Coursen-Nef, 'Preventive Measures Pertaining to Unconventional Threats to the Peace Such as Natural and Humanitarian Disasters' (1998) 30(3–4) *New York University Journal of International Law and Politics* 645, 677–82; ND Kristof, 'Chinese Disclose That Quake in 1970 Killed about 10,000' *New York Times* (19 November 1988) www.nytimes.com/1988/11/19/world/chinese-disclose-that-quake-in-1970-killed-about-10000.html.

[26] 'China Delayed Releasing Coronavirus Info, Frustrating WHO' *The Associated Press* (2 June 2020) https://apnews.com/article/united-nations-health-ap-top-news-virus-outbreak-public-health-3c061794970661042b18d5aeaaed9fae.

[27] See, eg, Tampere Convention (n 5) art 3(2); Nuclear Accident Convention (n 5) art 2(2); Civil Defence Assistance Convention (n 5) art 4(a)(1); AADMER (n 5) arts 4, 5(3); Inter-American Convention (n 6) art 11(b); Shanghai Agreement (n 5) art 3; BSEC Agreement (n 5) art 4; IDRL Guidelines (n 11) art 7; UN OCHA, 'Guidelines on The Use of Foreign Military and Civil Defence Assets In Disaster Relief' (November 2007) (hereinafter 'Oslo Guidelines') para 54. See also ILC, 'Memorandum by the Secretariat on the Protection of Persons in the Event of Disasters' (11 December 2007) UN Doc A/CN.4/590, paras 158–59.

[28] *Agreement between Denmark, Finland, Norway and Sweden on Cooperation across State Frontiers to Prevent or Limit Damage to Persons or Property or to the Environment in the case of Accidents* (20 January 1989) art 6(1).

[29] Tampere Convention (n 5) preamble.

about natural hazards, health hazards and disasters among the States Parties and with other States, non-State entities and intergovernmental organizations, and the dissemination of such information to the public, particularly to at-risk communities'.[30] Similarly, the IDRL Guidelines emphasise that:

> [I]n order to minimize transboundary impacts and maximize the effectiveness of any international assistance that might be required, all States should have procedures in place to facilitate the expeditious sharing of information about disasters, including emerging hazards that are likely to cause disasters, with other States and assisting humanitarian organizations as appropriate, including the United Nations' Emergency Relief Coordinator.

The Draft Articles do not explicitly refer to the subject of communication, but the commentaries suggest that information sharing may be considered a form of cooperation under the duty to cooperate.[31]

Yet, instruments take different approaches to when and what type of information must be shared. Several treaties require parties to notify others of the threat or onset of disasters, particularly where events risk causing transboundary harm.[32] For example, the *Convention on the Transboundary Effects of Industrial Accidents* stipulates:

> In the event of an industrial accident, or imminent threat thereof, which causes or is capable of causing transboundary effects, the Party of origin shall ensure that affected Parties are, without delay, notified at appropriate levels through the industrial accident notification systems.[33]

Similarly, the *Convention on Early Notification of a Nuclear Accident* – drafted in response to the 1986 Chernobyl disaster – obligates states to notify 'those States which are or may be physically affected' of nuclear accidents and provide 'such available information relevant to minimizing the radiological consequences

[30] ibid art 3(2).

[31] ILC (n 14) 42.

[32] *International Health Regulations (2005)* (23 May 2005) (IHR 2005) art 6; *Convention on Early Notification of a Nuclear Accident* (26 September 1986) art 2; *United Nations Convention on the Law of the Sea* (10 December 1982) art 198; *Convention on the Law of the Non-navigational Uses of International Watercourses* (21 May 1997) art 28; *International Convention on Oil Pollution Preparedness, Response and Cooperation* (30 November 1990) art 5; *Convention on the Transboundary Effects of Industrial Accidents* (17 March 1992) art 10; *Convention on the Protection and Use of Transboundary Watercourses and International Lakes* (17 March 1992) art 14. See also Conference on Environment and Development, 'Rio Declaration on Environment and Development' (14 June 1992) UN Doc A/CONF.151/5/Rev.1, principle 18; ILC, 'Draft Articles on Prevention of Transboundary Harm from Hazardous Activities' (2001) UN Doc UN Doc A/56/10, art 17. See further UN Human Rights Committee, 'General Comment No. 36 on Article 6: Right to Life' (3 September 2019) UN Doc CCPR/C/GC/36, para 62: 'States parties should therefore . . . provide notification to other States concerned about natural disasters and emergencies and cooperate with them, provide appropriate access to information on environmental hazards and pay due regard to the precautionary approach.'

[33] Convention on the Transboundary Effects of Industrial Accidents (n 32) art 10(2).

in those States'.[34] Under the EU Civil Protection Mechanism, Member States must report events that are 'likely to result in a call for assistance from one or more Member States'.[35] Other treaties foresee information sharing once international assistance is sought. For example, both the Nuclear Accident Convention and the AADMER stipulate that, when requesting assistance, the affected state shall 'specify the scope and type of assistance required' and, where practicable, provide 'such information as may be necessary for that party to determine the extent to which it is able to meet the request'.[36]

Details on the type of information that should be shared vary significantly across instruments. Some treaties, such as the *Framework Convention on Civil Defence Assistance*, adopt a general approach, simply noting that: 'The Beneficiary State shall provide all necessary information available relating to the situation, so as to ensure smooth implementation of the assistance.'[37] Others are far more specific. For example, the BSEC Agreement requires the affected state to provide details on 'the place, time, character and scale of the Disaster, and current state of the Emergency in the afflicted area', as well as 'actions already carried out, specification of the required Assistance, [and] setting the priorities of the requested Disaster relief'.[38] States are expected to keep this information updated 'following the development of the situation'.[39] The *Convention on Early Notification of a Nuclear Accident* is exceptionally detailed, obligating states to report 'the nuclear accident, its nature, the time of its occurrence and its exact location where appropriate' as well as share relevant data for the response, such as 'the assumed or established cause and the foreseeable development of the nuclear accident relevant to the transboundary release of the radioactive materials', 'general characteristics of the radioactive release', 'information on current and forecast meteorological and hydrological conditions' and 'the off-site protective measures taken or planned'.[40] States must notify others and provide this information without delay as soon as they become aware of the threat or onset of a disaster.[41]

Viewed through the lens of solidarity, the exchange of information must be understood as more than a practical step to facilitate disaster response; it is an essential expression of the shared responsibility for protecting people affected by disasters and a commitment to international cooperation. Sharing information

[34] Convention on Early Notification of a Nuclear Accident (n 32) art 2.

[35] EU Civil Protection Mechanism (n 5) art 14(2).

[36] Nuclear Accident Convention (n 5) art 2(1); AADMER (n 5) art 11(3). See also BSEC Agreement (n 5) art 4(2).

[37] Civil Defence Assistance Convention (n 5) art 4(a)(1).

[38] BSEC Agreement (n 5) art 4(2).

[39] ibid art 4(4).

[40] Convention on Early Notification of a Nuclear Accident (n 32) arts 2, 5(1).

[41] ibid art 2. See also IHR 2005 (n 32) art 6(1); International Convention on Oil Pollution Preparedness, Response and Cooperation (n 32) art 5(1)(c); Convention on the Transboundary Effects of Industrial Accidents (n 32) art 10(2); Convention on the Protection and Use of Transboundary Watercourses and International Lakes (n 32) art 14; United Nations Convention on the Law of the Sea (n 32) art 198; Convention on the Law of the Non-Navigational Uses of International Watercourses (n 32) art 28(2); ILC (n 32) art 17.

recognises that disaster response is not solely a sovereign undertaking of the affected state, but a common objective in which all states have an interest. As a result, other states should be informed about disasters to enable them to contribute towards the common objective – for example, by offering assistance where appropriate and needed. Seen in this way, sharing information acknowledges the part that third states and assisting actors play in disaster response and, importantly, it can serve as the starting point for dialogue, exploring whether international cooperation is necessary and, if so, in what forms and to what extent.

In addition, sharing information is an essential component of the duty to cooperate that flows from the principle of solidarity. Without timely and accurate information on the scale and effects of disasters, as well as on ongoing response efforts, meaningful cooperation becomes difficult, if not impossible. If states are truly committed to international cooperation in disaster response, they must actively share relevant information with others and facilitate effective (tele)communication to support information exchange between local authorities and relief workers.[42] Doing so would itself constitute 'a concrete expression of the duty to cooperate',[43] as suggested by several IDRL instruments that explicitly link information-sharing to this obligation.[44]

In light of this solidarity-based approach, the obligation to share information should be interpreted broadly: any information relevant to international cooperation in disaster response ought to be disclosed. This includes the threat or onset of a disaster, regardless of whether there is a risk of transboundary harm. Whereas the objective of several treaty-based reporting obligations is to warn other states mainly about potential cross-border impacts,[45] a solidarity-based interpretation assigns a different purpose: to inform others so that they can explore how to support the affected state if needed.

In terms of content, states should provide any information relevant to the response, including the nature, scope and effects of the disaster, as well as the needs of affected persons, insofar as this information is available.[46] States should

[42] Tampere Convention (n 5) art 3(2)(d).

[43] G Bartolini, 'A Universal Treaty for Disasters? Remarks on the International Law Commission's Draft Articles on the Protection of Persons in the Event of Disasters' (2017) 99(3) *International Review of the Red Cross* 1103, 1119.

[44] Tampere Convention (n 5) art 3(2)(b); AADMER (n 5) art 4(1). See also ILC (n 14) 42.

[45] IHR 2005 (n 32) art 6; Convention on Early Notification of a Nuclear Accident (n 32) art 2; United Nations Convention on the Law of the Sea (n 32) art 198; Convention on the Law of the Non-Navigational Uses of International Watercourses (n 32) art 28; International Convention on Oil Pollution Preparedness, Response and Cooperation (n 32) art 5; Convention on the Transboundary Effects of Industrial Accidents (n 32) art 10; Convention on the Protection and Use of Transboundary Watercourses and International Lakes (n 32) art 14. See also 'Rio Declaration' (n 32) principle 18; ILC(n 32) art 17.

[46] This interpretation is supported by existing treaty law, see IHR 2005 (n 32) art 6; International Convention on Oil Pollution Preparedness, Response and Cooperation (n 32) art 5(1)(c); Convention on the Transboundary Effects of Industrial Accidents (n 32) art 10(2), annex IX; Convention on the Protection and Use of Transboundary Watercourses and International Lakes (n 32) art 14. However, some treaties merely obligate states to notify other states of the threat or onset of disasters; see United Nations Convention on the Law of the Sea (n 32) art 198; Convention on the Law of the Non-Navigational Uses of International Watercourses (n 32) art 28(2). See also ILC (n 27) para 50.

provide such information without delay to enable timely and effective cooperation. The duty to share information is two-directional: it applies not only to affected states but also to other states and non-state actors that possess information relevant to disaster response. Affected states should disclose timely and accurate details about the disastrous event and their response efforts, consistent with its primary role. At the same time, other states and non-state actors, such as UN agencies, should share information that can assist the affected state and others in planning or carrying out relief operations. This may include satellite imagery, scientific data, meteorological forecasts or technological assessments. This interpretation finds precedent in existing treaty law, where states have a duty to notify others of (potential) disasters.[47] The reciprocal nature of this duty recognises the shared responsibility of all for disaster response, ensuring that all actors contribute to a shared pool of knowledge that strengthens disaster preparedness and response.

Furthermore, the duty to share information should apply not only to sudden-onset events, but also to slow-onset events such as droughts, desertification or sea-level rise. While it may appear less obvious to share information about slow-onset processes when they have not yet constituted a 'disaster' under its legal definition,[48] doing so is nonetheless essential for timely and effective action. These events often unfold gradually, but their impacts can be severe and predictable, meaning that early information exchange is critical to preventing foreseeable harm and protecting vulnerable populations. By sharing data on emerging risks, environmental changes and long-term hazard trends, states can enable coordinated mitigation strategies and adaptive measures that reduce future disaster impacts.

Although a duty to share information is sensible from a solidarity-based perspective, its implementation faces significant challenges rooted in the political realities of state behaviour during disaster response. The primary concern is that some states may perceive the obligation to share information as an encroachment on sovereignty, viewing it as external interference in matters traditionally regarded as internal.[49] Sovereignty implies full control over a state's territory and decision making, including how disasters are managed. Sharing disaster-related information might expose vulnerabilities, security risks or governance shortcomings, potentially undermining national authority or inviting internal or external scrutiny and pressure. Additionally, states may fear that such transparency could

[47] International Convention on Oil Pollution Preparedness, Response and Cooperation (n 32) art 5(1)(c); Convention on the Protection and Use of Transboundary Watercourses and International Lakes (n 32) art 14; United Nations Convention on the Law of the Sea (n 32) art 198. See also 'Rio Declaration' (n 32) principle 18.

[48] The Draft Articles define a disaster as 'a calamitous event or series of events resulting in widespread loss of life, great human suffering and distress, mass displacement, or largescale material or environmental damage, thereby seriously disrupting the functioning of society': Draft Articles (n 5) art 3(a). See a discussion of the legal definition of disasters in ch 1, section II.A.

[49] See generally R Knuth, 'Sovereignty, Globalism, and Information Flow in Complex Emergencies' (1999) 15(1) *The Information Society* 11.

trigger obligations – such as the duty to seek assistance – that they did not consent to, or even lead to international intervention, thereby limiting their autonomy. For these reasons, some governments may choose to restrict or refuse the dissemination of disaster information to maintain control and protect their sovereign prerogatives.

These sovereignty-related concerns have already played out in practice, with states invoking sovereignty to justify withholding disaster-related information or data. A notable example occurred in 2008, when Indonesia refused to share avian flu (H5N1) virus samples with the WHO's Global Influenza Surveillance Network, citing fears that pharmaceutical companies would use these samples to develop vaccines that would then be sold back to Indonesia at prohibitive prices.[50] Indonesia defended its position by claiming 'viral sovereignty', aimed at securing equitable access to vaccines.

These concerns can pose real challenges to the successful implementation of the duty to share information. Nonetheless, a proper interpretation of IDRL that reflects the principle of solidarity should alleviate some of these fears. First, the obligation to share information does not conflict with the principle of sovereignty. Disclosing information is intended to provide relevant data to other states and assisting actors to help determine an appropriate response; it should not be understood as a request for international assistance or as consent for the provision of such assistance. Therefore, the affected state does not relinquish any control over disaster response by sharing information. Although transparency may invite internal or external scrutiny of the affected state's response – particularly regarding whether it is doing enough to protect those affected – this does not undermine sovereignty as such. On the contrary, allowing others to scrutinise responses acknowledges the legitimate interest of the international community in protection and can enhance compliance with obligations under international law.[51]

Furthermore, solidarity leaves room for exceptions to the duty to share information, particularly where disclosure would involve sensitive data affecting national security interests. Examples could include information relating to affected military resources or critical infrastructure, which could expose vulnerabilities if shared. As shown in Chapter 4, section II, solidarity does not override or diminish state sovereignty; where the two principles clash, they must be carefully balanced.[52] Applied to this context, states may be justified in withholding information for legitimate reasons, provided that such withholding is proportionate and does not compromise the protection of disaster-affected populations. Where withholding information would cause disproportionate harm to those affected, states should

[50] See generally MF Rourke, 'Restricting Access to Pathogen Samples and Epidemiological Data: A Not-So-Brief History of "Viral Sovereignty" and the Mark it Left on the World' in M Eccleston-Turner and I Brassington (eds), *Infectious Diseases in the New Millennium* (Springer, 2020) 167.

[51] As discussed in ch 6, section III.D, there are no formal mechanisms to review or scrutinise response to disasters under international law.

[52] On how national interests can be balanced with solidarity, see the discussion in ch 5, section III.C.

disclose it to enable effective international cooperation necessary to ensure adequate protection.

However, in other instances, the motives for state withholding information are less clear. Rather than openly refusing to share information, states are more commonly secretive in their behaviour – delaying disclosure, withholding parts of the data or claiming an inability to retrieve information. These practices can create significant frustration among other states and assisting actors who rely on timely and accurate information to determine an appropriate response. A prominent example is the handling of the early stages of the COVID-19 outbreak by the Chinese authorities. China has been accused of suppressing information about the initial outbreak and withholding critical genomic data relating to the SARS-CoV-2 virus.[53] While Chinese officials asserted that they shared all the available information, the WHO criticised the country for being slow to release data essential for understanding the virus and developing vaccines and treatments.[54] Other states also accused China of obstructing the release of information regarding the origins of the virus, prompting a WHO-led investigation.[55] These controversies highlight how political sensitivities and sovereignty concerns can manifest in more subtle forms of non-cooperation, undermining global efforts to respond effectively to disasters.

As argued in the previous chapter, solidarity alone cannot overcome the lack of compliance by states that refuse to act in solidarity with others.[56] Nonetheless, it should be clear that states must disclose all available information without delay. Failure to do so not only breaches the state's international obligations but also affects the international community as a whole. Withholding critical information can hinder the effectiveness of international cooperation in disaster response and, ultimately, undermine the protection of disaster-affected persons. Frustrating cooperation for whatever reason subverts the spirit of solidarity and could eventually erode a state's position to benefit from the solidarity extended by the international community. In this sense, transparency is not merely a legal obligation, but a cornerstone of mutual trust and solidarity in disaster response.

Besides concerns over sovereignty and national interests, the risk of negative consequences may also discourage states from sharing information. Disclosure can trigger immediate reactions from other states that adversely affect the reporting state's economy, trade or international reputation. For example, after South Africa dutifully reported the discovery of the Omicron variant of the SARS-CoV-2 virus in late 2021, many states responded by swiftly imposing travel bans

[53] See generally TM Brown and S Ladwig, 'COVID-19, China, the World Health Organization, and the Limits of International Health Diplomacy' (2020) 110(8) *American Journal of Public Health* 1149.

[54] 'Covid-19 Pandemic: China "Refused to Give Data" to WHO Team' *BBC* (14 February 2021) www.bbc.com/news/world-asia-china-56054468.

[55] 'Australia Pushed for a WHO Probe into Coronavirus' Origins – Here's What the Investigation is up to' *ABC News* (27 August 2020) www.abc.net.au/news/2020-08-27/world-health-organization-coronavirus-investigation/12598616.

[56] This argument was developed in ch 6, section III.D.

on persons travelling from South Africa and neighbouring countries.[57] These measures, while intended to contain the spread of the variant, went against advice of the WHO and had severe economic and diplomatic repercussions for the region, possibly creating a disincentive for early reporting in future scenarios. It should be obvious that a negative backlash to disclosing information must be avoided. Taking restrictive measures against states that report emerging threats not only discourages transparency but also undermines the spirit of solidarity, which emphasises international cooperation and support – not punitive or retaliatory actions. States should have followed the advice of the WHO and, instead of imposing travel bans, offered assistance to South Africa to contain the spread of the new variant.

Finally, the obligation to share information can only be meaningfully fulfilled when states are able to collect relevant information. Sharing presupposes possession; if a state does not actively collect relevant data – such as situational assessments and risk analyses – it cannot provide the needed information that underpins effective cooperation. Gathering such information can therefore be considered a key component of the affected state's primary role in disaster response. There is a growing understanding that information gathering should be a continuous process that spans all stages of the disaster cycle. Effective international cooperation depends not only on post-disaster assessments but also on systematic efforts to identify risks and monitor hazards before a disaster occurs. This understanding is increasingly reflected in both binding and non-binding instruments. The Sendai Framework, for example, emphasises that 'in order to reduce disaster risk, there is a need to address existing challenges and prepare for future ones by focusing on monitoring, assessing and understanding disaster risk and sharing such information and on how it is created'.[58] Similarly, the Draft Articles affirm that states have a duty to reduce disaster risk, including through 'the conduct of risk assessments, the collection and dissemination of risk and past loss information, and the installation and operation of early warning systems'.[59]

Treaties also increasingly codify obligations to identify risks, monitor hazards and establish early warning systems.[60] For instance, the AADMER obligates parties to 'take appropriate measures to identify disaster risks in its respective territories', including through regular disaster risk assessments, early warning information systems and communication networks for timely delivery of information.[61] It further specifies that: 'Parties shall co-operate, as appropriate, to

[57] Z Adamu and S Busari, 'Anger Simmers over Omicron Travel Bans in Southern Africa' *CNN* (4 December 2021) https://edition.cnn.com/2021/12/04/africa/africa-travel-ban-omicron-variant-intl-cmd/index.html.

[58] Sendai Framework (n 16) para 14.

[59] Draft Articles (n 5) art 9(2).

[60] See, eg, International Convention on Oil Pollution Preparedness, Response and Cooperation (n 32) art 4; Convention on the Transboundary Effects of Industrial Accidents (n 32) art 4(1).

[61] AADMER (n 5) art 5(1).

monitor hazards which have trans-boundary effects, to exchange information and to provide early warning information through appropriate arrangements.'[62] In the health domain, the *International Health Regulations (2005)* (IHR 2005) require that '[e]ach State Party shall develop, strengthen and maintain . . . the capacity to detect, assess, notify and report' potential public health emergencies of international concern, such as outbreaks of contagious diseases.[63] Under the newly adopted *WHO Pandemic Agreement*, states are similarly obligated 'to progressively strengthen pandemic prevention and surveillance measures and capacities, consistent with the International Health Regulations (2005)'.[64] If states detect events that may constitute a public health emergency of international concern within their territory, they must notify the WHO, triggering a decision-making process on how to respond.[65]

While states bear primary responsibility for identifying and monitoring hazards within their own territories, this responsibility is complemented by a broader duty to cooperate internationally.[66] The duty to cooperate in this context may entail sharing relevant data, harmonising monitoring systems and engaging in joint risk assessments. It also includes supporting capacity-building in states with limited resources, participating in regional or global early warning mechanisms and coordinating the dissemination of information. Several IDRL instruments already foresee such cooperation. For example, state parties to the Tampere Convention have agreed to cooperate in 'the deployment of terrestrial and satellite telecommunication equipment to predict, monitor and provide information concerning natural hazards, health hazards and disasters'.[67] Similarly, the AADMER stipulates that state parties have a duty to cooperate in 'developing and implementing measures to reduce disaster losses including identification of disaster risk, development of monitoring, assessment and early warning systems'.[68] It goes even further by committing parties to:

> [I]ndividually or jointly, including in co-operation with appropriate international organisations, promote and, whenever possible, support scientific and technical research programmes related to the causes and consequences of disasters and the means, methods, techniques and equipment for disaster risk reduction[69]

The Sendai Framework also calls on states 'to promote the strengthening of, as appropriate, international voluntary mechanisms for monitoring and assessment of disaster risks, including relevant data and information'.[70] Practice reflects this

[62] ibid art 7(2).
[63] IHR 2005 (n 32) art 5(1).
[64] WHO Pandemic Agreement (20 May 2025) art 4(1).
[65] IHR 2005 (n 32) art 6(1).
[66] ILC (n 14) 50.
[67] Tampere Convention (n 5) art 3(2)(a).
[68] AADMER (n 5) art 4(a).
[69] ibid art 19(1).
[70] Sendai Framework (n 16) para 28(f).

commitment through numerous initiatives for joint global and regional forecasting and early warning systems on a voluntary basis.[71] One prominent example is the Global Tsunami Early Warning and Mitigation Programme, in which states and international organisations collaborate to establish networks of early warning systems for tsunamis worldwide.[72]

Such cooperation is particularly crucial for states that lack the capacity and resources to independently monitor risks and hazards. These states may become extra vulnerable to disasters when they are unable to collect, process and disseminate the data necessary for effective preparedness and response. Acting in solidarity, other states must support these states by providing technical assistance, sharing technology and engaging in joint monitoring and assessment initiatives.[73] This cooperation cannot remain purely voluntary; if states genuinely commit to solidarity, such collaboration must be understood as a legal duty stemming from the shared responsibility for disaster response.

In sum, the exchange of information is a clear example of how the duty to cooperate must cover all aspects of disaster response to facilitate effective collaboration, and why limiting cooperation to the response phase is too restrictive. Collecting and sharing information prior to disasters is crucial for reducing risks, mitigating impacts and preparing for effective response. Cooperation in this area is particularly critical because not all states have the resources or technical capacity to identify and monitor risks. By working together on information collection and exchange, states not only improve their ability to manage disaster risks but also help address structural inequalities between states, ensuring that all can benefit from timely and accurate data to protect their populations. Viewed in this light, cooperation is both a reflection of shared responsibility and a contribution to advancing international social justice.

B. Facilitation of International Cooperation

Among the most persistent challenges in international disaster response is the delayed and inefficient facilitation of international cooperation.[74] Despite the growing recognition of the need for cooperation in disaster response, few states are adequately prepared to facilitate a prompt and effective international

[71] See also UN General Assembly Res 46/182 (n 4) paras 19–20.

[72] Intergovernmental Oceanographic Commission, 'Global Tsunami Early Warning and Mitigation Programme' https://ioc.unesco.org/our-work/global-tsunami-early-warning-and-mitigation-programme.

[73] See also Sendai Framework (n 16) para 40.

[74] Fisher (n 2) 13; DP Fidler, 'Disaster Relief and Governance after the Indian Ocean Tsunami: What Role for International Law?' (2005) 6 *Melbourne Journal of International Law* 458, 471; D Fisher, 'Domestic Regulation of International Humanitarian Relief in Disasters and Armed Conflict: A Comparative Analysis' (2007) 89(866) *International Review of the Red Cross* 345, 355 ff; R Barber, 'Legal Preparedness for the Facilitation of International Humanitarian Assistance in the Aftermath of Vanuatu's Cyclone Pam' (2016) 8(1) *Asian Journal of International Law* 143.

response.[75] The most persistent and practical obstacles arise during the actual delivery of assistance, particularly in large-scale emergencies where needs are acute and significant volumes of aid flow into the affected state. In these situations, entry and distribution often become bottlenecks. Strict visa requirements, cumbersome customs procedures and import levies frequently delay the arrival of relief personnel and essential goods. These challenges can be compounded by the limited administrative capacity of local authorities to process the sudden influx of aid – a problem that is often exacerbated by the strain on resources caused by the disaster itself. For instance, during the severe COVID-19 outbreak in India in 2021, authorities were overwhelmed by the arrival of vast quantities of international assistance.[76] Although medical equipment and supplies were urgently needed in affected communities, their distribution was stalled for days due to 'unnecessary bureaucracy, human error, or time-consuming protocol'.[77]

Problems also frequently extend into the distribution of aid within the affected state. Third states and assisting actors often encounter restrictive rules that hinder their ability to operate effectively on the ground.[78] Securing temporary authorisation to legally function in the territory, for example, can be fraught with legal and administrative barriers, limiting their capacity to open bank accounts, enter into contracts and leases, acquire or dispose of property, and initiate legal proceedings for the purposes of delivering disaster relief and early recovery assistance.[79] In addition, unnecessarily restrictive regulations can disrupt ongoing operations. A striking example occurred in the aftermath of the 2004 Indian Ocean Tsunami, when foreign relief workers in Indonesia were forced to leave and re-enter the country every 60 days due to lengthy and costly visa procedures.[80]

Another recurring challenge lies in the coordination of disaster response activities and the distribution of aid.[81] While the affected state has the primary role in the direction, control, coordination and supervision of international assistance,[82] this principle often encounters practical difficulties. In many cases, it is unclear which government entity holds the mandate to lead coordination efforts, while capacity constraints of already overwhelmed authorities further

[75] Fisher (n 2) 14. See also IFRC, 'Annotations to Guidelines for the Domestic Facilitation and Regulation of International Disaster Relief and Initial Recovery Assistance' (26 October 2007) 3.

[76] J Hunter, 'India Covid Aid: Is Emergency Relief Reaching Those in Need?' *BBC* (6 May 2021) www.bbc.com/news/world-asia-india-56999104.

[77] J Yeung, 'The World Sent India Millions in Covid Aid. Why is it Not Reaching Those Who Need it Most?' *CNN* (5 May 2021) https://edition.cnn.com/2021/05/05/india/india-covid-foreign-aid-distribution-intl-hnk-dst/index.html.

[78] Fisher (n 2) 13.

[79] See also IDRL Guidelines (n 11) art 20.

[80] Fisher (n 2) 116.

[81] ibid 150.

[82] The primary role of the affected state was discussed in ch 5, section II.

undermine effectiveness.[83] Poor coordination can result in confusion, duplication of efforts and inefficient allocation of resources, where some communities are overserved while the needs of others are missed.[84]

The challenges in facilitating international assistance are not exclusively legal; mounting a rapid response to disasters has always posed significant operational difficulties. Nevertheless, evidence suggests that law is a critical component of the problem – and a potential solution. A comprehensive study by the IFRC on legal and practical issues in disaster response found that only a few states have adequate legal and institutional frameworks to enable effective international cooperation.[85] The study observed that:

> Recent experiences indicate that national laws and institutions are generally unprepared to handle the special issues incident to the receipt of international disaster relief and recovery assistance. While most states have disaster laws and/or plans of some sort, few have put sufficient advance thought into how to balance local control with the need for any international assistance that is required to be as speedy as possible. Instead, these dilemmas are commonly addressed for the first time in the charged and chaotic environment immediately following a disaster. This results in ad hoc rule-making, confusion and delay just when it can least be afforded.[86]

For example, following the devastating earthquake in Haiti in 2010, authorities were willing to cooperate and generously accepted international aid. However, they fell short on the facilitation of the influx of assistance. Although Haiti ratified a range of conventions seeking to facilitate the provision of international assistance, fragmented and ad hoc legislation fell short in terms of implementing these obligations, lacking clarity and enforceability and creating bureaucratic bottlenecks that delayed visa and customs procedures for relief personnel and supplies, impeding timely aid delivery.[87]

In the absence of established frameworks, states often resort to improvised measures, undermining efficiency and effectiveness. As Bill Clinton, in his role as UN Secretary-General's Special Envoy for Tsunami Recovery, remarked in his

[83] Fisher (n 2) 152. For example, a review of the international response to the 2004 Indian Ocean Tsunami found that '[i]n each tsunami-hit country, the government's ability to coordinate effectively was constrained by its own capacity and access to information': J Bennett et al, *Coordination of International Humanitarian Assistance in Tsunami-Affected Countries* (Tsunami Evaluation Coalition, 2006) 41.

[84] J Telford and J Cosgrave, *Joint Evaluation of the International Response to the Indian Ocean Tsunami: Synthesis Report* (Tsunami Evaluation Coalition, 2006) 57; D Fisher, 'The Law of International Disaster Response: Overview and Ramifications for Military Actors' (2007) 83 *International Law Studies Series – US Naval War College* 293, 306.

[85] Fisher (n 2) 14. See also IFRC (n 75) 3.

[86] Fisher (n 2) 14.

[87] I Granger, *IDRL in Haiti: A Study on the Legal Framework for the Facilitation and Regulation of International Disaster Response in Haiti* (IFRC, 2012).

formal review of relief operations in the aftermath of the 2004 Indian Ocean Tsunami:

> The aftermath of a crisis is the wrong time to create new institutions, establish new policies and legal frameworks, and recruit new staff, as all of this takes time. Confusion over responsibilities between new and existing institutions can also create major bottlenecks and delays, not to mention uncertainty among international partners that must deal with national, provincial, and local officials.[88]

The urgency of improving the facilitation of international assistance has never been greater. Climate change is driving an increase in both the frequency and intensity of disasters, while the humanitarian landscape has expanded dramatically. As the IFRC observes:

> Whereas a century ago there were only a handful of states and humanitarian actors regularly involved in disaster response, large disasters today can attract hundreds of international responders, ranging from states and humanitarian organizations to private companies and individuals.[89]

This proliferation of actors has introduced significant complications in the facilitation and coordination of disaster response. The sheer number of actors can create overlapping mandates, fragmented efforts and even competition for visibility and funding in a 'rat race' for the most sought-after projects, facilities, resources, staff and publicity.[90]

In light of these developments, there is growing attention to the facilitation of disaster cooperation in treaties and soft law instruments.[91] Nearly all IDRL instruments address common facilitation issues – albeit to varying degrees of detail – such as the entry of relief personnel (including visas, work permits and recognition of professional qualifications),[92] the admission of goods and equipment (including temporary admission, customs clearance, and exemptions

[88] WJ Clinton, 'Lessons Learned from Tsunami Recovery: Key Propositions for Building Back Better' (2006) https://reliefweb.int/report/thailand/lessons-learned-tsunami-recovery-key-propositions-building-back-better, 8.

[89] IFRC (n 75) 5.

[90] ibid; Telford and Cosgrave (n 84) 57.

[91] Draft Articles (n 5) art 9; IDRL Guidelines (n 11) arts 13-21; Tampere Convention (n 5) arts 3(1), 5, 9; Nuclear Accident Convention (n 5) arts 3(b), 8–9; Civil Defence Assistance Convention (n 5) arts 4(3), 4(7); AADMER (n 5) arts 12(2), 14, 16; Inter-American Convention (n 6) arts II(c), IV(c), V–VII; BSEC Agreement (n 5) arts 9–10; ACS Agreement (n 5) art 3; Arab League Agreement (n 5) arts 3, 7–9; Shanghai Agreement (n 5) art 9(2); *Protocol of Amendment to the International Convention on the Simplification and Harmonisation of Customs Procedures of 18 May 1973* (26 June 1999) Annex J.5; *Convention on Temporary Admission* (26 June 1990) Annex B.9; *Agreement Establishing the Caribbean Disaster Emergency Management Agency* (4 July 2008) (CDEMA Agreement) arts XXII(3), XXVII, XXXII, XXXIV.

[92] Draft Articles (n 5) art 14(1)(a); IDRL Guidelines (n 11) art 16; Nuclear Accident Convention (n 5) art 8(5); Civil Defence Assistance Convention (n 5) art 4(3); AADMER (n 5) art 14(b); Inter-American Convention (n 6) art VII; BSEC Agreement (n 5) art 9; Arab League Agreement (n 5) art 8.

from import and export duties, taxes and other restrictions),[93] and access to legal privileges, immunities and facilities (including immunity for foreign relief personnel, tax exemptions and temporary domestic legal status for non-state actors).[94] Other treaties that are dedicated to the subject of disasters are also relevant in this context as they foresee simplified entry and customs procedures for international aid in emergencies.[95] While covering a wide range of issues, these frameworks remain incomplete. For example, the temporary recognition of foreign professional qualifications, such as medical licenses or driver's licences, continues to be a major obstacle to effective international disaster response, yet it is rarely addressed in IDRL instruments.[96]

The IDRL Guidelines in particular play a key role in efforts to strengthen the facilitation of international assistance. Adopted in 2007 as a non-binding instrument by the IFRC,[97] the Guidelines aim 'to contribute to national legal preparedness by providing guidance to States interested in improving their domestic legal, policy and institutional frameworks concerning international disaster relief and initial recovery assistance'.[98] To achieve this, they outline nine key legal facilities that states should provide to assisting states and eligible humanitarian organisations, covering areas such as personnel, goods and equipment, transport, temporary domestic legal status, taxation, security and costs.[99]

Complementing the IDRL Guidelines is the Model Act for the Facilitation and Regulation of International Disaster Relief and Initial Recovery Assistance, developed by the IFRC in 2013.[100] The Model Act is intended 'to help states to be prepared for the most common legal and regulatory issues that arise in major international disaster operations'.[101] It provides a detailed legislative template, comprising 71 articles that address a wide range of topics relevant to the prompt and effective facilitation of international disaster cooperation.

[93] Draft Articles (n 5) art 14(1)(b); IDRL Guidelines (n 11) arts 17–18; Convention on Temporary Admission (n 91) Annex B.9; Protocol of Amendment to the International Convention on the Simplification and Harmonisation of Customs Procedures of 18 May 1973 (n 91) Annex J.5; Nuclear Accident Convention (n 5) art 8(3)(a); AADMER (n 5) art 14(a); Inter-American Convention (n 6) art V; BSEC Agreement (n 5) art 10; Arab League Agreement (n 5) art 7; Shanghai Agreement (n 5) art 9(2).

[94] Draft Articles (n 5) art 14(1)(a); IDRL Guidelines (n 11) arts 20–21; Tampere Convention (n 5) art 5; Nuclear Accident Convention (n 5) art 8; AADMER (n 5) art 14; Arab League Agreement (n 5) art 9; CDEMA Agreement (n 91) art XXVII.

[95] Protocol of Amendment to the International Convention on the Simplification and Harmonisation of Customs Procedures of 18 May 1973 (n 91) Annex J.5; Convention on Temporary Admission (n 91) Annex B.9.

[96] Fisher (n 74) 363; ILC (n 27) paras 92–93; G Bartolini, 'Epidemics and the Future of International Disaster Law' (2022) 24(3) *International Community Law Review* 257, 273.

[97] IDRL Guidelines (n 11) art 1(1).

[98] ibid art 1(3).

[99] ibid arts 16–24.

[100] IFRC, 'Model Act for the Facilitation and Regulation of International Disaster Relief and Initial Recovery Assistance' (March 2013).

[101] ibid 8.

Although non-binding, the Model Act serves as a practical tool for lawmakers, offering concrete provisions that can be adapted to national contexts. Together with the IDRL Guidelines, it has influenced the design of domestic disaster legislation in numerous states, helping to close critical gaps in legal preparedness.[102]

States have several ways to facilitate international disaster response. While they retain discretion to tailor solutions to their national contexts, a critical first step is the establishment of appropriate legal and institutional frameworks that set out clear rules and procedures for facilitation. The IDRL Guidelines emphasise that:

> [A]s an essential element of a larger disaster risk reduction programme, States should adopt comprehensive legal, policy, and institutional frameworks and planning for disaster prevention, mitigation, preparedness, relief and recovery which take full account of the auxiliary role of their National Red Cross or Red Crescent Society, are inclusive of domestic civil society, and empower communities to enhance their own safety and resilience . . . These frameworks should also adequately address the initiation, facilitation, transit and regulation of international disaster relief and initial recovery assistance consistent with these Guidelines.[103]

At a minimum, this requires clearly assigning responsibilities and authority for different aspects of disaster response in order to enable effective coordination.[104]

In addition, states are encouraged to consider temporary adjustments or waivers of specific national legislation or regulations where these would unnecessarily impede assistance. In the commentaries to the Draft Articles, the ILC:

> [E]ncourages States to allow for temporary non-applicability of their national laws that might unnecessarily hamper assistance in the event of disasters and for appropriate provisions on facilitation to be included within their national law so as not to create any legal uncertainty in the critical period following a disaster when such emergency provisions become necessary.[105]

This recommendation applies particularly to overly stringent visa and customs requirements that delay the entry of relief personnel and essential goods,[106] but also to other regulatory barriers, such as licensing requirements for the use of radio and telecommunication networks during disaster operations.[107]

[102] In 2019, the IFRC reported that 37 states had drafted domestic legislation based on the IDRL Guidelines; see IFRC, 'Fourth Progress Report on the Implementation of the IDRL Guidelines' (14 November 2019) 4.

[103] IDRL Guidelines (n 11) art 8(1-2).

[104] ibid art 8(2). See also Inter-American Convention (n 6) art III(a); BSEC Agreement (n 5) art 6(1); Arab League Agreement (n 5) art 6; Shanghai Agreement (n 5) art 5(1).

[105] ILC (n 14) 66.

[106] Draft Articles (n 5) art 15(1).

[107] Tampere Convention (n 5) art 9(3)(f).

Prompt and effective facilitation of international disaster response is vital to realising solidarity in IDRL. Without timely entry of personnel, goods and equipment, and without clear legal and institutional frameworks to remove administrative, regulatory and bureaucratic obstacles, international cooperation risks being undermined by unnecessary barriers and bottlenecks. States must therefore prepare in advance by adopting comprehensive laws and procedures that address common barriers to the provision of assistance. This is not only a practical necessity for saving lives and reducing suffering in the aftermath of disasters; it is also imperative if states truly commit to solidarity in international disaster response.

Furthermore, preparing for and improving the facilitation of international disaster response flows from existing obligations under international law. States bear primary responsibility for the protection of persons affected by disasters within their jurisdiction, and this responsibility includes ensuring that adequate assistance reaches those in need.[108] Facilitation should therefore be understood as an integral component of this duty. Moreover, facilitation is essential to the implementation of the duty to cooperate by taking away common obstacles to effective cooperation.

However, facilitation should not be understood as compromising the primary role of the affected state in directing, controlling, coordinating and supervising disaster response. It does not imply that states must admit all relief personnel and goods or waive every regulation deemed cumbersome. Sovereignty remains a core principle, and affected states retain the right and responsibility to regulate the entry and distribution of aid in order to protect national interests and ensure that assistance is adequate. This is reflected in the IDRL Guidelines, which note that facilitation measures 'will be subject to the interests of national security, public order, public and environmental health, and public morals of the concerned affected, originating and transit States'.[109] As the IFRC explains, '[w]here specific activities or situations implicate the critical state interests listed in this paragraph . . . some level of exception to the recommended facilities is both appropriate and inevitable', citing the continuing responsibilities of states to protect citizens, inter alia, from foreign terrorists, unsafe medicines or smuggled contraband.[110] Moreover, affected states remain responsible for ensuring that humanitarian assistance meets minimum standards under international law: assistance must be appropriate, adequate and provided in accordance with the humanitarian principles.[111]

The effectiveness of facilitation ultimately depends on striking the right balance between state control and the imperative for international assistance

[108] Draft Articles (n 5) art 10(1).
[109] IDRL Guidelines (n 11) part V, chapeau.
[110] IFRC, 'Annotations' (n 75) 29.
[111] Draft Articles (n 5) art 6; IDRL Guidelines (n 11) art 4(2).

to be delivered as swiftly as possible. While affected states may and should retain authority over the entry and distribution of aid, any restrictions must be limited to protecting 'critical state interests' only and never imposed for political or arbitrary reasons.[112] Moreover, such restrictions should be 'as narrow as possible in order to reduce any unnecessary impediments to the alleviation of human suffering'.[113] As argued in Chapter 5, section III.C, this implies a proportionality test: states must weigh up the need to safeguard legitimate national interests against the protection of persons affected by disasters. Consequently, restrictions must not unnecessarily or disproportionately delay or obstruct the provision of essential international assistance. Achieving this balance is fundamental to ensuring that sovereignty and solidarity coexist harmoniously rather than in tension.[114]

Beyond establishing domestic legal and institutional frameworks to anticipate and remove barriers to international cooperation, it is equally necessary to strengthen the capacity of states to process and coordinate the influx of international assistance. Practice shows that authorities are often overwhelmed by the sudden arrival of large volumes of aid, creating bottlenecks in entry and distribution.[115] Yet not all states have the resources to build this capacity on their own. For this reason, states must cooperate in a spirit of solidarity to enhance national systems for facilitation and coordination.[116] Such support may include financial and technical assistance, including policy consultancy, help in drafting regulatory frameworks, managerial and technical training, and the development of information and administrative systems.

In conclusion, the facilitation of international cooperation in disaster response ultimately comes down to preparation – both in terms of establishing appropriate legal and institutional frameworks that assign responsibilities and set procedures ahead of time, and in terms of building the capacity to process incoming assistance and coordinate its distribution promptly and effectively. While each state bears responsibility for these measures, cooperation is essential to support states that lack the necessary resources. Such support requires both technical expertise and financial assistance. Enhancing preparedness through cooperation not only contributes to the protection of persons affected by disasters but also strengthens the resilience of states. As such, cooperation in this context advances social justice by addressing and ameliorating structural inequalities that leave some states less equipped to prepare for disasters due to limited expertise and resources.

[112] IFRC, 'Annotations' (n 75) 29.

[113] ibid. The IDRL Guidelines also note that '[m]easures to protect such interests should be tailored to the exigencies of the specific disaster and consistent with the humanitarian imperative of addressing the needs of affected communities': IDRL Guidelines (n 11) part V, chapeau.

[114] As discussed in ch 4, section II.

[115] Fisher (n 2) 133.

[116] See also AADMER (n 5) art 18.

C. Building National Response Capacities

The previous two sections have highlighted the importance of cooperation in preparing for disasters, both by collecting information and implementing appropriate legal and institutional frameworks. If cooperation is understood as a vehicle for fulfilling the shared responsibility of all states for the protection of affected persons within a framework of solidarity – as was argued in section II – then it is essential that cooperation also includes building states' national response capacities. The concept of national response capacity encompasses the combination of all strengths and resources available within a state to reduce the effects of a disaster.[117] This includes infrastructure, institutions, human knowledge and skills, and collective attributes such as social relationships, leadership and management.[118] These capacities vary significantly across states, creating stark global and regional inequalities. Data shows that low-income countries in the Global South in particular have weaker response capacities and are consequently disproportionately vulnerable to hazards.[119] These disparities are expected to deepen under the impacts of climate change, which will disproportionately affect low-income countries, placing even greater strain on their response capacities and amplifying their vulnerability.[120]

Building national response capacities is essential for the protection of people affected by disasters because states with stronger capacities are better positioned to ensure adequate protection without relying on international aid. Disaster response should therefore not be limited to actions taken after a disaster strikes, but must also focus on improving resilience and enhancing the ability to manage disasters effectively. While each state should invest in strengthening their own national response capacities, they also have a shared responsibility to support those that lack resources and expertise to do so. Such cooperation reflects solidarity, recognising that enhancing the response capacities of all states is directly linked to the shared responsibility for protecting persons in disasters.

There is a broad and consistent commitment by states to cooperate in enhancing national response capacities. The UN General Assembly, for example, routinely reaffirms 'the importance of international cooperation in support of the efforts of the affected States in dealing with natural disasters in all their phases, in particular in preparedness, response and the early recovery phase, and of strengthening the response capacity of countries affected by disaster'.[121] Its resolutions repeatedly reiterate 'the commitment to support, as a matter of priority, the efforts of countries, in particular developing countries, to strengthen their capacities at all levels in order to assess and reduce risks, prepare for and

[117] UNDRR, 'Definition: Capacity' www.undrr.org/terminology/capacity.
[118] ibid.
[119] European Commission, 'INFORM Report 2024' (2024) 21–22.
[120] ibid 25–26.
[121] UN General Assembly Res 78/120 (8 December 2023) UN Doc A/RES/78/120, preamble.

respond rapidly, effectively and safely to natural disasters and mitigate their impact'[122] and stress that:

> [T]o increase further the effectiveness of humanitarian assistance, particular international cooperation efforts should be undertaken to enhance and broaden further the utilization of national and local capacities and, where appropriate, of regional and subregional capacities for disaster preparedness and response, which may be made available in closer proximity to the site of a disaster, and more efficiently and at lower cost.[123]

States have also made clear commitments to capacity-building in the Sendai Framework for Disaster Risk Reduction.[124] Adopted at the Third UN World Conference on Disaster Risk Reduction in 2015, the Sendai Framework sets out 'a concise, focused, forward-looking and action-oriented post-2015 framework for disaster risk reduction'.[125] While non-binding, in it states have committed to pursue coordinated action under four priorities, of which the final priority – enhancing preparedness for effective response and addressing risk reduction across recovery, rehabilitation and reconstruction – is the most relevant for the present purposes.[126] This priority underscores 'the need to further strengthen disaster preparedness for response, take action in anticipation of events, integrate disaster risk reduction in response preparedness and ensure that capacities are in place for effective response and recovery at all levels'.[127] To achieve this, it sets out a range of activities for states and stakeholders at the global and regional levels, including developing and updating disaster preparedness and contingency plans, promoting regional and international cooperation for early warning systems, and strengthening technical and logistical capacities to ensure better response in emergencies.[128]

The Sendai Framework consistently emphasises that international cooperation is indispensable in an era of increasing global interdependence, calling for collaboration to build knowledge, capacities and motivation for disaster risk reduction, particularly in developing countries.[129] It stresses that 'given their different capacities, as well as the linkage between the level of support provided to them and the extent to which they will be able to implement the present Framework', developing countries require enhanced provision of resources through global partnerships and sustained international support.[130] Special attention is urged for disaster-prone developing countries – especially

[122] ibid para 23.
[123] ibid para 35.
[124] Sendai Framework (n 16).
[125] ibid para 1(a).
[126] ibid para 20. The other priorities are understanding disaster risk (priority 1), strengthening disaster risk governance (priority 2) and investing in risk reduction (priority 3).
[127] ibid para 32.
[128] ibid para 33.
[129] ibid para 22.
[130] ibid para 38.

least-developed countries, small-island developing states, landlocked developing countries, African countries and middle-income countries facing specific challenges – whose vulnerability often exceeds their capacity to respond and recover.[131] Similar assistance should also extend to other disaster-prone states with unique characteristics, such as archipelagic countries and those with extensive coastlines.[132]

This requires, in the first place, sustained financial support, predictable funding streams and investment in local authorities that can manage disaster risk effectively over time. As the Sendai Framework underscores:

> Financing from a variety of international sources, public and private transfer of reliable, affordable, appropriate and modern environmentally sound technology, on concessional and preferential terms, as mutually agreed, capacity-building assistance for developing countries and enabling institutional and policy environments at all levels are critically important means of reducing disaster risk.[133]

However, cooperation must go beyond financial assistance to include robust technical assistance. The Framework highlights in this context that:

> In addressing economic disparity and disparity in technological innovation and research capacity among countries, it is crucial to enhance technology transfer, involving a process of enabling and facilitating flows of skill, knowledge, ideas, know-how and technology from developed to developing countries in the implementation of the present Framework.[134]

Technical assistance should prioritise knowledge transfer and technology sharing, enabling developing countries to adopt advanced early-warning systems, risk and needs mapping tools and resilient infrastructure standards. Equally important is strengthening governance and coordination mechanisms, as well as the capacity of national authorities to manage the influx of international aid promptly effectively.

States have made similar commitments to capacity-building in other contexts, such as global health law. For example, under the IHR 2005, states must develop, strengthen and maintain the capacity to detect, assess, notify and report events that could constitute a public health emergency of international concern.[135] In the IHR 2005, states commit 'to collaborate with each other, to the extent possible, in . . . the provision or facilitation of technical cooperation and logistical support, particularly in the development, strengthening and maintenance of the public health capacities required under these Regulations',[136] and states are

[131] ibid para 41.
[132] ibid.
[133] ibid para 46.
[134] ibid para 40.
[135] IHR 2005 (n 32) art 5(1).
[136] ibid art 44(1)(b).

allowed to request assistance from the WHO.[137] The *WHO Pandemic Agreement* builds on this approach, obligating states to 'develop, strengthen and maintain a resilient health system, particularly primary health care, for pandemic prevention, preparedness and response',[138] and pledging that:

> The Parties shall cooperate, directly or through relevant international organizations, subject to national and/or domestic law and available resources, to sustainably strengthen the pandemic prevention, preparedness and response capacities of all Parties, particularly developing country Parties. Such cooperation shall include, inter alia, the promotion of the transfer of technology as mutually agreed, including transfer of relevant knowledge, skills, and technical expertise, and the sharing of technical, scientific and legal expertise, as well as financial assistance and support for capacity-strengthening for those Parties that lack the means and resources to implement the provisions of the WHO Pandemic Agreement, and shall be facilitated, as appropriate, by the World Health Organization in collaboration with relevant organizations upon the request of the Party, to fulfil the obligations arising from this Agreement.[139]

Capacity-building is also a central pillar of the Paris Agreement on climate change. Under the agreement, states have committed to enhance the capacity and ability of developing countries and those that are particularly vulnerable to the adverse effects of climate change 'to take effective climate change action, including, inter alia, to implement adaptation and mitigation actions'.[140] It further provides that: 'All Parties should cooperate to enhance the capacity of developing country Parties to implement this Agreement.'[141] This commitment is critical for disaster response because strengthening adaptive capacity can significantly reduce vulnerability to the impacts of climate change, which increasingly drive disaster risk. In this context, capacity-building is not limited to climate mitigation, but extends to adaptation measures that bolster resilience against extreme weather events, sea-level rise and other climate-related hazards.

Some regional IDRL treaties also provide a framework for cooperation in building national response capacities, with the AADMER taking one of the most progressive approaches. Unlike many instruments that focus narrowly on cooperation during the response phase, AADMER expands its scope to include broader collaboration 'in developing and implementing measures to reduce disaster losses', encompassing disaster risk reduction and preparedness.[142] In this context, state parties have agreed to 'jointly or individually, develop strategies to identify, prevent and reduce risks arising from hazards' and, to this end, that '[e]ach Party shall undertake measures to reduce losses from disasters which include . . . strengthening local and national disaster management capability

[137] ibid art 5(3).
[138] WHO Pandemic Agreement (n 64) art 6(1).
[139] ibid art 17(1).
[140] Paris Agreement (12 December 2015) art 11(1).
[141] ibid art 11(3).
[142] AADMER (n 5) art 4(a).

and co-ordination'.[143] Furthermore, parties commit to 'jointly or individually enhance their national capacities, as appropriate' to respond to disasters within their territory and to cooperate with other actors where necessary.[144] AADMER also pursues 'technical cooperation' among state parties to improve resilience, preparedness and national response capacities.[145]

Other regional agreements also create space for capacity-building, even if in less comprehensive ways. For example, under the EU Civil Protection Mechanism, financial assistance is available to Member States 'to enhance prevention of, preparedness for and effective response to disasters', signalling a commitment to strengthening national systems beyond immediate disaster relief.[146] Similarly, the *Agreement between Member States and Associate Members of the Association of Caribbean States for Regional Cooperation on Natural Disasters* provides that 'Parties shall promote scientific and technical activities' aimed at improving technical capabilities and expertise, including the ability to conduct needs assessments.[147] In 2005, members of the Association of Caribbean States recommitted to cooperation in the prevention and mitigation of disasters, pledging to 'foster international co-operation and capacity-building in the area of natural disasters, in enhancing the provision of humanitarian assistance at all stages of a disaster and in promoting a culture of prevention and early warning systems'.[148]

The IDRL Guidelines also emphasise the importance of cooperation in capacity-building, stating that:

> With a view to increasing resilience and reducing the need for international disaster relief and initial recovery assistance, the international community, including donors, regional and other relevant actors, should support developing States, domestic civil society actors and National Red Cross and Red Crescent Societies to build their capacities to prevent, mitigate, prepare for and respond to disasters domestically.[149]

By encouraging international actors to invest in preparedness and response capacities at the national level, the IDRL Guidelines reinforce the principle that effective disaster governance requires both facilitation of international assistance and sustained cooperation to empower states to manage disasters independently.

Despite broad and consistent commitments, international cooperation remains inadequate and piecemeal, falling short of delivering sustained improvements in national response capacities. Reporting on the implementation progress of the Sendai Framework, the UN Office for Disaster Risk Reduction (UNDRR) highlights that financing, technology transfer and capacity development are the least

[143] ibid art 6(1–2).
[144] ibid art 8(3).
[145] ibid art 18.
[146] EU Civil Protection Mechanism (n 5) art 20.
[147] ACS Agreement (n 5) art 5.
[148] Association of Caribbean States, 'Declaration of Panama' (29 July 2005) para 20d.
[149] IDRL Guidelines (n 11) art 9(1).

reported among its targets.[150] While there is a significant level of international cooperation among states,[151] the UNDRR points to a striking underinvestment in disaster risk reduction within international aid: only $0.50 out of every $100 in disaster-related official development assistance was allocated for disaster risk reduction.[152] Similarly, there is a significant underinvestment in international cooperation on climate adaptation.[153] In light of this, the UNDRR calls for increased and sustained financing, and better cooperation that combines funding, technology transfer and capacity development.[154]

However, it is unlikely that the funding gap will close anytime soon. As previously noted, there remains a persistent disconnect between rhetoric and action.[155] Despite consistent pledges, donor states have been reducing development aid budgets – particularly the US under the Trump administration – and prioritising their own resilience and domestic needs over global capacity-building efforts, often without facing meaningful consequences.[156] Another contributing factor is that capacity-building investments tend to receive lower political attention because their benefits are long-term and less visible, making them less attractive compared to short-term, high-profile investments. This short-term thinking is further reflected in the stark disparity between funding for disaster risk reduction and allocations for relief, reconstruction and rehabilitation.[157] While the latter is essential for saving lives in the aftermath of disasters, it should not overshadow sustained investment in capacity-building, which could significantly mitigate the impact of disasters and reduce the need for emergency aid in the future.

What is needed is a fundamental reframing of international cooperation for capacity-building as a shared responsibility rather than a charitable gesture or an extension of development aid.[158] When cooperation is understood as an investment in collective resilience and the protection of vulnerable populations, it shifts the narrative from benevolence to mutual interest. This perspective can create stronger incentives for sustained cooperation, as states recognise that solidarity in reducing disaster risks globally also safeguards their interests, both by improving the protection of affected people and reducing the needs of affected states for international assistance during and after disasters. By framing capacity-building as a strategic investment with long-term dividends, international actors

[150] UNDRR, 'International Cooperation in Disaster Risk Reduction: Target F' (2021) 14.
[151] ibid.
[152] ibid 8.
[153] The UN has reported that the needs of low-income states on climate adaption are 12 times greater than funding provided by donors: UN Environment Programme, 'Adaptation Gap Report 2025: Running on Empty' (October 2025).
[154] UNDRR (n 150) 15.
[155] See ch 6, section III.C.
[156] Active Learning Network for Accountability and Performance, 'Global Humanitarian Assistance Report 2025' (2025) vii.
[157] UNDRR (n 150) 8.
[158] Chapter 2, section III discussed the possible motivations for states to act in solidarity.

may be more willing to commit resources consistently and overcome the short-term thinking that currently undermines disaster risk reduction efforts.

Strengthening enforcement mechanisms is also essential to ensure that states honour their commitments to international cooperation. When states fail to keep their promises, this erodes the mutual trust and reliance that underpin solidarity and reduce the credibility of the many frameworks for international cooperation in this area. To prevent solidarity from becoming something to which states can pay mere lip service without following through, stronger accountability measures are needed to hold states to their word. Such mechanisms could include more robust monitoring, reporting and compliance systems, as well as consequences for persistent non-compliance. Without these safeguards, pledges risk remaining symbolic rather than translating into tangible action, undermining efforts to build resilience and protect vulnerable populations.

IV. CONCLUSION

This chapter has examined the nature and scope of international cooperation in disaster response. It has argued that solidarity seeks to transform cooperation from ad hoc and reactive humanitarian efforts into a proactive and continuous process encompassing all stages of disaster management. Cooperation serves as a vehicle for fulfilling the shared responsibility to protect persons in the context of disasters. Understood in this way, cooperation must become structured and systematic, moving beyond temporary arrangements in response to specific events. The ongoing process of formalising frameworks for disaster cooperation in bilateral and multilateral agreements is therefore not only instrumental in facilitating disaster response but also a prerequisite for the success of solidarity. Furthermore, a broader understanding of cooperation is needed – one that recognises protection as an ongoing process rather than a reactive project triggered only after disaster strikes. This reframing shifts emphasis towards supporting states in reducing vulnerabilities and building resilience. Cooperation in this sense is an expression of solidarity, acknowledging that sustained collaboration is critical to protect people in the context of disasters.

The chapter has also explored three key aspects of cooperation, illustrating what reframing cooperation through the lens of solidarity would look like in practice. Section III.A examined the exchange of information as a condition for effective disaster response, arguing that states should share relevant data to facilitate response efforts and emphasising that cooperation extends beyond the mere provision of assistance. At the same time, it highlighted the need for more sustained collaboration to enable states to collect and analyse information about hazards and risks. Section III.B addressed recurring challenges arising from inadequate preparedness to facilitate international cooperation. The influx and distribution of assistance are often delayed or obstructed by unnecessary administrative, regulatory and bureaucratic barriers and bottlenecks. While states bear individual responsibility for implementing legal and institutional frameworks that anticipate these issues, there is also an urgent need for support through technical and financial assistance. Finally, section III.C focused on capacity-building, underscoring that solidarity requires increased and sustained cooperation to strengthen national response capacities, enhance resilience and reduce reliance on international aid. Yet, despite broad and repeated commitments, states continue to fall short of their targets.

While states often signal commitment to cooperation in the context of disasters, the successful implementation of solidarity is far from guaranteed. There remains a risk that states will invoke sovereignty as a cover to avoid fully engaging in cooperation and an equally significant risk that they will fail to meet their pledges for assistance. Persistent gaps between rhetoric and practice – such as chronic underinvestment in capacity-building and the failure to remove barriers to assistance – underscore the danger that solidarity becomes aspirational or merely rhetorical. Without stronger accountability mechanisms, commitments to cooperate risk remaining symbolic rather than translating into tangible action. Addressing this enforcement gap is therefore essential to operationalising solidarity and ensuring that international cooperation delivers on its promise of protecting people in the context of disasters.

Finally, this chapter has demonstrated solidarity's transformative potential within IDRL. Beyond reframing cooperation from a voluntary or humanitarian gesture into a binding commitment grounded in shared responsibility – as discussed in the previous chapters – solidarity emphasises the need to expand cooperation beyond the reactive paradigm, recognising that protection begins long before disaster strikes. By using cooperation as a vehicle for improving states' preparedness and resilience, solidarity not only pursues its central objective of protecting people in the context of disasters but also addresses structural inequalities between states, recognising that national response capacities are unequal and facing rising pressure due to the effects of climate change. In doing so, solidarity ultimately seeks to advance international social justice, closing protection gaps across the globe and ensuring that all states are better equipped to reduce vulnerabilities and manage risks.

8

Conclusion

I. A FUTURE OF DISASTERS

As this book reaches its conclusion, it returns to the urgent backdrop against which it began: the world is facing a bleak future in which disasters are predicted to intensify in terms of both frequency and severity due to the accelerating effects of climate change, threatening more people than ever before.[1] The international community has arrived at a pivotal moment – one that demands urgent preparation for a future of disasters. Now more than ever, global cooperation is essential to reduce disaster risks, mitigate their impacts and protect those affected. In this context, solidarity cannot remain a political slogan or a rhetorical gesture of sympathy. It must be translated into meaningful commitments to international cooperation and assistance. This chapter synthesises the findings of the book's analysis, distilling its core arguments and reflecting on how solidarity can be developed from aspirational language into a principle that transforms IDRL from a sovereignty-centred regime characterised by state autonomy and voluntarism into one pursuing the protection of disaster-affected persons through differentiated international cooperation and assistance.

At its core, this book has sought to unpack what solidarity truly means for IDRL: its meaning, legal status, practical implications and potential to transform the regime. By developing a conceptual understanding of solidarity and scrutinising its standing as a principle of law, the book found that while solidarity is not generally regarded by states as legally binding, it can nonetheless play a crucial role as a broadly accepted normative foundation for international disaster response, shaping the interpretation and guiding the future development of IDRL. From this point, the book explored the transformative potential of solidarity if states were to fully embrace it as a principle of IDRL, examining both its high-level implications for the regime and its translation into concrete norms and practices. The aim was to demonstrate how solidarity could reshape

[1] IPCC, 'Summary for Policymakers' in *Climate Change 2021: The Physical Science Basis. Contribution of Working Group I to the Sixth Assessment Report of the Intergovernmental Panel on Climate Change* (Cambridge University Press, 2021) 27. As cited previously, the IFRC predicts that the number of people affected by disasters that need international humanitarian assistance could grow by more than 40 per cent by 2050: IFRC, 'The Cost of Doing Nothing' (2019) www.ifrc.org/document/cost-doing-nothing, 3.

IDRL and what it could achieve in doing so, while addressing concerns about implementation and its impact on state sovereignty. What emerges is an outline of a possible future IDRL grounded in solidarity, offered at a pivotal moment when cooperation and assistance in disaster response are more urgent than ever.

This chapter serves as the closing piece. Section II looks back at the findings of this book, aiming not simply to summarise but also to synthesise them in order to make sense of solidarity within IDRL. It addresses the fundamental question of what solidarity means in this context, both as a concept and legal phenomenon. From there, the discussion turns to the transformative potential of solidarity, or how grounding IDRL in this principle would reshape the way in which this regime is understood. In particular, it highlights the profound consequences of reconceptualising disaster response from a matter confined to the sovereign domain of the affected state to one of shared responsibility of all states. As revealed through the book's analysis, this shift would require expanded cooperation and embed differentiation in responsibilities to reflect and respect the varying capacities of states. These changes do not radically erase the core foundations of IDRL as it stands, especially state sovereignty, but they fundamentally alter the lens through which we interpret the roles of affected states, third states and assisting actors, as well as the scope of international cooperation.

Section III then looks forward, asking the critical question of how solidarity's transformative potential can be realised within IDRL. Simply declaring solidarity as a principle does not, by itself, change the regime – tangible action is needed to ensure that IDRL genuinely reflects this commitment. This section therefore explores what that action entails, emphasising that much can be achieved through (re)interpreting existing norms and developing new ones. The negotiations on the treaty on the protection of persons in the event of disasters present a unique and timely opportunity to make this transition. At the same time, this section confronts obstacles identified throughout the book, most notably the enforcement gap that solidarity leaves behind – a gap that risks states prioritising national interests over solidarity without consequence. Because solidarity alone cannot close this gap, the chapter proposes the creation of a 'custodian of solidarity': an independent international body mandated to oversee, promote and facilitate the practice of solidarity in disaster response. This would not be a body to force states to act in solidarity – such coercion would undermine the very spirit of solidarity – but rather a representative of the international community tasked with safeguarding the principle, ensuring it transcends rhetoric and fulfils its promise of cooperation and assistance.

II. THE TRANSFORMATIVE POTENTIAL OF SOLIDARITY

Solidarity is invoked so frequently in the discourse on disaster response that it has almost become a buzzword – used in diverse contexts and with seemingly different intentions. Sometimes it serves as an expression of sympathy for those affected; at other times, it functions as a call for action, an appeal for assistance.[2] Yet this varied and often superficial use risks reducing solidarity to a mere rhetorical device – a signal of support without the substance of action. This is why it was necessary to examine solidarity more closely and develop a conceptual understanding that can be meaningfully applied in the context of IDRL. The goal of this exercise was not to impose a rigid definition, but to establish a shared understanding of what solidarity represents and what is at stake when it is invoked, providing a foundation for interpreting and operationalising it within IDRL.

Drawing on sociological, political and legal theory, and examining its use across international law, this book conceptualises solidarity as both a relational and a normative notion. Relationally, solidarity describes the social bond that connects a community; normatively, it entails a commitment to mutual support within that community. In international law specifically, solidarity is generally understood as the pursuit of common goals by a community of states (and others) who support one another through differentiated cooperation and assistance. This model departs from traditional, transactional notions of cooperation, implying a willingness to provide support without an expectation of reciprocity, even when benefits are unevenly distributed. This approach acknowledges and responds to existing inequalities between states, meaning that contributions to collective efforts are not equal, but differentiated according to capacity and responsibility. Understood in this light, solidarity is not merely altruistic or a corrective to inequality, but also a pragmatic response to the realities of an interdependent world, where mutual support is increasingly essential to achieving shared objectives.

In the context of international disaster response, solidarity is fundamentally oriented towards the protection of persons affected by disasters. This commitment emerges clearly from binding and non-binding instruments, the long-standing practice of humanitarian assistance and consistent statements by states and non-state actors, all of which affirm that protecting those affected is a common objective of the international community and that there is a broad readiness to cooperate in pursuit of this goal without expectation of mutual benefit.[3] This book has shown that solidarity is progressively embedded in legal frameworks facilitating international cooperation and assistance – sometimes even explicitly referenced in treaties where state parties agree to act 'in the spirit of solidarity'.[4] Yet, despite these commitments, solidarity remains predominantly understood as a moral aspiration rather than a legally binding principle. This is reflected in the voluntary nature of cooperation under IDRL, which encourages but does not obligate states to act in solidarity.

[2] See examples in ch 3, section IV.
[3] Evidence for this claim has been presented in ch 2, section IV.
[4] See examples of explicit references to solidarity in ch 3, section IV.A..

This leaves a discernible gap between what states say and what they do – a discrepancy in the use of solidarity that is visible across international law.[5] While states consistently affirm their commitment to solidarity, they stop short of accepting that rights and obligations flow from it, preserving sovereignty and the discretion to choose whether, when and how to cooperate with others. Although solidarity cannot yet be regarded as a general principle of law capable of creating, modifying or confirming states' rights and obligations, it can nonetheless significantly shape IDRL. The evidence shows that solidarity carries real normative weight within the regime as states indicate that international disaster response should be underpinned by solidarity. This recognition opens the door to using solidarity as an interpretative lens – through a teleological approach that gives effect to the law's underlying rationale and protective purpose – and as a model for future norm development. Not as binding law, but as a broadly supported normative foundation upon which IDRL can be designed, interpreted and evolved to better realise cooperation and assistance in practice.

These findings are significant because they yield critical insights into what solidarity is – both as a concept and as a legal phenomenon – shifting the conversation beyond abstract theorisation towards concrete discussions of its functioning and implications within international law. By establishing a common understanding of solidarity and clarifying how its legal standing can be assessed, the book provides a shared analytical vocabulary and methodological footing for interpreting, applying and developing solidarity. These insights are relevant across international law, especially in regimes where solidarity is frequently invoked, yet remains underexamined and underutilised – most notably, global health law and international climate change law – offering a way to evaluate claims of solidarity, to identify the normative work it already performs and to map how it can be operationalised through differentiated cooperation and assistance without collapsing into mere rhetoric.

Crucially, however, using solidarity as an interpretive lens and a basis for future development is not a mandate to remake IDRL – or any other regime of international law – in the image of solidarity alone. Like all principles, solidarity operates in concert with others, and in IDRL that means it neither replaces nor overrides sovereignty, which remains a founding premise of the regime. This addresses concerns that embracing solidarity could lead to a borderless model of disaster governance run by internationally centralised mechanisms – as some strands of solidarist thought may imply[6] – by demonstrating that solidarity can be operationalised within a framework that still respects state sovereignty. At the same time, solidarity necessarily imposes reasonable constraints on unrestricted sovereignty: it commits states to cooperation and assistance oriented towards

[5] M den Heijer and H van der Wilt, 'Global Solidarity and Common But Differentiated Responsibilities' in M den Heijer and H van der Wilt (eds), *Netherlands Yearbook of International Law 2020* (TMC Asser Press, 2022) 3, 4.

[6] For a brief discussion of the solidarist reinterpretation of international law, see ch 2, section II.

protecting persons affected by disasters, and it informs how discretion should be exercised in light of shared responsibilities for this common objective. If states genuinely commit to solidarity in international disaster response, such curbs are both justified and proportionate, clarifying not only the responsibilities of affected states but also the roles of third states and assisting actors, and guiding the scope and modalities of international cooperation without erasing sovereignty's core functions.

With this in mind, the remainder of the book has explored what IDRL would look like if it were interpreted and developed through the lens of solidarity, demonstrating its potential to transform it from a sovereignty-centred regime characterised by state autonomy and voluntarism to one pursuing the protection of disaster-affected persons through differentiated international cooperation and assistance. Chapter 4 articulated five high-level implications of implementing solidarity in IDRL: first, placing constraints on state discretion over whether and how to cooperate in disaster response; second, developing the rights and duties of non-affected third states, clarifying their responsibilities in support affected states and their populations; third, centring the rights of disaster-affected persons in response; fourth, committing to a binding duty to cooperate that moves beyond voluntarism towards proactive and sustained cooperation across all stages of disasters; and, fifth, differentiating responsibilities according to states' respective capacities. Together, these implications sketch a regime that is grounded in the idea that the protection of persons affected by disasters is a shared responsibility, embedding disaster response in a framework of differentiated international cooperation and assistance.

Chapters 5–7 then examined how solidarity can be translated from an abstract principle into concrete norms and practices by analysing three core dimensions of IDRL through the lens of solidarity: the role of the affected state; the role of third states and assisting actors; and the scope of international cooperation. By zooming in on specific issues that remain contested or underexplored, this granular approach showed how solidarity can be operationalised credibly and realistically, moving from aspirational theory to practice through concrete rules. In doing so, the analysis illuminates how solidarity recalibrates IDRL down through its veins: reframing responsibility, reinterpreting duties to cooperate with others and redefining the breadth and depth of cooperation in disaster response. It also presents alternative interpretations of key issues that can break new ground in resolving persistent controversies and proposes new norms to further develop IDRL, demonstrating that solidarity provides not merely a guiding idea, but an architecture for more equitable disaster response.

Rather than repeating how solidarity reinterprets each aspect of IDRL here, it is more illuminating to step back and consider what this analysis reveals about the transformative potential of solidarity. First and foremost, while solidarity is undoubtedly transformative, it does not radically overthrow or replace the existing framework. Instead, it works within it, preserving the core principles of responsibility whereby the affected state retains the primary role in disaster response, with third states and assisting actors playing an auxiliary role, offering support where needed. Within this structure, solidarity affirms respect for sovereignty and the principles that flow from it – most notably, the affected state's sovereign rights to direct, control, coordinate and supervise all disaster response efforts on its territory and the principle of consent. What solidarity does *not* do is shift responsibility for protection to the international community or centralise disaster response at a global or regional level. The affected state remains in charge of responding to disasters within its jurisdiction.

Solidarity nonetheless fundamentally changes how these responsibilities should be understood, reshaping the interpretation of states' respective roles and the scope of international cooperation. It presupposes a dual structure of responsibility: each state is responsible for contributing to the common objective according to its own capacity, while all states share a responsibility to support others in pursuing that objective when needed. In practice, this means that while every state should first rely on its own resources, it can fall back on the support of others if necessary. Understood this way, the protection of disaster-affected persons – the common objective pursued through solidarity – becomes a shared responsibility of all states, with the affected state carrying the primary responsibility and other states bearing a duty to assist through cooperation. While this interpretation preserves the existing distribution of responsibilities under IDRL, it produces a profound shift: moving away from sovereignty as the central premise of the regime and placing common goals, shared responsibility and mutual support at its core.

As argued throughout the book, this changed perception of responsibility has cascading effects across IDRL, reframing disaster response from a matter that falls squarely within the sovereign domain of affected states to a matter of international concern in which all states share an interest. This reframing aligns with the recognition – already evident in IDRL instruments and practice – that disaster response is a global event of significance for the international community as a whole.[7] It signals that states do not enjoy absolute freedom in deciding how to respond to disasters or whether, when and to what extent to cooperate with others. Whereas international law often justifies restrictions on discretion as flowing from existing obligations, particularly the duty to protect human rights and dignity, solidarity adds another layer: it acknowledges that states must also respect the interests of other states in disaster response, who share responsibility for protecting affected persons. Constraints on sovereignty thus reflect not only legal obligations but also the reality that states are part of a community and owe duties to contribute to common causes. This represents a fundamentally different way of thinking about responsibility under IDRL, emphasising community interests and shared objectives.

[7] See also ILC, 'Fourth Report on the Protection of Persons in the Event of Disasters, by Mr. Eduardo Valencia-Ospina, Special Rapporteur' (11 May 2011) UN Doc A/CN.4/643, para 83.

However, this reinterpretation of responsibility should not be misconstrued as a licence for foreign interference. Even though disaster response is framed as a shared responsibility, the primary responsibility remains with the affected state at all times. Third states and assisting actors have an interest in protecting persons affected by disasters, but their role is auxiliary – supporting the affected state through cooperation and assistance. When an affected state is unable or even unwilling to ensure adequate protection, others cannot intervene under the banner of solidarity. They may remind the state of its responsibilities and exert diplomatic pressure to act in solidarity, but they have no right to circumvent the affected state or conduct humanitarian interventions. Doing so would undermine the dual structure of responsibility that solidarity envisages. This also means that the affected state retains its primary role in directing, controlling, coordinating and supervising disaster response after accepting international assistance. Cooperation is not an invitation to take over; all assisting states and actors engaged in response efforts must operate within the laws, policies and directions set by the affected state.

In this context, it is important to rethink international cooperation positively – as a means for states to secure the support they need to protect their populations rather than as a potential threat of interference. The fear of encroachment on sovereignty appears, at least in part, to underlie the strong emphasis on sovereign prerogatives in IDRL and the tendency of some states to delay or even reject international assistance.[8] Solidarity offers a different perspective: cooperation is not about surrendering control but about enabling states to fulfil their primary responsibility when their own capacities are overwhelmed. Framing assistance as a tool of empowerment rather than intrusion helps dismantle the misplaced zero-sum logic that pits sovereignty against cooperation and instead positions solidarity as a mechanism for reinforcing, rather than undermining, the ability of states to protect those within their jurisdiction. From the standpoint of third states and assisting actors, cooperation is likewise not a vehicle for advancing national interests or exerting influence, but a means of achieving the common objective of protecting persons affected by disasters. In this sense, solidarity should be understood as a facilitator of humanitarianism rather than intervention, enabling international actors to alleviate suffering and uphold human rights and dignity by delivering aid where it is most urgently required.

At the same time, this requires reinforcing the role of third states and assisting actors, who should bear duties alongside rights – in particular, a duty to assist when needed. Such a duty can no longer be understood as merely hortatory, encouraging cooperation without creating a corresponding legal obligation. Solidarity demands that international disaster response moves beyond the tradition of voluntarism, requiring states to make hard commitments to provide assistance where necessary to ensure the protection of persons affected by disasters. However, this does not mean that states must collectively respond to every

[8] T Nelson, 'Rejecting the Gift Horse: International Politics of Disaster Aid Refusal' (2010) 10(3) *Conflict, Security & Development* 379.

disaster. Because solidarity presumes that each state will first rely on its own resources, international assistance becomes compulsory only when the affected state's national response capacities are overwhelmed. Even then, expectations are not equal among all states, but are differentiated according to their respective capacities. States with greater resources are expected to contribute more, alleviating the burden on those with fewer means. This framework ensures that the shared responsibility for the protection of persons can be fulfilled while respecting different needs and capacities, embedding fairness and equity into its architecture of solidarity-based cooperation.

Treating disaster response as a shared responsibility also transforms the nature and scope of international cooperation, shifting it from ad hoc and reactive responses to proactive and sustained collaboration across all stages of disaster management. If the protection of persons affected by disasters is a common objective that all states work towards, cooperation cannot be limited to emergency relief – it must also extend to reducing disaster risks, mitigating their impacts and increasing resilience, including through efforts to strengthen national response capacities. Such an understanding recognises that protection does not begin only once disaster strikes, but that it is a continuous process that is inseparable from the conditions that create vulnerability to hazards. By better resourcing states to protect their own populations, international cooperation is not only an expression of shared responsibility but also reinforces the primary responsibility of affected states and reduces dependency on external aid. As such, solidarity embeds resilience into IDRL, ensuring that cooperation is not an exceptional emergency response, but a structural feature of disaster governance.

Taking all these changes together, the transformation sought by solidarity is, at its core, about reconceiving disaster response as a project of social justice, recognising that global structural inequalities imperil the protection of disaster-affected persons because not all states possess the capacity to ensure adequate protection. Against this backdrop, disaster response must be treated as a shared responsibility of all states, with solidarity serving as the vehicle for protecting human rights and dignity worldwide. By acting in solidarity, states acknowledge these structural inequalities and seek to ameliorate them through differentiated cooperation, placing greater burdens on those with the strongest shoulders. In this sense, solidarity is not charity but a form of justice: a principled commitment to redistribute responsibility in proportion to capacity so that protection is reliable rather than contingent, ensuring that all people receive the protection they need during and after disasters, regardless of where they are.

III. THE WAY FORWARD: REALISING SOLIDARITY

While the promise of solidarity is great, this section turns to the question of how it can be realised in practice. Developing a coherent theoretical understanding of solidarity and its implications for IDRL is one thing; bringing it into action is quite another. As this book comes to a close, this section looks forward and explores what is needed to operationalise solidarity within IDRL. In doing so, it acknowledges some of the barriers to implementation highlighted throughout the book – such as concerns over sovereignty and the enforcement gap – but ends on a hopeful note: states now have a unique opportunity to commit to solidarity in the forthcoming treaty on the protection of persons in the event of disasters, transforming solidarity from aspirational rhetoric into a foundational principle of international disaster response.

The most obvious way to realise solidarity in IDRL is through norm development. While solidarity lacks legally binding force and cannot by itself create, modify or confirm rights and obligations, states can give effect to it by adopting it into law or developing norms that reflect its concept. As discussed in Chapter 3, section IV.A, there is already a discernible trend of explicitly referencing solidarity in treaties and soft law instruments, often through formulations such as requiring states to act 'in the spirit of solidarity' when responding to disasters.[9] Through these references, solidarity can acquire binding force when incorporated into treaties, though as a largely open norm that remains subject to interpretation to determine the specific rights and duties it entails. Future treaties and soft law instruments could build on this trend, progressively codifying solidarity as a principle of IDRL. Doing so would not only strengthen states' commitment to solidarity but could also contribute to its evolution into a general principle of law.[10]

However, while codifying the principle of solidarity would signal commitment and solidify its legal status, its abstract nature and limited conceptual development also mean that, in practice, it risks becoming a dead letter, particularly when states disagree on the concrete rights and obligations that can be drawn from the principle, if any at all. To avoid this outcome, it is essential to complement codification with the development of norms that operationalise solidarity within IDRL. The book offers a template for such an approach, outlining how IDRL can be reimagined through the lens of solidarity. If existing and future provisions are shaped according to this understanding, solidarity will be implemented in practice even if it is not yet fully codified as a standalone legal principle.[11]

The need to codify solidarity in legally binding rights and obligations may seem antithetical to its very spirit, which is rooted in a social bond formed

[9] ILC, 'Draft Articles on the Protection of Persons in the Event of Disasters' (27 May 2016) UN Doc A/CN.4/L.871, preamble; *ASEAN Agreement on Disaster Management and Emergency Response* (26 July 2005) art 3(3); *Treaty on the Functioning of the European Union* (13 December 2007) art 222(1); *Inter-American Convention to Facilitate Disaster Assistance* (6 July 1991) preamble; *Framework Convention on Civil Defence Assistance* (22 May 2000) art 3.

[10] The codification of solidarity as a principle in treaty law could produce evidence of its recognition as a general principle of law, see ch 3, section III.

[11] This development too can contribute to the emergence of solidarity as a general principle of law as it produces evidence of its recognition through the acceptance of existing rules that reflect solidarity as a normative underpinning, see ch 3, section III.

through an experienced connection rather than imposed by formal rules. Yet nothing could be further from the truth. While solidarity indeed originates in an invisible bond and a normative belief that one should support others, translating these expectations into law serves to reinforce that bond and clarify responsibilities. At the national level, this is common practice: modern welfare states extensively codify legal and institutional frameworks that embody solidarity.[12] Similarly, scholars have noted that solidarity permeates numerous norms across different regimes of international law.[13] Importantly, however, developing such rules is not a prerequisite for solidarity – states and assisting actors can, and often do, act in the spirit of solidarity without any legal obligation. Nevertheless, translating solidarity into concrete norms strengthens its status as a principle of IDRL, creating a more predictable, robust and reliable framework for international cooperation based on solidarity.

Norm development also opens the door to exploring issues beyond the scope of this book. For instance, it invites reflection on how solidarity might apply to underexamined issues such as liability and accountability of relief workers,[14] or its role at the regional level. It also raises questions about the intersectionality of disaster vulnerability with systemic issues like economic inequality, political underrepresentation, social marginalisation and racial domination; the mission of social justice that solidarity advances could align with this particular topic. Moreover, this process provides an opportunity to extend the lessons learned here beyond international disaster response to related fields, such as disaster risk reduction.[15] Another critical area for future development is the legal position of assisting non-state actors, who are central to disaster response and participate in solidarity, yet cannot participate fully in IDRL due to limits on international legal personality.

Norm development is important to realising solidarity, but even if solidarity is codified and embedded in binding norms, there is no guarantee that states will act in its spirit in practice. Throughout its analysis, this book has highlighted potential obstacles to realising solidarity in IDRL. Acting in solidarity requires states to make sacrifices: balancing national interests with the collective interest in disaster response, committing to cooperation – whether by seeking or providing assistance – even when they may prefer not to, and investing in ongoing

[12] K Metz, 'Solidarity and History. Institutions and Social Concepts of Solidarity in 19th Century Western Europe' in K Bayertz (ed), *Solidarity* (Springer, 1999) 191.

[13] As discussed in ch 3, section II.

[14] This topic, while critical in practice, remains underexposed in practice and the academic literature, see G Bartolini, 'Attribution of Conduct and Liability Issues Arising from International Disaster Relief Missions: Theoretical and Pragmatic Approaches to Guaranteeing Accountability' (2015) 48(4) *Vanderbilt Journal of Transnational Law* 1029.

[15] Chapter 7 dealt with preparedness and capacity-building as two components of disaster risk reduction, but the topic of disaster risk reduction is much broader and also encompasses aspects such as identifying and monitoring disaster risk, strengthening disaster risk governance and investing in risk reduction. See World Conference on Disaster Risk Reduction, 'Sendai Framework for Disaster Risk Reduction 2015–2030' (18 March 2015) UN Doc A/CONF.224/L.2, para 20.

processes of preparedness and resilience. Yet not all states might be willing to make these sacrifices, even if they formally endorse solidarity on paper. Practice shows that while most states cooperate when disasters overwhelm national capacity, there have been instances of resistance, with states delaying or rejecting assistance.[16] Moreover, some states oppose changes implied by solidarity, especially where these possibly encroach on sovereignty.[17] It would therefore be naïve to simply assume that all states will fully embrace and comply with obligations under a solidarity-based IDRL.

Herein lies a potential weakness. As argued in Chapter 6, section III.D, solidarity leaves an enforcement gap: it presupposes a willingness to cooperate and assist in good faith, but when that willingness falters or disappears altogether, solidarity offers no remedy. The spirit of solidarity cannot be enforced because it ultimately depends on trust and mutual reliance rather than coercion. However, persistent failures or outright refusals to cooperate do have consequences. They risk eroding a state's standing within the solidarity-based community, potentially losing its own right of relying on solidarity and receiving assistance when struck by disaster. In the worst-case scenario, such breaches could even destabilise the very sense of solidarity that underpins international disaster response, causing cooperation and assistance to unravel as trust among states collapses.

While solidarity itself may be unenforceable, norms that reflect solidarity can be enforced. The challenge, however, is that IDRL lacks a framework for accountability and enforcement, creating the risk that states can ignore their obligations under international law without consequence. To ensure that states uphold their commitments and do not prioritise sovereignty over solidarity, this framework must be strengthened. One proposal advanced here is the creation of a 'custodian of solidarity' – an independent international body mandated to oversee, promote and facilitate the practice of solidarity in disaster response. Such an institution could serve as a focal point for monitoring compliance, encouraging best practices and reinforcing trust among states, thereby making solidarity not only aspirational but also operational. It should not be conceived as an enforcer of solidarity or an attempt to centralise disaster response; rather, this body would act as a custodian that performs a role of stewardship rather than control. A custodian safeguards something valuable – in this case, the principle of solidarity – by ensuring it is respected, nurtured and translated into practice. The term 'custodian' signals neutrality and independence: this body would not adjudicate or enforce compliance through coercion, but would serve as a guardian that monitors, advises and convenes dialogue on behalf of the international community. Its role would therefore reflect the understanding that

[16] Various examples have been discussed in ch 5, sections III.B and III.C, ch 6, sections III.C and III.D, and ch 7, sections III.A, III.B and III.C.

[17] Some states have already signalled opposition to some norms that would reflect solidarity; see ch 5, sections III.B (the duty to seek international assistance) and III.C 5.3.3 (the principle of consent), and ch 6, sections III.B (the right to offer assistance) and III.C (the duty to assist).

the protection of affected persons is a shared responsibility of all states and be their voice.

To fulfil this mandate, such an international body should be tasked with monitoring compliance with international obligations in disaster response and raising concerns when states appear to fall short. This role becomes particularly critical when states delay or refuse to seek or accept international assistance despite their national response capacity being overwhelmed. As explained throughout the book, there is a particular accountability gap in these instances that could jeopardise the protection of affected persons.[18] In such cases, an independent body, acting on behalf of the international community, could intervene diplomatically, avoiding the entanglement of geopolitical interests that often arises when individual states or non-state actors raise concerns. Rather than functioning as a 'police officer', this body could offer its good offices, bringing issues to the attention of states and facilitating diplomatic solutions in a cooperative manner. Practice demonstrates that diplomatic engagement is often more effective than coercion and better reflects the cooperative ethos of solidarity. Beyond oversight, the body could also facilitate effective cooperation by evaluating and reviewing disaster responses, identifying best practices, extracting lessons learned, highlighting persistent legal, administrative and bureaucratic barriers, and prioritising areas with an urgent need for cooperation – not to reprimand states, but to foster continuous improvement that contributes to the common objective central to solidarity. Additionally, it could promote the normative development of IDRL, ensuring that solidarity evolves from principle to practice.

It is equally important to clarify what this body should *not* be doing. First, it should not centralise international disaster response in the image of the former International Relief Union (IRU); disaster response must remain decentralised, with states retaining sovereign authority within their territory. Accordingly, the proposed body should not operate as a platform for mobilising and distributing aid, but rather should act as an independent advocate and custodian of solidarity. Second, it should not evolve into an overly formalised (quasi-)judicial body that reviews state conduct through rigid procedures. Such formalisation could be counterproductive, deterring participation due to sovereignty concerns. Instead, a cooperative model is better suited to the fast-moving and sensitive context of disasters, allowing oversight to strengthen solidarity rather than reprimand states. Finally, this body should not become a political forum composed of state representatives, as this risks politicising solidarity and disaster response. To preserve neutrality, it must remain an independent entity dedicated to safeguarding and promoting solidarity.

Such a mandated international body does not yet exist. While organisations like the UN Office for the Coordination of Humanitarian Affairs (OCHA) and

[18] See ch 5, sections III.B and III.C, and ch 6, section III.D.

the IFRC play a de facto leadership role in international disaster response, their focus lies on aid provision, mobilisation, coordination and improving technical standards, not on accountability and enforcement. A custodian of solidarity would fill this structural void by creating an institution explicitly mandated to hold states to their commitments, broker diplomatic solutions where necessary and improve disaster response through cooperation. It would be crucial for this international body to be designed as an independent and neutral institution. Lessons can be drawn from the model of the ICRC in armed conflict, which is mandated to 'work for the faithful application of international humanitarian law applicable in armed conflicts and to take cognizance of any complaints based on alleged breaches of that law'.[19] The ICRC operates with neutrality and impartiality, using its good offices to raise issues with parties to a conflict through diplomacy and confidentiality. Similarly, the custodian of solidarity should derive its authority from expertise, neutrality and its ability to mobilise reputational pressure through dialogue. This approach would prioritise trust and cooperation in promoting and safeguarding solidarity.

As for who should fulfil this role, two options present themselves: mandating an existing organisation such as the IFRC or creating a new body endorsed by states through a UN General Assembly resolution or another instrument. While the OCHA already plays a central role in mobilising, facilitating and coordinating international disaster response, its position within the UN system makes it vulnerable to politicisation, which could undermine the neutrality required for a custodianship over solidarity. Over time, regional organisations engaged in disaster response could also pilot similar mechanisms, reinforcing solidarity at the regional level and complementing global efforts.

It is tempting to give in to a degree of cynicism about the prospects of these two avenues for giving effect to solidarity in international disaster response – norm development and the creation of an international body. Historically, major attempts to reform IDRL have failed, and states have not even been able to agree on a universal framework instrument for disaster response. However, times have changed. Progress has been slow but steady, with IDRL gradually developing through bilateral and regional agreements as well as soft law instruments that enjoy broad support among states.

Today, a growing sense of urgency could accelerate this process. As the effects of climate change become increasingly visible and disasters rise in frequency and severity, the need to improve international disaster response and, crucially, to embed solidarity as a foundational principle has never been greater. Recent developments show that there is momentum for global action. The adoption of the *WHO Pandemic Agreement* following the COVID-19 pandemic is a striking example: the pandemic exposed the cascading risks of health disasters in an interconnected world and the crippling lack of preparedness and both international

[19] International Conference of the Red Cross, 'Statutes of the International Red Cross and Red Crescent Movement' (1986) art 5(2)(c).

and national capacity to respond.[20] In this new treaty, states expressly committed to work together to prevent, prepare for and respond to future pandemics on the basis of solidarity.[21] This achievement demonstrates that solidarity can and does operate within international law, presenting a unique opportunity to do the same for disaster response.

The international community is now presented with a unique opportunity to advance IDRL and commit to solidarity as the UN General Assembly has initiated negotiations on a treaty on the protection of persons in the event of disasters, scheduled for adoption by the end of 2027.[22] In this process, negotiators should not only embrace solidarity as a key principle of international disaster response but should also pay close attention to how it can be operationalised in the treaty's text and provisions. This book offers a starting point for that effort, providing a pathway to achieving solidarity in the age of climate change.

[20] *WHO Pandemic Agreement* (20 May 2025).
[21] ibid art 3(5).
[22] UN General Assembly Res 79/128 (4 December 2024) UN Doc A/RES/79/128, para 4.

Bibliography

Active Learning Network for Accountability and Performance, 'Global Humanitarian Assistance Report 2025' (2025)

Adamu, Z and Busari, S, 'Anger Simmers over Omicron Travel Bans in Southern Africa', *CNN* (4 December 2021)

Ajitoni, BD, 'Ubuntu and the Philosophy of Community in African Thought: An Exploration of Collective Identity and Social Harmony' (2024) 7(3) *Journal of African Studies and Sustainable Development* 1

Akande, D and Emanuela-Chiara, G, 'Oxford Guidance on the Law Relating to Humanitarian Relief Operations in Situations of Armed Conflict' (UN Office for the Coordination of Humanitarian Affairs, 2016)

Aldrich, Daniel P, 'Separate and Unequal Post-tsunami Aid Distribution in Southern India' (2010) 91(5) *Social Science Quarterly* 1369

Ali, Z et al, 'The Role of Islamic Values in Promoting Social Justice and Community Welfare' (2024) V(1) *International Research Journal of Management and Social Sciences* 575

Allan, C and O'Donnell, T, 'A Call to Alms? Natural Disasters, R2P, Duties of Cooperation and Uncharted Consequences' (2012) 17(3) *Journal of Conflict and Security Law* 337

Allan, C and O'Donnell, T, 'An Offer You Cannot Refuse: Natural Disasters, the Politics of Aid Refusal and Potential Legal Implications' (2013) 5(1) *Amsterdam Law Forum* 36

Alpa, G, *Solidarity: A Normative Principle* (Kluwer, 2023)

Alston, P, 'A Third Generation of Solidarity Rights: Progressive Development or Obfuscation of International Human Rights Law?' (1982) 29(3) *Netherlands International Law Review* 307

Ammann, O, *Domestic Courts and the Interpretation of International Law: Methods and Reasoning Based on the Swiss Example* (Brill Nijhoff, 2020)

Amnesty International, 'Nepal: Earthquake Recovery Must Safeguard Human Rights' (2015)

Arendt, H, *On Revolution* (Faber, 1963)

Arnsperger, C and Varoufakis, Y, 'Toward a Theory of Solidarity' (2003) 59(2) *Erkenntnis* 157

Aronsson-Storrier, M, 'Exploring the Foundations: The Principles of Prevention, Mitigation, and Preparedness in International Law' in KLH Samuel, KN Bookmiller and M Aronsson-Storrier (eds), *The Cambridge Handbook of Disaster Risk Reduction and International Law* (Cambridge University Press, 2019) 52

Association of Caribbean States, 'Declaration of Panama' (29 July 2005)

Atay Alam, H, 'Turkey Receives Offers of Quake Aid from Nearly 100 Countries', *CNN* (10 February 2023)

'Australia Pushed for a WHO Probe into Coronavirus' Origins: Here's What the Investigation is up to', *ABC News* (27 August 2020)

Badanova, I, 'Making Sense of Solidarity in International Law: Input from the Integration of the European Gas Market' (2019) 11(2) *European Journal of Legal Studies* 105

Banting, K and Kymlicka, W (eds), *The Strains of Commitment: The Political Sources of Solidarity in Diverse Societies* (Oxford University Press, 2017)

Barber, R, 'Legal Preparedness for the Facilitation of International Humanitarian Assistance in the Aftermath of Vanuatu's Cyclone Pam' (2016) 8(1) *Asian Journal of International Law* 143

Barber, R, 'The Responsibility to Protect the Survivors of Natural Disaster: Cyclone Nargis, a Case Study' (2009) 14(1) *Journal of Conflict and Security Law* 3

Bartolini, G, 'Attribution of Conduct and Liability Issues Arising from International Disaster Relief Missions: Theoretical and Pragmatic Approaches to Guaranteeing Accountability' (2015) 48(4) *Vanderbilt Journal of Transnational Law* 1029

Bartolini, G, 'Charting an Emerging Subject: The Role of the Yearbook of International Disaster Law' (2019) 1(1) *Yearbook of International Disaster Law* 1
Bartolini, G, 'Epidemics and the Future of International Disaster Law' (2022) 24(3) *International Community Law Review* 257
Bartolini, G, 'A Taxonomy of Disasters in International Law' in F Zorzi Giustiniani et al (eds), *Routledge Handbook of Human Rights and Disasters* (Routledge, 2018) 10
Bartolini, G, 'Toward a Universal Treaty on "Protection of Persons in the Event of Disasters"', *EJIL:Talk!* (17 December 2024)
Bartolini, G, 'A Universal Treaty for Disasters? Remarks on the International Law Commission's Draft Articles on the Protection of Persons in the Event of Disasters' (2017) 99(906) *International Review of the Red Cross* 1103
Bassiouni, MC, 'A Functional Approach to General Principles of International Law' (1990) 11(3) *Michigan Journal of International Law* 768
Bayertz, K, 'Four Uses of "Solidarity"' in K Bayertz (ed), *Solidarity* (Springer, 1999) 3
'Beirut Explosion: World Reacts to Deadly Blast in Lebanon Capital', *Al Jazeera* (5 August 2020)
Bennett, J et al, *Coordination of International Humanitarian Assistance in Tsunami-Affected Countries* (Tsunami Evaluation Coalition, 2006)
Benton Heath, J, 'Disasters, Relief, and Neglect: The Duty to Accept Humanitarian Assistance and the Work of the International Law Commission' (2011) 43 *NYU Journal for International Law & Politics* 419
Benvenisti, E and Nolte, G (eds), *Community Interests across International Law* (Oxford University Press, 2018)
Bernstein, S, 'The Responsibility to Protect after Libya: Humanitarian Prevention as Customary International Law' (2012) 38(1) *Brooklyn Journal of International Law* 305
Besson, S, 'Sovereignty' in *Max Planck Encyclopedia of International Law* (Oxford University Press, 2011)
Beyer, GJ, 'The Meaning of Solidarity in Catholic Social Teaching' (2014) 15(1) *Political Theology* 7
Biddulph, M and Newman, D, 'A Contextualized Account of General Principles of International Law' (2014) 26(2) *Pace International Law Review* 286
Biondi, A, Dagilytė, E and Küçük, E (eds), *Solidarity in EU Law: Legal Principle in the Making* (Edward Elgar, 2018)
Boisson de Chazournes, L, 'Responsibility to Protect: Reflecting Solidarity?' in R Wolfrum and C Kojima (eds), *Solidarity: A Structural Principle of International Law* (Springer, 2010) 93
Bourdieu, P, *On the State: Lectures at the Collège de France, 1989–1992* (Polity, 2014)
Brown, TM and Ladwig, S, 'COVID-19, China, the World Health Organization, and the Limits of International Health Diplomacy' (2020) 110(8) *American Journal of Public Health* 1149
Bull, H, *The Anarchical Society: A Study of Order in World Politics*, 2nd edn (Macmillan, 1995)
Burci, GL, 'Ebola, the Security Council and the Securitization of Public Health' (2014) 10 *Questions of International Law* 27
Campanelli, D, 'Principle of Solidarity' in *Max Planck Encyclopedia of International Law* (Oxford University Press, 2011)
Caribbean Disaster Emergency Management Agency and Office for the Coordination of Humanitarian Affairs, 'Grenada and Saint Vincent and the Grenadines: CDEMA and UNDAC Deployment' (2024)
Carnegie, A and Dolan, LR, 'The Effects of Rejecting Aid on Recipients' Reputations: Evidence from Natural Disaster Responses' (2021) 16(3) *Review of International Organizations* 495
Carvosso, R, 'The Reactive Model of Disaster Regulation in International Law and its Shortcomings' (2021) 34(4) *Leiden Journal of International Law* 957
Casini, L, 'Solidarity between States in the Global Legal Space' (2013)
Cave, D, Kwai, I and Nagourney, E, 'An Island Nation Covered in Ash Now Worries About a Covid Intrusion', *The New York Times* (18 January 2022)

Cedervall Lauta, K, 'Human Rights and Natural Disasters' in S Breau and K Samuel (eds), *Research Handbook on Disasters and International Law* (Edward Elgar Publishing, 2016) 91
Center for Disaster Philanthropy, 'Disaster Phases' (2021)
'China Delayed Releasing Coronavirus Info, Frustrating WHO', *The Associated Press* (2 June 2020)
Chinkin, C, 'The Challenge of Soft Law: Development and Change in International Law' (1989) 38(4) *International and Comparative Law Quarterly* 850
Clark, MJ, 'Pope Francis and the Christological Dimensions of Solidarity in Catholic Social Teaching' (2019) 80(1) *Theological Studies* 102
Clarke, B, Otto, F and Harrington, L, 'Pakistan Floods: What Role Did Climate Change Play?', *The Conversation* (3 September 2022)
Clement, C, 'International Disaster Response Laws, Rules, and Principles: A Pragmatic Approach to Strengthening International Disaster Response Mechanisms' in DD Caron, MJ Kelly and A Telesetsky (eds), *The International Law of Disaster Relief* (Cambridge University Press, 2014) 67
Clinton, WJ, 'Lessons Learned from Tsunami Recovery: Key Propositions for Building Back Better' (2006)
Cook, ADB, Shrestha, M and Htet, ZB 'An Assessment of International Emergency Disaster Response to the 2015 Nepal Earthquakes' (2018) 31 *International Journal of Disaster Risk Reduction* 535
Costas Trascasas, M, 'Access to the Territory of a Disaster-Affected State' in A de Guttry, M Gestri and G Venturini (eds), *International Disaster Response Law* (TMC Asser Press, 2012) 221
Coursen-Nef, Z, 'Preventive Measures Pertaining to Unconventional Threats to the Peace Such as Natural and Humanitarian Disasters' (1998) 30(3–4) *New York University Journal of International Law and Politics* 645
'Covid-19 Pandemic: China "Refused to Give Data" to WHO Team', *BBC* (14 February 2021)
Crawford, E, 'Proportionality' in *Max Planck Encyclopedia of International Law* (Oxford University Press, 2011)
Creta, A, 'A (Human) Right to Humanitarian Assistance in Disaster Situations? Surveying Public International Law' in A de Guttry, M Gestri and G Venturini (eds), *International Disaster Response Law* (TMC Asser Press, 2012) 353
Cubie, D, 'An Analysis of Soft Law Applicable to Humanitarian Assistance: Relative Normativity in Action?' (2011) 2(2) *Journal of International Humanitarian Legal Studies* 177
Cubie, D, 'An Enchanted Tool: Humanitarian Assistance and the ILC Draft Articles on the Protection of Persons in the Event of Disasters' (2009) 4 *Irish Yearbook of International Law* 119
Cubie, D, 'Identifying Principles of International Disaster Law' in M Aronsson-Storrier and S Breau (eds), *Research Handbook on Disasters and International Law*, 2nd edn (Edward Elgar, 2024) 11
Cubie, D, *The International Legal Protection of Persons in Humanitarian Crises: Exploring the Acquis Humanitaire* (Hart Publishing, 2017)
Cubie, D, 'Sources of IDL: Focus on General Principles of Law' (2024) 5 *Yearbook of International Disaster Law* 493
Cubie, D and Hesselman, M, 'Accountability for the Human Rights Implications of Natural Disasters: A Proposal for Systemic International Oversight' (2015) 33(1) *Netherlands Quarterly of Human Rights* 9
Czuczai, J, 'The Principle of Solidarity in the EU Legal Order: Some Practical Examples after Lisbon' in J Czuczai and F Naert (eds), *The EU as a Global Actor: Bridging Legal Theory and Practice* (Brill Nijhoff, 2017) 145
Da Costa, K, 'R.I.P. R2P: On the Controversial "Responsibility to Protect" Doctrine and Why It Adds No Value to Disasters' in F Zorzi Giustiniani et al (eds), *Routledge Handbook of Human Rights and Disasters* (Routledge, 2018) 27
Dann, P, 'Solidarity and the Law of Development Cooperation' in R Wolfrum and C Kojima (eds), *Solidarity: A Structural Principle of International Law* (Springer, 2010) 55

Davies, SE, 'Natural Disasters and the Responsibility to Protect' (2012) 55 *German Yearbook of International Law* 149
Dawidowicz, M, 'Third-Party Countermeasures: A Progressive Development of International Law?' (2016) 29 *Questions of International Law* 3
De Guttry, A, 'Surveying the Law' in A de Guttry, M Gestri and G Venturini (eds), *International Disaster Response Law* (TMC Asser Press, 2012) 3
De Sena, P and Acconciamessa, L, 'Balancing Test' in *Max Planck Encyclopedia of International Law* (Oxford University Press, 2021)
De Vattel, E, *Le Droit des Gens, ou Principes de la Loi Naturelle, Appliqués à la Conduite et aux Affaires des Nations et des Souverains* (1758)
Den Heijer, M and van der Wilt, H, 'Global Solidarity and Common But Differentiated Responsibilities' in M den Heijer and H van der Wilt (eds), *Netherlands Yearbook of International Law 2020* (TMC Asser Press, 2022) 3
Deng, F, 'From "Sovereignty as Responsibility" to the "Responsibility to Protect"' (2010) 2(4) *Global Responsibility to Protect* 353
Derpmann, S, 'Solidarity and Cosmopolitanism' (2009) 12(3) *Ethical Theory and Moral Practice* 303
Desportes, I, 'Getting Relief to Marginalised Minorities: The Response to Cyclone Komen in 2015 in Myanmar' (2019) 4(1) *Journal of International Humanitarian Action* 7
Dinstein, Y, 'The Right to Humanitarian Assistance' (2000) 53(4) *Naval War College Review* 77
Donmez, BB, 'World Leaders Voice Solidarity after Powerful Earthquake Strikes Türkiye', *AA* (6 February 2023)
'Donors Pledge More than $9bn for Pakistan Flood Recovery', *Al Jazeera* (9 January 2023)
Doucet, L, 'Crisis upon Crisis: Why It's Hard to Get Help to Syria after Earthquake', *BBC* (11 February 2023)
Dupuy, PM, 'International Law: Torn between Coexistence, Cooperation and Globalization. General Conclusions' (1998) 9(2) *European Journal of International Law* 278
Durkheim, E, *The Division of Labour in Society* (Free Press Collier Macmillan, 1964)
Dworkin, R, *Taking Rights Seriously* (Duckworth, 1977)
Eburn, M, 'International Law and Disaster Response' (2010) 36 *Monash University Law Review* 162
Eggett, C, 'Solidarity as an International Legal Norm' in E Kassoti and N Idriz (eds), *The Principle of Solidarity: The Principle of Solidarity: International and EU Law Perspectives* (TMC Asser Press, 2023) 29
ETO Consortium, 'Maastricht Principles on Extraterritorial Obligations of States in the Area of Economic, Social and Cultural Rights' (2011)
European Commission, 'European Commission and Swedish Presidency of the Council Will Organise a Donors' Conference for the People of Türkiye and Syria Affected by the Earthquake' (8 February 2023)
European Commission, 'INFORM Report 2024' (2024)
Farrall, J and Michaelsen, C, 'The UN Security Council's Response to COVID-19: From the Centre to the Periphery?' (2021) 39 *Australian Yearbook of International Law* 214
Fidler, DP, 'Disaster Relief and Governance after the Indian Ocean Tsunami: What Role for International Law?' (2005) 6 *Melbourne Journal of International Law* 458
Fisher, D, 'Domestic Regulation of International Humanitarian Relief in Disasters and Armed Conflict: A Comparative Analysis' (2007) 89(866) *International Review of the Red Cross* 345
Fisher, D, *Law and Legal Issues in International Disaster Response: A Desk Study* (IFRC, 2007)
Fisher, D, 'The Future of International Disaster Response Law' (2012) 55 *German Yearbook of International Law* 87
Fisher, D, 'The Law of International Disaster Response: Overview and Ramifications for Military Actors' (2007) 83 *International Law Studies Series. US Naval War College* 293
Fisher, D, 'The Right to Humanitarian Assistance' (2010) 41 *Studies in Transnational Legal Policy* 47

Ford, S, 'Is the Failure to Respond Appropriately to a Natural Disaster a Crime against Humanity? The Responsibility to Protect and Individual Criminal Responsibility in the Aftermath of Cyclone Nargis' (2010) 38(2) *Denver Journal of International Law and Policy* 227

Forman, L and Habibi, R, 'Revisiting the Legality of Travel Restrictions under International Law during COVID-19' (2022) 71(3) *International and Comparative Law Quarterly* 743

Forst, R, 'Solidarity: Concept, Conceptions, and Contexts' in A Sangiovanni and J Viehoff (eds), *The Virtue of Solidarity* (Oxford University Press, 2024) 35

Frowein, JA, 'Obligations Erga Omnes' in *Max Planck Encyclopedia of International Law* (Oxford University Press, 2008)

Gaja, G, 'General Principles of Law' in *Max Planck Encyclopedia of International Law* (Oxford University Press, 2013)

Gardiner, R, *Treaty Interpretation*, 2nd edn (Oxford University Press, 2015)

Gavshon, D, 'The Applicability of IHL in Mixed Situations of Disaster and Conflict' (2009) 14(2) *Journal of Conflict and Security Law* 243

Giang, SM and Grimmel, A (eds), *Solidarity in the European Union* (Springer, 2017)

Giossi Caverzasio, S, *Strengthening Protection in War: A Search for Professional Standards* (ICRC, 2001)

Gofman, A, 'Durkheim's Theory of Social Solidarity and Social Rules' in V Jeffries (ed), *The Palgrave Handbook of Altruism, Morality, and Social Solidarity* (Palgrave Macmillan US, 2014) 45

Gould, CC, 'Transnational Solidarities' (2007) 38(1) *Journal of Social Philosophy* 148

Government of Albania et al, 'Albania: Post-Disaster Needs Assessment' (2019)

Government of Pakistan, 'Joint Launch of 2022 Pakistan Floods Response Plan by Government of Pakistan and the United Nations' (30 August 2022)

Government of Tonga, 'Post Disaster Rapid Assessment: Tropical Cyclone Gita' (2018)

Granger, I, 'IDRL in Haiti: A Study on the Legal Framework for the Facilitation and Regulation of International Disaster Response in Haiti' (IFRC 2012)

Grimmel, A, 'Solidarity in the European Union: Fundamental Value or "Empty Signifier"' in A Grimmel and SM Giang (eds), *Solidarity in the European Union* (Springer, 2017) 161

Hakimi, M, 'Making Sense of Customary International Law' (2020) 118(8) *Michigan Law Review* 1487

Hallegatte, S et al, 'From Poverty to Disaster and Back: A Review of the Literature' (2020) 4(1) *Economics of Disasters and Climate Change* 223

Hardcastle, R and Chua, A, 'Victims of Natural Disasters: The Right to Receive Humanitarian Assistance' (1997) 1(4) *International Journal of Human Rights* 35

Harvey, P, *Towards Good Humanitarian Government: The Role of the Affected State in Disaster Response* (Overseas Development Institute, 2009)

Hayward, JES, 'The Official Social Philosophy of the French Third Republic: Léon Bourgeois and Solidarism' (1961) 6(1) *International Review of Social History* 19

Hesselman, M, 'A Right to International (Humanitarian) Assistance in Times of Disaster' in F Zorzi Giustiniani et al (eds), *Routledge Handbook of Human Rights and Disasters* (Routledge, 2018) 65

Hestermeyer, H, 'Reality or Aspiration? Solidarity in International Environmental and World Trade Law' (Max Planck Institute, 2012)

Hey, E, 'Common But Differentiated Responsibilities' in *Max Planck Encyclopedia of International Law* (Oxford University Press, 2011)

Hillgruber, C, 'The Right of Third States to Take Countermeasures' in C Tomuschat and JM Thouvenin (eds), *The Fundamental Rules of the International Legal Order: Jus Cogens And Obligations Erga Omnes* (Martinus Nijhoff Publishers, 2006) 265

Hoffman, MH, 'What Is the Scope of International Response Law?' in V Bannon (ed), *International Disaster Response Laws, Principles and Practice: Reflections, Prospects and Challenges* (IFRC, 2003) 13

Hunter, J, 'India Covid Aid: Is Emergency Relief Reaching Those in Need?', *BBC* (6 May 2021)
Hutchinson, JF, 'Disasters and the International Order – II: The International Relief Union' (2001) 23(2) *The International History Review* 253
Hutchinson, T and Duncan, N, 'Defining and Describing What We Do: Doctrinal Legal Research' (2012) 17(1) *Deakin Law Review* 83
IASC (Inter-Agency Standing Committee), 'IASC Operational Guidelines on Human Rights and Natural Disasters' (2006)
IASC, 'Protection of Internally Displaced Persons: Inter Agency Standing Committee Policy Paper' (1999)
ICISS (International Commission on Intervention and State Sovereignty), 'The Responsibility to Protect: Report of the International Commission on Intervention and State Sovereignty' (2001)
IDI (Institut de Droit International), 'Obligations and Rights *Erga Omnes* in International Law' (2005)
IDI, 'Resolution on Humanitarian Assistance' (2003) 86(856) *International Review of the Red Cross* 874
IFRC (International Conference of the Red Cross), 'Annotations to Guidelines for the Domestic Facilitation and Regulation of International Disaster Relief and Initial Recovery Assistance' (26 October 2007)
IFRC, 'The Cost of Doing Nothing' (2019)
IFRC, 'Fourth Progress Report on the Implementation of the IDRL Guidelines' (14 November 2019)
IFRC, 'Guidelines for the Domestic Facilitation and Regulation of International Disaster Relief and Initial Recovery Assistance' (2007)
IFRC, 'Law and Public Health Preparedness and Response: Lessons from the COVID-19 Pandemic' (2021)
IFRC, 'Model Act for the Facilitation and Regulation of International Disaster Relief and Initial Recovery Assistance' (2013)
IFRC, 'The Principles and Rules for Red Cross and Red Crescent Disaster Relief' (1996) 36(310) *International Review of the Red Cross* 102
IFRC, 'Res. XVIII International Relief Actions: Revision of Principles' (1965) 47(563) *International Review of the Red Cross* 581, 582
IFRC, 'Statutes of the International Red Cross and Red Crescent Movement' (1986)
IFRC, 'World Disasters Report 2020: Come Heat or High Water' (2020)
IFRC and the International Committee of the Red Cross, 'Code of Conduct for the International Red Cross and Red Crescent Movement and Non-Governmental Organisations (NGOs) in Disaster Relief' (1994)
Intergovernmental Oceanographic Commission, 'Global Tsunami Early Warning and Mitigation Programme'
International Institute of Humanitarian Law, 'Guiding Principles on the Right to Humanitarian Assistance' (1993) 33(297) *International Review of the Red Cross* 519
International Law Association, 'Statement of Principles Applicable to the Formation of General Customary International Law' (2000)
IPCC (Intergovernmental Panel on Climate Change), 'Summary for Policymakers' in IPCC, *Climate Change 2021: The Physical Science Basis. Contribution of Working Group I to the Sixth Assessment Report of the Intergovernmental Panel on Climate Change* (Cambridge University Press, 2021)
Jacobs, C and Almeida, B, 'Government-Led Resettlement after Natural Disasters as a Durable Solution? The Case of Cyclone Idai' (2021) 40(2) *Refugee Survey Quarterly* 239
Jansen-Wilhelm, S, *Accepting Assistance in the Aftermath of Disasters: Standards for States under International Law* (Intersentia, 2015)
Junk, J, 'Testing Boundaries: Cyclone Nargis in Myanmar and the Scope of R2P' (2016) 30(1) *Global Society* 78
Kälin, W, 'The Human Rights Dimension of Natural or Human-Made Disasters' (2012) 55 *German Yearbook of International Law* 119

Kälin, W, 'Protection of Victims of Disasters: The "Vertical" Dimension of the Draft Articles on the Protection of Persons in the Event of Disasters' (2019) 1(1) *Yearbook of International Disaster Law* 28
Kamminga, MT, 'Extraterritoriality' in *Max Planck Encyclopedia of International Law* (Oxford University Press, 2020)
Kassoti, E and Narin Idriz, N (eds), The Principle of Solidarity: International and EU Law Perspectives (TMC Asser Press, 2023)
Kelman, I, *Disaster Diplomacy* (Routledge, 2012)
Kelman, I, 'Hurricane Katrina Disaster Diplomacy' (2007) 31(3) *Disasters* 288
Kim, DD, *Arendt's Solidarity: Anti-semitism and Racism in the Atlantic World* (Stanford University Press, 2024)
Knuth, R, 'Sovereignty, Globalism, and Information Flow in Complex Emergencies' (1999) 15(1) *The Information Society* 11
Koroma, AG, 'Solidarity: Evidence of an Emerging International Legal Principle' in H Hestermeyer et al (eds), *Coexistence, Cooperation and Solidarity* (Martinus Nijhoff, 2012) 103
Koskenniemi, M, *The Gentle Civilizer of Nations: The Rise and Fall of International Law, 1870–1960* (Cambridge University Press, 2002)
Krishnan, M, 'Sri Lanka Cyclone Tragedy Exposes Government Failures', *DW* (12 December 2025)
Kristof, ND, 'Chinese Disclose That Quake in 1970 Killed about 10,000', *The New York Times* (19 November 1988)
Küçük, E, 'Solidarity in EU Law: An Elusive Political Statement or a Legal Principle with Substance?' in A Biondi, E Dagilytė and E Küçük (eds), *Solidarity in EU Law* (Edward Elgar, 2018) 38
Letsas, G, 'Strasbourg's Interpretive Ethic: Lessons for the International Lawyer' (2010) 21(3) *European Journal of International Law* 509
Loevy, K, 'The Legal Politics of Jurisdiction: Understanding ASEAN's Role in Myanmar's Disaster, Cyclone Nargis (2008)' (2015) 5(1) *Asian Journal of International Law* 55
Macalister-Smith, P, *International Humanitarian Assistance: Disaster Relief Actions in International Law and Organization* (Kluwer, 1985)
Macalister-Smith, P, 'Reflections on the Convention Establishing an International Relief Union of July 12, 1927' (1986) 54(4) *Legal History Review* 363
MacDonald, RStJ, 'Solidarity in the Practice and Discourse of Public International Law' (1996) 8 *Pace International Law Review* 259
Martin, G, 'International Solidarity and Co-operation in Assistance to African Refugees: Burden-Sharing or Burden-Shifting' (1995) 7 *International Journal of Refugee Law* 250
McAdam, J, 'Evacuations as Displacement: Conceptual and Legal Challenges' (2025) 44(2) *Refugee Survey Quarterly* 204
McAdam, J and Mulder, T, 'A Last Resort? Reframing Evacuations as an Anticipatory Disaster Risk Management Strategy' (2026) *Journal of International Humanitarian Legal Studies* (forthcoming)
Merkouris, P, 'Interpreting the Customary Rules on Interpretation' (2017) 19 *International Community Law Review* 126
Metz, K, 'Solidarity and History. Institutions and Social Concepts of Solidarity in 19th Century Western Europe' in K Bayertz (ed), *Solidarity* (Springer, 1999) 191
Minnerop, P, Roht-Arriaza, N and Aminzadeh, S, 'Solidarity Rights (Development, Peace, Environment, Humanitarian Assistance)' in *Max Planck Encyclopedia of International Law* (Oxford University Press, 2018)
Mishra, V, 'Cyclone Ditwah Brings Worst Flooding in Decades to Sri Lanka, Killing Hundreds', *UN News* (30 November 2025)
'Morocco Earthquake: Why Authorities Accepted Limited Foreign Aid', *Al Jazeera* (12 September 2023)
Mulder, T, '"In the Spirit of Solidarity": An Analysis of Solidarity as a Principle of International Disaster Response Law' (2023) 6(1) *Yearbook of International Disaster Law* 301

Mulder, T, Simm, G and Williams, S, 'Regime Interaction and the Protection of Refugees during COVID-19' (2020) 3 *Yearbook of International Disaster Law* 92
Murphy, SD, 'Protection of Persons in the Event of Disasters and Other Topics: The Sixty-Eighth Session of the International Law Commission' (2016) 110(4) *American Journal of International Law* 718
'Myanmar Quake Toll Passes 1,000 as Rescuers Dig for Survivors', *The Japan Times* (29 March 2025)
Mydans, S, 'Myanmar Faces Pressure to Allow Major Aid Effort', *New York Times* (8 May 2008)
Nasu, H, 'The Global Security Agenda: Securitization of Everything?' in R Geiß and N Melzer (eds), *The Oxford Handbook of the International Law of Global Security* (Oxford University Press, 2021) 37
Natoli, T, 'Non-state Humanitarian Actors and Human Rights in Disaster Scenarios' in F Zorzi Giustiniani et al (eds), *Routledge Handbook of Human Rights and Disasters* (Routledge, 2018) 149
Nelson, T, 'Rejecting the Gift Horse: International Politics of Disaster Aid Refusal' (2010) 10(3) *Conflict, Security & Development* 379
Neuhold, H, 'Common Security: The Litmus Test of International Solidarity' in R Wolfrum and C Kojima (eds), *Solidarity: A Structural Principle of International Law* (Springer, 2010) 193
O'Donnell, T, 'Solidarity, Duties to Assist and the Potential of the ILC Draft Articles on the Protection of Persons in the Event of Disasters' in M Aronsson-Storrier and SC Breau (eds), *Research Handbook on Disasters and International Law*, 2nd edn (Edward Elgar, 2024) 274
O'Donnell, T and Allan, C, 'A Duty of Solidarity? The International Law Commission's Draft Articles and the Right to Offer Assistance in Disasters' in S Breau and K Samuel (eds), *Research Handbook on Disasters and International Law* (Edward Elgar, 2016) 453
O'Donnell, T and Allan, C, 'Identifying Solidarity: The ILC Project on the Protection of Persons in Disasters and Human Rights' (2017) 49(1) *George Washington International Law Review* 53
OCHA (United Nations Office for the Coordination of Humanitarian Affairs), 'Glossary of Humanitarian Terms' (2008)
OCHA, 'Guidelines on the Use of Foreign Military and Civil Defence Assets in Disaster Relief' (November 2007)
OCHA, 'Informe de Misión: United Nations Disaster Assessment & Coordination (UNDAC) Lluvias, Inundaciones y Deslizamientos de Tierra en el Norte del Perú' (2023)
OCHA, 'Revised Pakistan 2022 Floods Response Plan: 01 Sep 2022–31 May 2023' (4 October 2022)
Papanicolopulu, I, 'The Duty to Rescue at Sea, in Peacetime and in War: A General Overview' (2016) 98(202) *International Review of the Red Cross* 491
Paul, A, 'An Analysis of Leon Duguit's Theory of "Social Solidarity"' (2021) 3(1) *Indian Journal of Law and Legal Research* 1
Pauwelyn, J, *Conflict of Norms in Public International Law: How WTO Law Relates to Other Rules of International Law* (Cambridge University Press, 2003)
Pauwelyn, J and Elsig, M, 'The Politics of Treaty Interpretation: Variations and Explanations across International Tribunals' in MA Pollack and JL Dunoff (eds), *Interdisciplinary Perspectives on International Law and International Relations: The State of the Art* (Cambridge University Press, 2011) 445
Pensky, M, 'Solidarity' in A Allen and E Mendieta (eds), *The Cambridge Habermas Lexicon* (Cambridge University Press, 2019) 427
Perez, A, 'In Defense of Concurrent Application: The ILC Draft Articles on the Protection of Persons in the Event of Disasters and International Humanitarian Law' (2018) 46(3) *Denver Journal of International Law and Policy* 259
Peters, A, 'Humanity as the A and Ω of Sovereignty' (2009) 20(3) *European Journal of International Law* 513
Pietropaolo, MG, 'A Human Rights-Based Approach to Humanitarian Assistance: Current and Prospective Scenarios' (2016) 7(2) *Journal of International Humanitarian Legal Studies* 257

Pill, M, 'Towards a Funding Mechanism for Loss and Damage from Climate Change Impacts' (2022) 35 *Climate Risk Management* 100391

Pomson, O, 'General Principles of Law Formed Within the International Legal System?', *EJIL: Talk!* (12 July 2022)

Pronto, A, 'Codification and Progressive Development in Contemporary International Law-Making: Locating the Draft Articles on the Protection of Persons in the Event of Disasters' (2019) 1(1) *Yearbook of International Disaster Law* 148

Rahman-Shepherd, A et al, 'Solidarity in Response to the COVID-19 Pandemic' (Chatham House, 2021)

Raustiala, K, 'Form and Substance in International Agreements' (2005) 99(3) *American Journal of International Law* 581

Razek, R et al, '"Secondary Disaster" Looms as UN Aid Finally Reaches Survivors Battling Frozen Conditions in Syria', *CNN* (10 February 2023)

Riley, D, 'The New Durkheim: Bourdieu and the State' (2015) 2(2) *Critical Historical Studies* 261

Rodenhäuser, T and Giacca, G, 'The International Humanitarian Law Framework for Humanitarian Relief during Armed Conflicts and Complex Emergencies' in S Breau and K Samuel (eds), *Research Handbook on Disasters and International Law* (Edward Elgar, 2016) 132

Romanin Jacur, F, 'Solidarity and Differentiation: Moral and Legal Obligations of States in Addressing Global Challenges – The Case of Climate Change' in M den Heijer and H van der Wilt (eds), *Netherlands Yearbook of International Law 2020* (TMC Asser Press, 2022) 75

Rourke, MF, 'Restricting Access to Pathogen Samples and Epidemiological Data: A Not-So-Brief History of "Viral Sovereignty" and the Mark it Left on the World' in M Eccleston-Turner and I Brassington (eds), *Infectious Diseases in the New Millennium* (Springer, 2020) 167

Ryngaert, C, 'Humanitarian Assistance and the Conundrum of Consent: A Legal Perspective' (2013) 5(2) *Amsterdam Law Forum* 5

Sandoz, Y, Swinarski, C, and Zimmermann, B (eds), *Commentary on the Additional Protocols* (ICRC, 1987)

Saracino, D, 'Understanding Solidarity in the European Union: An Analytical Framework' (2024) 53(5) *Theory and Society* 1093

Saunders, I, 'International Disaster Relief Law and Article 38(1)(c) of the Statute of the International Court of Justice: The Forgotten Source of International Law' in DD Caron, MJ Kelly and A Telesetsky (eds), *The International Law of Disaster Relief* (Cambridge University Press, 2014) 29

Saunders, I, *General Principles as a Source of International Law: Art 38(1)(c) of the Statute of the International Court of Justice* (Hart Publishing, 2020)

Seglah, HA and Blanchard, K, 'Sexual and Gender Minorities and the Right to Non-discrimination: A Shortfall of Disaster Risk Reduction?' (2024) 5 *Yearbook of International Disaster Law* 133

Selth, A, 'Even Paranoids Have Enemies: Cyclone Nargis and Myanmar's Fears of Invasion' (2008) 30(3) *Contemporary Southeast Asia* 379

Shahzad, A, 'Pakistan out of Money for Flood Recovery, UN Boosts Aid Request – Minister', *Reuters* (5 October 2022)

Shue, H, 'Limiting Sovereignty' in JM Welsh (ed), *Humanitarian Intervention and International Relations* (Oxford University Press, 2004) 11

Simm, G, 'Disaster Response in Southeast Asia: The ASEAN Agreement on Disaster Response and Emergency Management' (2018) 8(1) *Asian Journal of International Law* 116

Simma, B and Alston, P, 'The Sources of Human Rights Law: Custom, *Jus Cogens*, and General Principles' (1988) 12 *Australian Year Book of International Law* 82

Sivakumaran, S, 'Arbitrary Withholding of Consent to Humanitarian Assistance in Situations of Disaster' (2015) 64(3) *International and Comparative Law Quarterly* 501

Sivakumaran, S, 'Techniques in International Law-Making: Extrapolation, Analogy, Form and the Emergence of an International Law of Disaster Relief' (2017) 28(4) *European Journal of International Law* 1097

Slaughter, AM, 'Security, Solidarity, and Sovereignty: The Grand Themes of UN Reform' (2005) 99(3) *American Journal of International Law* 619
Soguilon, WKD, 'The Compassionate Buddhist: A Preliminary Reflection on the Buddhist Concept of Karuna and its Implications' (2024) 11 *Open Access Library Journal* e12180
Sommario, E, 'Derogation from Human Rights Treaties in Situations of Natural or Man-Made Disasters' in A de Guttry, M Gestri and G Venturini (eds), *International Disaster Response Law* (TMC Asser Press, 2012) 323
Sommario, E, 'Limitation and Derogation Provisions in International Human Rights Law Treaties and Their Use in Disaster Settings' in F Zorzi Giustiniani et al (eds), *Routledge Handbook of Human Rights and Disasters* (Routledge, 2018) 98
Sommermann, KP, 'Some Reflections on the Concept of Solidarity and Its Transformation into a Legal Principle' (2014) 52(1) *Archiv des Völkerrechts* 10
Sphere Project, 'The Sphere Handbook: Humanitarian Charter and Minimum Standards in Humanitarian Response' (2018)
Spieker, H, 'The Right to Give and Receive Humanitarian Assistance' in HJ Heintze and A Zwitter (eds), *International Law and Humanitarian Assistance: A Crosscut through Legal Issues Pertaining to Humanitarianism* (Springer, 2011) 7
'St. Martin's Leader Quits over Irma Aid Spat', *DW* (25 November 2017)
Stephens, T, 'Disasters, International Environmental Law and the Anthropocene' in S Breau and K Samuel (eds), *Research Handbook on Disasters and International Law* (Edward Elgar, 2016) 153
Stjernø, S, *Solidarity in Europe: The History of an Idea* (Cambridge University Press, 2004)
Szpak, A, 'International Solidarity as the Basis for Millennium/Sustainable Development Goals' (2017) 26(1) *Polish Quarterly of International Affairs* 106
Task Force on Ethical and Legal Issues in Humanitarian Assistance, 'The Mohonk Criteria for Humanitarian Assistance in Complex Emergencies' (1994)
Telec, A, 'Challenges to State Sovereignty in the Provision of International Natural Disaster Relief' in DD Caron, MJ Kelly and A Telesetsky (eds), *The International Law of Disaster Relief* (Cambridge University Press, 2014) 270
Telford, J and Cosgrave, J, *Joint Evaluation of the International Response to the Indian Ocean Tsunami: Synthesis Report* (Tsunami Evaluation Coalition, 2006)
Tempone, E, 'Special and Differential Treatment' in *Max Planck Encyclopedia of International Law* (Oxford University Press, 2014)
Thierry, H, 'The Thought of Georges Scelle' (1990) 1(1) *European Journal of International Law* 193
Thirlway, HWA, *The Sources of International Law*, 2nd edn (Oxford University Press, 2019)
Thomson, M, 'The Obligation Not to Arbitrarily Refuse International Disaster Relief: A Question of Sovereignty' (2015) 16 *Melbourne Journal of International Law* 1
Tixier, C, 'The Legacy of Léon Bourgeois: From the Solidarist Doctrine to the Emergence of International Arbitration' in JQ Olmstead (ed), *Reconsidering Peace and Patriotism during the First World War* (Springer, 2017) 33
Tladi, D, 'The International Law Commission's Draft Articles on the Protection of Persons in the Event of Disasters: Codification, Progressive Development or Creation of Law from Thin Air?' (2017) 16(3) *Chinese Journal of International Law* 425
Tladi, D, 'In Search of Solidarity in International Law' in E Kassoti and N Idriz (eds), *The Principle of Solidarity: The Principle of Solidarity: International and EU Law Perspectives* (TMC Asser Press, 2023) 17
'Tonga Eruption, Tsunami: Images Appear to Show Most of Atatā Island Wiped Out', *Radio New Zealand* (19 January 2022)
Toshiya, U, 'Natural Disasters and the Theory of International Law' in DD Caron, MJ Kelly and A Telesetsky (eds), *The International Law of Disaster Relief* (Cambridge University Press, 2014) 21
Ud Din, A, 'Differential Treatment for Developing Countries as a Manifestation of Solidarity: Overcoming New Challenges by Going Back to the Basics' in E Kassoti and N Idriz (eds),

The Principle of Solidarity: The Principle of Solidarity: International and EU Law Perspectives (TMC Asser Press, 2023) 129
Ulrich, LM, 'The Customary International Law Obligation to Protect Foreign Disaster Relief Personnel and Their Equipment' (2014) 22 *Willamette Journal of International Law & Dispute Resolution* 343
UN (United Nations), 'Secretary-General's Press Encounter on the Earthquake in Türkiye and Syria' (9 February 2023)
UN Environment Programme, 'Adaptation Gap Report 2025: Running on Empty' (2025)
UN Office for the Coordination of Humanitarian Affairs (OCHA), 'End of Mission Report: United Nations Disaster Assessment & Coordination (UNDAC) 7.8 Earthquake (February 6, 2023)' (6 February 2023)
UNDRR (United Nations Office for Disaster Risk Reduction), 'Global Assessment Report on Disaster Risk Reduction - Our World at Risk: Transforming Governance for a Resilient Future' (2022)
UNDRR, 'The Human Cost of Disasters: An Overview of the Last 20 Years (2000–2019)' (2020)
UNDRR, 'International Cooperation in Disaster Risk Reduction: Target F' (2021)
UNFCCC (United Nations Framework Convention on Climate Change) Secretariat, 'COP27 Reaches Breakthrough Agreement on New "Loss and Damage" Fund for Vulnerable Countries' (20 November 2022)
Valencia-Ospina, E, 'The Work of the International Law Commission on the "Protection of Persons in the Event of Disasters"' (2019) 1(1) *Yearbook of International Disaster Law* 5
VanLandingham, R, 'Politics or Law: The Dual Nature of the Responsibility to Protect' (2012) 41(1) *Denver Journal of International Law and Policy* 63
Venturini, G, 'Disasters and Armed Conflict' in A De Guttry, M Gestri and G Venturini (eds), *International Disaster Response Law* (TMC Asser Press, 2012) 251
Verwey, W, 'The Principle of Solidarity as a Legal Cornerstone of a New International Economic Order' in *North-South Dialogue: A New International Economic Order* (Institute of International Public Law and International Relations of Thessaloniki, 1982) 487
Villani, S, *The Concept of Solidarity within EU Disaster Response Law: A Legal Assessment* (Bononia University Press, 2021)
Vitkovskaya, J, 'How the Soviet Union Stayed Silent during the Chernobyl Disaster' (25 April 2016)
Voigt, C and Ferreira, F, 'Differentiation in the Paris Agreement' (2016) 6(1–2) *Climate Law* 58
Walter, C, 'Subjects of International Law' in *Max Planck Encyclopedia of International Law* (Oxford University Press, May 2007)
Wellens, K, 'Revisiting Solidarity as a (Re-)Emerging Constitutional Principle: Some Further Reflections' in R Wolfrum and C Kojima (eds), *Solidarity: A Structural Principle of International Law* (Springer, 2010) 3
Wellens, K, 'Solidarity as a Constitutional Principle: Its Expanding Role and Inherent Limitations' in RStJ Macdonald and DM Johnston (eds), *Towards World Constitutionalism: Issues in the Legal Ordering of the World Community* (Martinus Nijhoff Publishers, 2005) 775
Wellman, C, 'Solidarity, the Individual and Human Rights' (2000) 22(3) *Human Rights Quarterly* 639
'Why Has Morocco Accepted Limited Foreign Aid So Far?', *Al Jazeera* (12 September 2023)
Williams, A, 'Solidarity, Justice and Climate Change Law' (2009) 10 *Melbourne Journal of International Law* 493
Williams, S and Simm, G, 'Assistance to Disaster Victims in an Armed Conflict: The Role of International Humanitarian Law' in F Zorzi Giustiniani et al (eds), *Routledge Handbook of Human Rights and Disasters* (Routledge, 2018) 43
Wolfrum, R, 'General International Law (Principles, Rules, and Standards)' in *Max Planck Encyclopedia of International Law* (Oxford University Press, 2010)
Wolfrum, R, 'International Law of Cooperation' in *Max Planck Encyclopedia of International Law* (Oxford University Press, 2010)

Wolfrum, R, 'Proportionality: Reconsidering the Application of an Established Principle in International Law' (2022) 99 *International Law Studies* 676
Wolfrum, R, 'Solidarity' in D Shelton (ed), *The Oxford Handbook of International Human Rights Law* (Oxford University Press, 2013) 401
Wolfrum, R, 'Solidarity amongst States: An Emerging Structural Principle of International Law' (2009) 49(1) *Indian Journal of International Law* 8
Wolfrum, R, *Solidarity and Community Interests: Driving Forces for the Interpretation and Development of International Law* (Brill Nijhoff, 2021)
Wolfrum, R and Kojima, C (eds), *Solidarity: A Structural Principle of International Law* (Springer, 2010)
Won, Y, 'Emergency Powers and COVID-19 Derogations' (2025) 23(1) *International Journal of Constitutional Law* 113
Wong, J, 'Reconstructing the Responsibility to Protect in the Wake of Cyclones and Separatism' (2009) 84(2) *Tulane Law Review* 219
World Bank, European Union and UN, 'Libya Storm and Flooding 2023: Rapid Damage and Needs Assessment' (2024)
'World Leaders Offer Solidarity after Devastating Morocco Earthquake', *France24* (10 September 2023)
WTO (World Trade Organization), 'Differential and More Favourable Treatment Reciprocity and Fuller Participation of Developing Countries' (28 November 1979)
Yamamoto, A, 'Fukushima Operator Admits It Didn't Reveal Meltdown for Months', *NBC News* (26 February 2016)
Yeh, MJ, 'Confucian Welfarism: Intellectual Origins of Solidarity for Health and Welfare Systems' (2023) 16(3) *Public Health Ethics* 232
Yerkes, MA and Bal, M (eds), *Solidarity and Social Justice in Contemporary Societies: An Interdisciplinary Approach to Understanding Inequalities* (Springer, 2022)
Zorzi Giustiniani, F, *International Law in Disaster Scenarios: Applicable Rules and Principles* (Springer, 2021)

Index

References are to page number.

www.ingramcontent.com/pod-product-compliance
Ingram Content Group UK Ltd.
Pitfield, Milton Keynes, MK11 3LW, UK
UKHW020805290926
15470UKWH00003B/957